ALWAYS MAGIC
IN THE AIR

ALSO BY KEN EMERSON

Doo-Dah!: Stephen Foster and the Rise of American Popular Culture

ALWAYS MAGIC IN THE AIR

The Bomp and Brilliance
of the
Brill Building Era

KEN EMERSON

VIKING

781.6409
EME

VIKING
Published by the Penguin Group
Penguin Group (USA) Inc., 375 Hudson Street, New York, New York 10014, U.S.A.
Penguin Group (Canada), 90 Eglinton Avenue East, Suite 700, Toronto, Ontario,
Canada M4P 2Y3 (a division of Pearson Penguin Canada Inc.)
Penguin Books Ltd, 80 Strand, London WC2R 0RL, England
Penguin Ireland, 25 St. Stephen's Green, Dublin 2, Ireland (a division of Penguin Books Ltd)
Penguin Books Australia Ltd, 250 Camberwell Road, Camberwell, Victoria 3124, Australia
(a division of Pearson Australia Group Pty Ltd)
Penguin Books India Pvt Ltd, 11 Community Centre, Panchsheel Park, New Delhi–110 017, India
Penguin Group (NZ), Cnr Airborne and Rosedale Roads, Albany, Auckland 1310, New Zealand
(a division of Pearson New Zealand Ltd)
Penguin Books (South Africa) (Pty) Ltd, 24 Sturdee Avenue, Rosebank,
Johannesburg 2196, South Africa

Penguin Books Ltd, Registered Offices:
80 Strand, London WC2R 0RL, England

First published in 2005 by Viking Penguin,
a member of Penguin Group (USA) Inc.

1   3   5   7   9   10   8   6   4   2

Copyright © Ken Emerson, 2005
All rights reserved

Information about song lyrics quoted in this book appears on pages 335–336.

ISBN 0-670-03456-8

Printed in the United States of America

FOR BEN GERSON

I thank God I have low tastes.

—Oliver Wendell Holmes Jr.

CONTENTS

INTRODUCTION

Turn the dial, push a button, click the mouse. Go to the movies or a restaurant, ride the subway or visit the mall. Throughout America (and a good bit of the rest of the world), chances are it won't be long before you hear a song composed by a remarkable group of songwriters who huddled in cubicles within a couple of blocks of each other in midtown Manhattan in the late 1950s and early '60s. It could be "On Broadway" (where "the neon lights are bright" and "there's always magic in the air") or "Stand By Me," "Save the Last Dance for Me" or "Walk On By," "Breaking Up Is Hard to Do," "Will You Love Me Tomorrow," "Do Wah Diddy Diddy," "You've Lost That Lovin' Feelin'," or "(You Make Me Feel Like a) Natural Woman.". . . Popular music thrives on novelty, yet songs such as these—instantly identifiable, endlessly replayed on radio, recycled in commercials and film sound tracks, and rerecorded by new generations of performers as well as many an older artist—have enjoyed a run of nearly half a century.

The music reminds baby boomers of their youth, of sock hops and slumber parties, of transistor radios and tail fins, of good girls who said no and the nice boys who took that for an answer, of not-so-nice girls wearing too much mascara and the bad boys with DAs who whisked them away on motorcycles. While an older generation fondly remem-

bers snapping its gum and fingers to the beat, younger ones are captivated by what sounds like exhilarating innocence.

Nostalgia and naïveté cannot entirely explain these songs' persistence. Professional craft and artistry have also made them endure. And
so has the way the music not only embodies a long-gone era but antic-
ipates and speaks to our own. Expressing the optimism and outrage of
the early civil rights movement, it amalgamated black, white, and Latino
sounds before multiculturalism became a concept, much less a cliché,
and integrated audiences before America desegregated its schools. It
helped create a youth market—teenagers were a new breed of human
being and a brand-new consumer category—and trafficked in teen idols
from whom Justin Timberlake and the Simpson sisters directly descend.
In addition to making life fun for teenagers, the music made life more
real for them by introducing racial and economic themes that encouraged a political as well as a consumer consciousness. The combination
was in keeping with a period when fear and frivolity, Sputniks and hula
hoops, simultaneously girdled the globe. "Get me another drink," said
a character in Nevil Shute's *On the Beach,* a best-selling 1957 novel that
depicted the dying days of the human race as radioactive fallout swept
the world. "I want to go somewhere—do something—*dance!*"

This is the story of seven songwriting teams, fourteen men and
women who helped create the sound of a city, a nation, and an era: Jerry
Leiber and Mike Stoller, Doc Pomus and Mort Shuman, Burt Bacharach
and Hal David, Neil Sedaka and Howard Greenfield, Carole King and
Gerry Goffin, Barry Mann and Cynthia Weil, Jeff Barry and Ellie Greenwich. The book is about the world that made these songwriters and
the world they in turn made in their music.

Most of these songwriters and much of their music are still alive
and kicking. After 2,036 performances on Broadway, *Smokey Joe's
Café,* a revue of the songs of Leiber and Stoller, is playing in various
venues around the world. In 2004, Sedaka appeared at Carnegie Hall (as
well as in the pop charts with a remake of one of his hits by *American
Idol* runner-up Clay Aiken), Mann and Weil performed their songs on
another Manhattan stage, and King crossed the country playing benefit
concerts for John Kerry's presidential campaign. His contribution to
the sound track of *Grace of My Heart,* a 1996 film based very loosely
on King's life, helped spark a revival of popularity for Bacharach that

shows little sign of subsiding. Performing and rerecording the songs he wrote with Hal David, collaborating with Elvis Costello, popping up in Austin Powers movies, Aimee Mann lyrics, and even a White Stripes album, the suave septuagenarian is ubiquitous.

Many other important pop music songwriters were active in New York City during the 1950s and '60s. Otis Blackwell, who wrote or cowrote such memorable songs as "Fever," "Don't Be Cruel," "Great Balls of Fire," and "Handy Man," comes immediately to mind. So do Bob Crewe and Bob Gaudio, who wrote most of the Four Seasons' hits. But this book is intended as a narrative, not an encyclopedia.

Another thing it is not is a string of biographies, although several of these songwriters deserve one. Instead of studying them individually, *Always Magic in the Air* paints a group or family portrait. For not only did these writers know, collaborate and compete with, and sometimes marry and divorce one another, but they also share a family likeness.

In many ways they *were* a family. Jerry Leiber and Mike Stoller were the patresfamilias, influencing and inspiring all these writers (with the exceptions of Neil Sedaka and Howard Greenfield), hiring some of them, working with others, and producing some of their greatest songs. All but one of them was Jewish, and Greenwich, the odd woman out, is half Jewish. Most of them were born or grew up in Brooklyn. Like one of the protagonists in Michael Chabon's novel *The Amazing Adventures of Kavalier and Clay,* they "dreamed the usual Brooklyn dreams of flight and transformation and escape." As Brooklyn Jews, raised on the Rosenbergs and Jackie Robinson, they developed a political and racial awareness to varying degrees. As the children and grandchildren of immigrants, they had some respect for, and in several instances training in, classical European music, which they did not forsake even as they fell in love with African-American and, at the height of Puerto Rican emigration to New York, Afro-Cuban music.

The black music that initially bowled over the older of these songwriters was jazz, jump, and rhythm and blues. The younger ones were enthralled by the doo-wop they heard on Alan Freed's *Rock and Roll Show* after the obstreperous disc jockey moved from Cleveland to New York in 1954 and, as the *New York Times* noted, "jumped into radio like a stripper into Swan Lake." Doo-wop's wobbly vocal harmonies encompassed a grave sentimentality and a giggling nonsensicality that reflected the emotional extremes of their own—and most people's—adolescence. Eventually nearly all these writers also became infatuated by Latin rhythms and incorporated them into their music. That's why Buddy Borsalino, a character in *The Wanderers,* Richard Price's vivid account of teenage life on the wild side of the Bronx in the 1960s, filed records under "F" for fast, "S" for slow, and "C" for cha-cha, assigning to this last category Goffin and King's "Will You Love Me Tomorrow," Leiber and Stoller and Ben E. (not to be confused with Carole) King's "Stand By Me," and all the Four Seasons' songs.

Their origins and enthusiasms prepared these writers to become the last gasp in the grand tradition of the Great American Songbook, the heirs of Irving Berlin, Jerome Kern, George and Ira Gershwin, Harold Arlen, and others. And some of their songs are standing the test of time as well as "Bewitched, Bothered, and Bewildered" and "All the Things You Are." But unlike their antecedents in a different technological era, these composers became keenly conscious that they were writing records, not songs. A 45 rpm single had to be played on AM radio and Dick Clark's *American Bandstand* in order to be heard. Almost inevitably, many of these songwriters developed into arrangers and producers, if only in self-defense: to preserve their music as they intended it to sound and to sell.

This music is commonly called "the Brill Building sound," a misnomer I perpetuate in the subtitle of this book with great reluctance. Although a lot of these songs originated in the legendary shrine of the music publishing business at 1619 Broadway, as many if not more emanated from 1650 Broadway and other nearby buildings with only addresses for names. The catch-all term has created such misunderstanding that both the definitive history of the American popular music business and the late editor of the recording industry's authoritative trade magazine mistakenly located Aldon Music—home to Sedaka, Greenfield, King, Goffin, Mann, and Weil—in the Brill Building rather than 1650 Broadway. This book, in turn, may be guilty of oversight if not error in concentrating on the songwriters of the Brill Building and 1650 while neglecting the denizens of 1697 Broadway, but, again, this is a narrative, not an omnibus.

Street numbers are one potential source of confusion. Nomenclature and genre are another. Although these writers' songs are staples of rock "oldies" radio, Bacharach, for one, and Gerry Goffin (with less justification) have insisted they never wrote a rock song. Leiber and Stoller's "That Is Rock & Roll" is one of the weakest records they wrote and produced for the Coasters. To some rock 'n' roll diehards, the music written in the Brill Building and 1650 Broadway during this era is at best pop and at worst pap. In neither case is it to be confused with rock 'n' roll, which was "all but dead" by 1958, according to one critic, and lay dormant until the Beatles revived its rude energy in 1964.

Songwriters who are by no stretch of the imagination head-banging rockers have cast similar aspersions. Paul Simon, a bit player on the Brill Building/1650 scene during this period, once observed, "Rock and roll got very bad in the early '60s, very mushy." In his recent memoir, Bob Dylan agreed: "Things were pretty sleepy on the American music scene in the late '50s and early '60s. Popular radio was sort of at a standstill and filled with empty pleasantries. It was years before The Beatles, The Who or The Rolling Stones would breathe new life and excitement into it."

Although "rock 'n' roll" and "rock" are legitimate historical, taxonomic, and descriptive terms, they should not be brandished as value judgments. They are merely categories or subsets of popular music, and using them to disparage pop music is as illogical as decrying jazz because it isn't bebop or classical music that is not symphonic. However disparate their music, Clay Aiken and the White Stripes are equally pop.

If the music of the Brill Building and 1650 Broadway consisted merely of "empty pleasantries," Stoller and Leiber's "Yakety Yak," Shuman and Pomus's "This Magic Moment," David and Bacharach's "The Look of Love," Greenfield and Sedaka's "Calendar Girl," King and Goffin's "Loco-Motion," Weil and Mann's "We Gotta Get Out of This Place," and Greenwich and Barry's "Out in the Streets" would not be so perdurable, and there would be little point to this book. Yet these criticisms, however ill-founded, illuminate one of this book's major themes.

Rock 'n' roll erupted in the mid-1950s. One music historian called it "the dynamite that blew apart the structure of an industry." When Elvis Presley entered and dominated the charts in 1956, record sales rose by roughly $100 million from the previous year's $227 million. The market for such records consisted of roughly 13 million teenagers, whose estimated annual spending power ranged from $7 billion to $10 billion.

Rock 'n' roll reared its head unpredictably, however, in regional markets and on independent record labels. In order to maximize profits, the market had to be consolidated and the product commodified. The need to rationalize rock 'n' roll became all the more urgent in 1957–58 when Elvis Presley entered the Army; Jerry Lee Lewis was banned from the airwaves for having taken his thirteen-year-old third cousin as his third wife before his second divorce became official; Buddy Holly was killed in a plane crash; Little Richard got religion; Chuck Berry was arrested for "motor-vatin'" across state lines with an underage girl; and, after an uproarious concert in Boston—headlined by Berry and Lewis—Alan Freed was charged under a Sacco-and-Vanzetti–era anti-anarchy statute with "inciting the unlawful destruction of property during a riot." The interruption of these rock 'n' roll stars' careers and the indictment of one of their most passionate promoters left a yawning void to be filled—or at least papered over.

This is where the Brill Building and 1650 Broadway came in. The music publishers and songwriters who worked there routinized the creation and production of rock 'n' roll. They smoothed the rough edges of black R&B performers to help them appeal to a white audience, and they roughed up white performers just enough to create a tousled titillation. Reining in the unruliness of rock 'n' roll made it safe for teenage America and profitable in the mass marketplace. A biographer of Phil Spector noted of Don Kirshner, the publisher who employed Sedaka, Greenfield, Goffin, King, Mann, and Weil and peddled their songs, "More than anyone else Kirshner . . . made rock and roll a profession rather than just a vehicle of rebellion."

But concentrating entirely on how these songwriters tamed the wildness of early rock 'n' roll ignores how much they brought to the music as well. They enriched it not only with a Latin savor but also with strings and echoes of classical music. They contributed to a second flowering of doo-wop and the blossoming of groups such as Dion and the Belmonts. They pioneered a distaff doo-wop, the girl-group sound of the Shirelles, the Crystals, the Ronettes, and the Shangri-Las. Working with black artists such as the Drifters, Ben E. King, and Dionne Warwick, they helped create modern soul music and gave it an uptown urbanity. Their songwriting craft set a standard to which John Lennon and Paul McCartney aspired, and it paved the way for the British Invasion that would roll right over many of them.

Another element these songwriters added was women. Apart from Dorothy Fields and Kay Swift, the great American songwriters of the 1920s through the '50s composed a men's club. Sun Records in Memphis, where Elvis and many other early rock 'n' rollers started out, was a boys' club. The prominence of Carole King, Cynthia Weil, and Ellie Greenwich was unprecedented in American popular music, all the more so because King and Greenwich not only wrote but arranged and produced songs. (Their prominence did not prevent their husbands from receiving first billing, however. It was always Goffin and King, Mann and Weil, Barry and Greenwich.)

It would be simplistic to argue that these women imbued the music of the Brill Building and 1650 Broadway with a female or feminist perspective. Sometimes the men did. "I always admire that Gerry could really get inside the head of a woman," King said of her husband. Hal David wrote the defiant lyric to Dionne Warwick's "Don't Make Me Over": "Accept me for what I am / Accept me for the things that I do." These songwriters, male as well as female, often explored emotions and behavior that did not conform to the blustering macho stereotypes that had characterized much of early rock 'n' roll.

Finally, and ironically, these songwriters who calculatedly cranked out hit after hit with assembly-line efficiency also brought to popular music a new authenticity. They were young people, for the most part, writing for young people. In the best of their work, as we shall see, they often drew upon, dramatized, and shared their own experiences, be it Doc Pomus's polio and marriage in "Save the Last Dance for Me" or Carole King's premarital pregnancy in "Will You Love Me Tomorrow." Such songs sounded real when they were originally recorded, and the records still sound real today.

The genius of the songwriters portrayed in this book lay in their ability to assimilate and project rock 'n' roll into the mainstream of American popular music, thereby extending and expanding both. If there is some truth to the charge that these songwriters ended up nearly killing the very thing they loved before the Beatles and Bob Dylan rescued it, purists who prefer the raw to the cooked and deplore accommodation and domestication forget that the greatest American music is seldom pure. A product of mixed races and mixed motives (making

noise, making art, making money), American culture is by its very nature impure, "sophisticated" in the original meaning of the word: mixed
and adulterated.

The proof of these songwriters' success does not lie in this book's attempt to chronicle and explicate their accomplishments. It's in the music, which I hope I will help readers understand and enjoy more fully.

Chapter One

THE ORIGINAL COOL CATS

★

In October 1957, New York traded the Brooklyn Dodgers for the Los Angeles–based songwriting team of Jerry Leiber and Mike Stoller. The ball club's farewell season in Ebbets Field was dispiriting. The Dodgers' third-place finish was their worst showing in a decade. But the twenty-four-year-old songwriters were on a streak that had begun eighteen months earlier when Elvis Presley sauntered into the lounge of the Sands Hotel in Las Vegas and heard Freddie Bell and the Bellboys fooling around with a song about a feckless lover who was "nothin' but a houn' dog."

This stroke of good fortune was soon followed by another when a United Fruit Company freighter rescued Stoller and 128 other passengers from the *Andrea Doria.* The Italian ocean liner bearing him and his wife, Meryl, back from a belated honeymoon in Europe had collided with the *Stockholm* and sunk in dense fog sixty miles south of Nantucket. When the *Cape Ann* deposited Stoller safely in New York on July 26, 1956, a relieved and elated Leiber greeted his bedraggled partner with a silk suit and news that Presley's stripped-down, speeded-up version of the song they had written four years earlier for Willie Mae "Big Mama" Thornton was a stupendous hit. Three weeks later, "Hound Dog" reached No. 1 on *Billboard*'s pop singles chart.

Now, as Leiber and Stoller arrived in New York intending to stick around, Presley's "Jailhouse Rock" became their second No. 1 song. By year's end the team would have more hit pop singles—eleven in all—than any other songwriters in 1957.

Overnight they had graduated from inadvertent beneficiaries of Presley's spectacular success to witting accomplices, writing songs to order for Elvis. A pretty ballad to croon? "Loving You" fit the bill and became the title of Presley's second film. A Christmas novelty? Leiber and Stoller concocted "Santa Claus Is Back in Town" in the nick of time for the holidays. Stoller even shaved off his hipster's goatee to play piano with Presley's on-screen band in his third (and best) movie, *Jailhouse Rock*.

Elvis was only the half of it. Leiber and Stoller also wrote pop hits in 1957 for the Coasters, the Drifters, Ruth Brown, Gale Storm, and Perry Como. Storm, star of the TV sitcom *My Little Margie*, and Como were, like Elvis, white. The Coasters, the Drifters, and Ruth Brown were black rhythm-and-blues performers on the roster of Atlantic Records (or, in the case of the Coasters, its subsidiary, Atco). The small, independent, New York–based record company specializing in R&B had engaged Leiber and Stoller as writers and producers on a nonexclusive basis since late 1955, and now this relationship was beginning to pay off for everyone.

The success of their work with Elvis persuaded RCA Victor, Presley's label (as well as Como's) and one of the nation's largest record companies, to offer Leiber and Stoller jobs at its New York City headquarters in A&R (Artists and Repertoire), selecting and producing material for RCA artists. Because these performers were overwhelmingly white and Atlantic was scarcely considered competition for one of the so-called Big Six labels, an exception in Leiber and Stoller's otherwise exclusive one-year contract with RCA allowed them to continue their association with Atlantic.

And so, while the Soviet Union lofted Sputnik I into orbit and the 101st Airborne and the National Guard protected nine black students at Little Rock's Central High School, Leiber and Stoller moved from L.A. to Manhattan. They were eager to enjoy and profit handsomely from the best of all worlds: corporate perks and feisty independence; pop, rock 'n' roll, and rhythm and blues; black and white artists; white and black audiences. Stoking the fires of the Elvis phenomenon, they inspired the singer and his teenage fans with their funky facility. They could lend middle-aging mainstream singers a little rock 'n' roll oomph. And they could tweak R&B acts until they crossed over to the pop charts from the rankings of what only eight years earlier had still been stigmatized as "Race Records."

Their backgrounds made Leiber and Stoller feel at home yet out of place in every camp. Born on April 25, 1933, Jerry Leiber grew up in a Yiddish-speaking household in a largely Catholic neighborhood on the edge of Baltimore's black ghetto. He felt less affinity for his "really anti-Semitic" neighbors than for the African Americans to whom his mother's grocery store extended credit and he delivered groceries and kerosene. "I identified with the blacks. I felt very sympathetic to them, and they were sympathetic to me." The blues and boogie-woogie that Leiber overheard on the radios in his customers' homes sounded a lot more inviting than the Polish, Russian, and Jewish folk music played in the immigrants' social club his family frequented. "Those radios were like magic boxes to me; they played music I never heard anywhere else." The death of his father when Leiber was only five, abandoning him to the ministrations of a mother and two older sisters, may have heightened the appeal of R&B's manly bravado.

Mike Stoller was born six weeks before Leiber, on March 13, in Belle Harbor, Long Island. He moved when he was four to Sunnyside, Queens, where he was reared on Red Seal records (RCA's classical line) and Richard Strauss. His father was a contractor, his mother a former model and actress who had appeared in the chorus of George Gershwin's 1927 musical comedy, *Funny Face,* and her sister was a conservatory-trained pianist. While economic necessity introduced Leiber to black music and culture, in Stoller's case it was the political principles of his liberal parents, who sent him at age seven to an interracial summer camp in New Jersey where he heard black teenagers playing boogie-woogie on an upright piano. Fascinated, he took several piano lessons from James P. Johnson, the great stride pianist who had tutored Fats Waller. Bebop enthralled Stoller when he entered his teens, and he began to sneak into jazz clubs on Manhattan's Fifty-second Street and hang out at a Harlem social club.

Leiber's family moved to Los Angeles in 1945, Stoller's in 1949. When Leiber, on the recommendation of a drummer and fellow student at Fairfax High School, appeared on Stoller's doorstep in the summer of 1950 and urged Stoller to write songs with him, each was "astonished by the other person." According to Meryl Stoller, "It was like, 'Wow! Where did you come from, soul mate?' In other respects they were diametrically opposite." Manic, impetuous, and aggressive, Leiber was a motormouth with curly red hair. One eye was blue, the other brown, and there was a crazy glint in both of them. (Asked what he put down for eye color on his passport, Leiber told a friend: "Assorted.") Stoller, on the other hand, was so laid-back he could scarcely be bothered to raise his eyelids, much less his voice. His manner was retiring and so, even in his early twenties, was his hairline. Over the years some people found Stoller's impassivity intimidating. "I was afraid of Mike," recalled Kenny Vance, a member of Jay and the Americans, a vocal group Leiber and Stoller produced. "Mike was deadpan. He was like a jazz guy, very dry. Jerry was more outgoing." "They were the original cool cats," said Steve Tyrell, a record promoter, producer, and pop singer. "Especially Mike—he was a beatnik."

They differed in tastes as well as demeanor. Stoller was deeply interested not only in modern jazz, sitting in once with trumpeter Chet Baker, but also in contemporary classical music. Caring little for music he couldn't dance to, Leiber demanded a beat. But Leiber and Stoller shared a passion for what they later called, in a song they improvised for the b-side of a single, "alley music." Even before blackface minstrels sang about Shinbone Alley in the 1830s, the alley was where African Americans could get down, get high, and get laid. On the eve of World War I, homesick South Carolinians at New York's Jungles Casino would cry, "Now, put us in the alley!" when they wanted James P. Johnson to get funky. "They'd dance, hollering and screaming until they were cooked," Stoller's teacher recalled. The alley was where the Clovers, one of the most popular R&B vocal groups of the 1950s, went "ballin' 'til half past three" and Little Richard's Uncle John ducked with Long Tall Sally when he saw his missus coming.

For Leiber, perhaps, "alley music" was a reminder of the backdoor deliveries he had made and the backstreet music he had heard in Baltimore. For Stoller, it echoed his boyhood in Queens when, huddled under his blankets past bedtime, he listened surreptitiously to Symphony Sid Torin's jazz program on a battery radio. One commercial extolled the sartorial splendors to be found at Alley's Pants on Brooklyn's Fulton Street. "Alley, Alley, Alley, you been so good to me" went the bluesy jingle. "You got those three-ring bottoms . . ." Exactly what "three-ring bottoms" were was as mystifying as the origins of the singer. Identified by Torin as "Doc Pomus," he became "a mythical figure" in Stoller's young imagination. When Leiber and Stoller were transplanted to California, Central Avenue, the main street of Los Angeles's black ghetto, Watts, became their alley.

The relaxation of discriminatory hiring practices in the aircraft and other defense industries drew African Americans in droves to Los Angeles during World War II. The city's black population more than doubled between 1940 and 1946, and its spending money and numbers made L.A. a hotbed of rhythm and blues. Melding the Kansas City swing of touring territory bands with the blues and boogie-woogie of migrants from Texas, Oklahoma, and Arkansas, R&B flourished in Central Avenue nightclubs such as the Club Alabam and on local independent record labels like Modern and Aladdin. Critics haggle over when and where jazz and blues spawned R&B and R&B in turn helped spark rock 'n' roll. The evolution (or devolution, according to detractors) was continuous and occurred on many fronts, while the lines dividing genres are blurred and arbitrary. But Los Angeles was where much of the action transpired, and local performers played principal roles: Charles Brown; Roy Milton and his Solid Senders; Joe Liggins (whose "The Honeydripper" has as strong a claim as any to being the first rhythm and blues record); Joe's brother, Jimmy Liggins; Johnny Otis; Percy Mayfield; and Jesse Belvin. According to one prominent producer, "The big, first surge of R&B was on the West Coast in L.A., not in New York."

"People talk about the blues in Chicago," blues singer Jimmy Witherspoon once told an interviewer, "but do you know that 99 percent of the blues was recorded right here in Los Angeles? I didn't say 'a lot.' I said *99 percent.*" Witherspoon idolized Big Joe Turner and sat at his feet when the blues shouter from Kansas City opened a club, The Blue Room, on Central Avenue. He also discovered Johnny Otis, the Greek-American impresario of L.A. R&B. "He's a white guy who's passing for black," Witherspoon noted, "and a great drummer." Witherspoon became the first performer to record (though not to release) a song by Leiber and Stoller, "Real Ugly Woman," at a concert at L.A.'s Shrine Auditorium in December 1950, only months after the teenagers met. "She's three hundred pounds of meat," Witherspoon hollered, "And she's my female Frankenstein." "When Jerry and I started writing," Stoller once said, "it was a kind of spontaneous combustion."

With Lester Sill, the national sales manager for Modern Records, acting as their mentor and guide, the duo explored Los Angeles's bustling R&B scene. "It was a *secret world,*" Leiber recalled. That was alley music's greatest appeal: It concealed and disclosed secrets about life and death, love and sex, and racism that were unmentionable in the mainstream popular music sung by Dinah Shore, Patti Page, and Perry Como. Like the femme fatale in Walter Mosley's first Easy Rawlins mystery, *Devil in a Blue Dress,* which vividly evokes Central Avenue just before Leiber and Stoller began to haunt it, the young songwriters had "a predilection for the company of Negroes." They, too, liked "jazz and pigs' feet and dark meat, if you know what I mean." "We used to argue between the two of us over which one was the blackest," Leiber said. Who won? According to Stoller, "*We* did." On one of the rare occasions they performed and recorded one of their own compositions, the sardonic "Too Bad Sweet Mama," Jerry Leiber styled himself "Billy Black."

Leiber and Stoller cruised Central Avenue while the best minds of Allen Ginsberg's generation dragged themselves "through the negro streets at dawn"—as "Howl" famously began. A new crew of ostensibly hip and defiantly beat writers was beginning to trumpet their love of black culture and their conviction that it was superior to their own. In 1957, the year Leiber and Stoller moved to New York, Norman Mailer published "The White Negro" and effectively dismissed the discipline, intelligence, and artistry of Louis Armstrong, Duke Ellington, and Charlie Parker by declaring, with what he thought was high praise, "Jazz is orgasm, it is the music of orgasm, good orgasm and bad." That same year saw the publication of *On the Road,* in which Jack Kerouac demonstrated greater knowledge of jazz but little more understanding of African Americans: "At lilac evening I walked with every muscle aching among the lights of 27th and Welton in the Denver colored section, wishing I were a Negro." Kerouac wrote that he yearned to "exchange worlds with the happy, true-hearted, ecstatic Negroes of America." (When Orval Faubus barred these happy Negroes from Little Rock's Central High School, Louis Armstrong sounded more angry than ecstatic: "The way they are treating my people in the South, the government can go to hell." He added, "It's getting almost so bad a colored man hasn't got any country.")

But Leiber and Stoller were more than just another couple of thrill-crazy kids in search of what Kerouac called "old-fashioned spade kicks."

Their experience of African-American culture was more intimate and less patronizing than the Beats', and it continued a time-honored musical tradition of envy and emulation. Thirty years earlier, Bix Beiderbecke had shared rotgut with Milton "Mezz" Mezzrow and wondered "why white musicians are so corny." According to Mezzrow's account, the great white jazz cornetist said, "Hell, you even feel better physically when you get in a colored café. The people all seem to be enjoying everything in a real way. . . . goddamn, those people know how to live."

Listen to Leiber in 1990: "I felt black. I *was,* as far as I was concerned. And I wanted to be black for lots of reasons. They were better musicians, they were better athletes, they were not uptight about sex, and they knew how to enjoy life better than most people."

Musicians like Johnny Otis and Mezz Mezzrow who passed for black were models for the young Leiber and Stoller. If Mezzrow's 1946 memoir, *Really the Blues,* is to be believed, his draft card read "Race, Negro." Arrested at the 1940 World's Fair with his pockets full of reefer, Mezzrow, who played Dixieland clarinet and saxophone when he wasn't peddling marijuana, convinced his jailers he was black so he could share a cell block with his buddies on racially segregated Rikers Island. Years before James P. Johnson gave Stoller lessons, the stride pianist's recording of "Bleedin' Hearted Blues" and "You Can't Do What My Last Man Did" inspired Mezzrow to try, for the first of many times, to kick his opium habit. Leiber and Stoller's occasional use of the songwriting pseudonym Elmo Glick suggests that they had read *Really the Blues,* which features a poolroom proprietor and good friend of Mezzrow's named Emil Glick. Just as Mezzrow was, according to one jazz critic, among "the first self-conscious *students* of jazz," Leiber and Stoller were precocious pupils of rhythm and blues.

Dropping out of Los Angeles City College, Leiber and Stoller spent the early 1950s writing mostly for local R&B performers such as Otis, Witherspoon, Charles Brown, Little Esther, and Little Willie Littlefield. Under the gaze of a photograph inscribed by George Gershwin, Stoller puttered on an upright piano in his parents' apartment while Leiber shouted words until licks and lyrics coalesced in as many as five songs a day. As their titles—"Corn Whiskey," "Back Door Blues," "Fast Women and Sloe Gin," "Flesh, Blood and Bones," "Hollerin' and Screamin'," "Blood Is Redder Than Wine"—suggest, many of these lurid blues and boogies were generic celebrations of juice and jelly roll.

"We felt, in some cases, very successful if people thought that what we wrote was traditional," Stoller once said. "We wanted people to hear that we were part of a tradition, rather than imitating something that wasn't ours."

Yet Bobby Nunn and the Robbins' "That's What the Good Book Says," the very first Leiber-Stoller composition to be released (Witherspoon's "Real Ugly Woman" was recorded earlier but issued later), displayed a hip impudence that was distinctly Leiber and Stoller's and would become a hallmark of their career. The Robins, as they were usually and officially known, had been discovered by Johnny Otis, who played vibes on "That's What the Good Book Says." Inspired perhaps by that Gershwin photo, "That's What the Good Book Says" married George and Ira's "It Ain't Necessarily So" with the jive harmonies of the Golden Gate Quartet, a gospel group that was a formative influence on the Robins. Leiber and Stoller's riff on Scripture included hemp-smoking Hebrews and an impenitent Eve who opined, "This apple cider taste mighty fine."

Leiber and Stoller's breakthrough came on August 13, 1952, when Big Mama Thornton recorded "Hound Dog," a song it had taken them less than fifteen minutes to write. Their "novelty jump," as one trade paper called it, reached No. 1 on the national R&B charts. Set to a relaxed rumba beat, the original "Hound Dog" was about sass and sex. Thornton, a three-hundred-pound "female Frankenstein" notorious for her foul language, scars on her cheeks that a razor may have incised, and mannish garb of khaki trousers and plaid shirts, sang with a deep growl and a broad wink. She inveighed against her shiftless lover, but she didn't get too hot and bothered. Imbued with the realism and the comedy of rhythm and blues, her rendition acknowledged that she had been done wrong before and would probably be done wrong again, yet it recognized that grit and good humor would prevail.

Presley's version, on the other hand, "disappointed" Leiber and Stoller because it sounded "terribly nervous, too fast—and too white." But that's what made it rock 'n' roll. Performing for white teenagers to whom everything in life and love was happening for the very first time, Presley packed innocence, outrage, and apocalyptic urgency into "Hound Dog." He sang as if he couldn't believe his lover's perfidy. And by garbling the lyrics and repeating emphatically six times "Well, they said you was high-classed / But that was just a lie" (Thornton sang "You told me you was high class / But I can see through that" twice and left it at that), he expanded a sexual salvo into a class manifesto.

The original "Hound Dog" was a breakthrough on at least two additional counts. When Leiber and Stoller, dissatisfied with the drummer on the date, urged Johnny Otis, the session's producer, to fill in on drums, they replaced Otis in the recording booth and for the first time became de facto producers. When the record became a hit, they were displeased once again. The label of the 78 (the 45 rpm record had not yet become the pop music standard) rendered Stoller's name as Stroller and credited Johnny Otis as coauthor. (The musical accompaniment was attributed to Kansas City Bill & Orchestra, a reminder not only of the enduring influence of the territory bands but also of another song that Leiber and Stoller wrote in 1952: "K.C. Lovin'," later and better known as "Kansas City.") Adding injury to insult, the record company's owner stopped payment on a check to the duo. This injustice provoked Leiber and Stoller to form their own publishing company, Quintet Music, and record company, Spark. According to Stoller, "The idea was that Jerry and I shouldn't end up being screwed out of our royalties again." It was as producers, publishers, and entrepreneurs as well as songwriters that Leiber and Stoller put their stamp on rock 'n' roll.

The third single Leiber and Stoller wrote, produced, and released on Spark, in 1954, reunited them with the Robins. Just prior to their signing with Spark, the group was on RCA and Leiber and Stoller had penned for them "Ten Days in Jail," in which a convict complains only semi-comically, "I don't dig this bread and water / I like my meals made to order." Now Leiber and Stoller took this a step further and created a calling-card style: a comic narrative, set to a black rhythm, that pokes fun at cultural and racial stereotypes. Exploding with sound effects of swirling sirens and the rat-a-tat-tat of tommy guns, swaggering to a Muddy Waters beat, the Robins' "Riot in Cell Block #9" is at once hilarious and ominous. Although the jailhouse rebellion it describes is quashed by record's end and the inmates, obviously black, return to their cells, guest singer Richard Berry warns with a basso profundo drawl that they will surely rise up again. (Berry, best remembered as the composer of "Louie Louie," was not a member of the group, but Leiber and Stoller enlisted him when the Robins' Bobby Nunn sounded too tentative.) Sly and the Family Stone recalled this insurrectionary threat seventeen years later when, as America's cities were burning, they appropriated the song's chorus for the title of their 1971 album, *There's a Riot Goin' On.* Nearly two decades after that, "Riot in Cell Block #9" reverberated, however subliminally, in California gangsta rap like Niggaz with Attitude's "Fuck tha Police."

Early, pre-Leiber and Stoller Robins records, such as "Courtroom Blues," drew on old vaudeville and chitlin' circuit skits. There were many antecedents and analogues apart from the group's own recordings for Leiber and Stoller's combination of black humor, narrative, and a rocking chorus: the Clovers' "One Mint Julep" (written by Rudy Toombs) and "Your Cash Ain't Nothin' but Trash" (by Jesse Stone), for instance, and the Treniers' "Uh Oh (Get Out of the Car)" (by Claude and Cliff Trenier). Leiber himself cited as an influence the dialogue between Jimmy Ricks's bass voice and the rest of the Ravens, one of the very first doo-wop and so-called bird groups that inspired the Robins' and many other groups' names. (Indeed, the Robins had originally been called the Bluebirds.)

But "Riot in Cell Block #9" took such storytelling to new, dramatic heights. Until he heard Amos Wilburn sing "Bad Bad Whiskey" on the radio, Leiber had aspired to be an actor. Now he was writing "playlets." In the Robins, he and Stoller discovered and developed "a little company of players, a vaudeville troupe," in Stoller's words. Leiber and Stoller's theatrical imagination, the ensemble's malleability, and relentless rehearsing made the Robins and the group into which they would shortly evolve, the Coasters, an extraordinary comic vehicle. The comedy might be an affectionate parody of popular culture in the contemporaneous spirit of *Mad Magazine* (launched in 1952). Or it might have a sharper, more subversive point, skewering racial discrimination. Half a century later the Robins/Coasters remain the most consistently and uproariously funny group that R&B and rock 'n' roll have ever known, recalling Mezz Mezzrow's characterization of jazz in the 1920s as "a collectively improvised nose-thumbing at all pillars of all communities, one big syncopated Bronx cheer for the righteous squares everywhere."

Kenny Vance of Jay and the Americans described how Leiber directed the group a few years later. Though their name and personnel had changed, the modus operandi remained the same:

Jerry Leiber would actually transform himself into this character. He would slink and dance around the office, singing the part that he wanted Billy Guy or Carl Gardner to become. Jerry Leiber would go into that place and he would become that guy that he wanted them to imitate. I had never really seen anybody break character like that. I had never really seen anybody transform himself into a black guy. . . . It was wild to watch his abandon, to watch him do his work and not be self-conscious about it. . . . It sort of gave me permission to find that part of me inside myself.

Leiber later sought on several occasions to blunt the racial edge of "Riot in Cell Block #9," claiming that all he had intended was to spoof the *Gangbusters* radio show of his youth. "Those voices just happened to be black. They could have been white actors on radio. . . . We used to write cartoons." But D. H. Lawrence's dictum about American literature applies to American music as well: "Never trust the artist. Trust the tale." Only a couple of years earlier, Leiber had dallied with a left-wing commune seeking to convert Mexican workers at a Lockheed plant to Marxism. Neither he nor Stoller—whose uncle, Hollywood screenwriter and novelist Guy Endore, fronted a script for the blacklisted Dalton Trumbo and wrote pamphlets defending Chicano rights—was a political naïf. If racial injustice was the furthest thing from their minds, they probably would not have hired Richard Berry to provide such a lowering lead vocal, and they certainly would not have followed up "Riot in Cell Block #9" with "Framed," in which a white judge (in 1954, was there any other kind?) throws the book at a hapless black defendant. The social criticism as well as the cartoonishness of Leiber and Stoller's black humor anticipated the more celebrated and entirely Caucasian "black humor" of writers like Terry Southern and Joseph Heller, who also made a mockery of political, racial, and sexual hypocrisy.

Yet Leiber's insistence on the innocuousness of "Riot in Cell Block #9" and popular music's long, wretched history of exploiting black artists raise the question of how black Leiber, Stoller, and the music they made in Los Angeles actually were. Leiber himself recalled that when he ventured a suggestion during the recording of "Hound Dog," Big Mama Thornton glared at him "like looks could kill and said—and this was when I found out I was white—'White boy, don't you be tellin' *me* how to sing the blues.'"

Although Presley's recording of "Hound Dog" sounded "too white" to them, Leiber and Stoller had worked with ofays before. When a wealthy Los Angeles businessman put up the money to record his son and two fellow UCLA students, Leiber and Stoller wrote two pop hits for the Cheers: "Bazoom (I Need Your Lovin')" and "Black Denim Trousers and Motorcycle Boots." "You couldn't get three whiter people in this life," according to Buddy Bregman, who arranged and conducted the orchestra on "Bazoom." Oblivious to R&B, as most white teenagers still were in 1954 and 1955, the Cheers were a pre–rock 'n' roll pop vocal group that loved show tunes. One member, Bert Convy, would later appear in the original Broadway productions of *Fiddler on the Roof* and *Cabaret*.

"Black Denim Trousers and Motorcycle Boots" lampooned motorcycle movies like *The Wild One*, culminating in the fatal crash of a Marlon Brando–like character who "never washed his face and . . . never combed his hair" and "had axle-grease embedded underneath his fingernails." Another Cheers song that Leiber and Stoller cowrote, "Chicken," parodied James Dean and *Rebel Without a Cause.* The cool cats of Central Avenue couldn't take the pop culture of white teenagers seriously, yet they profited from it. The Cheers recorded on a major label, Capitol. In addition to being covered by Vaughn Monroe, "Black Denim Trousers and Motorcycle Boots" was the first song recorded and released by a vocal quartet from Toronto, the Diamonds, who would become famous a couple of years later for their delirious rendition of "Little Darlin'." It was also an unlikely hit in France for Edith Piaf after Leiber and Stoller sold the song's foreign rights for $15,000 to Jean Aberbach, the dapper Viennese co-owner with his brother, Julian, of Hill and Range Songs. Leiber and Stoller's relationship with the Aberbachs, who were shortly to become Elvis Presley's music publishers, preceded their involvement with Presley.

Leiber and Stoller's irreverence toward icons of white teenage culture extended even to Elvis. Three years after "Riot in Cell Block #9," "Jailhouse Rock" reduced a prison uprising to a party. Instead of rioting, the inmates were rocking, having such a good time behind bars that they didn't want to escape: "I wanna stick around a while and get my kicks." Prison had turned into a playground, and the prisoners, including Presley, into pussycats.

Leiber and Stoller worked extensively with the Cheers, composing or coauthoring at least eight songs for the group and two more that the Robins also recorded. Simultaneously they wrote "cartoons" for the black as well as the white group. "Riot in Cell Block #9" was far too incendiary to be played on radio stations catering to white listeners, but Leiber and Stoller smoothed the rougher edges of the Robins' racial humor on most of their subsequent records. No matter how much they prided themselves on being "race" men and how little they identified with white teenagers, they recognized rhythm and blues was beginning to appeal to a larger audience that it would be folly to ignore—especially as they began to settle down and assume adult responsibilities.

They had a record company to run, partners to please (Lester Sill, Sill's friend Jack Levy, and Stoller's father), pressing plants to pay, and distributors to dun—often to little avail. And in May 1955, Stoller married Meryl Cohen, a bookkeeper with a fondness for jazz who often attended their recording dates. "Every session was like a live performance," she recalled. "It was like sitting in a club. There might have been twenty takes on the same song, but it didn't matter. It was never exactly the same. And then you had these two careening idiots in the recording booth, dancing around and waving their arms and screaming. They were an act in themselves. They never knew it, but they were. Jerry *never* sat still. Even Mike couldn't sit still if [he] wasn't . . . at the piano."

It was at such a session on September 28, 1955, that the Robins recorded "Smokey Joe's Café," which dramatizes a diner's close call when he makes the mistake of ogling the proprietor's girl. Carl Gardner's bug-eyed lead vocal quivers with lust and then fright when Bobby Nunn's deadpan bass warns him to "eat up all your beans, boy, and clear right on out." The group's harmonies provide a theatrical as well as a musical chorus, swarming over octaves and filling the café with buzzing spectators. Even the musicians are players. Barney Kessel's guitar tartly punctuates the proceedings, and Gil Bernal's slinky saxophone solo prolongs them. "Smokey Joe's Café" is a rich record and a cunning one, too. By putting the song's black protagonist on the receiving end of a threat, it disarmed white fears that "Riot in Cell Block #9" had aroused.

Although "Smokey Joe's Café" was a local success, Spark Records lacked the resources to win the song a wider hearing. But the record caught the ear of Nesuhi Ertegun, whose brother, Ahmet, had co-founded Atlantic Records. Nesuhi had befriended Leiber and Stoller and solicited from them a song, "Ruby Baby," that the Drifters recorded for Atlantic only a few days before the Robins cut "Smokey Joe's Café." Nesuhi brought the record to Atlantic's attention and Ahmet, who had tried unsuccessfully to acquire "Riot in Cell Block #9" for national distribution, leased "Smokey Joe's Café." Rereleased on Atlantic's Atco label, it was only a minor hit, but it was the first time the Robins reached even the lower rungs of the national pop charts.

It was also the last time. Largely on Nesuhi's recommendation, Ahmet and his partner, Jerry Wexler, hired Leiber and Stoller to provide material and produce records for Atlantic. Unusual for its era, the arrangement was not exclusive, and it stipulated that Leiber and Stoller receive a producers' royalty of two cents per record sold. If Leiber and Stoller were not the first independent record producers, they certainly became the first highly successful ones. The royalty agreement and Atlantic's wider distribution also relieved them of the burden of managing their own record company. When Spark was dissolved, however, three of the Robins and their manager declined to sign with Atco. Casting their lot with Leiber and Stoller, Carl Gardner and Bobby Nunn were joined by new singers and dubbed the Coasters, a name that echoed the Drifters' and described their bicoastal status as a Los Angeles group on a New York label.

Within days of their agreement, Leiber and Stoller were writing songs for Atlantic's stable of artists. On November 3, 1955, Big Joe Turner—whom Atlantic had nudged from jazz and blues into rhythm and blues and, with "Shake, Rattle, and Roll," to the threshold of rock 'n' roll—recorded a jump blues by Leiber and Stoller, "The Chicken and the Hawk (Up, Up and Away)." According to Jerry Wexler, who produced the New York session with Ahmet Ertegun, Leiber was "Mr. Disorderly, . . . a charming mess—extravagantly verbal, always in a flamboyant dither," while "[w]ith his Robert Oppenheimer visage— the huge forehead and penetrating eyes—Stoller was the taciturn virtuoso, an enigmatic keyboard wizard who looked as though he'd just arrived from Venus or Jupiter."

The following year, Leiber and Stoller songs propelled Ruth Brown and the Drifters from the rhythm-and-blues to the pop charts. "Lucky

Lips" was an uncharacteristic attempt by Leiber and Stoller to pen a formulaic pop song. "Fools Fall in Love," on the other hand, cast a jaundiced eye on Frankie Lymon and the Teenagers' "Why Do Fools Fall in Love" and on the sentimentality that was mother's milk—along with Strontium 90—for most adolescents, black and white, in the 1950s:

> *Fools fall in love in a hurry.*
> *Fools give their hearts much too soon.*
> *Just give them two bars of "Stardust";*
> *Just hang out one silly moon,*
> *And they've got their love torches burning,*
> *When they should be playing it cool.*

Once again the cool cats expressed their disdain for the sentimentality of teenage culture—fourteen-year-old Lymon was an early "teen idol"—and, with their dismissal of "Stardust," for that of their parents. Meticulous taskmasters, Leiber and Stoller demanded fifty-six takes of their song, and their perfectionism yielded rewarding results. The Drifters had been left rudderless by the departure of their original lead singer, Clyde McPhatter, but they landed higher in the pop charts with "Fools Fall in Love" than ever before—while failing altogether to make the R&B rankings. The song seemed to appeal more strongly to white teenagers than to the Drifters' black base. When Leiber and Stoller not only wrote but also produced the Drifters' "Drip Drop" in 1958, the group fared even better with pop audiences.

Despite their dedication to black music and their dismissal of teenage pap, Leiber and Stoller's greatest contribution to Atlantic Records was to make black music more alluring to white kids, and to help the company make the transition from an R&B specialty label to a rock 'n' roll powerhouse. Leiber and Stoller straddled and synthesized both strains of music, and never more brilliantly than with the Coasters.

Less than ten minutes were left at the end of the Coasters' last recording session in Los Angeles on February 15, 1957. They had recorded three songs, which left them one song shy of a second single. Studio time was too costly to waste, so with Stoller at the piano and Leiber in the booth, the group rushed to perform a song the pair had written invoking the celebrated sleuths of their childhood: Sherlock Holmes, Charlie

Chan, Boston Blackie, and Bulldog Drummond. Perhaps because there was no opportunity to prepare anything more elaborate, the music was radically simplified. Recorded on the fly, it sounds, in Leiber's words, "really funky, cranky, trashy." The clubfooted rhythm, pounding on every other beat, makes it clear that the singer is going to be trudging on the trail of his sweetheart for quite a while. For the first time on a Robins or Coasters record there is no saxophone, no instrumental solo. The vocal harmonies are elementary, too, endlessly repeating "Gonna find her." The rudimentary setting spotlights the rubbery lead vocal of Billy Guy, a newcomer to the group and a great clown; he hammers some words with flinty precision, stretches others as if they were Silly Putty, and toward the end veers unexpectedly into falsetto. Stripped of most of the accoutrements of rhythm and blues, "Searchin'" achieves the simplicity and the incessancy of rock 'n' roll. Yet it also (and here lies Leiber and Stoller's genius) gets down to the barest essentials of funk. It reached No. 3 on the pop charts in the summer of 1957, higher than any record Atlantic had ever released, and proved that Leiber and Stoller did not need Elvis Presley to make a song a hit.

That summer Leiber and Stoller produced a Coasters record that failed even to dent the charts. Although "What Is the Secret of Your Success?" ostensibly expresses a black bum's befuddlement at Elvis Presley's stardom ("How come you make all the little girls faint?"), it is also at least semiautobiographical. The lead is sung by Billy Guy, who Jerry Wexler once observed "really was an expression of Jerry Leiber." You can almost see Guy scratch his head in disbelief as he sings:

> *People point at you and say you'll sure go far*
> *Just a year ago you was an awful mess*
> *What is the secret of your success?*

Bobby Nunn reveals the answer in his most sepulchral bass:

> *Some cats got it and, uh, some cats ain't.*

Leiber and Stoller had it, and they were taking it to New York.

Chapter Two

A BROADWAY DIVIDED

★

Leiber and Stoller moved to New York for the same reason Elvis Presley left Memphis-based Sun Records for RCA; Alan Freed, the disc jockey who coined the term "rock 'n' roll," graduated from WJW in Cleveland to WINS in New York; and Dick Clark commuted from Philadelphia to broadcast *The Dick Clark Saturday Night Show* live from Manhattan.

Power and opportunities in the music business were concentrated in New York. Most of the Big Six record companies were headquartered there. So were most of the major music publishers (including Presley's); the two major performing rights licensing organizations, the American Society of Composers, Authors and Publishers (ASCAP) and Broadcast Music, Inc. (BMI); the television networks; and the radio stations with the nation's biggest audiences. As Leiber and Stoller had discovered to their dismay with Spark, it was much harder to break a Los Angeles record on the right side of the Rockies than to distribute and promote across the country a record originating in New York. As rock 'n' roll grew in popularity, it inevitably followed the money, gravitating toward and consolidating in New York.

Tin Pan Alley did not roll out the welcome mat for alley music. The very month Leiber and Stoller arrived, Frank Sinatra denounced rock 'n' roll as "written for the most part by cretinous goons." "[B]y means of its almost imbecilic reiteration, and sly, lewd, in plain fact, dirty lyrics," he fulminated, "it manages to be the martial music of every sideburned delinquent on the face of the earth. It is the most brutal, ugly, desperate, vicious form of expression it has been my misfortune to hear."

Rock 'n' roll was an easy target in an era of anxiety over China's Great Leap Forward, the Soviet Union's great leap into space, Cuba's revolution, and, within America's borders, the racial unrest that reared its head in Little Rock and the juvenile unrest epitomized by Charles Starkweather's murderous spree. Little evidence linked rock 'n' roll to a Communist plot, but conspiracy theorists would have had a field day if they had discovered Leiber's dalliance with a leftist commune. The music was clearly culpable, however, of promoting racial mixing and miscegenation, and of corrupting the minds and morals of kids who should have been hitting the books in order to take back the lead in the space race.

"[I]f we do not get off our soft fannies in this country and get down to basic things and get down to business and perhaps turn back the clock a bit to the old times when we had family life and the father was the head of the family," a judge warned a U.S. Senate subcommittee investigating juvenile delinquency, the Russians "will not beat us only with sputniks, and with missiles, they will also beat us in the markets of the world."

Although juvenile delinquency was nothing new—New Yorkers founded the Society for the Reformation of Juvenile Delinquents in 1824—juvenile arrests more than tripled in New York City between 1950 and 1959, while juvenile court cases more than doubled nationally between 1948 and 1957. "Never in our 180-year history has the United States been so aware of—or confused about—its teenagers," a popular journalist observed. One poll indicated that juvenile delinquency ranked behind only national defense and world peace as Americans' greatest concern.

Rock 'n' roll was widely viewed as synonymous with juvenile delinquency. In 1956, Frankie Lymon and the Teenagers recorded a song protesting "I'm Not a Juvenile Delinquent." Some listeners were skeptical—in this instance, with good reason. A heroin overdose would kill Lymon at age twenty-five, and one Teenager died in prison. When Harrison Salisbury published a book about juvenile delinquency in 1958, the Pulitzer Prize–winning *New York Times* correspondent entitled it *The Shook-Up Generation* after Elvis Presley's No. 1 hit of the previous year, "All Shook Up."

Concern for America's moral fiber was probably not what triggered Frank Sinatra's outburst against rock 'n' roll, however. He had personal and professional reasons to resent the upstart music. For Sinatra, 1957 was a very bad year. His ABC television series flopped, and only one of his records managed to break into *Billboard*'s Top Ten while Presley boasted five, two of them composed by those "cretinous goons," Leiber and Stoller. Sinatra was also speaking for many of his cronies in the citadel of popular music publishing, the Brill Building.

Named after its owners, men's haberdashers who initially occupied the ground floor, the Brill Building opened for business in 1931, the same year as the Empire State Building. Art Deco ornamentation enlivened its ten-story white brick façade, and a handsome bronze and slate entrance dared the Depression to do its worst. The Great White Way was crammed throughout the 1930s and '40s with nightclubs, vaudeville houses, and movie palaces. Directly across Broadway from the Brill Building was the Rivoli Theatre, "the Parthenon of Times Square," and on New Year's Eve, 1932, The Paradise, renowned as the home of, count 'em, "50 Girls 50—World's Most Beautiful Girls," opened on the Brill Building's second floor. The upper stories at 1619 Broadway housed the lower orders of show business and street life: bootleggers, bookmakers, agents, promoters and, as Tin Pan Alley inched up Broadway from its original home on Twenty-eighth Street, music publishers, songwriters, and performers.

A. J. Liebling regaled readers of *The New Yorker* in the 1940s with tales of "The Jollity Building," a composite that drew heavily on the Brill Building. Here, Liebling wrote, "the small-scale amusement industry nests like a tramp pigeon." The Jollity Building's denizens were "the petty nomads of Broadway," some of whom camped out in the third floor's cubicles, which were "formed by partitions of wood and frosted glass which [did] not quite reach the ceiling" and were "furnished with a desk and two chairs." These rented "for $10 and $12.50 a month, payable in advance." An office on a higher floor might accommodate two desks, "four theatrical agents, a band leader, a music arranger, a manager of prize fighters, and a dealer in pawn tickets." According to the Jollity Building's rental agent, "Nobody would be in this building unless he had already hocked his watch."

In his autobiography, Jerry Wexler described the men who peddled, published, and plugged pop songs amid the hurly-burly of the early 1950s as "right out of John O'Hara's *Pal Joey.*" Commanding the second table on the right in Lindy's at Fifty-first and Broadway, they sported "smooth felt hats with tapered crowns, double-breasted gabardine suits, wide white-on-white collars and big-knotted hand-painted ties, shiny black wing tips and ultrasheer rayon socks, always a smile, always a story to tell and a song to sell."

The 1958 Manhattan Yellow Pages listed Sinatra Songs, Inc., as one of ninety music publishers at 1619 Broadway, and many others who couldn't afford a phone clustered there. Two of Sinatra's favorite songwriters, Johnny Burke and Jimmy Van Heusen, were tenants. So were Irving Caesar, the man who wrote George Gershwin's lyrics before Ira did, and Charles K. Harris Music, whose founder had published in 1892 "After the Ball," the first pop song deliberately conceived and marketed as a million seller. Racing season saw an early-afternoon exodus from the Brill Building as Caesar, Jule Styne, and other old-timers bolted to the track.

In the late 1950s, the Brill Building retained a certain raffishness. A bookie would interrupt songwriting sessions to retrieve the betting slips he stashed in a piano. Enterprising writers continued to start on the top floor and work their way down. "If they had a song that was so-so but they could sell it," recalled Ed Cramer, an attorney who became head of BMI, "they'd get $25 for an advance, and they'd sell it five times before they hit the first floor. It was like *The Producers*. The song wasn't going to make it, so no one would ever know the difference." Still, by now the Brill Building had settled into stodgy semirespectability. One major publisher nearly fired a young secretary for wearing a sweater to work. "It could just as well have been an insurance company," she recalled.

The two restaurants at the base of the Brill Building illustrated its divided nature. To the left was the Turf Restaurant, where writers congregated because the food was cheap and traded tips about who was looking for new material. "The Turf was for people with less money," one habitué recalled, "though it had two sections. For cats that did have money, it was seafood, surf and turf, and you could sit at a table. The guys who could get roast beef on a bun for 50 cents were standing at the counter." "There were about twenty phone booths," Kenny Vance remembered. "So everybody who didn't have an office in the Brill Building had their own office, because they'd be working out of the phone booth." The Turf made life easier for impecunious patrons by listing a public telephone number in the Yellow Pages.

To the right you entered Jack Dempsey's Restaurant and Bar, where the champ held court in a corner booth and only big shots and tourists could afford the fare. If Dempsey looked out the window, he might see Quincy Jones and other arrangers and songwriters who, Jones wrote in his autobiography, "hung out in front of the Brill Building doorway like Mafia hit men, hands in pockets, collars up, freezing their asses off, broke, hungry, always looking for the next job."

Before he found success in 1959 singing the novelty number "(Seven Little Girls) Sitting in the Back Seat," Paul Evans, a songwriter and performer, made the rounds with his guitar. "I started knocking on doors in the Brill Building. I knew that this was the center of publishing. However, I remember distinctly in a couple of instances—'Come in!'—opening the door and finding guys playing cards in the middle of the day. And they were not interested in listening to material. These were old-line guys, mostly, who saw a kid with a guitar [and were] *praying* rock 'n' roll would go away."

"Some of them could not accept the fact that their music was not as popular as it once was," Ed Cramer said, "and the only explanation that they could accept was a conspiracy to keep them off the air. It was a convenient excuse, but I felt sorry for many of those people. There's an expression I heard: 'The older you get, the better you were.'"

"The Brill Building was the real old-timers," one writer observed, "the 'Shine On, Harvest Moon' guys." Many of them belonged to ASCAP, the oldest and most exclusive performing rights organization, whose membership requirements and old-boy network strongly favored traditional Tin Pan Alley, Broadway, and Hollywood composers. "They never let country songwriters in, and rock 'n' roll neither," said one record company executive. "It had nothing to do with 'artistic.' They didn't want to share the pie." Gene Autry once complained it was easier to get into the White House than into ASCAP. BMI, on the other hand, had been founded by radio broadcasters, and its open-door policy made it a haven for writers of country-and-western music (like Autry) and rhythm and blues and rock 'n' roll (like Leiber and Stoller). The competition between the two organizations regularly spilled over into Congress and the courts. At one point Sinatra's lawyer, Mickey Rudin, sued BMI on behalf of thirty-three ASCAP songwriters. The wrangles pitted generation against generation, genres against genres. While the Brill Building was a bastion of ASCAP writers and publishers, BMI probably represented a greater percentage of the tenants at 1650 Broadway, two blocks uptown and across the street, just past the Winter Garden, where *West Side Story* opened on September 26, 1957.

Many of 1650's occupants then were as young as the musical's Sharks and Jets. Built in 1922, 1650 Broadway was nearly a decade older than the Brill Building and a couple of stories taller, but many of the Brill Building writers looked down on it. Nameless and opening on Fifty-first Street rather than Broadway, it appeared as if it had been "dropped in by helicopter," one songwriter recalled, contrasting its anonymity to the "very plush and regal" Brill Building.

The sixty-six music publishers listed at 1650 Broadway in 1958 included W. C. Handy and Irving Berlin. Handy died that year, however, and Berlin, always tight with a buck, probably hung on because the rent was cheap. Many tenants were too young to buy a drink at the Turf or Jack Dempsey's, and too broke to spring for a meal at either eatery. Instead, they bellied up to the soda fountain at Hanson's Drug Store, on the corner of Fifty-first Street and Seventh Avenue, shared an egg salad sandwich, and played the jukebox as they eyed the actresses who came in to buy cosmetics.

Like the Brill Building, 1650 was a model of what one music historian called "vertical integration." Among its warren of offices you could find publishers to buy a song, arrangers to arrange it, and musicians and singers to record on cheap acetate in a bare-bones studio a "demo," or demonstration record, that served as the song's calling card and blueprint. A demo could cost as little as $60 and became increasingly valuable with the rise of rock 'n' roll, whose impresarios, producers, and performers were often unable to read music.

"Sixteen-fifty to me was the hip building," recalled Hank Medress, a founding member with Neil Sedaka of the Tokens. "The Brill Building was really holding on to the past of Tin Pan Alley. The Brill Building is always depicted as *the* place, but actually it was cornier. Sixteen-fifty was cool, more progressive." Singer Tony Orlando, who worked in 1650 but married a Brill Building secretary, said there "was a little bit of a competitive thing" between the two addresses. "They were much like two high schools. It was like, 'The people in that building aren't as contemporary as the people in *our* building.' Sixteen-fifty saw the Brill Building as old-line publishers." In his autobiography, Orlando wrote that the big, bright, fluorescent directory in the lobby of 1650 "fairly screamed excitement. Then, when you went up to the different floors, all the doors were painted with a black gloss paint, with the company name in gold letters."

The youthfulness and glitz of 1650 Broadway made it more receptive, by and large, to rock 'n' roll. According to Jay Siegal, another member of the Tokens, "Sixteen-fifty was a little easier to get access to. . . . At the Brill Building you needed an appointment. You had to know the secretary to get in. At Sixteen-fifty, you banged on the door and most people would let you in and say, 'Well, whaddya got?'"

"You might aspire to be able get into the Brill Building, but if you were a kid from Queens," said someone who grew up there, "or a kid from Brooklyn, Sixteen-fifty Broadway was the cat's meow." "Sixteen-fifty was more of a workman's place," Ed Cramer said. Freddy Bienstock, the Aberbachs' young cousin and chief lieutenant at Hill and Range, agreed: "All the schleppers were at Sixteen-fifty." Bienstock was one of them, for Hill and Range, a BMI affiliate, was on the eighth floor, to which Jean Aberbach climbed the stairs for exercise. Leiber and Stoller sometimes wrote in Hill and Range's offices amid canvases by Bernard Buffet and other modern European painters whose works Jean and Julian Aberbach collected. An unlikely couple of connoisseurs to publish bluegrass, honky-tonk, and rockabilly, the Viennese brothers had replaced the other original investors in Quintet Music and were now partners in Leiber and Stoller's publishing company. By forming such partnerships, first with country-and-western acts (hence Hill and Range) and then with rock 'n' roll performers like Presley and writers like Leiber and Stoller, the Aberbachs pieced together a publishing empire. "Their philosophy," recalled one employee, "was that it was better to have a percentage of something than 100 percent of nothing."

The differences between the Brill Building and 1650 Broadway should not be exaggerated. Although most of the Brill Building's occupants, according to Jerry Wexler, "had been brought up on Tin Pan Alley ballads and were afraid of the new music," rock 'n' roll had begun to infiltrate the classier address. Alan Freed had an office there. On the first Monday of every month, Wexler met the disc jockey in the cloakroom and handed over a paper bag containing $600 in cash. "It was purely a defensive move," Wexler said. "The baksheesh didn't guarantee play for any particular record; we were only buying access." Freed's manager, Morris Levy, who owned Patricia Music, Roulette Records, and the famous jazz club Birdland, was also at 1619 Broadway. An associate of the Genovese crime family, Levy claimed a cowriter's credit (and publishing royalties) for Frankie Lymon and the Teenagers' "Why Do Fools Fall in Love?" and sole credit for "I'm Not a Juvenile Delinquent." There was nothing juvenile about the delinquency of Levy, "the best-looking Jewish gangster I ever saw," according to Jerry Leiber, "except Bugsy Siegel."

Still, it's appropriate that not long before Leiber and Stoller arrived in New York the Brill Building was where two older ASCAP writers began to make names for themselves. They were affiliated with Famous Music, the music publishing arm of Paramount Pictures and one of the first publishers to settle in the Brill Building. Eddie Wolpin, an executive at Famous, had suggested in 1956 that the thirty-five-year-old Hal David and Burt Bacharach, twenty-seven, try collaborating and offered them a room and a piano.

"My whole history in New York was in the Brill Building," David said. But the lyrics to his first hit song, "The Four Winds and the Seven Seas" in 1949, sounded so antique they might have been composed when Tin Pan Alley was still on West Twenty-eighth Street: "We vowed and said someday we'd wed / In the church in the vale." "Vale"? The word was more redolent of the middle of the nineteenth century than the middle of the twentieth.

Born in Manhattan within sight of the Polo Grounds on May 25, 1921, David moved to Brooklyn at the age of one and grew up in East New York. His father, an Austrian immigrant (as was his mother), owned a delicatessen. David and his three siblings all played the violin. "It was a form of Jewish culture," he recalled. Hal's brother, Mack, nine years his senior, became a prolific songwriter, penning hits throughout the 1940s and '50s for Bing Crosby, Benny Goodman, the Dorsey Brothers, Glenn Miller, Dinah Shore, and the Ames Brothers. His "I Don't Care if the Sun Don't Shine" was a bigger hit for Patti Page in 1950 than it was for Elvis Presley in 1956. Principally a lyricist, Mack David translated into English Edith Piaf's signature song, "*La Vie en Rose*," and provided words for Max Steiner's theme to *Gone with the Wind*, Jerry Livingston's theme for the television show *77 Sunset Strip*, and Pérez Prado's internationally best-selling cha-cha "Cherry Pink and Apple Blossom White."

"He was a role model to me," said Hal David, but Mack discouraged him from following in his footsteps. "He thought I'd be smarter getting into advertising, that's where the big money is. . . . Songwriting he didn't think was quite legitimate for his kid brother." Hal David studied journalism at New York University, dropped out, and landed a job as a copywriter at the *New York Post*. Drafted in 1943, he was stationed during the war in Oahu, Hawaii, where he found a berth in Maurice Evans's Special Services unit. Writing songs, skits, and shows to entertain the troops in the Pacific Theater, he rubbed shoulders with Carl Reiner, Howard Morris, Werner Klemperer, and other young GIs in a show-business boot camp. "It changed my life," David said, and when he was demobilized in 1946, he was determined to become a songwriter.

David's first song to be recorded, with music by Lou Ricca, was "Horizontal," performed by jazz singer and pianist Bunty Pendleton. Although it ostensibly described a returning soldier's eagerness to take it easy and stretch out horizontally, the double entendre caused the record to be banned in Boston and elsewhere. Hal became an ASCAP member like Mack, one of the ASCAP writers who sued BMI. In 1948, David married a schoolteacher, Anne Rauschman, who did not have to support him for long before "The Four Winds and the Seven Seas," which David wrote with Guy Lombardo's singer, Don Rodney, became a hit for Lombardo and was also recorded ("vale" and all) by Vic Damone, Mel Tormé, Herb Jeffries, and Sammy Kaye. For the better part of a year David worked for Kaye's publishing company, writing songs and special material for $50 a week, but preferring the freedom of freelancing, he eventually settled into an arrangement with Famous Music, which had the right of first refusal of David's songs and was generous with advances. By the time he met Burt Bacharach, Hal David was not nearly as successful as Mack, but he had written hits with a variety of partners for Frank Sinatra ("American Beauty Rose"), Teresa Brewer ("Bell Bottom Blues"), and other well-established performers. He commuted to the Brill Building from the suburban comfort of Roslyn, Long Island.

If Mack David was a tough act to follow, Bert Bacharach was a showstopper. That's Bert with an "e," the songwriter's father: all-Southern Conference fullback at Virginia Military Institute, U.S. Marine, radio show host, syndicated newspaper columnist, author of *Bert Bacharach's Book for Men* and *Right Dress: Success Through Better Grooming*, and recognized in the 1950s as "*the* authority on men's clothing." It was the songwriter's mother, Irma Bacharach (née Freeman), an amateur painter and singer, who insisted on naming their child "Burt," thereby distinguishing her son from her husband but also suggesting he could never match his father. And it was Irma Bacharach who insisted that Burt with a "u" take lessons and practice on their Steinway when he would rather have been outside playing sports, in which he was not big enough to excel. "I ate jars of peanut butter to try and grow taller," Bacharach said, but he was too short to make the football team or, until a belated growth spurt finally elevated him to five feet ten inches, attract girls.

Bacharach also felt excluded by his Jewishness in Forest Hills, Queens, where his family eventually settled after moving to New York from Missouri a year after Burt's birth in Kansas City on May 12, 1929. All his friends at Forest Hills High School, which he attended a few years before Mike Stoller, were Catholic. "They always got to do things together, like go to midnight mass, and I couldn't go. Even in a football huddle, they'd say, 'Let's kick the hell outta those Jews,' and I'd say, 'Yeah, let's get 'em.' Now I look back and can't understand why it was so important to belong to those guys faking their I.D.'s to get rye and ginger ales at the bowling alley, but *wow*, it was then. So, to be the life of the party, I played piano in a Friday night dance band." A band member who was the son of Jack Conn, a principal in Bregman, Vocco, and Conn, a prominent Brill Building music publisher, provided the stock arrangements they played.

Other than as a means to win popularity, music did not inspire Bacharach profoundly until he heard *Daphnis et Chloé*. Ravel's airy chromaticism and Rachmaninoff's melodicism dispelled his conception of classical music as something to listen to somberly on the car radio as darkness fell while the family returned from an outing to Philadelphia or the Jersey Shore. And on Fifty-second Street, Bacharach discovered the quirky, darting rhythms of Dizzy Gillespie, Charlie Parker, Thelonius Monk, and Miles Davis. "Hearing them . . . was like a window opening." Impressionism and bebop lit a fire that Brahms and Basie had not kindled.

Bacharach studied composition for three years at McGill University in Montreal; during summers at Tanglewood, the Music Academy of the West in Santa Barbara, California, and the New School for Social Research in Manhattan; and, after his discharge from the U.S. Army, at

New York's Mannes School of Music. His most important teachers were Henry Cowell, Darius Milhaud, and Bohuslav Martinů. What did these Californian, French, and Czech composers have in common? Cowell, with his interest in Asian and folk music; Milhaud, steeped in Brazilian music and African-American ragtime and jazz; and Martinů, influenced by ragtime, jazz, and Debussy, were all eclectic, open-minded, and adventurous. And none of them disdained popular music. Gershwin had studied with Cowell, and Dave Brubeck with Milhaud, who encouraged Bacharach, the songwriter recalled, "to let the melody shine through."

Such formidable training might have prepared Bacharach to become a classical composer, but he never forgot, he said, that he "got into music in the first place to be popular." Subsisting on commissions, grants, and academic appointments would never provide the affluence or even the wardrobe to which the son of the author of *Right Dress: Success Through Better Grooming* was accustomed from birth. Somehow Bacharach found time during the summers to play standards in hotels and restaurants in the Catskills and on Cape Cod.

Basic training was a torment when Bacharach left McGill to enter the Army. "I have written practically nothing with the exception of little fugues, simple canons, and colorless counterpoint," he wrote Cowell. "All very dry and uninventive." He was desperate to transfer to Special Services because "I just have to make contact with music again. Just these two weeks, which incidentally seem like two years, have made me feel completely divorced from music." Bacharach's wish was granted, and he steered clear of Korea by entertaining officers in the United States. When he was shipped off to Germany, he wrote arrangements for a German dance band and paid other soldiers to clean his M-1 rifle.

Bacharach met Vic Damone in Germany and, after his discharge in 1952, worked briefly as the singer's accompanist. "I was probably one of forty-three piano players he fired," Bacharach said. "It really hurt." He accompanied Polly Bergen (on whom he developed a deep crush), Imogene Coca (whom Hal David's Special Services compatriots, Carl Reiner and Howard Morris, helped propel to stardom with the material they wrote for the television shows on which she appeared with Sid Caesar), Georgia Gibbs, Joel Grey, Steve Lawrence, and the Ames Brothers. He also performed solo in nightclubs such as Nino's Continental in Manhattan and the Bayview on Fire Island, New York. In 1953, he married Paula Stewart, one of many less well-known singers who hired him as a rehearsal pianist.

Working with the Ames Brothers, a quartet from Malden, Massachusetts, whose blood ties were stronger than its vocals, Bacharach was so unimpressed by the quality of the songs they were recording that he felt sure he could do better. He had written a song at McGill, "The Night Plane to Heaven," and there was nothing to it. Renting a cubbyhole in the Brill Building, he worked at the piano every day with any lyricist willing to write with him. The first of several collaborators was Jack Wolf. "My family knew his brother-in-law or something like that. . . . I wrote some really bad songs." He toiled for ten months without coming up with a single song a publisher would buy, until finally Patti Page cut "a terrible song" he had composed with Wolf, "Keep Me in Mind," and Mel Tormé recorded "Desperate Hours," a song written with Wilson Stone to promote a Paramount film, William Wyler's suspenseful *The Desperate Hours.*

When Eddie Wolpin put Hal David together with Burt Bacharach, Famous Music and David were doing Bacharach a big favor by taking a chance on a writer with such an undistinguished track record. Famous offered Bacharach $50 a week for the right of first refusal, eventually raising this to $75 for exclusive rights. "It may have been we guaranteed to place six songs with them a year," Bacharach recalled. "It was more like they gave us a place to work. There was an office space there."

One cannot imagine opposites more polar than Leiber and Stoller and the unpromising team of David and Bacharach. The performers Bacharach had accompanied and for whom David had written were singing music that time was rushing by, and their first collaborations, recorded in 1956, did not seize the moment in popular music. "The Morning Mail" disappeared on the b-side of a single by a minor doo-wop group, the Gallahads. Although Alan Dale sang their "I Cry More" in *Don't Knock the Rock,* he was by far the most sedate and old-fashioned performer in the exploitation film that Alan Freed screened at mobbed rock 'n' roll shows at Times Square's Paramount Theatre in February 1957. While Bill Haley and the Comets, Little Richard, and the Treniers lit up the screen, Frankie Lymon and the Teenagers, as well as Ruth Brown and the Cadillacs, wrecked the stage. "I was lousy as a Rock and Roll hero," confessed Dale, an Italian crooner born Aldo

Sigismondi who had recorded a hit version of "Cherry Pink and Apple Blossom White" with Mack David's lyrics.

Yet in 1957, Bacharach and David, meeting in the Brill Building every morning at eleven, managed to write Top Twenty hits in rapid succession for Marty Robbins, Perry Como, and Patti Page. Though Robbins's "The Story of My Life" and Como's "Magic Moments" were produced by different people for different labels, both records begin inauspiciously with whistling. Lyrically as well as musically they sound trifling and retrograde, as if the composers were whistling past the graveyard of their own obsolescence.

"The Story of My Life" was produced by Mitch Miller, the powerful head of Columbia Records' Popular Division. Remembered today for his long-running series of "Sing Along with Mitch" records, Miller has often been maligned as a maestro of 1950s schlock who disregarded the sophisticated artistry of the Great American Songbook yet resisted the elementary energy of emergent rock 'n' roll. Even today his description of a popular song as "a 32-bar commercial" is off-putting, if only because it is so undeluded. Yet Miller injected elements of rhythm and blues and country music, however diluted, into mainstream pop. He persuaded Tony Bennett, for instance, to record Hank Williams's "Cold, Cold Heart" and created a new market for country songs. With Marty Robbins, Miller did the opposite, giving a country artist pop songs. Robbins became one of the first country singers to "cross over" to pop success. While "The Story of My Life" reached No. 15 on the pop charts in 1958, it went all the way to No. 1 in the country rankings. "When we wrote 'The Story of My Life,'" David recalled, "I did not know we were writing what would be considered a country song. I'd never been to Nashville. It was just something I liked, and they put a name to it." Bacharach and David would not have a No. 1 pop hit for a decade.

Yet Robbins, who would soon become famous for the ballad "El Paso," sounds characterless on "The Story of My Life," and Bacharach and David were as much if not more to blame than Mitch Miller for the blandness. They pitched the song to the lowest and oldest common denominator, as they did Perry Como's "Magic Moments." Although the latter has an interesting rhythmic pattern and an ingenious mouthful of a David couplet ("The way that we cheered whenever our team was scoring a touchdown, / The time that the floor fell out of my car when

I put the clutch down"), novelist Richard Russo nailed "Magic Moments" when a character in his novel *Empire Falls* betrays his age and inanity by crooning the ditty.

These songs and Patti Page's "Another Time, Another Place" pale in comparison to Leiber and Stoller's songs from the same period. Despite their initial commercial success, Bacharach and David thought so little of the potential of their partnership that it nearly lapsed while they collaborated with other songwriters and Bacharach leapt at an offer to become musical director for fifty-six-year-old Marlene Dietrich. Certainly the sophomoric nostalgia in which they trafficked could not hold a candle to the street-corner immediacy of "Searchin'" or its flip side, "Young Blood," on which the Coasters leer at a girl and compete for her attention with come-ons that the singers deftly pass from one to the other and dribble from the upper to the lower register until the girl's dad, like the cook in "Smokey Joe's Café" and played once again by bass Bobby Nunn, puts his foot down and an end to their amorousness. "Young Blood" made Bacharach and David's music seem old hat and their future unpromising.

Chapter Three

LONELY AVENUE

★

Doc Pomus was honeymooning in the Catskills in the summer of 1957 when he entered a luncheonette and dropped a dime in the jukebox. As he was about to punch in his selection, another title caught his eye. Curious, he played "Young Blood" by the Coasters. What he heard sounded dimly familiar. He had made a demo of a song with that title which Leiber and Stoller had rewritten almost beyond recognition. They had helped him out before, suggesting a change in the chorus of a ballad Pomus had written for LaVern Baker, but this was different. Rhythm and blues records rarely made it to rural Northern jukeboxes. "Young Blood" had to be a national pop hit. Pomus excitedly telephoned Atlantic Records, which wired him more money—$1,000 in one of his accounts, $1,500 in another—than he had ever earned in a lump sum for a single song.

How much credit Pomus deserves for "Young Blood" is unclear. According to Leiber and Stoller, he provided nothing but the title, which Jerry Wexler insisted *he* gave them. Pomus himself acknowledged gratefully that it "was a very average hack song until Jerry and Mike helped me and did a serious rewrite." What matters most are that Leiber and Stoller, unlike many people in the record business, had the honesty and generosity to share the credit and that the song, plus Pomus's marriage to a beautiful blond actress and the songwriting partnership he had formed a year earlier with Mort Shuman, gave Jerome Solon Felder, at thirty-two, a new lease on life and on music.

Jerome Felder was born on June 27, 1925, in Williamsburg and grew up at 75 Manhattan Avenue, at the corner of McKibbin Street. It was the only elevator building in the Brooklyn neighborhood, and his family moved there after polio crippled Jerry at the age of six. The Felders' four-room apartment was on the second floor, so Jerry could clamber up and down a single flight of stairs if the elevator failed.

To avoid an epidemic of infantile paralysis, Jerry's mother had sent him to summer camp, where he awoke one morning unable to move his legs. When his parents raced to his rescue in an ambulance, they were initially denied entry to the quarantined campground. Never again did Jerry walk unsupported by braces and crutches. Felder family lore includes encounters with Franklin and Eleanor Roosevelt at Warm Springs, but hydrotherapy at the Georgia clinic, where "Master Jerome Felder of Brooklyn, New York" was listed as a resident in November and December 1932, did not help. In later years, Pomus told of a surgeon who would enter his hospital ward and point to children whose limbs were to be amputated. Day after day he lay quaking in fear that the doctor would finger him. This sounds more like a nightmare than a real remembrance—amputation was not customarily prescribed for polio victims—but even if exaggerated, it underscores the fact that treatment for the disease when Pomus contracted it was nasty, brutish, and long.

Confined to bed at home, Jerry had to yell to attract his family's attention. He developed strong lungs and, although the Felders were not musically inclined, a strong interest in music, especially jazz and blues. He played clarinet, alto sax, and a baby grand piano that, according to his younger brother, Raoul Felder, was "the only decent piece of furniture in the house." Jerry would venture with Raoul to the Brighton Beach Baths on weekends to hear Harry James and Kay Kyser and "swing and sway" with Sammy Kaye years before the bandleader employed Hal David. It was a long subway ride from Williamsburg to Brighton Beach, and the elevated stations' stairs were arduous. "It was quite an ordeal," Raoul remembered. "He would fall and fall."

In his teens, Jerry led a dance band that rehearsed in the cramped Felder living room and played bar mitzvahs and weddings. He yearned for harder stuff, however—by now Big Joe Turner had become a favorite—and he found it in clubs where he could not yet legally buy a drink. George's Tavern in Greenwich Village launched his precocious and audacious career as a blues singer.

Hanging around the stage to hear another set by jazz trumpeter Frankie Newton and his band, Felder was a nuisance. The kid wasn't running up a tab, and his unsightly crutches must have inconvenienced customers who were. When the owner of George's Tavern threatened to throw him out, Felder protested that he was a singer. Newton overheard and out of generosity or in jest invited the youngster to sit in. What would he like to sing? Seizing the opportunity, Felder called "Piney Brown Blues." The squat Jewish teenager hoisted himself up and belted out the tribute that Big Joe Turner and his Fly Cats had paid in 1940 to their late friend, the proprietor of Kansas City's Sunset Café who had employed Turner and dubbed William Basie "Count":

> *I dreamed I was standing on 18th and Vine,*
> *I shook hands with Piney Brown,*
> *And I could hardly keep from cryin'.*

Asked to sing another song, Felder reprised "Piney Brown Blues" because it was the only blues whose lyrics he knew by heart.

Felder's performance can only have been a desecration of the song that jazz historian Gunther Schuller called "a poignant lament, a heartfelt jeremiad," and "[o]ne of the most remarkable and moving recorded performances in the history of jazz." Newton knew that history intimately. He had contributed to it by playing the muted introduction to Billie Holiday's original recording of "Strange Fruit." Jerry Felder was staking a claim to a musical experience that was historically, geographically, and racially alien territory. Yet his naïveté and nerve intrigued Newton and other listeners who invited him to come back. "I went home that night on the subway walking on air." His crutches were all but forgotten. Felder returned shortly, having doubled his repertory by composing a song he called "B. B. [for Brighton Beach] Blues."

Soon Felder was singing with Newton's band at George's Tavern for $5 a night and at Sunday afternoon jam sessions at another Greenwich Village club, the Pied Piper. The British jazz critic, songwriter, and impresario Leonard Feather heard him there and recorded him backed by veterans of Fletcher Henderson's, Count Basie's, and Chick Webb's bands. Feather provided the songs and played piano on the first record, released on the independent Apollo label, to bear the name "Doc" Pomus. Now a nineteen-year-old political science student at Brooklyn College, Felder had acquired the nickname "Doc" because of his learning and added the "Pomus" himself.

Over the years Pomus offered several explanations for his choice of an alter ego. "I come from . . . a very respectable middle-class family," he once said, "and had to use the name 'Doc' Pomus to keep my parents from finding out what I was up to. White kids just didn't sing the blues with negroes in . . . 1940." But it strains credulity that the Felders were entirely in the dark about their disabled son's doings, especially since getting him to gigs was a major production. Cabs didn't cruise the "slum" where they lived, according to Raoul Felder, who had to walk several blocks to a main thoroughfare, hail a taxi, and persuade the driver to pick up his big brother. If it didn't prevent his parents from learning about his singing career, at least the pseudonym spared them public embarrassment when he shouted the praises of marijuana in "My Good Pott" ("Long and thin, but awful sweet, / A perfume smell that can't be beat") or the "real great jelly roll" of "My New Chick":

> Well, we get home in the evening,
> We turn down all the lights,
> Screams, "Daddy, daddy, daddy, everything's all right!"
> And we boogie, yes, we boogie all night long,
> And when I get tired, my baby's still coming on strong.

The most persuasive explanation for Jerry Felder's pseudonym is that "Pomus" suggested something hard and gritty, like pumice or stone, and "Doc Pomus" sounded like "a hip, midnight character." Assuming the title of "Doc" also turned the tables on the physicians who had tyrannized Jerry Felder during his childhood. "If you ever feel stiff around your back, / Send for me and you'll hear it crack," Pomus boasted on "Send for the Doctor," promising to "soothe every ache and ease every pain / But my kinda cure's gonna drive you insane." It was a rebellious, escapist fantasy that Jerry Felder lived to the fullest, especially when he began to perform in black clubs like the Baby Grand in Harlem, the Verona Club in Brooklyn, and Cookie's Caravan in Newark, where he was frequently the only white person on the premises, but the patrons, Pomus recalled, "didn't object to whitey doing the indigo stuff."

In a competition with Leiber and Stoller over who was blackest, Doc Pomus wins hands down. He wasn't just writing the blues; he was singing and living them. "Doc Pomus . . . was a white Negro before it became fashionable," Mort Shuman wrote, still marveling more than thirty years later that his songwriting partner "sang in clubs that even some of his black friends were afraid to enter." It's fitting that two of the first people to recognize Pomus's talent, Frankie Newton and Leonard Feather, were friends of Mezz Mezzrow. Newton had even played in two of Mezzrow's short-lived bands. Performing a couple of weeks before her death, Dinah Washington paused while singing "Blowtop Blues," a Feather composition, when she spotted him in the audience. "Would you believe," she asked, "that a white man wrote this song?"

Pomus's identification with African Americans was deep and enduring. A 1940s *Journal of Pediatrics* article remarked of children hospitalized with polio that "being 'good' means being quiet and unenterprising while being 'bad' means indulging in the most modest imitations of a pre-school child's normal activity." An Association for the Aid of Crippled Children publication warned of a "social taboo" requiring that a handicapped person

> express his pain, his desires, his hopes, and his anguish only in the most superficial manner; if he expresses his bitterness deeply or with any sense of personal tragedy, he risks alienating the nonhandicapped. . . . As long as the handicapped individual is cheerful and lighthearted, he is, like the "jolly fat boy," usually accepted by his peers.

Jerry Felder refused to be the jolly fat boy. "I was never one of those happy cripples," he wrote years later. "I was too fucking mad." Rebelling against his fate and his family, he acted up and acted out, flicking unstubbed Chesterfields out his window and setting his apartment building's awning aflame more than once. Leonard Kriegel, a Bronx native who also contracted polio at summer camp and became an eloquent chronicler of the disease, once wrote, "To be doomed by illness is to learn how to refuse the temptation of the ordinary and settled." The blues became Doc Pomus's defiance of his disability.

The blues also embodied his empathy with African Americans. Racial discrimination was as unjust, undeserved, and devastating as polio. The disease, a sociologist observed, was "a kind of discriminatory barrier in the attainment of important social values; in short, it was 'un-American.'" The blues, according to Raoul Felder, "reached out and touched a depth" in his brother. "The plight of black people then was just terrible. I think black people were basically nicer to him than white people. The identification went both ways." In one of his notebooks Pomus imagined "a huge army with the blind and crippled marching hand in hand with the blacks and the other disenfranchised." He wrote, "To the world, a fat crippled jewish kid is a nigger—a thing—the invisible man—like Ralph Ellison says." The blues vanquished that invisibility. It "was the only way," he said, "I could express myself and . . . channel my feelings and tell the world who I was."

Yet Jerry Felder would have had much to rebel against even if polio had not stricken him. According to Shirlee Hauser, his closest companion in later years, "The darkness came before that." He grew up in an angry household. Morris Felder, his father, was born in Vienna. Raoul Felder described him as "an unsuccessful veterinarian—you never saw a Jewish person with a pet in Williamsburg—and then an unsuccessful lawyer." He ran repeatedly and unsuccessfully for political office, losing the 1942 Democratic primary for Congress because he could not secure the support of the Democratic organization. He was a short man who suffered from curvature of the spine and the scorn of his wife. Millie Goldstein, born in London, expected Morris to support her, their two children, and her widowed, skirt-chasing father in a grander style than he could manage. They fought frequently over money. As Millie became the family's main provider by managing a nursing home, Morris retreated into sullen silence. Their son's polio made matters even worse. Millie concentrated her affection on Jerry, making her husband, who saw his own deformity mirrored and magnified in his son's disability, feel all the more alienated. A lot of resentment was crammed into a small apartment. During the afternoon Jerry rehearsed his band in the living room, where his father saw clients in the evening and his grandfather slept at night.

The Felders were dismayed by their son's escape into music. Fearing he might end up selling pencils on the street, they hoped he would become an accountant. Though he was no less fearful of destitution, Jerry had different ideas. "My legs were lifeless, useless," Leonard Kriegel wrote, "but their loss had created dancing images in whose shadowy

gyrations I recognized a strange but potentially interesting new self."
The new self that "Doc Pomus" promised was far more interesting to
Jerry Felder than a career keeping books, and he dropped out of Brook-
lyn College to pursue a career in music.

Pomus worked with an extraordinary number of great jazz musicians in the 1940s, including Rex Stewart, Willie "The Lion" Smith,
Roy Eldridge, Milt Jackson, Horace Silver, Walter Page, and Buddy
Tate. On the few records he made during this period, he sounds delighted and somewhat amazed to be in such august company. He
became friends with Duke Ellington and briefly shared a manager with
Charlie Parker. As rhythm and blues became more popular in black
clubs and Pomus began sharing bills with the likes of Big Maybelle
and Roy Hamilton, his performances became more raucous. With a
blues singer named Andrew Tibbs he sometimes staged a "Battle of the
Blues," competing with improvised choruses for the favors of a woman
in the audience. "Sometimes it was hilarious and sometimes it was dangerous," Pomus recalled, conjuring up a scene out of "Smokey Joe's
Café" or "Young Blood": "[I]t got dangerous if she had an old man and
he took it the wrong way and waited for us at closing time with may-
hem on his mind."

Two of Pomus's best friends and drinking buddies were fellow
singers Jimmy Scott, whose androgyny made him nearly as freakish a
figure on the R&B scene as Pomus's pallor and polio, and Otis Blackwell, a performer with a fondness for country music as well as the blues
who pressed pants in a Brooklyn tailor shop to make ends meet. "[W]e
were the kings of Bed-Stuy, Williamsburg, and parts of Flatbush," Pomus said of Blackwell and himself. Two musicians with whom Pomus
worked frequently, guitarist Mickey Baker and tenor saxophone player
King Curtis, became most-favored session men at Atlantic Records as
well as recording stars in their own right.

To support his habit of singing songs, Pomus began writing them for
other performers. "[T]he songwriting came very hard to me," said Pomus, who could read music but found writing it down "tedious." It became more difficult to compose on the piano when he broke the fingers
in his right hand fending off a mugger after leaving a club late one night.

Gatemouth Moore, a blues-singing Baptist preacher, was the first
performer other than Pomus to record one of his compositions. Herb

Abramson introduced Pomus to Atlantic Records, which Abramson had cofounded with Ahmet Ertegun. The only partner with prior professional experience in the record business, Abramson had produced Big Joe Turner, the Ravens, and other acts for National Records. He encouraged Pomus to write for R&B singers on Atlantic such as Lil Green. Pomus would drop by and sing a song, perhaps playing halting accompaniment on piano. If the producer or performer liked it and the song was recorded, it became the property of Atlantic's publishing arm, Progressive Music.

On one visit to Atlantic's offices, Pomus bumped into Big Joe Turner, who had recently signed with the label. As chance would have it, Turner was describing a performance by Pomus that he had seen at Harlem's Baby Grand. "That's the guy!" Turner said. Pomus started writing songs for his idol, beginning with a slow blues, "Still in Love," that is as blunt, balanced, alliterative, and concise as a dispatch from Julius Caesar: "You loved me, then you left me, now you're laughin'."

Another song Pomus wrote for Turner, the rollicking "Boogie Woogie Country Girl," anticipated Chuck Berry's sketches of music-mad teenagers. Pomus shared writer's credit for the song with Reginald Ashby, a friend and frequent accompanist on piano who spent so much time at the Felders' apartment that Raoul forgot he was black. Pomus said he gave 15 percent of the song to Ashby in exchange for writing the lead sheet that guided the band. "Boogie Woogie Country Girl" was recorded at the same November 3, 1955, session as Leiber and Stoller's "The Chicken and the Hawk." Although these performances sound more like rock 'n' roll and less like rhythm and blues than any others Turner recorded, the drummer driving them was the newest member of the Modern Jazz Quartet, Connie Kaye.

It was about this time that Leiber and Stoller, now under contract to Atlantic, met Pomus, whose "Alley, Alley" commercial had thrilled Stoller a decade earlier. Although Pomus was eight years older than Leiber and Stoller, he was always deferential and grateful to the more successful songwriting team whom he called "the kids."

The greatest song Pomus composed without a collaborator was "Lonely Avenue," which Ray Charles recorded on May 16, 1956. It was based on a tune that the Pilgrim Travelers, one of the nation's most popular and widely touring gospel groups, had liked so much they used it twice. "Lonely Avenue" is Pomus's personal "Desolation Row":

Now my covers they feel like lead
And my pillow it feels like stone
Well I've tossed and turned so ev'ry night
I'm not used to being alone.

★

"Lonely Avenue," Pomus told an interviewer, "is about myself." His notebooks linked the song directly to his disability. "There's a street that the especially isolated people live on," he wrote. "The people who feel like they're always fighting the battle of life with limited physical equipment." On a television special a couple of years after recording "Lonely Avenue," Ray Charles identified discrimination as the inspiration of many of his performances:

> You sing about the woman, but you are really also talking about all the kicking around you've had, the humiliations that you've had, the throwing out of doors you've had, the hunger that you've had. You *think* about all these things, but you're still *singing* about that woman.

Pomus's perspective and Charles's converged in a bleak threnody.

Every aspect of the record's arrangement and production emphasizes the isolation and oppression of the lyrics. The instrumentation is stark: drums, bass, piano, and a saxophone solo. Charles's full band draws attention to its absence by not entering until the song's very last note. Echoing his vocal and mocking his loneliness, the Cookies—three young black women, two of whom would eventually become Raeletts—sound like voices in Charles's head rather than in his dreary room. The beat is a dull 2/4 thud as heavy as those covers of lead and that pillow of stone, yet only the bass, throbbing like a migraine, marks it, while the drummer weighs in with a rim shot on every other beat. The sparseness made Jerry Wexler, who produced the record with Ahmet Ertegun, apprehensive. "There's so much time between the downbeats," he said to Charles. "Don't we need eighth notes or something to fill in between them?"

Charles said, "No, brother. Trust me." And Ray Charles, as usual, was right.

Songs like "Lonely Avenue" won Pomus some renown in rhythm-and-blues circles, but little remuneration. His singing career was even less rewarding. In October 1955, he wrote and recorded a single for the Dawn label, "Heartlessly," which awkwardly amalgamated blues and rock 'n' roll. Lightening his voice and cleaning up his language, Pomus tried to sound sincere rather than raunchy. When Alan Freed began to play the song on WINS, it looked for a moment as though Pomus might pull it off. But when Dawn, like many a diminutive, undercapitalized independent with a potential hit on its hands, sold "Heartlessly" to a major label, RCA, the record stopped dead in its tracks. An RCA executive probably concluded that no amount of promotion could interest white teenagers or blacks of any age in a record by a thirty-year-old Jew on crutches.

Pomus was devastated. "I realized I was going to end up being absolutely impecunious for the rest of my life." Living in fleabag hotels and sharing bathrooms with diseased derelicts and hookers, Pomus subsisted on less than $5,000 a year, earning some of this by writing articles under a variety of pseudonyms for *Confidential* and other pulp magazines.

Moreover, since the introduction of the Salk vaccine in 1954, polio, like the blues and R&B, seemed on the verge of extinction. In 1957, new cases of the disease dropped by more than two-thirds. "[P]olio had ceased to be a vital concern," one historian observed. "Once lionized as heroic examples of human fortitude, the thousands of polio survivors who continued to need medical and financial help were suddenly ignored as embarrassing emblems of their own poor timing, clumsy enough to get polio before the vaccine that could have protected them was found."

Time seemed to be passing by Pomus in more ways than one. In desperation he turned to a teenager who was dating his cousin. "I had no instinct for rock 'n' roll because my antecedents were different," Pomus recalled. "I always considered myself a songwriter, period, not necessarily a songwriter for kids. Because when you write for black audiences, like I did write for Joe Turner and Ray Charles, your audience was people of all ages. . . . Mort was very much a part of young music, so I was able, in my own wonderfully schizophrenic way, to transcend myself into teenage stuff with the help of Mort Shuman."

★

Mortimer Shuman grew up on the top floor of an apartment building in Brighton Beach. Over his head the BMT clattered to its last stop, where Jerry Felder occasionally tumbled down the stairs. Born on November 12, 1936, Shuman was the only child of free-thinking, left-leaning Jews from Warsaw. Until he entered public school, he spoke Yiddish in Brighton Beach's "shtetl on the shores of the Atlantic Ocean," as he described the neighborhood in an unpublished autobiographical sketch.

At Abraham Lincoln High School, Shuman was a class ahead of Neil Sedaka, who remembered him as "very dynamic and popular." Sometimes the two of them loitered in Andria's Pizzeria on Brighton Beach Avenue and listened to the Wurlitzer jukebox, swapping opinions of the records. Louis Shuman played the mandolin and gave his son a guitar. Mort also took the piano lessons that were nearly inevitable at that time for a nice Jewish boy—or girl, for that matter. ("Everybody on my block played an instrument," a contemporary of Shuman's in Brooklyn recalled.) A violin-playing, bourbon-swilling uncle drilled him in the differences between Bach, Vivaldi, and Telemann. But Shuman felt more attracted to rhythm and blues.

Shuman was still a teenager when he met Doc Pomus, his father died, and he discovered marijuana. Under the influence of pot and Pomus, Shuman "became," he later recalled, "what Norman Mailer wrote about in one of his essays: a white negro." Eleven years older, Pomus gave Shuman a "blues education" that continued while Shuman desultorily studied a more conventional curriculum at City College. By his own account, Shuman "started to dress black, talk black, walk black, and eat black, because as everyone knew, black was 'soul' and white, Jewish, lower-middle-class America had none." At least white, Jewish, lower-middle-class America put food on the table. Famished after a long day attending classes and working a part-time job, Shuman would sometimes visit the Felder family apartment in Williamsburg, where he earned the nickname "the *fresser*" because he ate like a pig.

Pomus encouraged Shuman to write songs, and eventually the protégé became a partner. Pomus explained,

I decided that the best way to make a lot of money as a song-writer was to write with somebody else, and this way we'd write so many songs that we had to make a living at it. . . . I had him sit in the room with me while I wrote songs for a year, so he saw everything I did. He had a great ear for what was going on with young kids. After a year, I started giving him a piece of every song I wrote. And then he started contributing. And after about two and a half years, I made him a full partner. . . . He wrote about 75 percent of the melodies and about 25 percent of the lyrics, so it was a true collaboration.

A few months after the failure of Pomus's "Helplessly," on May 15, 1956, Andrew Tibbs, with whom Pomus had performed, and his brother Kenneth recorded on Atlantic the first song that Pomus and Shuman jointly copyrighted. "Get Hip, Miss Rip Van Winkle," the Tibbs Brothers sang, poking fun at a square who didn't care for rock 'n' roll. "You're a Model T in th'atomic age." In reality it was Pomus who was struggling to get hip to a new beat and new audience.

None of the songs Pomus and Shuman wrote during the first couple of years of their partnership equaled artistically or commercially the best material that Pomus had composed on his own. Writing for grown-up rhythm-and-blues singers whom they revered while trying to reach white teenagers whom Pomus, at least, held in little regard, they connected with neither artists nor audiences. Eight years older than Leiber and Stoller, Pomus did not have their agility; three years younger, Shuman had yet to acquire their expertise. They contributed two songs to Ray Charles, "You Be My Baby" and "Carryin' the Load," which sounded like pale imitations of songs Charles had written better himself (indeed, Charles shared songwriting credit for "You Be My Baby"). They wrote two numbers for Big Joe Turner, "Love Roller Coaster" and "I Need a Girl," that tried to transform the lusty blues man into a bouncy pop Romeo. Saxophone and guitar unison interludes make both songs sound like roller-rink renditions of the hokey-pokey.

It took another partnership to provide Pomus with the inspiration and incentive to achieve commercial success. Two weeks after Turner recorded "Love Roller Coaster" and "I Need a Girl," on May 27, 1957, Pomus married Wilma Burke in Saint Joseph's Roman Catholic Church in Greenwich Village.

Pomus had met Willi Burke the previous winter in the lobby of the Village's Broadway Central Hotel, where he was holed up and she had just arrived. She entered his life when it was going nowhere, which is probably what attracted him to someone so entirely his opposite. As unhip as Miss Van Winkle, Burke had never heard of Billie Holiday, much less LaVern Baker. The music in which she had received her college degree was strictly classical. A midwestern Catholic eight years younger than Pomus, the virginal Burke had thought of becoming a nun and looked like an angel to Pomus. An aspiring actress, she was so poor that her dinner often consisted of Campbell's soup, which she warmed on an iron in her room. When she returned at night from the restaurant where she worked as a hostess, Pomus would greet her with cookies, doughnuts, and, soon, a poem.

> We'd sit there in the lobby every night for months, talking. He was really a charming man and extremely intelligent. He was almost like a father figure to me. . . . He was such a dichotomy, in that he was this Brooklyn guy with a blues background, but he was college-educated. . . . The thing that attracted me so much to him was that this gruff bear of a person was at the same time extremely sensitive, intelligent. He didn't curse—except when he got mad. He had never thought he was going to get married. I didn't think I was going to marry him, actually. It just happened.

Burke did not inform her parents of their wedding, and his did not attend the Catholic ceremony, though they hosted a reception at a Lower East Side delicatessen. The couple spent their wedding night at the Waldorf, where Pomus, sitting down abruptly as his braces forced him to, broke the bed. When they summoned a bellboy for help, Burke hid in the bathroom in embarrassment.

Returning from their Catskills honeymoon, Pomus and Burke settled into the Felder apartment in Williamsburg (Pomus's parents had moved to Sheepshead Bay), where they had their first child, Sharyn, a year after their wedding. The neighborhood was deteriorating. "You'd come home at night," Pomus recalled, and "you had to have a police escort." When a bullet whizzed through Sharyn's window, they beat a hasty retreat to a ranch house in Lynbrook, New York. Pomus forsook black clubs and fleabag hotels for family life with a shiksa in a Long Island suburb. "When we got married," Burke said, "we had such a feeling about life that he'd never had before. So optimistic. Like we were going to build a family. I think that's when he started writing different stuff. He wanted to be more commercial."

Pomus launched a record label bankrolled by an acquaintance seeking an alibi to enjoy company other than his wealthy wife's. R&B Records shared an office with a film company in 1650 Broadway, an appropriate venue for such a dubious venture. Pomus was the president, and Shuman, still in college, the stock clerk. When a quintet from Harlem auditioned, they liked what they heard. Although the 5 Crowns had been around for years, recording with various personnel on sundry labels, they had recently added two promising singers, Charlie Thomas and Ben Nelson, and dropped the digit from their name. Pomus and Shuman wrote a doo-wop pastiche for the Crowns and recorded it with Thomas singing lead. "Kiss and Make Up" startled everyone by becoming a hit in Pittsburgh, but R&B Records lacked the funds to promote the record or press more copies. The single fizzled and the label folded.

A frequent visitor to the R&B Records office while it lasted was Pomus's old friend Otis Blackwell, who had graduated from singer to songwriter more swiftly and successfully than Pomus. Having written with various collaborators Little Willie John's "Fever" (covered by Peggy Lee), Presley's "Don't Be Cruel" and "All Shook Up," and Jerry Lee Lewis's "Great Balls of Fire," Blackwell didn't have to press pants anymore. He was ensconced at 1650 Broadway in the offices of Elvis Presley Music, a BMI-affiliated joint publishing venture with Hill and Range. Blackwell introduced Pomus and Shuman to Paul Case, the professional manager of Hill and Range, who scouted, acquired, and placed songs. Case took a liking to the pair and signed them to a three-year contract in late 1958 even though, Pomus acknowledged, "we had no track record, really." Shuman, who had recently been kicked out of City College, remembered loading crates at a temporary job all day and trudging through a snowstorm to 1650 Broadway. He looked so exhausted and malnourished on arrival that someone gave him $10 for dinner. Restored, he returned and signed on the dotted line. Only twenty-two, Shuman was so boyish that Jean Aberbach often fondly pinched his cheeks and called him "Mordecai."

Case was a "consummate music man," according to one Hill and Range colleague. He made the transition from big bands and show tunes to rock 'n' roll as easily as the move from his native Iowa to New York. Pomus relied on him heavily. "Paul always knew just how to tweak a song, how to rough an edge," Shirlee Hauser said. "He also had a wonderful instinct for who a song should go to."

It wasn't long before Case called Pomus and Shuman's attention to a surly fifteen-year-old who had been "discovered" on the stoop of his South Philadelphia row house just after an ambulance carried off his police officer father, stricken with a heart attack. "The first time I heard Fabian," Pomus said, "I couldn't believe that Paul would want to direct us to this guy. Paul had heard this guy singing and seen him at record hops, and Paul said that the right kind of song, written for Fabian, was going to be a hit."

Since Fabian Forte's first two singles had flopped, Case was clairvoyant. Fabian's third release, Pomus and Shuman's "I'm a Man," took off, and his fourth, "Turn Me Loose," which they also wrote, exalted him from a hometown favorite on Dick Clark's *American Bandstand* to national stardom. Both songs accommodated Fabian's narrow vocal range, yet even within those confines the teenager had little more control over his pitch than he did over his hormones. Fabian's macho blurt was so amateurish it inspired mirth in adults but commiseration and identification among adolescents. Who understands better than a kid how hard it is to act like a man? The crack professionalism of the New York studio band that played on both records offset but also accentuated Fabian's tune-deafness.

Fabian met Pomus when the songwriter auditioned "Turn Me Loose." "This little guy limped in," Fabian said, and played the song on the piano. "He was bright, extremely friendly, a lovable munchkin kind of guy. . . . I was just blown away, and the main reason was the way he sang it."

"Well," Pomus asked the singer half his age, "what do you think of the song?"

"It's so great," Fabian replied, "why don't *you* do it?"

Fabian recorded at least five songs by Pomus and Shuman, including a third hit, "Hound Dog Man," which was the title song for Fabian's motion picture debut. As that title indicates, Fabian was marketed as an Elvis knockoff. Pomus and Shuman may originally have intended some of these songs, especially "Turn Me Loose," for Presley. Pomus said as much in one interview, and so, it would seem, did Shuman. Additional evidence is the insistence of Fabian's manager that Pomus tone down the original, sexually suggestive lyrics of "Turn Me Loose" to suit a sixteen-year-old singer. Elvis was overseas, however, serving with the Third Armored Division's Thirty-second Tank Battalion in Friedberg, Germany, and Hill and Range had proven writers like Otis Blackwell to provide material for the publisher's biggest star. How low Pomus and Shuman stood in the pecking order is suggested by what happened when another writer, Paul Evans, learned that Hill and Range was planning to give Fabian a song that Evans had cowritten and Presley had recorded but not yet released. "I got hysterical," Evans said. "No, no! Elvis, Elvis!" Hill and Range relented, and "I Gotta Know" appeared on the flip side of Presley's "Are You Lonesome Tonight." Most likely Paul Case assigned Pomus and Shuman to Fabian as a rehearsal for Presley. "Elvis had to be impressed," Fabian said, by "I'm a Man" and "Turn Me Loose"; he added that "if it wasn't for Mort Shuman and Doc Pomus, I wouldn't have had the career that I had. Those two songs, especially 'Turn Me Loose,' put me on the map."

The success of those two songs also made Pomus and Shuman much sought-after songwriters for "the meatballs," as Fabian facetiously described his fellow Italian-American performers. Some of these singers were extenuations of the previous generation's Sinatras and Comos. Others were "teen idols," many of them recruited from South Philadelphia High School, who were promoted by *American Bandstand* and record labels based in heavily Italian Philadelphia. A third cluster consisted of harmony groups that translated doo-wop from the street corners of Harlem to Brooklyn and the Bronx. Until 1958, doo-wop had been primarily a black preserve. By 1959, Italian Americans had claimed it as their turf, too. Pomus and Shuman, two Jewish songwriters in love with African-American music, initially succeeded by adapting it for Italian Americans.

Bobby Darin (born Robert Walden Cassotto), who idolized and emulated Sinatra, recorded two negligible Pomus-Shuman ditties: "Plain

Jane," which pilfered the chorus of the nineteenth-century minstrel song "Buffalo Gals," and "I Ain't Sharin' Sharon," inspired by Pomus's six-month-old daughter, Sharyn. Now Fabian's fellow Philadelphians followed in his footsteps. Frankie Avalon (born Francis Avallone) recorded Pomus and Shuman's "Two Fools"; Bobby Rydell (Robert Ridarelli) recorded "I Dig Girls"; and James Darren (James William Ercolani), whose roles in films such as *Gidget* (opposite Bobby Darin's wife-to-be, Sandra Dee) had made him a star and landed him a record contract, recorded "Angel Face," "Teenage Tears," and his own version of "I Ain't Sharin' Sharon." When Rydell recorded but did not release "Go, Bobby, Go," Pomus resold the song to Jimmy Clanton. He met the Baton Rouge–born singer of "Just a Dream" backstage at an Alan Freed show at Brooklyn's Fox Theatre and said that he and Shuman had written the song especially for Clanton. "Go, Jimmy, Go" peaked at No. 5.

Most of the songs Pomus and Shuman wrote for these pretty boys, whom Pomus called "Philadelphia's beautiful singing and non-singing men," were piffle. The songwriters did not work well by long-distance telephone. Pomus complained that the co-owner of Rydell's record label would "call up and say 'Write songs' as though he was sending us to the grocery store with an order." He "treated New Yorkers like they possessed some highly infectious fatal disease. He would never let them near the artists or the recording studios."

Personal contact and a New York connection proved more inspirational. Gene Schwartz, the president of Laurie Records, solicited material for the Mystics, a doo-wop quintet from Bensonhurst, Brooklyn, that his label had recently signed. "We had no idea who they were," recalled Al Contrera, who sang bass with the group, "but when Doc and Mortie walked in, Mortie and I recognized each other. I knew him from the neighborhood."

"I know you guys," Shuman said. "You sing on the corner all the time." Shuman and Pomus listened to the group and returned a few days later with a song called "Teenager in Love." Earlier they had written a rather inanely upbeat song entitled "Great to Be Young and in Love." Adapting the tune, they turned the words entirely around so it *hurt* to be a teenager in love. "The new lyrics fit my philosophy," Pomus said, "because I felt it was *terrible* for young people to be in love. . . . [I]t was *torture* to be in love." Shuman played the song for the

Mystics. "They even had the background worked out, with the 'ooh-wahs' and all," said Contrera, who remembered Shuman's intensity: "When he sat down at the piano, he really hammered out a song as if he was recording it himself. He threw his whole body into it."

The group rehearsed "Teenager in Love" and sang it enthusiastically on the subway back to Brooklyn, convinced and thrilled that they had a hit song for their first single. The following day their manager called them with bad news: The song was being given to another doo-wop group, Dion and the Belmonts. "We were devastated," Contrera said. In Laurie's offices, Gene Schwartz explained that the label had such high hopes for "Teenager in Love" it didn't dare entrust the song to an unknown group. Dion and the Belmonts, named for their neighbor-hood in the Bronx, already had a modest hit, the ebullient "I Wonder Why," under their belts. Their success had won them fourth billing on the 1959 Winter Dance Party tour but not seats on the Beechwood Bo-nanza whose crash killed Buddy Holly, Richie Valens, and the Big Bop-per. (One of the headliners who filled in for the fallen stars was Fabian.)

Pomus and Shuman were at the Laurie meeting. It was to their ad-vantage for an already proven group to record their song, but according to Contrera, Shuman said, "We can't let these guys go away without something." Schwartz suggested that Pomus and Shuman write some-thing in the style of "Little Star," a No. 1 hit by the Elegants, an Italian group from Staten Island. The very next day Pomus and Shuman deliv-ered a delicate lullaby that may have come to Pomus as he sang Sharyn to sleep. Sung with tender devotion, "Hushabye" became the Mystics' first and only hit.

Meanwhile, Dion DiMucci felt less than grateful for the gift of "Teenager in Love" although he admired its composers. Pomus "was like a dad to me," he once said, and Shuman "was an amazingly talented guy. He had a photographic memory, spoke more than fifteen lan-guages and sang in even more. He'd take a guitar and suddenly become a flamenco virtuoso, or sit down at the piano and transform himself into a Mississippi blues master." But Dion had hung out on the fringes of the Fordham Baldies, a fabled street gang, and had taken his first snort of heroin at the age of fourteen. To such a tough guy "Teenager in Love" seemed maudlin, even "faggy," lacking the credibility of the mean streets on which he and the Belmonts had grown up.

Despite Dion's misgivings, "Teenager in Love" made a star of the "wary young man with a delicate face, an uneven complexion, and twice as much hair as President Kennedy," as *The New Yorker* described him. It was also a breakthrough for Pomus and Shuman, the first of their collaborations to strike a distinctive note. The first few measures of "Teenager in Love" plink along as innocuously as Bacharach and David's "The Story of My Life" and have a similar faint country feel that Dion, whose first musical idol was Hank Williams, accentuates by twanging the word "heart." But the very first verse announces that the stakes are perilously high:

> *Each time we have a quarrel*
> *It almost breaks my heart*
> *'Cause I am so afraid*
> *That we will have to part.*

When the band and the Belmonts drop out, Dion's solitariness as he sings a cappella the falling line, "Why must I be a teenager in love?" dramatizes his vulnerability. This fearfulness, fragility, and tremulous romanticism are at the heart of many of Pomus and Shuman's best ballads and contrast sharply with Leiber and Stoller's amused outsiders' perspective.

"Teenager in Love" was so successful that three versions of the song (the others by Marty Wilde and Craig Douglas) reached the Top Ten in England simultaneously, and Pomus and Shuman were invited to London to write for British television. The reporters and photographers who greeted them at the airport astounded Pomus, who was making his first and only trip overseas. "[A]ll the time I thought this music was second class. . . . [I]n America, nobody paid any attention to the people who were writing the songs." In London, however, where Shuman and the Pomus family stayed for a few months and hobnobbed with such West End theater luminaries as Lionel Bart and Anthony Newley, "Older people knew us. People knew songwriters, period. And rock music was music to them; it wasn't apologetic. So, man, I started thinking there may be something here that I'm just subconsciously aware of."

Pomus never spoke contemptuously of the teen idols and teenage girls for whom he and Shuman wrote. "As to a hierarchy of songs," he later observed in his journals, "that may get tricky—there are all degrees and one person's frothiness is another person's deepness." But most of the music he wrote was a source of income rather than pride. "If you're not writing songs for a teenage audience," he said, "you can get yourself in serious trouble if you're trying to make a lot of money." Pomus and Shuman made money by mastering the transition from R&B to rock 'n' roll, which consisted, in the words of music historian Scott Saul, "at least in part, [of] stepping away from the bawdy 'plain talk' of the blues and exploring the pink swoon of adolescent romance." The popularity of his music gratified Pomus deeply. "I think he was trying very desperately to fit in the world in some way," Shirlee Hauser said. England's warm welcome encouraged Pomus to take himself and his music more seriously.

When Pomus and Shuman returned to New York, they rode the elevator to the top of the Brill Building. The fortune that Hill and Range had made from Elvis and his offspring had lofted the publisher from 1650 Broadway to the penthouse suite in 1619 Broadway. The ten Pomus-Shuman hits on *Billboard*'s pop charts during 1959 were surpassed only by Leiber and Stoller's twelve. "The old-time Broadway show songwriters," said Pomus, "hated us. They wouldn't even speak to us." The "cretinous goons" had taken over the Brill Building.

Chapter Four

"MY DAUGHTER BOUGHT IT. WHAT ARE YOU GOING TO DO ABOUT IT?"

★

Well, let's see what other garb—uh—rock-and-roll music we have. This one is by the Coasters, four fugitives from a hog caller seminar and they've come up with an ear-caressing little dandy. . . . Well, now I just don't know who wrote that little opus but I bet six months' pay against the chance of an ice cube in you-know-where that it wasn't Cole Porter or Gershwin.

The unnamed writers were Leiber and Stoller, their "little opus" was "Yakety Yak," and a Washington, D.C., radio announcer maligned them on a recording distributed to national advertisers by the sales department of the NBC radio network, which was pushing Perry Como. In actuality, Leiber and Stoller held Porter and Gershwin in such high regard that they belittled their own compositions. According to Stoller, "[W]e said that what we wrote were records and that these records were like newspapers or magazines in that they'd last a month and then they'd be gone. . . . All the standards had been written, *we* thought."

Leiber and Stoller followed Hill and Range to the Brill Building, frequently working out of their briefcases in the offices of the publisher that was now their partner not only in Quintet Music but also in Tiger Music, a joint venture with Atlantic's publishing arm. They opened their own office above a brassiere shop on Fifty-seventh Street. When it rained, they couldn't hear their piano for the clatter on the skylight. They moved in 1961 to the ninth floor of the Brill Building, two flights below Hill and Range, and presided over their own publishing company, Trio Music.

Too free-spirited to be contained by the corporate structure of a major record company, they had abandoned the A&R jobs at RCA that had brought them to New York after only six months. "I couldn't even find my office because they all looked the same," Leiber said. "By the time you filled out a requisition for something, the idea was stale." The handful of records they produced—by Jaye P. Morgan, Georgia Gibbs, Varetta Dillard, and others—did not enter the charts, and apart from Presley, RCA's roster of artists was much too middle-of-the-road for mavens of alley music.

Leiber and Stoller's relationship with Presley was also short-lived, largely because Elvis's manager, "Colonel" Tom Parker, and the Aberbachs would not countenance anyone getting close to the King and unsettling the goose that was laying one golden egg after another. Leiber had the temerity to suggest that Budd Schulberg might be enticed to script and Elia Kazan to direct a film of Nelson Algren's *A Walk on the Wild Side* starring Presley as the novel's antihero in "hide-tight jeans." It was insightful to recognize that Dove Linkhorn's innocence and garishness, his racial ambiguity and tolerance, were akin to Elvis's. But the notion that Presley might portray a "studbum" deflowering make-believe virgins for the entertainment of Peeping Toms on New Orleans's Perdido Street indicates how poorly Leiber understood Colonel Parker's plans for Elvis—or how eager he and Stoller were to no longer play a part in them. The Aberbachs were unimpressed that a reunion of Schulberg and Kazan might do for Presley what *On the Waterfront* had done for Marlon Brando. Since Presley was already a star, what need was there to *make* him one? According to Leiber, Jean Aberbach threatened, "If you ever try to interfere with the business or artistic workings of the process known as Elvis Presley . . . you will never work with us again."

Leiber and Stoller contributed three numbers to Presley's third film, *King Creole*, which translated the Jewish boxer from Brooklyn in Harold Robbins's 1952 novel, *A Stone for Danny Fisher*, into a poor-white-trash pop singer in, coincidentally, New Orleans. Their songs were not nearly as memorable as those they had written for *Jailhouse Rock*. In January 1958, while Presley was preparing to record them in California and Leiber was hospitalized with pneumonia in New York, life uncannily imitated art (if Herbert Baker and Michael Gazzo's script for *King Creole* can be called that). In a scene from the movie that owes nothing to the novel, a nefarious nightclub owner played by Walter Matthau bullies Presley: "All you got to do is sign this little piece of paper. There's nothing on it, but don't worry: I'll fill it out later." According to Leiber, Colonel Parker pulled the same stunt but less successfully, sending him and Stoller a blank contract that they refused to sign. "We never worked with him again." Thereafter Leiber and Stoller submitted only a couple of original songs to Presley, though they were delighted by the remuneration they received from the many songs he covered that they had already recorded.

Leiber and Stoller may have been emboldened by Presley's draft notice. No one could predict whether his unprecedented popularity would survive a prolonged absence or military flattop. But artistic pride and boredom played a greater role than commercial calculation in Leiber and Stoller's defection. "It was demoralizing," Stoller recalled. "As Jerry has said, it was a license to print money. They'd show us these scripts that were just godawful and they got *worse* by the time they got to the screen."

Spurning RCA and Presley engendered few hard feelings at Hill and Range because the publisher profited from the strong ties and great success Leiber and Stoller enjoyed at Atlantic. Their first New York recording session with the Coasters yielded nothing to equal "Searchin' " or "Young Blood," but their second struck pay dirt. Leiber was boiling water for tea in his Washington Square duplex when Stoller, fooling around at the piano, played a lick—a "funny shuffle, *oom-paka-oom-paka*"—that tickled Leiber's ear. A current hit single, the Silhouettes' "Get a Job" (whose doo-wop chorus of "sha na na na na na na na na" would give the popular oldies revival group of the 1970s its name) may have inspired Leiber. For the necessity of finding employment, a harsher reality in black families than in many white ones, he substituted the household chores that were a hassle for white as well as black teenagers. "Take out the papers and the trash," he yelled. Picking up the rhyme from the Clovers' "Your Cash Ain't Nothin' but Trash," Stoller shouted back, "Or you don't get no spendin' cash!" Within fifteen minutes they composed a song that gave voice to every adolescent's frustration with nagging parents. All but three of the thirty-three notes in the melody are the same hectoring high C. The record Leiber and Stoller produced on March 17, 1958, is animated by the Coasters' harmonies and voicings (especially the paternal put-down—"Don't talk

back!"—by William "Dub" Jones, who had replaced Bobby Nunn as
the group's bass singer), the roisterous rhythm section, and King Curtis's stuttering tenor sax. Doc Pomus's old friend and former accompanist played so integral a role on "Yakety Yak" and subsequent Coasters
recordings that Leiber and Stoller considered him the group's "sixth
voice." Stoller called Curtis's solos "bluegrass" because they sounded
like a bowed fiddle.

"Yakety Yak" became Leiber and Stoller's fourth No. 1 pop single
and meant more than its predecessors because Presley's huge popularity had helped make those hits. The Coasters, on the other hand, were
Leiber and Stoller's creation, an expression and extension of their own
sensibilities. "Yakety Yak" made such an impact that it even figured in
a United States Senate hearing. Testifying before a panel considering an
ultimately unsuccessful bill that sought to clip BMI's wings to the benefit of ASCAP, a witness singled out "Yakety Yak" for scorn.

"My daughter bought it," noted Senator John O. Pastore, chairman
of the Subcommittee on Communications of the Committee on Interstate and Foreign Commerce. "What are you going to do about it?"
The junior senator from Rhode Island continued:

> I think rock and roll is a fashion and a fad that appeals to
> younger people. It certainly does not appeal to me too much,
> but the fact of the matter is that I do not know what we are go-
> ing to do about it in this hearing to cut it out. . . . I said from
> the beginning, when these hearings opened, that the only thing
> I was interested in was the free choice on the part of the listen-
> ing public to listen to the music that it chooses to hear.

Leiber and Stoller were indebted to this begrudging defense to the
fourteen-year-old daughter of a Republican senator—a far cry from the
original cool cats' target audience before they moved to New York. But
the songwriters were beginning to have kids of their own. Mike and
Meryl Stoller had their first child, Amy, the same month that "Yakety
Yak" was recorded. Soon Leiber married and started a family with the
German-born actress Gaby Rogers, best known for her portrayal of a
pistol-packing Pandora whose curiosity kills her when she opens a box
containing radioactive material at the end of Robert Aldrich's 1955 film

adaptation of Mickey Spillane's *Kiss Me Deadly*. (It's typical of their contrasting temperaments that Leiber's first wife was an actress and Stoller's was a bookkeeper.)

While Pomus and Shuman were writing songs sung by teenagers, in "Yakety Yak" and later Coasters records Leiber and Stoller mastered Chuck Berry's trick of writing songs sung by adults *about* teenagers. (Like Berry, the Coasters' senior member, Carl Gardner, was in his thirties.) They did so with incomparable verbal and musical wit. Consider "Fee fee fi fi fo fo fum / I smell smoke in the auditorium," the lines that introduce "Charlie Brown," Leiber and Stoller's tribute to every high school's class clown and cutup. The heavy tread of half-note monosyllables abruptly accelerates in a polysyllabic rush of quarter notes that scamper down the scale as if toward the excitement (or out the door in obedience to the fire alarm). An equally unforgettable couplet, "It's gonna take an ocean / Of calomine lotion," appears in "Poison Ivy," their allegorical admonition against sexually transmitted discomforts. Recognizing "poison ivy" as code for the crabs introduced many a teenager to metaphor. Leiber once partly attributed his precision and fascination with words to the fact that English was his second language, which he studied as closely as he would study R&B.

Other Coasters songs, such as "The Shadow Knows" and "Along Came Jones," continued the sport that "Searchin'" had made of pop culture. Hilarity disrupted the session at which they recorded "Along Came Jones," a travesty of Hollywood Westerns syndicated on TV. One of the musicians hired for the date was George Barnes, a jazz guitarist who detested rock 'n' roll and often protested, "What am I playing this shit for?" For the money, obviously, and Barnes was so gifted that rock producers put up with him. Asked to lug both a guitar and a banjo to the Coasters session, on arrival Barnes demanded a double fee plus cartage. He ran stone-faced through the parts he was supposed to play, only to dissolve in laughter when the Coasters started singing. Tom Dowd, the Atlantic engineer who manned the controls on most Leiber and Stoller dates, had to stop the tape. "George Barnes has tears rolling down his eyes," Dowd recalled, "'cause he hasn't heard the lyric. Now he's hearing the lyric, and he's busting up laughing while we're recording. He just went to pieces in two seconds, and that date was over. He walked out the door. He says, 'Next time this group is in town, you got to let me know. I don't want to ever miss one of their dates.'" Barnes phoned Dowd monthly, asking when he could play with the Coasters again.

"I think the most fun we ever had working with any artists, including Elvis Presley, was with the Coasters," Stoller said. "We'd be falling on the floor—all of us—and staggering around the room holding our bellies because we were laughing so hard." But it was also hard work. "It took a lot of preparation," Stoller explained. "Harmony was not their forte, and I used to rehearse them for weeks until they could remember who had which note." Despite their fierce drilling, the Coasters sang as if they could scarcely contain their glee and might at any moment burst, like George Barnes, into gales of laughter. The genius of Leiber and Stoller's production of the Coasters—which was "their shining hour," according to session musician and arranger Artie Butler, who played piano on many Leiber and Stoller dates—was their ability to create and choreograph painstakingly the illusion of high-spirited spontaneity.

Leiber and Stoller overcame the Coasters' vocal limitations more easily than the demographic demands of the pop marketplace. What was original in the humor of "Along Came Jones" was not its parody of shoot-'em-ups; the 1945 Gary Cooper film from which the song took its title was itself a spoof. What was new were black voices mocking an iconic Caucasian genre fifteen years before Mel Brooks's *Blazing Saddles.* Leiber's original lyrics sharpened the racial angle by calling attention to the hero's white hat, white boots, and faithful white horse. Those lines did not pass muster with Jerry Wexler, the executive producer at Atlantic to whom Leiber and Stoller generally reported. Although Wexler's veto may have been artistically correct—why belabor the obvious, subtlety is all, and so forth—commercially it was unquestionably on the money: Don't ask for trouble.

Leiber once said that he and Stoller "started drifting away from exclusively black-oriented rhythm-and-blues subject matter, and after we moved to New York, the focus of our work began to shift toward a more universal rock & roll style." Their New York sessions with the Coasters exhibited ambivalence rather than a concerted tendency.

When the Coasters cut "Charlie Brown," they also recorded "Hey Sexy," a punchy song whose title and lubricious lyrics ("I swear I never saw so much potatoes and meat / There oughta be a law against you walkin' down the street") made it unreleasable for the pop market in 1958, though rhythm-and-blues radio stations might well have played it. Another song recorded on the "Poison Ivy" date, "What About Us," indicted racial and economic inequality. While "Poison Ivy" reached No. 7 on the pop charts, "What About Us" made it only to No. 47. "Shoppin' for Clothes," a comic dialogue conducted over a slinky instrumental vamp in which a slick department store salesman, played by Dub Jones, denies credit to Billy Guy, a sucker for "pure herringbone," peaked at No. 83. Humiliation, however humorous, was not hit material because white teenage consumers experienced it infrequently.

The Coasters' last major hit was "Little Egypt (Ying-Yang)" in 1961. By then Leiber and Stoller had transcended theatrical "playlets." "Little Egypt" was positively cinematic as it spun the yarn of a yokel who falls for an aging sideshow siren. Leiber's internal rhymes are as intricate as any Broadway lyricist's, yet they are extremely idiomatic and street-savvy: "Little Egypt came out struttin' wearin' nuttin' but a button and a bow." The hootchy-kootchy girl may have harked back to Stoller's childhood when he was mesmerized by hearing on the family Victrola Strauss's Salome perform her dance of the seven veils.

Leiber and Stoller's success with the Coasters was so great that it spilled over and gave one of the groups that had influenced them, the Clovers, a brief new lease on life. Leiber and Stoller had written a new song for the Coasters when an old friend called. Lou Krefetz managed the Clovers, who had moved from Atlantic to United Artists Records and, well past their prime, were desperate for a hit. Leiber and Stoller obliged by producing "Love Potion Number Nine," in which a gypsy's aphrodisiac provokes the singer to kiss a cop. Although the song is delightful, the Clovers' performance falls short of the Coasters' humor and hubbub. The group subsequently released a sanitized version of "Hey Sexy," reentitled "Lovey."

Leiber and Stoller were not so lucky with many of the veteran black artists on Atlantic. Stoller considered it "quite an honor" to play piano on forty-six-year-old Big Joe Turner's recording of "Teenage Letter," but the song attracted little attention. Neither did a ballad sung by Turner that Leiber and Stoller produced. They also worked with Ruth Brown and LaVern Baker, although they failed to reignite their careers. "LaVern Baker was *tough*," Leiber said, "but Ruth Brown was a sweetheart." Leiber and Stoller's "I Can't Hear a Word You Say," a brassy blues in which Brown spurns the advances of a lounge lizard claiming to be a talent scout ("You may not know it from the looks of my clothes / But I taught Nat King Cole everything he knows"), was too hip and adult to enjoy the crossover pop success of "Lucky Lips," which they had written for Brown three years earlier. They wrote and produced a duet for Baker and Jimmy Ricks, doo-wop's prototypical bass voice with the Ravens; it became an R&B hit but scarcely registered on the pop charts. A Baker solo single, "Saved," which Leiber and Stoller produced a couple of months before the Coasters' equally ambitious "Little Egypt," was a send-up of salvation in which the evangelizing singer, "beatin' on that big bass drum," sounded like one of the "Big-voiced lasses" in Vachel Lindsay's poem, "General William Booth Enters into Heaven," who "made their banjos bang, / Tranced, fanatical they shrieked and sang." Baker's preacher used to "dance the hootchy-koo" like Little Egypt, and the ferocity of her vocal left little doubt that she could still dance up a storm, but the song proved only a modest hit. Time and teenagers were passing by the rhythm-and-blues performers who had originally drawn Leiber and Stoller to Atlantic.

Leiber and Stoller might have suffered the same commercial disappointment with the Drifters, but the group Atlantic enlisted them to produce in 1959 was no longer the Drifters who had recorded "Ruby Baby," "Fools Fall in Love," and "Drip Drop." The group's manager, George Treadwell, fired those Drifters in June 1958, alleging drunkenness and dereliction during a weeklong engagement at the Apollo Theater, and replaced them with four of the five Crowns who had recently recorded "Kiss and Make Up" for Pomus and Shuman's short-lived R&B Records and were performing on the same bill in Harlem. Treadwell, a former jazz trumpeter who had managed jazz singer Sarah Vaughan before they divorced, owned the Drifters' name and could do with it as he pleased. "The Drifters were not a legitimate group like the Coasters," Leiber once said. "They were a name doing business. . . . The personnel was constantly changing because the group was on a weekly salary."

"They got no royalties," Stoller added. "It was almost . . . slave labor."

When Treadwell's new employees hit the road singing the old Drifters' hits, baritone Ben Nelson started working on an up-tempo song called "There Goes My Baby." When he played it for Leiber and Stoller, the producers heard something new that Nelson had never imagined. They heard strings. "I started playing this counter-line on the piano during the rehearsal," Stoller recalled, and it reminded him of Borodin or Rimsky-Korsakov. "Jerry said, 'That sounds like violins.' I said, 'Why not?'" Despite Stoller's modest shrug, their decision was momentous.

Although the Orioles had used strings as early as 1951 and Buddy Holly had recorded with a string section six months before Leiber and Stoller produced "There Goes My Baby," they were a rarity in R&B and early rock 'n' roll. Commonplace accompaniment in middle-of-the-road and middle-aged pop music, string sections represented a considerable expense and required musical charts, which seemed inimical to the informality of most records appealing to black and young audiences. To many such listeners, violins suggested "longhair" music, which still meant Toscanini and Stokowski (or even Mantovani) rather than the Beatles.

But Mike Stoller was still interested in classical music and even wrote some. A quartet he composed received its premiere in 1962 at the Lexington Avenue Young Men's and Young Women's Hebrew Association as part of violinist Max Pollikoff's "Music in Our Time" series. Stoller was in distinguished company. The composers featured in the showcase of contemporary classical music that year included Elliott Carter and Charles Wuorinen. While Jerry Leiber and Gaby Rogers tended to socialize with actors and painters, Mike and Meryl Stoller were friends with composers Morton Feldman and Earle Brown. Stoller studied with Stefan Wolpe, a brilliant Berlin-born composer whose dynamic eclecticism drew jazz musicians like Eddie Sauter and George Russell as well as classical composers to his studio on 125th Street.

Unsure how to indicate the bowing for the strings on "There Goes My Baby," Stoller turned to another Wolpe student, arranger Stanley Applebaum. Charlie Thomas, one of the old Crowns and new Drifters, recalled how Applebaum "just came into our life and—boom! He came into the studio with his little short pants on, in his sneakers and his T-shirt, and had all his papers. He'd just lay them out and give the band weird stuff to do. I'd sit up there and look at him and say, 'Where does this man get all these ideas from?'"

According to Applebaum, "There Goes My Baby" was nothing special—"an assignment that I did like anything else." The unison string line that he wrote, "because of the key it was in, took advantage of the low string on a violin, so it had the guts on the G string. Pop-pop-pop-pop-pop-POP-pop-pop: G-A-B-B-G-A-B-B." The dramatic urgency of the strings on "There Goes My Baby" prompted what song-writer Jimmy Webb, discussing a subsequent Leiber-Stoller produc-tion, called a "striking realization: Rock 'n' roll and the string ensemble are not antithetic after all. To the contrary, the rough, self-taught tex-tures of rock vocalists are ineffably complemented by the silken tones of the orchestra and vice versa." Strings expanded the musical palette of rock 'n' roll, adding novel colors and imbuing the music with a new, sumptuous sweep. They also extended pop's racial and cultural range, encouraging songwriters and producers who were the sons and grand-daughters of Jewish immigrants to draw on their familiarity with clas-sical music, derived from their European heritage and the music lessons that were obligatory in many of their households. But you didn't have to be Jewish to like "There Goes My Baby." "When I heard strings on R&B," Steve Tyrell recalled, "I knew I had to get the fuck out of Texas and come to New York."

Strings were not the only innovation that Leiber and Stoller brought to "There Goes My Baby." In the studio where they recorded the song were timpani that no one knew quite how to tune. That did not deter the producers from asking a percussionist to belabor one beat on the kettle drums throughout the song, and not just any beat but the rhythm of the Brazilian *baion.* "The *baion* beat is a very simple, specific beat," Applebaum explained, "a dotted quarter with an eighth note going into a quarter." BOM-be-bom.

Leiber and Stoller borrowed the beat from *Anna,* a 1952 Italian tear-jerker (released in the United States in 1953) in which Silvana Mangano's opulent bosom made a less enduring impression than the rhythm of the film's theme song. Mangano, playing a nightclub singer turned novice nun, performed it in an interlude that the *New York Times* found "frisky." Her recording of the song proved successful and inspired cover versions by LeRoy Holmes, Paul Weston, and Pérez Prado, among others, while Mack David cowrote "Silvana Mangano Mambo" to pro-mote another film, Robert Rossen's *Mambo,* in which she starred. By the time Leiber and Stoller recorded "There Goes My Baby," the *baion* beat was no longer a novelty, but no one had ever been so audacious as to wed the Italian bastardization of a Brazilian samba to an ersatz Russian string orchestration on a rhythm-and-blues record by an African-American quartet.

It was so outlandish that Charlie Thomas, who was supposed to sing lead vocal on the song (and did so on two other songs recorded on March 6, 1959), choked. "They said I got shook up and nervous. I probably did, 'cause I was young and fast." Leiber and Stoller turned to the song's initial author, Ben Nelson. "I was a baritone-bass singer," Nelson once recalled, "who never considered himself a lead singer." By now "There Goes My Baby" bore scant resemblance to Nelson's original conception, but he leapt boldly into the breach. The result was one of the most influential singles in the history of rock 'n' roll and a long, successful career for Nelson, best known by the stage name he soon adopted: Ben E. King.

Even today, "There Goes My Baby" sounds wild and weird. The presence of strings is not as striking as the absence or inaudibility of nearly everything else. An upright acoustic bass is dimly detectable, but a guitar can be heard only faintly for a couple of measures. There's no piano, no saxophone, and if there's a conventional drum kit, it doesn't register. Suspended between the churning violins and cello and the timpani's hollow thud, the lead vocal seems to echo out of some desolate limbo. The lyrics, too devastated to rhyme consistently, repeat and trip over themselves ("I need her *beside* my side" rather than "*by* my side"), and at one point King (as he would be known from then on) enters early and beats a hasty retreat, leaving an embarrassed half-syllable hanging in midair.

"There Goes My Baby" is a sonic adventure into a world almost antithetical to the Coasters records that Leiber and Stoller produced concurrently. The record is not cool, it is not hip, it is not humorous, and it is not (except perhaps in its ungainliness) particularly adolescent. An anonymous string ensemble supplants King Curtis's idiosyncratic saxophone, and the sound trumps the lyrics. An intense, engaged romanticism replaces wit, wordplay, and bemused detachment. From a marketing point of view, "There Goes My Baby" represented brilliant product differentiation. No one would ever mistake the Drifters for the Coasters, even though the same team produced them for the same record company. But the difference between Leiber and Stoller's work for the two groups owed less to commercial cunning than to their own restless imaginations and love of experiment.

Atlantic Records was as nonplussed as Charlie Thomas by "There Goes My Baby." When Leiber and Stoller played it for Jerry Wexler, he gagged on his tuna fish sandwich. "I totally misprized the record. I thought it was a horrible abortion. Out of tune, which it was, ... it sounded like two radio stations." Ahmet Ertegun was scarcely more encouraging but allowed Leiber and Stoller to remix the record with engineer Tom Dowd. Even then, Wexler delayed its release for months. "It was not a favorite record of the executives," according to Dowd. "Atlantic had a history of doing the unusual, and this was another of the unusuals, though Atlantic wasn't party to it. It was Jerry and Mike."

The song's prospects seemed so dim and the salary he received from George Treadwell was so paltry that Ben E. King tried to peddle his writer's interest in the song. Although he had instigated "There Goes My Baby," four other people finally shared composing credit, some (Leiber and Stoller) more deservedly than others (Treadwell and Lover Patterson, who had managed the Crowns and now road-managed the Drifters). Wexler said that in order to prevent King from selling out to a "shyster," he personally purchased King's interest for $200, drew up a contract, put it in a drawer, and tore it up when the song became a hit. "Because never would I countenance a thing like that. There were a lot of scoundrels in the business who put their names on songs."

The Drifters were performing in Mobile, Alabama, when they learned that "There Goes My Baby" had belatedly broken into the charts. A disc jockey invited them to his radio station for an interview and played the record. Charlie Thomas said they were bowled over. "Wow! We hadn't even heard it yet!" The deejay said, "The record company has been calling, looking for you guys." They hightailed it back to New York.

Three weeks after Leiber and Stoller recorded "There Goes My Baby," they went into the studio with the Coasters and produced a song that referred explicitly to the earlier session. "Ever hear those strings / Doin' crazy things?" the Coasters sang. "Baby, that is rock and roll." Yet "That Is Rock & Roll" is one of the Coasters' least convincing recordings. The prominent banjo (played by George Barnes) smacks of Dixieland pop rather than rock 'n' roll, and Leiber, who barks a few lines in the chorus, sounds more like Jimmy Durante than Howlin' Wolf. For the first time the Coasters' high spirits seem forced. The record's falsity reflected the beginning of a shift that "There Goes My Baby" marked but no one recognized at the time.

Leiber and Stoller were at the top of their form in 1959. Twelve recordings of their songs, more than by any other composer(s), made the pop charts that year, surpassing the eleven they had scored in 1957. As if these weren't enough, they produced another three charting pop singles that they did not write, including a No. 3 hit, "Lavender-Blue," sung by the R&B crooner Sammy Turner, one of several performers they produced for Hill and Range's record label Big Top.

Yet Leiber and Stoller's biggest hit in 1959 was a song they had written at the very outset of their career, and they played no role in its revival. King Curtis alerted them at a Coasters session that someone had just recorded "K.C. Loving," a Leiber-Stoller blues that Little Willie Littlefield had released in 1952. Although the song had not been a big hit, a Newark-based singer named Wilbert Harrison remembered it (though not the original recording's title) and recut it as "Kansas City." He remembered it because Stoller had intended people to. "[I]t *is* a twelve-bar blues, but it's a *melodic* one, as opposed to a traditional blues melody, which is basically just a series of inflections. I wanted to write something that, if it was played on a trumpet or trombone, people could say it was a particular song, instead of that's just a blues in E flat or F." Leiber thought this was a lousy idea. "I wanted it to have a traditional straight blues contour, that any blues singer would sing in his own style with just changes and the words." Stoller prevailed and set to a jaunty tune Leiber's lyric about a man eager to "be standin' on the corner / Twelfth Street and Vine"—six blocks from the intersection where Big Joe Turner dreamed he shook hands with Piney Brown— "with my Kansas City baby / and a bottle of Kansas City wine."

Leiber and Stoller had been toying with the idea of rerecording the song with Joe Williams, Count Basie's vocalist, before Wilbert Harrison beat them to the punch, and Williams did indeed eventually release a version of the song. But by breaking the even 4/4 of the original recording into a brusquer rhythm stressing every other beat, replacing the tenor saxophone with an electric lead guitar, and dropping an adult verse about walking out on one's "old lady" as she sleeps, unsuspecting,

Harrison updated and transformed Littlefield's languid R&B into rock 'n' roll for audiences who no longer associated Kansas City with Basie, Charlie Parker, territory bands, or even jazz.

"At least 60% of our stuff is rock 'n' roll," Leiber complained to *Time* magazine, "and we're sick of it. But consumers dictate the market: kids nine to 14 make up our market, and this is the stuff they want." As the 1960s dawned, Leiber and Stoller's songwriting was already becoming, albeit imperceptibly, a thing of the past. Beginning with the Drifters, their importance and influence as producers, publishers, and entrepreneurs gradually eclipsed their preeminence as composers.

Chapter Five

PARTNERS IN CHUTZPAH

★

In the spring of 1958, Doc Pomus and Mort Shuman bumped into two dejected songwriters at Hill and Range shortly before the publisher moved from 1650 Broadway to the Brill Building. Neil Sedaka had been a class behind Shuman at Abraham Lincoln High School, and Howard Greenfield had graduated two classes ahead of him. Both were friendly with their schoolmate and awed by Pomus. "Anyone who wrote those Ray Charles songs to me was a god," Sedaka recalled. Sedaka was a short, bright-eyed chipmunk. Greenfield was tall and pudgy. Together they looked like Mutt and Jeff (as did, for that matter, the roly-poly Pomus and string-bean Shuman). Sedaka had just played and sung several songs at the piano but failed to interest Paul Case in the material he and Greenfield had written. Pomus and Shuman commiserated and suggested they try their luck with a new outfit on the sixth floor. Sedaka and Greenfield descended and knocked on the door. A man in short sleeves opened it, informed them that the office's occupants were in conference, and asked them to come back in a couple of hours. Although the conference evidently consisted of sweeping the floor of a minuscule room into which two desks and a piano had been crammed, Sedaka and Greenfield did as directed. When they returned and asked to see the publisher, the broom pusher, who was only a couple of years older than Greenfield, said they were looking at him.

Don Kirshner was the second half of Aldon Music, a publishing company he had just formed with Al Nevins, a music business veteran forced by heart trouble to retire from the Three Suns, an instrumental trio that had entertained nightclub audiences and record buyers for two decades with pleasant pop fare. No short sleeves for the suave Nevins, whose Japanese houseboy yanked a cord in his penthouse apartment to rotate winter clothes and spring-summer garb. Despite their disparity in dress and age, Kirshner and Nevins were equally impressed and in-credulous when Sedaka played a fistful of songs for them. This fortu-itous meeting of two novice publishers and two fledgling songwriters laid the foundation for one of popular music's most fabled publishing firms.

★

Howard Greenfield, born on March 15, 1936, and Neil Sedaka, born March 13, 1939, grew up at 3260 Coney Island Avenue in a six-story brick apartment building close to the boardwalk. In sight of the sea that their families had crossed and in earshot of the screeching elevated train that linked Brighton Beach to Manhattan, they were raised in a way sta-tion between two worlds. "I thought the whole world was Jewish," Sedaka recalled, "because I lived in Brighton Beach and we were all Jewish."

Sedaka shared a cramped apartment on the second floor with his father, Mac, a cabdriver whose Sephardic parents had emigrated from Turkey, a grandfather, and eight women: his mother, Eleanor, of Russian-Polish descent, his older sister, five aunts, and a grandmother. He was a mama's boy whose mama, feeling crowded and fearing for her health, had not wanted him. According to Sedaka, she rode a roller coaster in hopes of inducing a miscarriage. Surrounded by women and domineered by his mother, Sedaka was, by his own admission, a "sissy" and "a very, very babyish person." Listening to the radio and singing along with the Andrews Sisters on Martin Block's *Make-Believe Ballroom,* he sang Patti's part while his sister Ronnie took Maxene's. Not knowing whether the singer who sobbed "Cry" was a woman or a man did not deter him from imitating Johnny Ray. When Sedaka's second-grade teacher noted his musical talent, his mother took a part-time job in an undergarment factory to buy a $600 secondhand upright piano. Envisioning a career as a classical pianist and teacher, she made sure he practiced every afternoon when he started taking Saturday classes at the Juilliard School of Music.

It was Howard Greenfield's mother, Ella, who overheard Sedaka practicing the piano at the Kenmore Lake Hotel in the Catskills and, in-troducing herself to the boy, said, "My son Howard is a poet. We live in the same building as you. . . . I'm going to have him ring your bell, and perhaps you can write songs together."

Greenfield, who lived on the fifth floor, rang Sedaka's bell on November 11, 1952. "I was thirteen, he was sixteen," Sedaka said. "I didn't get along well with him. We called him 'Fat Howie.' He was very heavy and kind of a recluse. And I said to myself, 'What is he doing here?'" Greenfield had a Webcor wire recorder, however, and the novelty of the device helped persuade Sedaka to put aside his Chopin and compose his first melody, "My Life's Devotion," set to Greenfield's lyric. Sedaka recalled it as "a combination of a bastardized bolero in a minor key, a ruptured rhumba, and probably a fragment of a bad 1940s movie." Soon they were writing a song a day.

"Why are you writing songs with him?" their Spanish teacher at Abraham Lincoln High School asked Sedaka. "He's last in the class. He's a terrible student." When Sedaka defended Greenfield as a talented lyricist, she replied, "Oh, you should write with my brother." Her brother happened to be Irving Caesar. Born on the Fourth of July, 1895, Caesar wrote the words to more than a thousand songs, ranging from "Swanee" with George Gershwin to "Tea for Two" with Vincent Youmans. Sedaka visited Caesar in the Brill Building. Though they never collaborated, Sedaka sang on several demos of songs by Caesar, who probably hoped that someone forty years his junior might win them a hearing in an increasingly youth-oriented marketplace. Lyrics that Sedaka recalled and sang about a moonshiner's "busy little still" sounded creaky and showed why Caesar's hopes were in vain.

While Sedaka became acquainted with Caesar, Greenfield idolized Caesar's exact contemporary, Lorenz Hart, also born in 1895. Greenfield may not have known when he was in his teens that Richard Rodgers's first lyricist had been a homosexual, just as he may not yet have recognized that he himself was gay. Both Greenfield and Sedaka adored Broadway musicals. Sedaka directed and performed selections from Rodgers and Hammerstein's *Carousel* at Abraham Lincoln High School and oversaw performances of *Pajama Game, Annie Get Your Gun,* and other shows as a music counselor at a Lake George, New York, summer camp.

In 1954, however, hanging out at Andria's Pizzeria with a skinny, buck-toothed girl from James Madison High School named Carol Klein, Sedaka heard something startling on the Wurlitzer. "Earth Angel" by the Penguins (another "bird" group, this one, like the Robins, from Los Angeles) transfixed him. Sedaka felt comfortable with classical music, Broadway musicals, and Tin Pan Alley tunes, but the crudity and paradoxical delicacy of the Penguins' yearning doo-wop ballad unsettled and excited him. Its simplicity rebuked his precocious facility while inviting him to give the music a try. Greenfield dismissed doo-wop as disgusting and off-key, but his partner persisted and convinced him to collaborate on a song they entitled "Mr. Moon." When Sedaka performed it with a saxophone player and drummer at a high school assembly, his schoolmates, to borrow an expression from a later Sedaka-Greenfield song, went ape. "All the black-leather set started to do their bump-and-grind," Sedaka recalled. The ruckus so disturbed Abraham Lincoln's principal, Abe Lass, that he summoned Sedaka to his office and ordered him not to repeat the number at a second assembly. No rock 'n' roll allowed. But students insisted, Sedaka reprised "Mr. Moon," and "for a few moments the sissy was a hero." Italian "toughies" with duck's-ass do's even welcomed Sedaka to the Sweet Shoppe, a hangout across the street from Abraham Lincoln that many students felt too intimidated ever to enter. Sedaka's local celebrity lasted longer than "a few moments" or Andy Warhol's fifteen minutes. The high school newspaper, *The Lincoln Log,* devoted as much if not more coverage to Sedaka during his senior year as to any other student.

Abraham Lincoln was New York City's rock 'n' roll high school, alma mater of Mort Shuman, Howard Greenfield, Neil Sedaka, the Tokens, and Neil Diamond. Music teacher Ben Goldman was an aspiring though untalented songwriter who secured jobs for his students playing proms, bar mitzvahs, and, during the summers, in the Catskills. Unlike Leiber and Stoller and Pomus and Shuman, from the very outset Neil Sedaka wrote (and performed) music in order to be accepted by his peers. This is a critical difference between the elder generation of "white Negroes" (including Shuman, even though he was only two and a half years older than Sedaka and eight months younger than Howard Greenfield) and Sedaka, as well as most of the songwriters who would follow him to Aldon Music. Sedaka and his cohort were not for the most part rebelling against their families, their crowd, or even the mainstream pop music that Leiber and Stoller and Pomus and Shuman scorned. Nor, in embracing rock 'n' roll, did they reject Tin Pan Alley.

To the contrary, they were eager to update the Great American Song-book by adapting it to changing times. And although they loved black music—with Carol Klein, Sedaka sought out R&B records in Harlem that stores in white neighborhoods did not stock, and sometimes he played hooky from Juilliard, then located at 122d Street, to catch Ray Charles or Clyde McPhatter at the nearby Apollo—they did not live it. Most of the neighborhoods they grew up in and the schools they at-tended were not racially mixed. Sedaka's graduating high school class was reminded of its "permanent obligation to see to it that every man—regardless of his race, creed, or color—can walk erect and free in peace, in dignity, and in security," but the obligation was rather abstract. Abraham Lincoln was 80 to 85 percent Jewish. Sedaka and most of his songwriting contemporaries did not experience during their adoles-cence the intimacy with African Americans that Leiber and Stoller and Pomus and Shuman (through Pomus) had enjoyed. Alan Freed, ac-cording to songwriter and producer Richard Gottehrer, exposed him and other offspring of middle-class Jewish families in the boroughs to "a culture we knew nothing about. We learned about it secondhand, thirdhand." One consequence of this racial and ethnic isolation, as well as of these songwriters' youth, was that they had little knowledge of or interest in jazz. The music they would write owed less to Big Joe Turner than to Irving Berlin. Though it often rocked, it seldom swung.

★

While Sedaka diligently practiced the piano every afternoon, a kid from around the corner played punchball beneath his window in the narrow alleyway between their buildings. Although Hank Medress couldn't sing or play an instrument, he convinced Sedaka to form a group. En-listing Eddie Rapkin and Cynthia Zolotin, they dubbed themselves the Linc-Tones in honor of their high school and began rehearsing in Sedaka's apartment. Instead of singing the hits of the day as most start-up groups did, they performed Sedaka-Greenfield originals exclusively. Sedaka played, sang, and taught them their parts, recording the pro-ceedings on a Wollensak tape recorder. "It wasn't like we'd all go there and go 'woo-oo-woo,'" Medress said. "We had to learn it." Although Sedaka was the group's leader, Eddie Rapkin sang most of the lead vo-cals while Sedaka, despite his high, girlish voice, essayed the bass lines.

Greenfield did not play an active role in the sessions. "Howie was tone-deaf," Sedaka said. "I had to teach him how to carry a tune."

Rehearsals began promptly at five, after Sedaka completed his classical practice under his mother's watchful ear. "Neil's life was run by his mother," Medress recalled. "His father was a very weak guy—nice man, but she was the balls. When she said 'jump,' everybody jumped. Neil had school, he had his classes on Saturdays at Juilliard; we had the time allotment when we could rehearse; and Howie and Neil had their time allotment to write." Despite the regimentation, the Linc-Tones occasionally escaped to harmonize on the beach or in a Forest Hills subway station where the echo was thrilling. Such impromptu performances probably outnumbered their engagements at bar mitzvahs and sock hops. Appearing at the Ocean Avenue Jewish Center, Sedaka impressed the accordion player with the dance band that was sharing the bill. "Neil was always very cocky," Jack Keller recalled. "He said, 'We'll see who gets the first hit.'" (A couple of years later, when Sedaka and Greenfield auditioned unsuccessfully for Paul Case, Keller, who had already cowritten a hit for the Chordettes, happened also to be peddling his songs at Hill and Range. "The first thing Neil said was 'Congratulations, but we're going to get the next one.'")

Through Cynthia Zolotin's family the Linc-Tones connected with a Brill Building hustler whose name—Happy Goday—A. J. Liebling would delightedly have added to the Hy Skys, Hockticket Charlies, and Judge Horumphs who populated the Jollity Building. Goday signed the group to a short-term contract and may or may not (memories vary) have renamed them the Tokens—as in "affection," he insisted, not the fare from Brighton Beach. Before they knew it, the foursome was huddled around a single microphone in a basement recording studio that "reeked of marijuana and alcohol," in Sedaka's recollection. Backed by a bored black quintet, they recorded four Sedaka-Greenfield songs in two hours for producer Morty Kraft, the proprietor of Melba Records.

Melba released two of these songs as a single. Rapkin gasped, gulped, and whooped the lead vocal on the frenetic a-side, "I Love My Baby." Sedaka sang more sedately on the b-side, a ballad, "While I Dream," which included lines—"Daylight makes us strangers / And moonlight makes you mine"—that demonstrated Greenfield's growing knack for juxtaposing, compacting, and playing with opposites such as day and night, devil and angel. The production was so crude, however, and the arrangements so desultory that it's surprising the record received some local airplay.

The Tokens performed on Ted Steele's *Teen Bandstand,* a New York version of *American Bandstand,* wearing black chinos, red button-down oxford shirts, and gray crew-neck sweaters—the collegiate look. When Eddie Rapkin departed for college, however, the Tokens began to unravel. Playing Bach, Chopin, Debussy, and Prokofiev in auditions judged by an extraordinary panel that included Arthur Rubinstein, Rudolf Serkin, and Jascha Heifetz, Sedaka was named one of the metropolitan area's fifteen outstanding young musicians by the *New York Times* and its radio station, WQXR. According to Sedaka, Rubinstein complimented him on his rendering of Chopin's G-minor *Ballade.* Sedaka performed live on WQXR and, after graduating from Lincoln, enrolled full-time at Juilliard even though his heart and ambition did not lie in the conservatory. The Tokens, who recorded the perennial hit "The Lion Sleeps Tonight" two years later, would by then include only one original member of the Linc-Tones, Hank Medress.

Sedaka may have been a sissy, but he had a will of steel. The plummets and swerves of the Cyclone, Coney Island's famous roller coaster, terrified Medress but not Sedaka, whose in utero experience may have inured him. "He would go on it over and over again," Medress recalled, "and he said he would tell everybody if I didn't go on it. How could I live that down?" Sedaka's fearlessness and the recommendation of a songwriting secretary whom Greenfield had befriended at the Brill Building, where he had landed a clerical job with Famous Music, led Sedaka and Greenfield to Atlantic Records. Jerry Wexler bought several of their songs and recorded them with the Cookies, a trio of young women from Coney Island who returned the favor by appearing with the Tokens at an Abraham Lincoln High School dance; the Cardinals, a "bird" group from Baltimore whose biggest doo-wop hits were several years behind them; and the Clovers. None of these singles was a significant hit, nor was another song that Sedaka and Greenfield wrote with their Abraham Lincoln music teacher, Ben Goldman, which Jerry Dorn recorded on King Records.

Sedaka was equally keen to succeed as a songwriter and a performer. He bought a copy of Mickey and Sylvia's "Love Is Strange" (Mickey was Doc Pomus's former guitarist, Mickey Baker), scratched the name of the song's author off the label, and substituted his own to see how it would look on a hit single. Likewise, he rubbed out the name of the artist with the No. 1 record in *Billboard* or *Cashbox,* the record industry's rival trade magazine, and wrote in "Neil Sedaka."

Pitching songs to Atlantic, Sedaka tried in vain to interest Wexler and Ahmet Ertegun in his potential as a performer. "I used to make demos, and they would say, 'Who's the girl on the demo?'" Two Sedaka singles were released on other labels. Dick Clark, a partner in another venture with the owners of the Philadelphia-based label that picked up the second Sedaka single, gave the hyperkinetic "Ring A Rockin'" a spin on *American Bandstand* and invited Sedaka to lip-synch it on his Saturday night show. Yet these records fared even more poorly than other artists' renditions of Sedaka-Greenfield songs. If Sedaka stuck it out at Juilliard, he could expect to make some kind of living as a musician and teacher, but Greenfield, now four years out of high school and working as a messenger for National Cash Register, had nothing to fall back on. So it was with desperation as well as determination that the two of them knocked on Aldon Music's door in the spring of 1958.

★

Until he met Sedaka and Greenfield, Don Kirshner had been more successful on the basketball court than in the music business. The son of a tailor whose Harlem shop counted Pearl Bailey and Dinah Washington among its clientele, Kirshner grew up in the Bronx and then Washington Heights. After a year at City College, an athletic scholarship took him to Upsala College in East Orange, New Jersey, where he ended up captain of the basketball team.

Two chance encounters diverted Kirshner from sports to music, which he could neither play nor read. Swimming in the pool at Long Island's Surf Club while he was working there as a bellhop, Kirshner was captivated by a melody he overheard a younger boy play on a piano. He made up words to complete the song, and the two teenagers played it for Frankie Laine, who was performing at the resort. The pop star, famed for his brawny renditions of "Mule Train," "Jezebel," and other hits, kindly explained what a demo was and encouraged them to make one. With $50 from his father, Kirshner recruited the Surf Club's bartender to sing, cut a demo in Manhattan, and managed to get the song published, although it was never recorded.

Shortly thereafter, Kirshner met Robert Walden Cassotto in a Washington Heights candy store. With a single published song to his credit, Kirshner was one up on Cassotto in professional credentials, but he had met his match and ideal partner in chutzpah. Songwriting, singing, acting, and dancing were all arrows in Cassotto's quiver. His target was stardom; his bull's-eye, Sinatra. Stricken by rheumatic fever as a child, Cassotto had not been expected to live past the age of sixteen, and his sickly heart stoked his resolution to become "the most important entertainer in the world," a legend before he turned twenty-five.

Although he had no appreciable musical talent, Kirshner harbored a deep conviction that he could discern it in others. Like the Supreme Court justice who couldn't define obscenity but knew it when he saw it, Kirshner saw talent in the disheveled Hunter College dropout. "Bobby," Kirshner said, "became the brother I never had. He could sing, he could play instruments, he could act, he could do everything that I couldn't do that I wished I could. I used to split my allowance with him." Together they began to write commercial jingles, mainly for furniture stores and other New Jersey emporia. Kirshner lugged the tape recorder when they hawked their wares because it was too heavy for the fainthearted Cassotto.

In 1956, Kirshner graduated from Upsala with a degree in business administration, and his partnership with Cassotto progressed from commercials to pop songs. They copyrighted their first such collaboration, "Bubblegum Pop," in January and followed it up with songs that were recorded by LaVern Baker, Bobby Short, Gene Vincent, and several others. With the exception of "Wear My Ring," a b-side ballad for Vincent, Capitol Records' answer to Elvis, none of these entered the charts. Intent on a singing career, Cassotto secured professional management and adopted the name Bobby Darin. Although they remained close friends and continued to write together occasionally (Leiber and Stoller would record their "Wait a Minute" with the Coasters), Kirshner was adrift.

Darin's smashing success, starting with "Splish Splash," convinced Kirshner all the more of his infallible ability to identify a star, and it impelled him to discover more. Decades later, Kirshner told *The New Yorker* that his "idols were people like Walt Disney, and I feel that what he did with Pinocchio and Mickey Mouse and Minnie Mouse I had the ability to do in my own right—build the stars as a star maker. And maybe it's because, you know, I don't read or write music—and I guess I live vicariously through these people, 'cause I don't have the talent myself—but, you know, I'm the man with the golden ear."

According to Doc Pomus, Kirshner asked him whether he thought he could make more money as a songwriter or a singer. After listening to his songs, Pomus charitably suggested that he consider publishing. To Leiber and Stoller's surprise, Kirshner stopped them on Fifty-seventh Street one day and asked if they wanted to join him in a publishing company he was starting. Knowing Kirshner as little more than an errand boy delivering lead sheets to Atlantic Records, the vastly more accomplished Leiber and Stoller did not take the offer seriously. Kirshner also approached Pomus and Shuman, "but he wasn't offering us enough money," Pomus recalled, "because I had a pregnant wife." (Nonetheless, Pomus, Shuman, and a third writer, Allen Norman, published a song, "Stampede," with Kirshner in November 1958, just before they signed with Hill and Range.)

"Everybody laughed at me," Kirshner conceded. "Who's this brash kid? What does he think he's doing?" He persisted, however, and persuaded Al Nevins to become his partner. Though slowed by his heart problems, Nevins was feeling particularly flush at the time. The Three Suns' signature tune, "Twilight Time," which Nevins wrote with his brother and cousin, the two other Suns, had sold more than three million copies in 1944. With lyrics added by Buck Ram, it had also been a hit for Doris Day with Les Brown's band and for Teddy Walters with Jimmy Dorsey's. Now, in April 1958, it was a hit once again, a No. 1 single for the Platters (managed, not coincidentally, by Buck Ram). And even though he no longer appeared with the Three Suns, the group maintained its "reputation for palatable sounds," according to the notes for one of its albums, which Nevins continued to produce. Sales of the Three Suns' mood music and quirky arrangements of standards were as respectable in the later 1950s as the group itself. (Their make-out music for the middle-aged would win new listeners in the 1990s when a new generation discovered "lounge music.")

Kirshner had everything to gain from Nevins's money, reputation, experience, and connections. "The guy who was the brains of that operation was Al Nevins," Hank Medress said. "It wouldn't have been called Aldon if it was all Donnie, and Donnie, to his credit, got an education."

"Al was a respected figure in the industry," explained Dick Asher, an attorney for Aldon Music. "Don was a brash kid in the beginning." While Nevins "played the front-man role with the rest of the industry," Kirshner "was the front man with the writers." Nevins also knew how to produce records. "Somebody had to show them which dials to turn," Asher continued. "I don't think Don knew the studio. He was a kibitzer in the studio more than a force."

Nevins was "very suave—just the complete opposite of Kirshner," said Larry Kolber, the third writer (his writing partner, Larry Martin, was the fourth) signed to Aldon, after Sedaka and Greenfield. "Donnie was a street kid. Al was very, very hip, bordering on English." He sometimes wore an ascot, and Kolber, who never quit his day job as a salesman for Four Roses bourbon, noted Nevins's appreciation of rare wines, cognacs, and imported cordials.

"Al was like a father figure to me like I was to my writers," Kirshner said, yet Nevins also profited enormously from their unlikely partnership. Although Kirshner could muster only $50 as an initial investment in Aldon, he also contributed his energy, his youth, and his ear for what teenagers wanted to hear. These gave Nevins a second lease on life, a helping hand across the generation gap, and a major role in shaping popular music.

★

When the four of them met in 1650 Broadway, Kirshner and Nevins were more impressed than Sedaka and Greenfield. Aldon Music had yet to publish a song, while Sedaka and Greenfield had written many, and several had been recorded. They insisted, therefore, that Kirshner and Nevins prove themselves. If they could place one of the songs Sedaka had played for them within three months and it made the charts, the duo would sign long-term contracts. Kirshner and Nevins negotiated an extension of the deadline for another month, and the clock started ticking.

On an unusually sweltering day, Sedaka, Greenfield, and Kirshner trekked by train and bus to Newark, New Jersey, and waited for a couple of hours at Bamberger's department store while Concetta Maria Franconero had her hair done. The nineteen-year-old Newark native whom Arthur Godfrey had renamed Connie Francis was the nation's hottest young female singer. Kirshner had first met Francis when he and Bobby Darin had sold her a song, "My First Real Love," that sank like a stone, failing as nine others did before "Who's Sorry Now" buoyed her to the top of the charts. That flop notwithstanding, Francis, whose heart seemed to throb in her multitracked voice, had fallen in love with Darin. Although her tyrannical Calabrian father squelched their romance, Francis still carried a torch for Darin and felt fondly toward "Kirsh," as she called him. Winning an audience with Francis was the best shot Kirshner, Sedaka, and Greenfield had at getting their careers off the ground.

On the drive to her home, a nervous Sedaka told Francis that Dinah Washington had just released a song he had written. That failed to impress her, and so did the songs Sedaka played when they arrived. "Who's Sorry Now," selected by her father, had been written in 1923. Her follow-up, which hearkened back to 1918, had not done nearly so well, and Francis wanted to get with it. As Sedaka played one old-fashioned ballad after another, she grew increasingly bored, even leafing through her diary. Finally, in desperation, he played an up-tempo song they had promised to a bouncy blond trio called the Shepherd Sisters. "Stupid Cupid" was a rocker that vaguely recalled Jerry Lee Lewis's recent hit, "Great Balls of Fire." As unlikely as the conjunction of the Brooklyn mama's boy and the hell-raising redneck might seem, it's entirely understandable that Sedaka emulated one of the few early white rock 'n' roll stars who was, like Sedaka, a pianist—and inevitable that the outcome sounded diminished and domesticated. The coauthor of "Great Balls of Fire" was Otis Blackwell, Doc Pomus's friend and a Hill and Range associate, which may help explain why Paul Case turned down "Stupid Cupid" and Sedaka and Greenfield's other material. It sounded too familiar. Francis, on the other hand, whose romance with Darin had turned her on to rhythm and blues, leapt at the chance to establish her rock 'n' roll credentials with young listeners. "I knew there was no way I could ever sound like LaVern Baker or the others I liked. So I decided to just wing it on 'Stupid Cupid.'" Morty Kraft produced the recording session, during which Sedaka ripped off a fingernail playing glissandos and sprinkled blood on the piano.

"Stupid Cupid" hit No. 14 in the pop charts in September 1958. Francis sounded perky and as exhilarated as listeners were by the novelty of a girl sneaking into the boys' room of rock 'n' roll. Francis, Kirshner gratefully acknowledged, "really started me in the publishing business and record business." She launched Sedaka and Greenfield's careers as well. Aldon signed a long-term deal with the duo and also contracted to manage and produce Sedaka as a performer. Sedaka persuaded his parents to allow him to leave Juilliard, promising that he would return to the conservatory if he didn't capitalize on his success within six months. "And in those six months, I just wanted it so badly that I knocked and broke down doors. I was a very pushy little Jewish kid."

Francis followed up "Stupid Cupid" with a second Sedaka-Greenfield song, the bluesy "Fallin'," and soon recorded a third, "Frankie." Noting how many hit songs included a person's name, Francis had suggested the maudlin ballad's title, thinking of Frankie Avalon but perhaps also, subliminally, of Sinatra and her own moniker. Sedaka took Francis to Coney Island, where they rode the Cyclone and stopped at Nathan's Famous Hot Dogs. With pride, Sedaka told the vendor his companion was Connie Francis, and a crowd gathered. With envy, he told himself, "You know, I want to be famous, too. This is wonderful."

Sedaka won his own first taste of fame because George Goldner was out of town. A pioneering R&B entrepreneur whose discoveries had included the Crows, Frankie Lymon and the Teenagers, and the Chantels, Goldner owned End and Gone Records, whose offices were on the top floor of 1650 Broadway. Little Anthony and the Imperials, a group on the End label, were regulars at Hanson's Drug Store. Bobby Darin had recorded the demo of the stately ballad that became their first big hit, "Tears on My Pillow." Sedaka and Greenfield borrowed liberally from this song when, taking a leaf from Connie Francis's diary, they wrote "The Diary," which Little Anthony and the Imperials recorded and Goldner designated as their next release. When he left New York on business, however, one of Goldner's lieutenants, producer and songwriter Richard Barrett, substituted a song that he had written as the group's follow-up single.

Goldner was outraged, Sedaka and Greenfield were stung, and Al Nevins suggested that Sedaka record the song himself. Nevins, who had considerable clout with RCA because the Three Suns were on the label, convinced the company to sign not only Sedaka as an artist but Nevins-Kirshner as his producer. The deal was sealed one year after Leiber and

Stoller began their abortive association with RCA. Nevins and Kirshner were following Leiber and Stoller's lead as independent producers but going several steps further by owning a piece of the performer as well as of the publishing and the record. (Indeed, according to Sedaka, the entire advance from RCA went to Nevins-Kirshner.) In addition to receiving as publishers the standard mechanical royalty of two cents per record sold and giving a penny to the songwriter(s), Nevins and Kirshner were soon able to command as producers and packagers a royalty of roughly 10 percent, which they split more or less evenly with the performer(s). Such a deal gave them another advantage in that it enabled them to put an Aldon song on both sides of a single.

Nevins knew more about the record business than he did about rock 'n' roll. The Three Suns, according to the liner notes for one of their many albums, represented "a pinnacle of musical taste." Nevins hired a host of session musicians and background singers, and produced a version of "The Diary" that struck Sedaka as entirely too tasteful. "It just didn't sound like rock 'n' roll." Sedaka persuaded Nevins to let him rerecord the song with only a rhythm section and several friends singing backup. Sedaka's melody mirrored "Tears on My Pillow," and his vocal even imitated Little Anthony Gourdine's finicky enunciation, yet the intensity of Sedaka's performance, especially his bravura "woah-woah-woahs" and falsetto fillips at the end of the song, announced the arrival of a voice to be reckoned with.

Kirshner took Sedaka on the road to promote "The Diary." "Those were terrible days," Kirshner said, recalling the winter of 1958–59. "Neil and I were freezing, going from Pittsburgh on planes, walking the streets all over to get it played." RCA took the unusual step of printing a photograph of Sedaka on the single's label (something it had not done even for Elvis) and spent $100,000 promoting the record, giving away refrigerators and televisions to ensure and reward airplay. The extra push boosted "The Diary" to No. 14 in February 1959.

Sedaka's following two singles, "I Go Ape" and "Crying My Heart Out for You," faltered. Greenfield and he were still selling material to other performers, and LaVern Baker, Clyde McPhatter, and the R&B balladeer Roy Hamilton all made the charts with their songs in 1959. But as a singer in his own right, Sedaka was in danger of becoming a one-hit wonder. "I'll tell you one thing about that era," said Hank Hunter, a songwriter who knew and collaborated with Sedaka. "Once an artist was cold, forget it. It would take a miracle to bring them back. Once they were off the charts, they very rarely ever came back."

In a panic, Sedaka skimmed the international charts in *Billboard*, bought the top three records in every major country, and studied them closely. "I decided to write a song that incorporated all these elements in one record," he said, and in two and a half hours he composed the melody of the song that would become "Oh! Carol." Sedaka often worked this way, picking songs apart, figuring out what made them tick, and reassembling them like so many watches—some of them counterfeit. "Neil and Howie would pick up *Cash Box* or *Billboard*," Hank Medress recalled, "and they'd go down the chart, and because Neil was such a great musician, he could take a song that was already a hit and write it sideways. He'd just restructure it. . . . He would literally play the song that he was copying from and then start changing the chords."

A simpler and equally plausible explanation of the origins of "Oh! Carol" is that Don Kirshner urged Sedaka to write a song like the Diamonds' "Little Darlin'." Kirshner himself said he did, and according to another Aldon songwriter, Kirshner repeatedly urged his stable to "write 'Little Darlin'.' He always thought that was the prototype of the great pop song." It was characteristic of Kirshner to consider a white Canadian quartet's cover version of a record by a black doo-wop group, the Gladiolas, a "prototype," even though the Diamonds' opportunistic imitation teetered on the brink between rip-off and delirious parody. Kirshner's ears were keenly attuned to commercial appeal and insensitive to issues of color. It's unquestionable that "Oh! Carol" appropriates the melody, the bass line, the cha-cha beat, and the deadpan spoken interlude of the Diamonds' rendition of Maurice Williams's "Little Darlin'." This is "writing sideways," which hardly bothers to disguise its original inspiration, and Kirshner, Nevins, Sedaka, and company employed as the record's arranger the same man, Chuck Sagle, who had arranged the Diamonds' single. (The Diamonds retaliated by recording a lackluster version of "Oh! Carol" and releasing it in Australia.) Yet it's also characteristic of Sedaka's magpie facility and musical education that he darted for a measure into 6/4 time and kicked off the chorus with a pianistic flourish from a classical piece, Heitor Villa-Lobos's *A Prole do Bebê* (The Baby's Family), Suite No. 1 (The Dolls).

Sedaka played the song for Greenfield and suggested that the lyric be "an ode to my old high school girlfriend, Carol Klein." Once again, another plausible (but by no means contradictory) explanation exists. Connie Francis had pointed out how frequently songs celebrating names became hits, and "Stupid Cupid" had scaled the charts in tandem with a song by Chuck Berry, "Carol." Sedaka-Greenfield's "Oh!" distinguished their song from Berry's and echoed, however subliminally, "Oh! Susanna," the song that had launched more than a century earlier the career of Stephen Foster, one of Sedaka's favorite composers. In any event, Sedaka and Greenfield smoothed out and slicked up "Little Darlin'," dignifying the Diamonds' send-up with a superficial sincerity.

Anxiety over Sedaka's future and uncertainty about "Oh! Carol" were so acute that at the same session Sedaka recorded for the first time someone else's song, "One Way Ticket (to the Blues)," which Hank Hunter and Jack Keller had composed with Frankie Avalon in mind. The same Jack Keller who had met Sedaka at the Ocean Avenue Jewish Center and again at Hill and Range had become Aldon's fifth writer. Impressed by "The Diary" and Sedaka's picture on the label, Keller had noted the Nevins-Kirshner production credit and tracked down their office. When he played for Kirshner the demo he and Hunter had made for $60 of "One Way Ticket," he was hired.

Greenfield was upset that his partner was recording someone else's song. Aldon attorney Dick Asher recalled a wrangle over which song to release as the a-side of Sedaka's next single. RCA initially promoted both sides with the intention of pushing whichever song caught fire first. "One Way Ticket" was by far the bigger hit overseas, but "Oh! Carol" won out in the United States and went Top Ten. Sedaka knew he was a star when, pressing the buttons on the radio in his Chevy Impala, he heard "Oh! Carol" on three stations simultaneously. He celebrated by buying a Thunderbird.

★

Two weeks before "Oh! Carol" peaked at No. 9, Alan Freed interrupted playing Little Anthony and the Imperials' "Shimmy, Shimmy, Ko-Ko-Bop" to announce, amid sobs, his resignation from WABC. He had refused to sign an affidavit that he had never received money or other gifts in exchange for spinning records. The Grand Payola Inquisition was under way.

There was nothing new about payola. The word itself dated back to 1916, when song-plugging rather than record promotion was the principal vehicle of corruption. This time around, the investigation was egged on by aging performers, writers, publishers, and record executives who were convinced that only bribery could account for the airplay rock 'n' roll was receiving at the expense of *their* music. Payola was indeed rampant, but by no means restricted to rock 'n' roll. RCA, according to a Cleveland disc jockey's testimony, dispensed color televisions and cash through its local distributor to win airplay for older acts like the Ames Brothers and Dinah Shore. RCA executives assured Sedaka that the label's similar largesse on his behalf was "legitimized payola." It may indeed have been within the law, which was unclear about exactly what constituted "commercial bribery" and bore down on the recipients of such bribes more heavily than on the people who tendered them. The victims of the investigation were for the most part disc jockeys who received payola rather than the record company executives, distributors, and promoters who doled it out. Thus George Goldner, after detailing in executive session the payments he had made to disc jockeys and the copyrights he had assigned to Dick Clark, concluded his testimony, "I personally don't see anything to hurt me personally from what I have said." He emerged unscathed, while a deejay who testified that he had solicited a $4,000 "loan" from Goldner was convicted on thirty-five counts of commercial bribery. Only after he had lost his job and his house was he let off with a six-month suspended sentence and a $500 fine.

Artie Ripp, who worked for Goldner at Gone and End Records, painted a vivid picture of payola in action:

> Promotion meant first of all that you came in with a great record by a great artist with a great song. It did not mean that you came in with a piece of shit, put money on the table, and go to some disc jockey or program director and get that person to play the record. That was not in [Goldner's] game plan at all. . . . Rather than saying, "I'm paying you to play my record," we'd take the guy from, let's say, Pittsburgh over the West Virginia line to Wheeling and go to a gambling place. So he'd turn around and say, "Artie, give the guy a thousand. Let him go over and play."

It wasn't some kind of a blatant action: Here's the envelope with the money, here's the record, play the record. . . . George's style was much more [to] fill up a hotel floor with chicks. There's a redhead in this room. There's a blonde over here. There's a girl with brunette hair over there. There's a girl with black hair over there. There's a black girl over there. There are two broads over in that room. What's your flavor today? You could go into that room, and one of the girls might turn and say, "You know, George really appreciated . . . Not only am I going to make you happy, but George wanted for you to go out and get yourself a great suit so we can go out together." . . . I can't say unequivocally that George never sent an envelope, but he had a sensitivity that he didn't want the disc jockey to feel like he was a hooker.

Usually you'd get close enough to these guys that they'd say, "Jesus, I really would love to have that down payment on the car." And the guy would be giving you the hint of what kind of help he'd like to have. And then somehow, someway, we would find the way, if he was a strong enough guy, to take care of his wish and his need.

As the producer of *American Bandstand* until the payola scandal broke, Tony Mammarella was certainly "a strong enough guy." According to his widow, Agnes Mammarella, Goldner "wanted to put in a swimming pool for us, and he wanted to buy us a Cadillac. He said to Anthony, 'Look at all the money I have made. I want to do something [for you]!'"

What were Don Kirshner and Al Nevins doing while RCA was handing out refrigerators? Publishing, Goldner once told his daughter, was "the clean side of the [music] business." As publishers, Kirshner and Nevins had fewer opportunities to dirty their hands, and Nevins had a long-standing reputation for probity. In the early 1940s, the Three Suns had fingered five song pluggers for violating their union's rule against paying for songs to be played. "We couldn't control what the record company was doing," Kirshner acknowledged, "but even when I would go on the road with Sedaka or a disc jockey would want to get paid for a record or slip me five or slip me this or that, we'd walk away. We'd hate that we wouldn't be on the playlist, but we had too much pride in our work ethic, too much pride in the song."

Artie Ripp, who later worked for Kirshner, agreed:

> It would amaze you how naïve and squeaky clean Donnie could be. . . . Donnie's sense was, in a kind of crass way, that the song, the artist, and the record were the big pair of tits. If you walked in with a big pair of tits to somebody who was really a breast man, you didn't need anything else to move that guy. If in fact that disc jockey or program director needed to be schmoozed, that was the record company's job. Donnie was not the record company. Donnie would have acted in an incorrect, demeaning manner had he greased the guy. Now, he could turn around to the promotion guy at RCA and say, "What do we have to do to take care of this guy?" That would not be beyond Donnie's creative thinking. But Donnie himself [was] really like P. T. Barnum bringing his artist into town.

The payola hearings briefly depressed record sales. Hardest hit were the independent labels accustomed to purchasing airplay for rhythm-and-blues records with "a bottle of Jack Daniels and a polyester shirt"—the going price, according to Jerry Wexler, for a black deejay at a small southern radio station. The scandal hastened the departure and self-destruction of Alan Freed and the ascendancy of Dick Clark, Aldon Music, and Neil Sedaka, merchants of rock 'n' roll who reassured consumers and their parents that their product was good, clean fun.

Chapter Six

THE YOUNG LOVERS

★

"Oh! Carol" did not take Carol Klein's name in vain. Sedaka's friend had followed in his footsteps by writing songs and, under the name Carole King, making records, although with less success. Now, at the suggestion of Chuck Sagle, who had taken a job at Epic, a subsidiary of Columbia Records, she recorded "Oh, Neil," a riposte to the song Sagle had arranged five months earlier. Although Sedaka was delighted by the additional publicity and even helped promote the single, the lyrics, written by King's husband, Gerry Goffin, a few months after their marriage, were more jeering than flattering. "I'd even give up a month's supply of chewin' tobacky," King sang with a cornpone twang, "just to be known as Mrs. Neil Sedacky." The travesty did not make the charts, but it did bring Mrs. Gerald Goffin to the attention of Don Kirshner. Soon Carole King and Gerry Goffin joined Sedaka and the other writers at Aldon.

Born on February 9, 1942, the daughter of a firefighter and a school-teacher, Carol Klein began playing the piano at age four, even earlier than Sedaka. When they became friends during their teens, Sedaka was impressed by her perfect pitch. He would pound his fists randomly on the keyboard, and she would identify every note he struck: "You're playing F, A, A, B flat, B, C, E, and G with the right hand and two perfect fifths, C and G and G and D, with your left." Or they would sing. "We used to do a half-tone," Sedaka remembered. "She would sing a C and I would sing a C sharp, and if you sing a half a tone between two people, you'll hear waves—beats—in the air."

According to Sedaka, Carol Klein became his girlfriend. "She was a groupie," he wrote ungallantly in his autobiography, "a Neil Sedaka groupie." On another occasion he recalled, "Her mother told me I was a bad influence on her, because she would neglect her schoolwork to write songs and chase me from bar mitzvahs to weddings. And my mother would say, 'Why do you like her?' Because she wasn't particularly great-looking in those days, and she was a chain-smoker." Hank Medress confirmed that "Carol was enamored with Neil, because Neil was *the* man, and Carol could hardly play. . . . Carol wasn't on the same level as Neil in the beginning."

Carole King denied indignantly any romantic involvement with Sedaka. "I went out on *one* date with him! But I did admire what he was doing with his fellow school members, who turned out to be the Tokens. And I started a little group in my school, doing something similar." She and other female students at James Madison High School formed the Co-Sines, whom Sedaka saw perform in a synagogue.

Carol Klein played piano for the freshman entry in Madison's Sing, an annual contest in which classes vied for honors in elaborate musical productions. Two murals flanked the stage in the auditorium where Klein performed. "The Sacrifice of Youth for Democracy" commemorated World War II, while "The Fulfillment of Youth Under Democracy" displayed a chorus singing, a young woman dancing, and a young man reading a book, all beneath a blazon of quarter notes. The message to the high school's preponderantly Jewish students was loud and clear: Parents and previous classes at Madison had endured the hardships of emigration, war, and the Holocaust so their children and successors could make art and have fun.

Klein contributed an essay to her senior yearbook that elaborated a musical metaphor and concluded that, as graduation neared, "from the mellow chords a transformation occurs . . . each note sounds out its individual glory. The sweet jazz chords become louder and faster and more progressive as each senior finds his note and holds." Her yearbook photo leaves little doubt that Klein's note was rock 'n' roll. Her hair is swept back over the left side of her head and curled over her right brow in emulation of a DA.

By then Carol Klein had released her first single on ABC–Paramount Records as Carole King. Since Paul Anka was the label's biggest star and she worked with the same producer, Don Costa, it's not surprising that she sounded a little like Anka (as well as Frankie Lymon). Both of her records for the label paired a ballad with a rocker, words as well as music composed by King, and neither registered on the charts.

Entering Queens College with the intention of becoming a teacher like her mother "and marry[ing] some doctor," King recorded several demos of other people's songs with a classmate, Paul Simon. He and Art Garfunkel had been unable to duplicate the modest success of their first single (as Tom and Jerry), "Hey, Schoolgirl." While majoring in English, Simon recorded extracurricularly under the names Jerry Landis and Tico and the Triumphs. In addition to singing on these demos, for which King and Simon were paid $25 apiece, King played piano and drums, while Simon played guitar and bass. One song they demoed, "Just to Be with You," became a minor hit for the Passions, a doo-wop group and friends and neighbors of the Mystics in Bensonhurst.

During spring semester of her freshman year, King was introduced in the student lounge to a shy chemistry major three years older than she. Gerry Goffin was looking for someone to set to music the lyrics he was writing for a musical based on *The Young Lovers,* a sentimental first novel by Julian Halevy that reminded a few reviewers of *Catcher in the Rye.* The protagonist, an N.Y.U. sophomore who receives his draft notice hours after learning that his girlfriend is pregnant, may have reminded Goffin of himself: "tall, with a gangly air of just having finished growing."

"I showed her the play, and Carole said, 'Well, I'm not really interested in writing for plays. You know, I write rock 'n' roll songs. Besides, my father doesn't want me to write songs anymore.'" Nevertheless, King let Goffin drive her home in his black-and-white 1955 Mercury. Soon she was writing tunes for his musical, and he was writing lyrics for her songs.

Gerald Goffin knew little about rock 'n' roll. Born on February 11, 1939, he had grown up in Jamaica, Queens. His mother had moved into her parents' house there after divorcing when Goffin was five. As a youngster Goffin toiled in the basement for his grandfather, "an oppressive Russian Jew" who was a furrier. He carved out of cork little "skulls" that slipped into and reinforced the pelts in mink stoles. Resenting the task and the pay—75 cents an hour—Goffin whiled away the time by listening, like Neil Sedaka, to *Make-Believe Ballroom.* He enjoyed Eddie Fisher, Perry Como, Frank Sinatra, and "a lot of Sammy

Cahn and Jimmy Van Heusen tunes." He became interested in Broadway when his salesman father occasionally took him to a Rodgers and Hammerstein musical. By the time he was eight, Goffin began making up lyrics "like some kind of game in my head. I'd think of them as songs—they'd have a kind of inane melody. Sometimes I would sing the melodies over chords, but they were pretty horrible." Hot-tempered yet retiring, speaking with a slight stammer, and as tone-deaf as Howie Greenfield, the teenaged Goffin never found a kindred spirit or collaborator to draw out his creativity.

Graduating from Brooklyn Tech, an elite all-boys high school concentrating on math and science to which he commuted by subway, Goffin attended Queens College. He did not dream except idly of becoming a professional lyricist. "I never knew what I wanted to do. Neither did Carole, really. She never assumed she would make it. That's the furthest thing from your mind when you're a wannabe: actually becoming." As Goffin and King got to know each other, he became less interested in his musical and more interested in rock 'n' roll. Under her influence, he listened to Chuck Berry, Little Richard, and Jerry Lee Lewis.

Rock 'n' roll led to romance. King became pregnant in the summer of 1959, and the young lovers, only seventeen and twenty, wed on August 30. Dropping out of college, she worked as a secretary until late in her pregnancy, while Goffin tested polymers and epoxies at a chemical plant. After living in a basement on Flatbush Avenue, they moved up to a ground-floor apartment at 2635 Brown Street in Sheepshead Bay. The row of identical semi-attached three-story brick buildings was ten blocks from King's parents' apartment and close to Brighton Beach.

Their day jobs left Goffin and King time to write in the evenings. She was more driven by ambition than he, but financial desperation was a powerful incentive for both of them to collaborate—all the more so after the birth of their daughter, Louise, on March 23, 1960—and so was the fun they had doing it. "We were having a ball," Goffin said, "but we were too panicky to realize it." Remarkably, they sold two songs right off the bat.

Mickey Baker liked "The Kid Brother," but he recorded it after Sylvia Vanderpool had left the best-selling duo. Fans would accept no substitutes, and a single by Mickey and Kitty (Noble), with King and Goffin's song on the b-side, flopped. Then they thought they had placed a song with the Drifters, only to learn that Atlantic Records had decided "Show Me the Way" would be recorded not by the famous group but by its departing lead singer, Ben E. King. With Jerry Wexler producing, Ben E. King cut "Show Me the Way" at his very first session as a solo artist and sang the amiable trifle more impassionedly than it deserved. Ben E. King had not yet become a star in his own right, however, and the song was ignored.

So much for beginners' luck. The young couple wrote "a couple of cheap shots," as Goffin characterized them, for King herself to sing. RCA released "Short Mort," which parodied "Tall Paul," the hit record by former Mouseketeer Annette Funicello, while paying tribute to Leiber and Stoller's "Charlie Brown." Not only did Goffin's lyric mention the mischievous Charlie by name, but the saxophone break carbon-copied King Curtis's work with the Coasters. The flip side, "Queen of the Beach," was uncannily clairvoyant, anticipating the beach blanket movies that Funicello had not yet begun to make with Frankie Avalon. The record sold poorly, and RCA was apparently uninterested in a repeat performance.

"Oh, Neil" transported "Oh! Carol" from Brooklyn to Tennessee and ended with gunfire as a hillbilly pursued with his shotgun the singer who had infatuated if not impregnated his daughter. Although Sedaka said he "felt flattered" and thought the record was "very funny," the insulting edge to Goffin's lyrics is unmistakable. The other side of the single was sentimental rather than satirical. King wrote her first orchestral arrangement for "A Very Special Boy" and pulled out all the stops on this 3/4 ballad. Strings shimmer, chimes cascade, and what sounds like the Mormon Tabernacle Choir aaahs in the background. The persistent flatness of King's vocal makes the solemnity with which she pledges lifelong love seem both endearingly unaffected and slightly comic. "Donnie loved that side," according to Goffin, "and thought it showed a lot of promise."

Although Sedaka welcomed King and Goffin to Aldon, King's old friend and new husband bristled at each other. "Gerry and I were in competition," Sedaka said, "because we were both going out with Carole, or I had just stopped. . . . He scared me, Gerry." While Sedaka sensed Goffin's volatility, Goffin resented Sedaka's superciliousness and prickly condescension.

"Gerry was a bit introverted, but his lyrics did the talking for him," Kirshner said. "Carole was very sure of herself. I don't want to use the word 'cocky,' [but] she knew she had the goods. All she needed was the right break." The break was Kirshner's offer of a guaranteed advance against royalties of $1,000 a year, to be doubled if Aldon opted to renew the deal for a second year and tripled if the publisher renewed it for a third. King and Goffin jumped at the opportunity.

Few of the songs they wrote during their first year with Aldon were recorded, and none of them dented the charts. Typical of their clinkers during this trying period was "Bobby, Bobby, Bobby," a mash note to Bobby Darin sung by Jo-Ann Campbell. Dubbed the Blonde Bombshell by Alan Freed and featured prominently in his stage shows, Campbell was a dancer turned singer who replaced Connie Francis in Darin's affections for a spell but did not rival her vocal talent.

Yet Goffin and King persisted while Kirshner gave them encouragement and an extra $100 or so at the end of the month to help pay their bills. King put in long hours at the piano they had purchased for $35, while Goffin clung to his day job. "I don't know if Gerry would have got into the business if Carole hadn't had such a drive to make music," Tony Orlando observed. Orlando frequently visited 2635 Brown Street after Kirshner signed the pudgy, half–Puerto Rican, half-Greek sixteen-year-old and shortened his name from Michael Anthony Orlando Cassivitis. "I remember going into that house and I would hear Carole listening to classical music. She would find things and kind of play them sideways, because the strings and timps were so classical in nature that she was finding new things from old. Her own classical training was a major part of her success. She was my first professor." Orlando sang many of King and Goffin's demos. "They had a little four-track recorder, and we'd do the demos live."

One evening in the fall of 1960, according to Goffin, King went off to play mah-jongg. "How Jewish can you get?" Goffin returned home between nine and ten, having worked all day and then gone bowling with friends. "We had a bowling league. Typical Brooklyn scene." A note on their Norelco tape recorder said that Kirshner needed a lyric by tomorrow for the Shirelles. "Normally I would have let it slide to the next day, because I was really tired." But the prospect of writing for the Shirelles, a black "girl group" that had recently had a hit with

"Tonight's the Night," excited him, and so did the melody King had left on the tape. "Just piano, no bridge. She had the first verse, second verse, and last verse." Recognizing immediately that King had composed something new and different, Goffin began writing. "The lyric came out so easy." He was finished well before King came home at midnight, and he had some ideas for the bridge. Together they completed "Will You Love Me Tomorrow" and fell in bed by two.

Although they had written the song with the Shirelles in mind, Kirshner had another idea. "Will You Love Me Tomorrow" was so striking he hoped it might win him an audience with Mitch Miller and access to Columbia Records. "I thought it was a great song for Johnny Mathis. . . . I walked in to Mitch. He was very nice and I was very—I don't usually get nervous, but he was, like, God in those days, controlling A&R, Artists and Repertoire, which was a new word to me, and picking songs. He was very cordial and said, the same way I did eventually, 'I've got to be loyal to my writers. I like the song, but it's not for Johnny.' Which is the best thing he ever did for me." (It's indicative of Kirshner's insignificance at the time that Miller did not recall this encounter.)

Tony Orlando was eager to sing "Will You Love Me Tomorrow" at his first recording session, but Kirshner nixed it. A sorely disappointed Orlando asked why. Kirshner, repeating something Mitch Miller had probably said that he himself had been slow to realize, explained that it was "a girl's lyric. No teenage boy says that to a teenage girl. A girl says that to a boy."

So it was that "Will You Love Me Tomorrow" ended up where it had originally been intended. King played the song and two others for the Shirelles' producer, Luther Dixon, who quickly singled it out. Rock 'n' roll was still a small, tight world. Not only were the offices of the Shirelles' record label, Scepter, conveniently located in 1650 Broadway, but Luther Dixon had been urged to take up arranging and producing by Mickey Baker. When the Shirelles heard the simple piano-and-voice demo that King made for them, their lead singer, Shirley Owens, feared it was too country for four young black women from Passaic, New Jersey. King played the song slowly and sang it slower, drawling behind the beat. Owens whispered to Dixon, "I can't do this song because I don't think it's a Shirelles song."

Dixon overcame Owens's objections and asked King to write a string arrangement. King and Goffin were delighted. "We had some pretty definite ideas about doing a nice string arrangement à la Jerry and Mike," Goffin said, "'cause we loved the string arrangements that they did on the Drifters. . . . Carole wrote it down, of course, but I had some layman ideas that I could translate to her, especially where I wanted the cellos to play. . . . And after the string arrangement was on it, we knew it was a hit."

In January 1961, "Will You Love Me Tomorrow" became the first song by a female group to hit No. 1 on the pop charts since the McGuire Sisters in 1958, and the first ever by a group of black women. The string arrangement greatly enhances the song's emotional impact. While the violins heighten the romance of the intimate encounter that the song dramatizes, the cello adds an insistent undercurrent of anxiety to the singer's plea. The quaver in Shirley Owens's lead vocal and the dramatic ironies and deliberate contradictions in Goffin's lyrics ("Tonight with words unspoken / You swear that I'm the only one") create a tension that aches to the point of excruciation and exemplifies what Norman Mailer called in "The White Negro" "our contradictory popular culture (where sex is sin and yet sex is paradise)." This is an experience not only wholly imagined but fully lived by two writers all too familiar with teenage sex and pregnancy, yet determined, like the couple in *The Young Lovers,* to make a teenage marriage succeed. King and Goffin were no longer writing from the outside when they composed "Will You Love Me Tomorrow." When King had become pregnant, Goffin loved her tomorrow and for years to come. This was an inside job as surely as Doc Pomus's "Lonely Avenue." The difference was that record buyers cared less about the estrangement of an African American or a cripple than they did about the anxiety of young lovers. And Goffin, who had been writing words with and for a woman from the very outset of his career, had "the happy chore of writing female lyrics," as he described it, at a time when young women were the principal consumers of popular music.

When "Will You Love Me Tomorrow" topped the charts, Kirshner and King took a limousine to the chemical plant where Goffin toiled and told him he didn't have to work anymore. "We got a nice advance and we got credit cards, and I never had to do an honest day's work since."

Chapter Seven

PUTTING THE BOMP IN THE BOMP, BOMP, BOMP

Sheepshead Bay seemed as remote and outlandish to Cynthia Weil as Botany Bay. It had taken her well over an hour to get there, and never before had she ridden the subway so far alone. In a cramped apartment on a cramped block, Carole King was playing a promising melody on the piano, but Weil was worrying less about fitting words to it than about how she was ever going to make it home.

"I can read music," the slender, stylishly dressed Weil reassured the frowzy teenage mom. "Why don't you just write this out for me, and I'll take it home. I'll fool around with it, and I'll get an idea and call you."

When Weil returned to her Manhattan apartment, the phone was ringing. "I know this is no way to start a writing relationship," King said, "but Gerry came home from work, and he really likes that melody and said I shouldn't have given it to you and he wants it back."

"Really?"

"Well, he happens to have a very good idea for it."

"Oh yeah, what is it?"

"It's called 'Take Good Care of My Baby.' "

"That's a pretty good idea, so I'm giving it back to you."

"Take Good Care of My Baby" became Goffin and King's second No. 1 single in 1961, and the first (and only) one for Bobby Vee, a singer and guitarist who had subbed for Buddy Holly when Holly's plane crashed en route to Vee's hometown of Fargo, North Dakota. ("When I knew him, he was a great rockabilly singer," recalled Bob Dylan, who briefly played piano in Vee's band.) Vee's producer, Snuff Garrett, heard the demo in Kirshner's office and arranged for King to come in the following day to hammer out an introductory verse. "I'm sure I screamed and yelled," he recalled, "and I remember Carole crying. I wanted to get a hit quick, right now, boom!"

The failure of their first attempt at collaboration did not prevent Weil from becoming an intimate friend of King and Goffin. Alone among the pop songwriters who were her friends and peers, she was born (on October 18, 1940) and raised in Manhattan. Growing up in considerable comfort on West Ninety-fourth Street, she was indulged by a German nurse to whom she felt closer than to her straitlaced mother. Her father, who owned a couple of furniture stores, died when she was seven. Weil attended the progressive, private Walden School, took piano lessons and, until she hurt her back, ballet. Starstruck by her first Broadway musical, Rodgers and Hammerstein's *The King and I,* and inspired by a maternal aunt who had scandalized the family by becoming a chorus-line dancer and nightclub choreographer, she set her heart on show business. After attending the University of Michigan for a year, she transferred to and graduated from Sarah Lawrence, majoring in theater.

While still in college, Weil performed in nightclubs, dancing and singing Cole Porter and Vernon Duke songs that she updated with additional lyrics of her own. "My mother was having conniption fits. This was not what nice Jewish girls do." Weil, it seemed, was "a chip off the bad seed" of her aunt.

An agent she auditioned for urged her to become a lyricist. "All my life I had been encouraged to write," Weil said. "I thought it was too lonely. But it started looking more appealing. And I just naturally knew how to write because I had loved all these Broadway composers. I studied everything they had done."

Weil met Frank Loesser, the irascible composer of *Guys and Dolls, The Most Happy Fella,* and *How to Succeed in Business Without Really Trying,* over breakfast. Loesser detested rock 'n' roll and dismissed the teenagers who listened to it as "pimplefarms." His last, uncompleted musical would include a song containing the scornful lines: "I only know, babe / I only know / Three chords on the guitar." This was fine by Weil, who "was not into rock 'n' roll at all." Although Loesser did not hire her, he gave Weil the run of his publishing firm and the opportunity to collaborate with several staff writers, but none of their efforts was published.

From there Weil went briefly to Hill and Range, where she wrote to little avail with John Gluck Jr., whose best-known song would be Lesley Gore's "It's My Party." She also met Beverly Ross, a young woman whom Hill and Range had recently signed on the strength of her coauthorship of songs such as "Dim, Dim the Lights (I Want Some Atmosphere)" by Bill Haley and the Comets and "Lollipop" by the Chordettes. Ross visited Weil at the tony dress shop next door to El Morocco where Weil worked to support herself. "I always loved fashion," Weil said, adding that if she had not taken up songwriting, "I think I would have worked for *Vogue.*"

A friend of her renegade aunt introduced Weil to Ken Greengrass, the manager of Steve Lawrence, Eydie Gorme, and Teddy Randazzo. An aspiring teen idol with the looks of a Frankie Avalon but a stronger voice, Randazzo had appeared in Alan Freed's quickie film *Rock, Rock, Rock,* billed beneath Frankie Lymon, Chuck Berry, and LaVern Baker but above Connie Francis. Weil wrote "a terrible song" called "Cherie" with Randazzo and was sitting in Greengrass's office when Howard Greenfield walked in with another Aldon songwriter named Barry Mann. Sitting down at the piano, Mann played a song that Greenfield and he had composed for Randazzo, "The Way of a Clown." He was "*so* cute," Weil recalled, "and I'm bowled over. Who *is* this guy?"

★

Barry Imberman was born in Flatbush on February 9, 1939, two days before Gerry Goffin, and graduated from James Madison High School in 1956, two years ahead of Carol Klein. He did not know Klein then, but everyone knew Imberman, a Big Man on Campus (though somewhat short of stature) who was president of his senior class, leader of the chorus for the Junior and Senior Sings, and a member of the Go-Getters, a cheering squad that greeted visitors to the school and performed community service.

Imberman's father was an accountant "from a shtetl background"; his mother's family included several capable classical musicians. According to Artie Resnick, a childhood neighbor who would also grow up to write songs (most notably "On the Boardwalk"), Barry's mother was "very influential" and "took a big interest" in her son's life. She also took Barry and Artie to Resnick's first Broadway musical, Rodgers and Hammerstein's *Oklahoma!*

Imberman took piano lessons sporadically and never, he insisted, developed Carol Klein's proficiency, much less Neil Sedaka's. "I can barely read and write music," he once told an interviewer. He did, however, acquire "a real knowledge of chords and their relationships to each other. I also picked up the ukulele and learned every chord there is in different keys." He listened, as all his contemporaries did, to *Make-Believe Ballroom*. "My idols when I was a kid were Frankie Laine, Johnnie Ray, Patti Page—very melodic, very pop." When a friend urged him to tune in Alan Freed on WINS, he discovered doo-wop. "Because of the background I came from, kind of classical, I thought, Boy, they sing flat! But for some reason after a week I got to like it, and it grew on me."

Barry Imberman was a straight arrow who seemed destined for conventional success. He was not moody and withdrawn like Gerry Goffin. He was not a bohemian like Mort Shuman, a homosexual like Howard Greenfield, or a sissy like Neil Sedaka. Yet he was driven—above all else, perhaps—by a desire to escape. The postage-stamp-sized subdivided house at 2063 Homecrest Avenue in which he grew up was so suffocating, and the surrounding blocks so oppressively regimented and inland from the ocean breezes and vista that uplifted residents of Brighton Beach, that Imberman was determined to get out of that place. In anticipation of more wide-open spaces, he wore cowboy boots.

Working as a busboy in the Catskills—Zalkin's Birchwood Lodge in Ellenville, New York—to earn money for college tuition, Imberman was befriended by Jack Keller, who had progressed from accordion to piano and was performing in the hotel band. Keller heard Imberman playing a song while the other waiters and busboys circled around the piano in the dining room; it was something he had written in imitation of Paul Anka's "Diana" entitled "Eileen." Keller offered to try to peddle his songs in New York. Imberman said he had to call his mother. "He was very leery," Keller recalled.

A guest at Zalkin's who was in music publishing gave Imberman his phone number and encouraged him to call if he ever wanted to work professionally. The phone number and the friendship with Keller came in handy when Imberman, deciding that college and a career in architecture were not for him, dropped out of Pratt Institute in 1957. "I was kind of freaking out. My mother didn't know what to do." Friends of the family, one of them a guidance counselor, suggested that his songwriting might turn out to be more than a hobby.

The publisher who had given Imberman his number was in the Brill Building. He fancied one of Imberman's songs and told him to make a demo. When Imberman asked what a demo was, the publisher hired a band and cut "The Ecstasy of Love." Although the song failed to find a buyer, Imberman used his unspent tuition money to book time in a Brill Building studio and record the rest of his songs, overdubbing ukulele and piano. A songwriter named Lou Stallman walked into the studio, liked what he heard, and invited Imberman to join Round Music, a publishing company Stallman had recently formed with his partner, Joe Shapiro, and named after a No. 1 song they had written for Perry Como, "Round and Round." Imberman worked at Round for the better part of a year, writing with Shapiro and another Round writer, Sid Jacobson, and abbreviating his name to Mann.

"I always wanted to be a songwriter," Mann said, "but in the back of my mind I thought, 'Well, maybe I could also be a singer and make it as an artist.'" When he made his first attempt, "Mann" was not sufficient. He released "Dix-A-Billy," a song that Paul Evans had a hand in writing, and performed the up-tempo ditty at record hops as far south as Baltimore under the name of Buddy Brooks. From Israel Berline to Robert Zimmerman and beyond, many Jews in the music business, especially those like Jerome Felder and Carol Klein who performed publicly, have anglicized or otherwise altered their names. Klein and Imberman did not change their names as a repudiation of their Jewishness or a safeguard against anti-Semitism so much as to seem as all-American as Concetta Maria Franconero, Robert Walden Cassotto, Robert Ridarelli, and the teenagers to whom all of them appealed.

"Stranded," Mann's first composition to be recorded and released, by Bobby Pedric Jr., was a collaboration with Round's Sid Jacobson. Billy "Crash" Craddock, an Elvis-imitating rockabilly singer from North Carolina, recorded a negligible ballad by Mann and Joe Shapiro, "Don't Destroy Me," that inched into the charts at No. 94. As Mann made the rounds of record companies, studios, and managers, he repeatedly bumped into Mort Shuman, who had attended the same junior high school, and he met Don Kirshner in the Brill Building offices of Morris Levy's Roulette Records. "I remember him saying he was starting this company, and I forgot all about it."

Mann didn't write his first hit until he switched publishing companies and partners. Teaming up with Mike Anthony, he wrote "She Say

(Oom Dooby Doom)" for the Diamonds, who had graduated (as had many white teenagers) from cover versions to original material. A novelty number that parodied doo-wop more explicitly than the Diamonds had on "Little Darlin'," it was the group's last successful single, reaching No. 18 in March 1959.

Then Jack Keller reentered Mann's life with news that he had just been hired as a writer by an outfit called Aldon. "What really got me," Mann said, "is he told me he signed for $200 a week in advance money—which was incredible! I go up there and meet Donnie Kirshner, play him a couple of songs, and he says, 'Great!' So he signed me for $150 a week, and it would go up to $200 the next year if I made up my advance. Coming from a family where my father's an accountant, you think of security and getting a salary and getting a job. It was really nice."

Mann did not mind earning less money than Keller, but he did become upset when his songs did not earn back his first year's advance and Aldon refused to give him a raise. "I was very pissed off. Al [Nevins] was part of that negotiation. He was very sweet, very suave, very cool."

Arriving at Aldon several months before King and Goffin, Mann collaborated with whoever was hanging around, including Keller and Greenfield. "Howie loved work," Mann said, recalling that when Greenfield came up with a good lyric, he would get excited, draw very close, and sing it in his collaborator's face. With Hank Hunter, the cowriter with Keller of Sedaka's "One Way Ticket (to the Blues)," Mann composed "Footsteps" for Steve Lawrence (né Leibowitz), a close friend of Kirshner. This rather insipid song wafted all the way to No. 7 in January 1960. Soon Hunter, who had been working at Aldon on a freelance rather than a contractual basis, went his own way. ("It became almost like a factory," he said. "The competition was ridiculous.") "Come Back, Silly Girl," another Steve Lawrence song for which Mann wrote the words as well as the bland music, did not chart until the Lettermen recorded it a year later.

Mann partnered frequently with Larry Kolber. "He could have been a really good lyricist," Mann said, "but writing songs was a side venture for him." For his part, Kolber described Mann as "very reticent at the beginning" and rather nervous. Whenever Mann played Kolber a song, he would say, "I'm faking it, I'm faking it." Their first collaboration was "Patches," a lachrymose tale of star-crossed love. "It was *Romeo and Juliet* sideways," said Kolber. "Teen Angel" and "Tell Laura I Love Her," two tearjerkers that established death rock as an undying genre, provided additional inspiration as Kolber wrote the words to the melody, in his head, of Marty Robbins's "El Paso." Producers and singers shied away from the intimations of suicide in "Patches," however, and it was not until a couple of years later that a Tennessee singer, Dickie Lee, recorded the song, which became his first and biggest hit.

In the meantime, Mann and Kolber wrote two songs, "Forty Winks Away" and "Sweet Little You," that Sedaka recorded. According to Kolber, Sedaka, who was loath to cut anyone's songs but his own, cut these at Kirshner's insistence. "Sweet Little You" was only a minor success, but it was funkier than anything else Sedaka sang, with a raucous pungency that contrasted sharply with Sedaka-Greenfield's candy-coated compositions.

Mann and Kolber were indebted for their biggest hit to a man who stole it from under their noses. Kirshner and Nevins's success with Sedaka at RCA had enabled them to wangle a recording deal for Tony Orlando at Epic, a subsidiary label that was more hospitable to rock 'n' roll than its parent, Columbia, where Mitch Miller held sway. Orlando's first single, Goffin-King's "Halfway to Paradise," peaked at No. 39—not bad for a pimply kid just turned seventeen. There's a lot of "Will You Love Me Tomorrow" in King's string arrangement for "Halfway to Paradise," and a little in her melody. Orlando's seductive yet oh-so-sincere and even abject plea—"Don't lead me halfway to paradise / So near, yet so far away"—might have invited the Shirelles' wary question. "Carole King sang harmonies," Orlando recalled. "We had strings and harps. We used the timpani percussion that got popular after the Drifters' 'There Goes My Baby.' It was like rock 'n' roll gone symphonic."

Eager to secure the follow-up to "Halfway to Paradise," Mann and Kolber played Kirshner a song whose lyrics Kolber had written in five minutes on a napkin in Hector's Cafeteria. Kolber crossed the street to 1650, intending to hand the verses to whichever melodist he found at Aldon. Mann was on the premises and set "I Love How You Love Me" to a lively tune he hoped was appropriate for Orlando.

Kirshner concurred and promised Mann and Kolber that Orlando would record "I Love How You Love Me" at his next session. Suddenly a man lying semi-concealed on a couch in Kirshner's office—a stranger whom Kolber, at least, had not noticed and certainly did not recognize—raised his hand. He wanted the song, he said, and Kirshner gave it to him. "I was pretty pissed," Kolber recalled.

The interloper was an odd, ugly duckling of a young man from Los Angeles who had been hanging around New York City for most of the past year. Phil Spector, according to Dion, was "little and squirrely, with a big nose and funny hair, the kind of guy that always got picked on where I came from." He impressed New Yorkers with the intensity and extravagance of his musical vision, intrigued them with his personal eccentricity, and infuriated them with his professional untrustworthiness.

Spector had come to 1650 Broadway seeking a follow-up to a minor hit he had produced for the Paris Sisters, a namby-pamby California trio. He knew that Aldon possessed a trove of promising material because he had recently gone into Bell Sound, a recording studio on West Forty-sixth Street, with a Goffin-King ballad, an up-and-coming singer from Connecticut named Gene Pitney, and a militia of musicians and kibbitzers. Many grueling hours (most of them overtime) later, Spector emerged with a titanic single that lumbered only because it took such giant steps. "Every Breath I Take" established Pitney as a keening virtuoso vocalist and gave listeners their first inkling of the epic sound that would make Spector world-famous.

Spector's production of the Paris Sisters' "I Love How You Love Me" bore little resemblance to the sprightly song that Mann and Kolber had intended for Tony Orlando. He retarded the 3/4 tempo to a crawl that an appalled Kolber likened to "a funeral dirge." But Spector knew better than the song's composers what he was doing. The narcoleptic beat and Priscilla Paris's hushed lead vocal echoed Spector's first hit, the Teddy Bears' "To Know Him Is to Love Him." From its very first line, "I love how your eyes close whenever you kiss me"—which Spector told Kolber had sold him on the song—"I Love How You Love Me" captured the otherworldly innocence and rapt devotion of first love, when dancing cheek to cheek slows to a trance. The song reached No. 5 in October 1961. By then Mann had exchanged Kolber for another partner.

★

Cynthia Weil wasted little time after her first encounter with Barry Mann in the office of Teddy Randazzo's manager. She made an appointment at Aldon and showed Kirshner some lyrics. "My whole career really started because I was stalking Barry," she said. Kirshner said he had the perfect collaborator for her. Weil tried to conceal her disappointment when he told her it was "this little girl and she's a wonderful writer, but her husband's a chemist and he works during the day, so they can only write at night." Like Tony Orlando, Weil was to keep King company and work with her during the day.

Shortly after Weil's initial unproductive visit to Sheepshead Bay, Goffin, King, and their infant daughter took the subway one evening to Manhattan and called on Weil in her studio apartment on East Fifty-seventh Street. Weil's mother, who lived down the hall, took care of Louise while they wrote because King and Goffin, according to Weil, couldn't afford a babysitter. Their first three-way collaboration was a song called "Echoes." Jerry Landis recorded the demo, which went no further, and it was years before Weil learned that Landis was Paul Simon. Jackie De-Shannon, a Kentucky-born, California-based singer and songwriter who had recorded her first single for George Goldner's Gone Records, released a subsequent Goffin-King-Weil song, "Heaven Is Being with You."

Weil hung around Aldon without actually being hired in hopes that Mann would notice her. It was not long before he recognized who was staring him in the face. They started to date and then to write. John Gluck Jr., Weil's collaborator at Hill and Range, was heartbroken, believing that Weil and he had the potential to become a superb songwriting team. Larry Kolber, who said he never exchanged "more than five sentences" with Weil, was more philosophical, in part because he did not rely entirely on songwriting for his living. The liquor salesman's collaboration with Mann was strictly "B.C."—before Cynthia—and they never wrote together again.

Brooklyn and Manhattan, Mann once said, are "two different countries." Weil and he came from different musical backgrounds as well. Although he loved Elvis and she thought Presley was silly, Mann suspected that "the kind of lyrics she was writing, which had this Broadway kind of quality, would be really interesting to write with rock 'n' roll." He educated her with records by the Drifters and the Everly Brothers, and she also learned from Gerry Goffin. "Gerry was a tremendous influence on me," Weil said.

> From Gerry I learned how to be commercial. One thing that
> I am is a quick learner, and I get it fast. And I suddenly knew

everything I had been doing wrong and everything that I needed to do to get these kinds of songs written. I had to be much less sophisticated. My ideas had to be much simpler. What Gerry always wrote with, which I think I learned from him, was a great deal of humanity. I just picked up on that. I stopped being as clever, as smart-ass, as I-can-show-you-how-many-ways-I-can-rhyme, and got to the heart of it. Part of me wishes that I hadn't. I enjoy writing for the theater more than I ever enjoyed writing pop records.

Mann and Weil wrote a song together, "Mine Till Monday," which sounded a lot like "Will You Love Me Tomorrow," and recorded a demo on which Weil sang lead. Mann played it for Kirshner, who liked it and asked, "Who's the singer?" He signed Weil for $50 a week.

Mann shuttled between his family's home in Brooklyn and Weil's apartment on Fifty-seventh Street, where the couch opened up into a bed and a little piano was crammed. Weil's mother looked askance at Mann's cowboy boots, fearing they were orthopedic shoes. God forbid her grandchildren might inherit weak ankles! "I bring home this guy who is a songwriter and who is not a college graduate. . . . It was not exactly what she would have chosen for me."

On the heels of their deals for Sedaka at RCA and Orlando at Epic, Nevins and Kirshner signed Mann to ABC-Paramount. His first two singles, collaborations with Howie Greenfield, flopped, but his third, "Who Put the Bomp (in the Bomp, Bomp, Bomp)?" an affectionate spoof of doo-wop with lyrics by Gerry Goffin, reached No. 7 in September 1961.

Goffin and Mann's recollections of the song differ. According to Goffin, it originated in a contest. "We used to kid each other around. I said, 'I bet you we could write three songs in half an hour.' So he plays something on the piano, and I start singing over it, 'Who put the bomp in the bomp . . .' It took us about ten minutes, and we didn't talk about it too much because we had to get on to the next song. So I said something about 'aardvark, aardvark. . . .'"

Mann said that Goffin showed him a half-written lyric he was reluctant to complete. "This is a hit, Gerry," said Mann, who desperately needed one after two strikes at ABC-Paramount. "You're crazy. Let's write it." The song pushed the parody of "She Say (Oom Dooby

Doom)" a step further, poking particular fun at the Marcels' recent doo-wop send-up of Rodgers and Hart's "Blue Moon." The Edsels, an Ohio group whose "Rama Lam Ding Dong" had anticipated if not inspired the Marcels, sang backup vocals, lending a note of authenticity to Mann's amiable tenor.

Novelty songs, even one as ebullient and amusing as "Who Put the Bomp," are seldom the springboards for lasting careers. Their performers are frequently one-hit wonders. Nevins, Kirshner, and ABC-Paramount rushed out an album whose liner notes pandered to teenagers by pretending that the twenty-two-year-old Mann had just turned nineteen. Mann's next two singles flopped. Weil as well as Goffin contributed lyrics to the third, which turned Ricky Nelson's "Teen Age Idol" into "Teen Age Has Been" and kvetched, "My first record sold a million / My second one just sold three." More prophetic and pathetic than ironic, "Teen Age Has Been" never entered the charts.

Tony Orlando worked closely with Mann and Weil as well as with Goffin and King. "Their relationship seemed to blossom around the time I remember being in the studio cutting a demo," Orlando said. "I looked up over the mike into the booth, and there was Cynthia, crying, because I was nailing the song. I was never so flattered, to think I moved the writer! I remember Barry putting his arm around her and holding her, and I got this feeling, 'Boy, what a nice couple!'"

Mann and Weil succeeded where Mann and Kolber had failed, through no fault of their own, in composing a follow-up to Orlando's "Halfway to Paradise." "Bless You" was a bigger hit, and the first that Mann and Weil wrote together. When an Aldon artist cut an Aldon song in the company's early days, production was a family affair. "Jack Keller produced my first records," Orlando said, "with Al Nevins and Donnie Kirshner. . . . He was the guy that Donnie and Al were grooming as not only a songwriter but a producer. . . . Carole was arranger/ writer. Barry was artist/writer. These categories were all being slotted and fitted. . . . They were grooming everybody as they saw what their strengths were."

"We'd all contribute," Mann said. "We had all this energy." Weil added, "There'd be a take, and everybody would come running out. 'Why don't you try this?' 'Why don't you play that?'" The second-guessing at one Orlando session grew so vociferous that George Barnes, the veteran session guitarist whom Leiber and Stoller had cracked up, rolled his eyes and said, "Here comes 'Juvenile Jury.'"

Despite the talent overflowing Columbia Records' new recording studio on Fifty-first Street, no one could figure out how to kick off "Bless You." "It just wasn't working," Orlando said. "There were thirty musicians in this room, and each song got an hour. If you didn't make it in that hour, as a writer or producer or singer, it was on to the next song. Can you imagine? Everyone was singing live. No overdubs. One, two, three takes, and that's it. No fixing. You better be in key, and you better be singing from the heart, 'cause this is a live show, baby!"

Nodding to King, who was conducting the orchestra, Keller left the recording booth and played a rhythmic lick on the piano. A startled Mann said, "That's 'Hava Nagila'!" It was indeed. The unison timpani-bass figure that plays throughout "Bless You" is a bar mitzvah beat, which would reappear a year later (along with the opening notes of Mann's melody) in the Crystals' "He's a Rebel," written by Gene Pitney and produced by Phil Spector. Thus a traditional Jewish dance was transmogrified into an anthem of teenage rebellion.

An exhilarating song that rouses the spirit as it races up the scale, "Bless You" was a breakthrough for Mann personally as well as for Mann and Weil professionally. Although Mann had taken songwriting and his singing career seriously, he had never seemed deeply engaged by pop music and its expressive possibilities. His music had been aloof. If his songs weren't parodies, they went through the motions of emotion. The melody of "Bless You" was much more expansive than most of Mann's previous work and much more successful. "Bless You" reached No. 16 in October 1961. The first royalty check Weil and Mann received for the song was for $3,000, and Mann never had to worry again about earning back his advances from Aldon.

On October 29, Mann and Weil wed. As the bride strolled down the aisle, her mother stage-whispered, "You can still change your mind."

Chapter Eight

IN THE GARDEN OF ALDON

★

When Aldon Music moved from the sixth to the tenth floor of 1650 Broadway, Neil Sedaka and Howie Greenfield were awarded a cubicle with a window. For the first year or so, Sedaka and Greenfield were, for most intents and purposes, Aldon Music. They wrote a few songs for other performers. Jimmy Clanton, the Louisiana singer on whom Pomus and Shuman had fobbed "Go, Jimmy, Go," recorded their bluesy ballad "Sleepless Nights" and the puppyish "What Am I Gonna Do." Bobby Darin released Sedaka-Greenfield's "Keep A Walkin'," and Sedaka played piano on the March 5, 1959, session that yielded Darin's hit single "Dream Lover" and its flip side "Bullmoose."

More importantly, Sedaka and Greenfield composed two songs featured in Connie Francis's first motion picture, *Where the Boys Are*. The film's producer, Joe Pasternak, wanted a Hollywood veteran to write the title song, but Francis held out for her buddies from Brighton Beach. Pasternak asked scornfully whether she really believed they could write a better song than Sammy Cahn, one of Sinatra's favorite lyricists, who was up for the assignment. "Maybe not better," Francis replied, "but it'll sell more records. It'll make the picture a hit no matter what the picture's like." Working without a script, just the title, Sedaka and Greenfield submitted two different theme songs, preferring one that Sedaka described as "a Johnny Mathis kind of thing." Pasternak chose the other, a soaring ballad that Greenfield's unusually direct lyric, which eschewed his characteristic wordplay and imagery for overt emotional expression, and Francis's pull-out-all-the-stops performance infused with far more passion than the film's setting (spring break in

Fort Lauderdale), though not its subject (the attractions and dangers of premarital sex), deserved. The single (with a b-side by Pomus and Shuman) as well as the movie became hits.

Sedaka concentrated primarily on writing for himself, however. "Neil always thought that the song should be his rather than the other artist's," Aldon attorney Herb Moelis recalled. He did so with spectacular success. The highly derivative "Oh! Carol" had been a happenstance hit, but Sedaka followed it up with five Top Ten singles, all written with Greenfield, between 1960 and 1962. Beginning with "Stairway to Heaven" (No. 9 in May 1960), he developed a distinctive style and sound that were fully realized on "Calendar Girl" (No. 4 in February 1961) and reached their apotheosis on "Breaking Up Is Hard to Do" (No. 1 in August 1962). All three records plus "Little Devil" (No. 11 in May 1961), "Happy Birthday, Sweet Sixteen" (No. 6 in January 1962), and "Next Door to an Angel" (No. 5 in November 1962) feature a xylophone, glockenspiel, celeste, or some other kind of chime. The tinkle proclaims that these are sparkling trifles; coupled with a strutting drumbeat, it conjures up images of prancing majorettes. Sedaka's high, overdubbed harmonies could be cheerleaders.

These songs are not set in the real world like Goffin and King's "Will You Love Me Tomorrow." There are no blue notes in Sedaka's cotton-candy scale, no traces of actual experience in Greenfield's imagery of angels and devils and cutie-pies. These are fantasies whose only urgency is their extreme eagerness to please. Yet the craftsmanship lavished on the sheer surfaces of this music without depth or subtext provides pleasures that are far from superficial. It's nearly impossible not to smile, for instance, as Sedaka draws upon his technical proficiency to interweave almost contrapuntally the melody of "Breaking Up Is Hard to Do" with "comma, comma, down-doo-be-doo-down-down."

Sedaka came up with that vocal obbligato the night before the recording session. He telephoned arranger Allan Lorber, sang the line, and asked him to write a guitar part. The following day he taught the Cookies their parts as they drove from Coney Island to Manhattan. The Cookies were no longer the same trio that had recorded Sedaka and Greenfield's "Passing Time" in 1956 and "King of Hearts" in '57. Only Dorothy Jones remained from the original group; she was joined now by her cousin, Margaret Ross, and Earl-Jean McCrea, whose older sister had left the Cookies to become one of Ray Charles's Raeletts. Recruited by Sedaka, these Cookies sang backup vocals on many Nevins-Kirshner productions.

Producing a Sedaka record—or any record—could be a harrowing experience in those days. "You had only two hours," Jack Keller recalled. "There wasn't any digital, so you couldn't go back. You had to get it that night, on the spot." No wonder Al Nevins told Keller, "To be a producer, you have to have the stomach of a peasant, the nerves of a matador, and the patience of a saint."

In the recording studio, Nevins was "king," Tony Orlando said. "That was his world. Prior to that, finding the talent and picking the talent, I think Al sensed a generation gap. He stayed out of the picture a bit because he felt older than all those people, while Donnie was this twenty-six-year-old kid who had the energy and understood that young thing." Kirshner, on the other hand, was "Mr. Quiet. The only time we would look for Donnie in the studio would be not for what he'd say but for what he'd do with his head. When Donnie closed his eyes and swayed his head, you knew you'd hit the pocket. He'd get this look of delight like someone tasting a fine wine, and you'd go, 'Oh my God, I've got a hit!' But if he didn't do that, you were still searching."

If Kirshner didn't like what he heard, Keller explained, "he had not a clue what to do about it. Nevins was knowledgeable, understood everything, but Nevins was old. I was the young horse. I would turn to Nevins and say, 'The guitar player is holding it too tight. *Ching-ching-ching*. Gotta let it ring!' Nevins says, 'Run out and tell him.' And I would then [run] out the door, into the studio, and tell the guitar player. Run back from the studio, play it, and [Keller clapped his hands] that's a hit! Everybody's dancing."

Nearly all the Aldon writers participated in Nevins-Kirshner productions. "I wanted them to learn production," Kirshner said. "I wanted them to learn about hooks, riffs, timing, where they were more musically inclined than I was. And everybody was rooting for each other." According to Stanley Applebaum, who arranged "Calendar Girl" and many other Sedaka songs, Sedaka was "very professional, very competent. He would always play piano on the dates. One of the things that I was always careful to do was make certain that whatever bass lines he wrote were covered. I did not invent bass lines for him, because his bass lines were very important to the structure of the songs that he wrote."

"There was a Neil Sedaka sound, certainly," Sedaka said. "My left hand was the bass lines, so [arrangers] respected it exactly. And my right hand was the sweeteners. The 'dooby-doos' and the 'tra-la-las' were a trademark. It was original. The multiple voices were original. The dance beat was very important. Tempo is very important to me, and not rushing the tempo. I wanted them to hear every word. I learned from Dinah Washington, and enunciation was very important to me."

"Rather than just writing songs, I was now starting to write records," Sedaka wrote in his autobiography. With him, as with Roy Orbison and Buddy Holly, "sex appeal was not the key." (Kinescopes of Sedaka's mincing performances in the early 1960s confirm this.) "We sold records because our songs were musically solid and had more than four chords." The bridge of "Breaking Up Is Hard to Do," he boasted, marked "the first time in rock 'n' roll that a minor seventh chord was used."

Twelve days after Sedaka recorded "Next Door to an Angel," the soundalike follow-up to "Breaking Up Is Hard to Do," he married Leba Strassberg, the daughter of the proprietors of the Esther Manor Hotel in Monticello, New York. He had met her while performing there in the summer of 1958, as "Stupid Cupid" was climbing the charts. Since then they had been dating, Strassberg had gotten a nose job, and Sedaka had become a star, losing his virginity in Curitiba, Brazil, to a pubescent hooker who said, "I wanted to make fork with you since I first hear your voice on the radio." Sedaka's writing as well as his marital partnership had originated in the Catskills; now his wedding reception was held—where else?—at the Catskills' Concord Hotel. After honeymooning in Europe, the couple moved into an apartment on Brooklyn's Ocean Parkway.

Not long afterward, Howie Greenfield also found a partner with whom to share his life. Tory Damon was a handsome midwesterner, a dapper dresser, and a would-be cabaret singer. Together they eventually settled in an apartment on East Sixty-third Street in Manhattan. "We all adored Tory," said Sedaka. Jack Keller, who with his fiancée and soon wife, Robi, frequently double-dated with Greenfield and Damon, agreed: "Tory was totally fun, always happy."

While Sedaka's stardom made him aloof, Greenfield was more convivial. His colleagues at Aldon were as accepting of his homosexuality as they were of Sedaka's effeminacy. "Neil seemed to be a little 'up there' all the time," Larry Kolber recalled. "Howie was one of the people. He assimilated more with the troops." Hank Hunter, who wrote a song with Sedaka, agreed that Greenfield "was warmer. We could meet for a hamburger and talk like old friends. I don't think you could do that with Neil."

Greenfield made friends because he needed collaborators when Sedaka was busy performing. Even when Sedaka was available, writing was like pulling teeth. "We always fought over the songwriting," Sedaka admitted, "but the end product was great. He would have to force me to write. I had a love-hate relationship with writing. I was afraid that I couldn't do well, and I had to top the last Top Ten record." On another occasion Sedaka said the pressure made him feel like "a surgeon performing a very delicate operation with absolutely no training and the patient could die at any second."

"Howie would lock Neil in the room, make him write, and not let him out until they were finished," Keller said. When Sedaka went on the road to promote "Oh! Carol," he left Greenfield at loose ends. Kirshner asked Keller to work with him, and the second song they wrote together became a No. 1 hit more than two years before Sedaka-Greenfield's "Breaking Up Is Hard to Do." For the next six years Greenfield and Keller collaborated every Monday and Wednesday, beginning at ten with coffee and working through the day.

"Everybody's Somebody's Fool" was originally a slow number in 3/4 time that Keller and Greenfield thought might interest LaVern Baker. Greenfield showed Connie Francis the lyrics when they were at the movies and dialed Keller from a phone booth in the lobby. "She loves the lyrics," Greenfield said, but added that Francis had asked, "What kind of music does Jack write? Is it like 'Heartaches by the Number?'" Francis was referring to a recent hit for Guy Mitchell composed by Nashville songwriter Harlan Howard. Could an R&B ballad be turned into a country-western song? "Hold on," said Keller. He put the phone down, went to the piano, and noodled. He returned to the phone and said, "Yeah, you can do it. Okay, good-bye."

Francis recorded "Everybody's Somebody's Fool" at the same session she cut a song Greenfield had written with Barry Mann, "The Millionaire." Francis wanted to release "Everybody's Somebody's Fool" as a single, but MGM president Arnold Maxin pressed for "The Million-aire" and warned that "Everybody's Somebody's Fool" was so cornball it could ruin her career. When Greenfield played the song for Sedaka, he was so flabbergasted by its "hokey" sound—the roller-rink organ, the ricky-ticky rhythm and sing-along chorus—that he predicted it would turn out to be a great hit or "the biggest flop of all time." Francis stuck to her guns as stubbornly as she would when Joe Pasternak disparaged Sedaka and Greenfield, and she was vindicated when "Everybody's Somebody's Fool" became her first No. 1 single.

Greenfield and Keller wrote Francis's second No. 1 hit, too. With "My Heart Has a Mind of Its Own" Francis became the first female singer ever to score two consecutive No. 1 singles and was second only to Presley as the top-performing singles artist of 1960. This time Greenfield and Keller decided they should do some research, so they bought three Hank Williams albums and played them in Greenfield's apartment before attempting their second country song. Their third, Francis's "Breakin' in a Brand New Broken Heart," peaked at No. 7.

Greenfield and Keller's "Broadway country" songs (as Sedaka characterized them) became so popular that Ernest Tubb, Patti Page, and Brenda Lee also recorded them. "We wrote the same song for three years, because country's I-IV-V," recalled Keller, referring to the genre's rote chord progression. As the titles "My Heart Has a Mind of Its Own" and "Breakin' in a Brand New Broken Heart" demonstrate, Greenfield was adept at the turns of phrase, the verbal hooks, that country music traditionally favored. And Francis sang them as if her life and her love depended on them, overdubbing duets and trios with herself. "She just has that *tear* in her voice," Keller said.

What were two Brooklyn Jews and an Italian from Jersey doing, writing and performing country music? It is frequently forgotten how popular country music was in urban America during the 1950s and early 1960s—as originally recorded by Hank Williams and others or as reinterpreted by Mitch Miller for pop singers like Tony Bennett and Frankie Laine. "There's Gold in Them Thar Hillbilly Tunes," a national magazine noted. As a child, Francis listened to country music on the radio, and her father had convinced her to record an entire album, *Connie Francis Sings Country and Western Golden Hits,* in 1959. Although Doc Pomus's friend Otis Blackwell was an African American, born and raised in Bedford-Stuyvesant, he idolized singing cowboy Tex Ritter.

Dion was a Hank Williams fan before he discovered doo-wop. Shirley Owens feared "Will You Love Me Tomorrow" was too country for the Shirelles. And remember Barry Mann's cowboy boots. "If a Woman Answers (Hang Up the Phone)," an early song written with Cynthia Weil, was a honky-tonk hit for country singer Leroy Van Dyke. "That's what was great about Aldon Music," Mann explained. "It was a school and we wrote in all genres."

Greenfield and Keller wrote a fourth country song for Francis, "Standing in the Footsteps of a Fool," which she never recorded. Although they were old friends, she and Kirshner fell out over publishing profits from the songs she was turning into hit after hit. "It was not uncommon at the time for performers to take a percentage of the publishing," recalled one of Kirshner's attorneys, Dick Asher. "Some of it was business, some of it was ego, but Nevins-Kirshner thought their songs were responsible for her success." Determined to get her due, Francis spurned Aldon and hired Hank Hunter to supply her with material.

If Keller could transform R&B into country, turnabout was fair play. "Standing in the Footsteps of a Fool" became a pop song for Eddie Fisher (Keller, who produced the date with Greenfield, recalled it as "one of the worst sessions of all time") and a soulful ballad for Ben E. King. "Jack could turn anything into anything," said Larry Kolber, who collaborated with Keller every Friday after Mann began working exclusively with Weil. Such facility was a liability as well as an asset for Keller, a journeyman whose melodies were seldom as distinctive as Mann's or Carole King's.

The most successful song other than Connie Francis's that Greenfield and Keller wrote in the early '60s shows how everyone at Aldon got in on the act of writing, plugging, arranging, and producing a hit. On this occasion Greenfield and Keller set out to parody Paul Anka. "There was a giant competition between Paul and Neil," Keller said. "Neil and Howie felt their hits were teenage, but they were intelligent lyrics. Anka was 'love' and 'above,' 'moon' and 'June.' He was getting No. 1's, and it was killing Sedaka and Howie." Keller's unusually lithe melody was no joke, however, and Greenfield's lyric—"Venus in blue jeans / Mona Lisa with a ponytail"—was a catchy compendium of pop tropes from Nat King Cole's "Mona Lisa" to Frankie Avalon's "Venus." Barry Mann sang lead and the Cookies the backups on the demo. Kirshner and Nevins were out of town when Jimmy Clanton arrived in New York looking for material, but the singer knew Greenfield from "Just a Dream." Greenfield and Keller played "Venus in Blue Jeans" for Clanton, who loved it. That night they played the demo for King, who dashed off an opulent arrangement for brass and a rippling harp. "Gerry came up with the muted trumpets on the bridge," Keller recalled. The next day, without a contract or agreement, Clanton recorded the song, which became his last big hit.

Greenfield found other writing partners at Aldon. With Helen Miller, a middle-aged housewife and mother of three who commuted from Westbury, Long Island, he composed the piddling "Rumors" for Johnny Crawford, an original Mouseketeer with Annette Funicello who had graduated to the role of Chuck Connors's son on the television Western *The Rifleman*. They also wrote the charming "Foolish Little Girl," in which the rest of the Shirelles gang up on Beverly Lee and scold her for abusing and losing her boyfriend.

On one memorable occasion Greenfield collaborated with Carole King. On a lark, Greenfield, Keller, King, and Goffin switched partners and went into separate rooms to write. When they emerged, Greenfield and King had written "Crying in the Rain" and Goffin and Keller had come up with "I've Got My Pride" (a line that also crops up, curiously enough, in "Crying in the Rain" as well as in an early Mann-Weil song, "Like I Don't Love You").

The Everly Brothers approached Aldon after a rift with Wesley Rose, their manager and publisher, denied them access to the Acuff-Rose catalog and Boudleaux and Felice Bryant, the couple who had written most of their hits. When they recorded "Crying in the Rain" in Los Angeles in November 1961, they followed nearly note for note King's demo, on which she had even overdubbed the duo's harmonies. King's eloquent melody, which rises like a sob that refuses to be stifled, Greenfield's insistent internal rhymes, and the Everlys' exquisite harmonies made "Crying in the Rain" a major hit. Goffin and Keller's "I've Got My Pride" was recorded by crooner Jack Jones and failed miserably. Goffin had his pride, too, and King never collaborated with Greenfield again.

Goffin wrote with Keller, however, on Tuesdays and Thursdays, when Keller was not busy with Greenfield or Kolber. Keller would show up at Goffin and King's Sheepshead Bay apartment around one in the afternoon and start working with Goffin while King did the dishes or tended to the children (Louise was soon followed by Sherry). "If we didn't get anything after a couple of hours," Keller said, "we'd go out and shoot pool and then come back about a quarter to five and sit down and—boom!—get the chorus. And then when I'd see him on Thursday, he'd have the bridge done and the song would be finished." The collaboration couldn't have been more different from Keller's with Greenfield. "It was work for him," Keller said. "We didn't go out and shoot pool."

Goffin and Keller followed up "Crying in the Rain" with several songs for the Everly Brothers, none of which rivaled King and Greenfield's commercial or artistic success. Although it was the b-side of their next record, Don Everly hated the rocking "How Can I Meet Her?" perhaps because its attempt to recapture the spirit of the Everlys' early hit "Bird Dog" was too forced. Goffin and Keller wrote both sides of the following single, "Don't Ask Me to Be Friends" and "No One Can Make My Sunshine Smile," and King arranged and conducted the recording session. Both songs were wan echoes of the brothers' glory days, which "Crying in the Rain" had capped and now were forever past.

Goffin and Keller enjoyed much greater success with a song they had originally intended for the Everly Brothers, and it is intriguing to speculate whether "Run to Him" could have revived the Everlys' flagging career if they had recorded it rather than Bobby Vee. The song was inspired by the guitar lick on a Peggy Lee record that Keller heard on the radio as he drove to Sheepshead Bay. "Four hours later, we worked the whole tune out. All of sudden, Carole comes out of the kitchen, bumps me off the piano bench, and says, 'You can go lie down on the couch. I know this song by heart. I can play it for Gerry while he writes the lyrics.'" Keller took a nap—"which I did a lot, 'cause once I had the tune done, man, I wasn't waiting around for them fucking guys to take that long to get the damn lyrics done." When King awakened Keller, she invited him to listen to his song and played "Run to Him."

With the Everly Brothers in mind, Goffin, King, and Keller cut a demo, one of several that Kirshner played for Vee's producer, Snuff Garrett. Asked if he liked "Run to Him," Garrett replied, "I smell fuckin' money." Since Vee had just had a No. 1 single with Goffin-King's "Take Good Care of My Baby," Kirshner was not about to turn down a chance to repeat its success. "Run to Him" nearly did, reaching

No. 2. While Goffin's lyric tapped the vein of mawkish self-pity and noble self-sacrifice he had opened in "Take Good Care of My Baby," Keller's melody and Ernie Freeman's arrangement tried something new. A song without a bridge, "Run to Him" builds drama and tension like a bargain-basement *Boléro,* bulking up incrementally while the singsong tune repeats maddeningly until the last verse modulates and accelerates in a rush of release.

Before "Run to Him" was issued, Keller visited the Brill Building and played the song for Burt Bacharach and Hal David, who reciprocated by playing Bobby Vinton's "Blue on Blue," also unreleased. "That's how it used to go," Keller said. "It was very friendly." The bridge of "Close to You," he pointed out, a song Bacharach and David wrote a couple of years later, is the melody of "Run to Him."

Clean-scrubbed and apple-cheeked, Bobby Vee, who dropped the rockabilly Bob Dylan remembered soon after he started recording in Los Angeles for the Liberty label, "epitomized," in the dismissive words of one rock critic, "the triumph of suburban values over the combined spirit of country and ghetto." But Snuff Garrett knew a good song when he heard one, and Vee was a lucrative franchise for Aldon. Vee recorded more than a dozen songs by King and Goffin, including the delightful "Walkin' with My Angel," to which simulated footsteps add pedestrian percussion. King provided vocal harmonies and a piano part indicating the string arrangement on most of the demos she and Goffin made of these songs. All Garrett and Vee had to do was connect the dots. "It was almost like architecture," said Brooks Arthur, the recording engineer for many such demos. "She would sing and do a demo that would be better than any of the records were. It was a blueprint, like building a home. She had a clear plan in mind."

"What do you want to do when you grow up?" Goffin once asked Keller, and then offered his own answer: "I don't want to write the next hit for Bobby Vee." Although many of the songs Goffin and King wrote for him were bland, they were seldom as vapid as the material they provided teen and TV idols such as Bobby Rydell, Annette, Paul Petersen (yet another Mouseketeer alumnus, who played Donna Reed's son on *The Donna Reed Show*), and *Hawaiian Eye* costar Connie Stevens. Kirshner and Nevins courted film and television stars assiduously because they knew that their celebrity could often make even a mediocre song a hit no matter how poorly it was sung. They cultivated a profitable relationship with Columbia Pictures' record label, Colpix, whose roster included Petersen, Shelley Fabares (Petersen's juvenile costar on *The Donna Reed Show*), and James Darren. When Darren had a hit with the ta-ra-ra-boom-der-ay marching-band novelty "Goodbye Cruel World," Goffin and King followed it up with a sarcastic sound-alike, "Her Royal Majesty," which was nearly as successful, although they ran out of luck when they wrote the same song sideways once again with "They Should Have Given You the Oscar."

Mann and Weil did a similar number with Fabares, writing the lackluster "Johnny Loves Me" as a sequel to the actress's winsome hit "Johnny Angel." Often they took up where Goffin and King left off, writing subsequent hits for Petersen ("My Dad") and Darren. Although Mann called it an ill-considered attempt to "do Broadway," "Conscience" sounded more like a Disney cartoon. It featured Darren singing two roles: a heartbreaker growling like the Big Bad Wolf and a tisk-tisking Jiminy Cricket admonishing the lady-killer to be "kind and sentimental." Mann and Weil belabored this theme in a second hit for Darren in which love conquers libido and reduces the singer to "Mary's Little Lamb."

Often the songwriters took turns. Much as Mann-Weil's "Bless You" succeeded Goffin-King's "Halfway to Paradise," King and Goffin wrote a Paris Sisters single after Mann and Kolber's "I Love How You Love Me." Not only the melody but even the song's title echoed its predecessor: "He Knows I Love Him Too Much." "We all wrote interchangeably," King said. "You'd sit there and write, and you could hear someone in the next cubbyhole composing a song exactly like yours. . . . The environment didn't exactly foster inventiveness."

Although the competition was friendly, it did create tensions. "On the surface we got along well," Goffin said, "but you could feel a little bit of jealousy . . . about who was gonna get the next record." One day Paul Evans bumped into Mann racing past the Winter Garden on Broadway. Evans congratulated him on having three songs in the Top Ten. An out-of-breath Mann said, "Yeah, but they're all on the way down. I gotta go do some demos." "He ran off and my jaw dropped," Evans recalled. "That's how nervous we all were."

Yet the two couples' careers were so aswirl that it seemed only they could understand each other. "Our entire life was built around writing and demoing," Weil said. "We had no friends except for Carole and

Gerry. They were the only people who lived the lifestyle we lived. We didn't have friends outside the business because nobody understood what we were doing." They often vacationed together, joking that it prevented the other couple from writing a hit song behind their backs. On a drive back from Sunapee, New Hampshire, where Mann and King, pregnant with Sherry, learned to ski (Weil had skied before, and Goffin demurred), the foursome held a contest. Which couple's songs would the radio play more frequently? According to Weil it was a dead heat until they pulled into New York and heard "Crying in the Rain," written by King, of course, though not with Goffin. "They beat us by a half!"

With an athletic coach's cunning that he learned as a sports fan and as the captain of the Upsala Vikings, Kirshner kindled this spirit of competition, not only between Mann and Weil and Goffin and King but among all Aldon's writers, while making sure it never burned out of control. "It was really a hotbed of creative craziness," Weil recalled. "I remember we used to wait around for Kirshner to see if he needed a song for someone. We used to wait for him in front of the men's room because we knew that sooner or later he'd have to go. But then the men would grab him and talk inside. Once I grabbed him and said, 'Look, I've been waiting here for three days,' and he finally said, 'Okay, come with me,' and we started to walk into the men's room together."

They waited for Kirshner, not for Nevins. His experience in the music business and the recording studio made Nevins indispensable to Aldon's success. "Nevins gave [Kirshner] a sense of maturity and security he did not otherwise have in this business," Ed Cramer said. But Kirshner was the master of motivation, the company's "electricity," by one employee's account, and its "magnetic North Pole." "We had this kind of sibling rivalry to please Daddy," Weil reflected. "He was like our surrogate father," Sedaka agreed. "He got very excited over music, and it was infectious. We would all go into his office and play our songs at the end of the day." Gathered around a garish red mahogany piano that Kirshner himself was unable to play, they vied for his favor. "You became his follower," Orlando said, "one of Donnie's kids."

Although he was only a few years older than most of his writers, Kirshner was a "father figure," he acknowledged, on whom they depended as "doctor, lawyer, psychiatrist, friend. 'What are we gonna do, Donnie?' 'Do you like the hook, Donnie?' And even though it was very competitive, the loser was always a winner. Because the secondary song would wind up No. 1 for another artist."

More than their insecurity and youth made the Aldon writers look up to Kirshner. The generosity that he and Nevins displayed, their paternalism, the doggedness with which Kirshner plugged writers' songs, and his invincible optimism inspired gratitude and dependency. Nevins and Kirshner helped Goffin and King with household expenses. They lent another employee money to fly a girl he had impregnated, and her mother, to Puerto Rico for an abortion. Jack Keller was floored when Kirshner, after meeting him for the first time and hearing the demo of "One Way Ticket (to the Blues)," ushered him into Nevins's office and Nevins's first question was "Need any money?" Before he could answer, Nevins ordered a check made out for $200 as an advance against future royalties, and another for $60 to cover the cost of the demo. "This was totally different from anything that had ever been done," Keller said. The deal was sealed days later in a taxi when Kirshner asked Keller what he wanted. "I want a Top Ten song," he answered. Kirshner upped the ante: "How about three?"

Kirshner delivered on that promise, as he had on his promise to Sedaka and Greenfield. "If he heard a song he liked, he would promise the moon," Hank Hunter said, remembering when Kirshner was excited by a song that Hunter had written with Keller and vowed, "If I don't get Frankie Avalon or Dion on this, I'm going out of business." Kirshner did not succeed in this instance, but he managed to place the song with another singer who had a Top Ten record to his credit. "Donnie Kirshner was probably one of the best song pluggers that ever lived," Keller said. "He always got us the records," Goffin agreed. "He could make somebody feel that they were going to make money by doing one of our songs."

"All the major labels had people on staff who produced records," explained songwriter and producer Richard Gottehrer, "and they were denying that this music we called rock 'n' roll was ever going to be anything of significance. They couldn't get the people internally to do it, so they'd have to say, 'Oh, get those kids from down the street. That Don Kirshner, he's got a couple of them. Let 'em write some songs and then we'll get the teenage feel for our artists.' Donnie seemed to be in the know. If you were an A&R person, he could make you feel he had the answer to your problems. And your problem, if you were signing teenage talent, was what in the hell were they going to record?"

Kirshner's machinations were often Machiavellian. "Donnie liked to use whatever advantage he had for leverage," Jerry Wexler said. "For example, if he gave you a good song to record, then the condition would be that he had to have either the b-side as well or the next single." But such dealings freed writers from fretting about pitching their songs. "The family encompassed everything," Keller said.

> We didn't have to promote ourselves. If you had anything pressing in life that would take your mind off the creative end of it, you went in to see Al. Al says, "Okay, write up a check." That took care of that. Go back and write. And then when you wrote, you could get a payoff right away by playing the song for Donnie on the red piano in his office, because he was available. I went in there, and to the right they had five attorneys with Nevins and Kirshner. And I say, "Hey, you gotta hear this song!" Donnie stands up and walks out of the room, and I play him the song. Never said no to hearing a song. For five years we had a Garden of Eden.

Paradise expanded rapidly. By 1962, Aldon had eighteen writers on staff, and even many of the less talented among them thrived. As the company grew, it occupied most of the tenth floor at 1650 Broadway. Though writers worked at home as often as they did in their cubicles, according to Cynthia Weil, "the great thing about going in was the music you heard through the walls." "It was like a bazaar," attorney Herb Moelis said, "or a lottery ticket: You never knew which little room was going to produce the next hit record."

Aldon was publishing songs, producing artists singing them, and managing the careers of those artists. Its demos, especially those crafted by King and Goffin, were often as fully realized as and sometimes even surpassed the records that were made on their basis. Its profits were not commensurate with its success, however. "The record company made all the money," Moelis said, explaining that a production company normally earned only 2 percent of a record's sales, and the artist 3 to 5 percent. Forming Aldon's own record company seemed an inevitable next step, which Kirshner and Nevins took in the summer of 1962, creating two labels, Companion and Dimension, in partnership with a New Jersey–based independent record company and distributor. "We wanted to go from a production company to earning a greater percentage on a record," Moelis said. Yet impatience and rejection played as great a role as the profit motive in impelling Aldon into the record business.

When Snuff Garrett hesitated to release Bobby Vee's recording of "It Might As Well Rain Until September" because another Vee single by Goffin-King, "Sharing You," had yet to run its course on the charts, Kirshner and Goffin, perhaps fearing that the song's seasonal sentiment would wear thin by autumn, grew frustrated by the delay. "I got mad," recalled Goffin, who told King, "We're going to add some strings to this and put out a Bobby Vee record, only you're going to be Bobby Vee."

"It Might As Well Rain Until September," the first release on Aldon's Companion label and King's first recording since "Oh, Neil" in 1959, does indeed sound a lot like a Bobby Vee record. Though multitracked, King's voice is rather scrawny—which she and Goffin may have meant to acknowledge by putting on the b-side a ballad entitled "Nobody's Perfect." Yet her vocal does not detract from her fluent melody and perky string arrangement, and the song reached No. 22 in the United States and was even more successful in England.

Encountering legal difficulties with the use of "Companion" as a moniker, Nevins and Kirshner reissued "It Might As Well Rain Until September" on the Dimension label to take advantage of the sensation created by the drumrolls and blaring saxophones of the first Dimension single, "The Loco-Motion." Goffin-King's third No. 1 single (after "Will You Love Me Tomorrow" and "Take Good Care of My Baby") was a dramatic departure for Aldon, Goffin, and King.

The dance craze that Chubby Checker's "The Twist" ignited in 1960 and supercharged when it hit No. 1 for an unprecedented second time in 1961 had left Aldon cold. At first it was a Philadelphia phenomenon dominated by a Philadelphia label, Cameo-Parkway, which had its own stable of writers and shared publishing begrudgingly. Even when The Peppermint Lounge, just six blocks from 1650 Broadway, became "the Temple of the Twist" and Leiber and Stoller and Pomus and Shuman leapt on the bandwagon with, respectively, Steve Lawrence's "The Lady Wants to Twist" and The Lone Twister's "Lone Twister" ("Move that torso / A little more so"), Aldon writers were evidently too busy and untrendy to gyrate with the slumming socialites and celebrities who forsook El Morocco for the 178-seat bar on West Forty-fifth Street. Moreover, the Aldon crew wrote very few flat-out dance records, sticking for the most part to mid-tempo numbers and ballads sweetened by strings. Although Sedaka released "Neil's Twist," Kirshner and Nevins were quicker than most of their charges to capitalize on the craze, composing Fabian's last single ever to make the charts, the bemused "Kissin' and Twistin'."

But when Dee Dee Sharp followed up her duet with Checker, "Slow Twistin'," with an even more popular solo single, "Mashed Potato Time," Goffin and King wrote a dance song with Sharp in mind. As they worked on it, they turned for advice and reaction to their nineteen-year-old babysitter, Eva Narcissus Boyd. Born and raised in Belhaven, North Carolina, Boyd had come to Coney Island to stay with her brother and his wife, who happened to be a friend of the Cookies' Earl-Jean McCrea. After auditioning by singing "Will You Love Me Tomorrow," Boyd joined the Cookies on backup vocals for a few recording dates, and Goffin and King hired her to babysit Louise and, shortly thereafter, Sherry for $35 a week. Boyd was hardly an accomplished singer, but King and Goffin chose her to sing the demo for "The Loco-Motion" because she sounded enough like Sharp to sell the song to Cameo-Parkway.

Shortly before recording the demo, Goffin and King caught Bobby Darin's act at the Copacabana. A sound startled Goffin. "What's that?" he asked his more musically knowledgeable wife. "Well, that's open fifths on saxophones," King replied. "We've got to use that on our record," Goffin said, and when they did, "It fit perfectly. We had that drumroll that sounded like an engine and then the horns that sounded like a railroad."

It's unclear whether "The Loco-Motion" was ever actually offered to or rejected by Cameo-Parkway. By one account the label passed because it refused to surrender a penny in publishing (though it didn't turn up its nose at Goffin-King's "[I've Got] Bonnie" or Barry Mann and Mike Anthony's "I'll Never Dance Again," both hits the same year for Bobby Rydell on Cameo). In any event, the demo was such an exhilarating rush of rhythm that Kirshner and Nevins decided to release it on Dimension and sent Goffin and King back to the studio to add a few finishing touches. Not too many, because its rough-edged, stripped-down sound is what makes "The Loco-Motion" so powerful. There are no strings, and the only instruments that make an audible impression are the saxophones and clattering drums, pushing and pulling the beat while the girlish lead vocal by Little Eva, as she was dubbed, is echoed and elevated by a swinging swirl of harmonies sung by Boyd and King.

When "The Loco-Motion" reached No. 1 in August 1962, it dislodged Sedaka's "Breaking Up Is Hard to Do." With two No. 1's, eight Top Ten, and eighteen Top Twenty songs, two of these on the Dimension label, Aldon owned the charts in 1962. And Al Nevins warned Goffin and King that they weren't going to be paying their babysitter $35 a week anymore.

Chapter Nine

"IT WAS JUST JEWISH LATIN"

★

It was the dream of many songwriters during the early 1960s to write for the Drifters. The group scored so many hits following "There Goes My Baby" that anything it recorded was likely to be lucrative. Adult, gifted, and black, they possessed an authenticity and artistry, despite continually shifting personnel, that made teen idols sound tinny. "All my writers idolized the black artist," Don Kirshner said. "The biggest thing was not to get a white artist's song but a soul record . . . because they felt that most black artists could express a tune with a soulful quality that nobody else could express." And writing for the Drifters meant working with Leiber and Stoller, the liveliest, most imaginative, and most generous producers of popular music during this period.

"I cut my eye-teeth learning how to make records from watching Mike and Jerry," said Artie Butler, a teenager from Flatbush who played piano on and booked musicians for many Leiber and Stoller sessions. "They were responsible for a lot of careers. We all learned from what they did." When Leiber and Stoller quickly realized that the satiric style of songwriting they had honed with the Coasters was not suited to the more romantic strains of the Drifters, Doc Pomus, Mort Shuman, Burt Bacharach, Hal David, Carole King, Gerry Goffin, Barry Mann, and Cynthia Weil eagerly enrolled in what Butler called "Record Business 1-A." With Leiber and Stoller as instructors, editors, and collaborators, they added a new chapter to the American Songbook.

The first writers Leiber and Stoller enlisted were their friends Pomus and Shuman, who had known and produced four of the Drifters when they were still Crowns. "Pomus loved the Drifters. That's who he understood," said Willi Burke, his wife at the time. "When he sang, he sounded very black. That's where he was coming from." And Pomus loved Leiber and Stoller. "I always thought they were geniuses," he said. "I never knew anybody who could do what they did on a record."

Congeniality encouraged Pomus to compose some of his most auto-biographical lyrics, summoning up once again the emotional intensity of "Lonely Avenue." The epiphany of a first kiss that the Drifters' "This Magic Moment" evokes amid fluttering violins epitomizes the redemptive role that grace plays in the memoirs of many polio survivors—grace that can take the form of a religious experience or conversion, a sudden self-awareness and self-acceptance, or simply falling in love. "I used to believe in magic," Pomus wrote in his journals years later, "and flying and that one morning I would wake up and all the bad things were bad dreams. . . . And I would get out of the wheelchair and walk and not with braces and crutches."

According to Burke, Pomus wrote "Save the Last Dance for Me" on their honeymoon. Their daughter, Sharyn, found half the lyric scrawled on the back of their wedding invitation. Whenever he wrote it, Pomus said it took only half an hour to compose the account of a man who serenely allows his lover to dance with other men because he knows it is he who will be taking her home. Leiber recounted that after hearing only four bars of the song, he recognized it was "a huge hit" and the story of Pomus's life—though he insisted that Pomus and Shuman rewrite part of it.

Leiber's enthusiasm notwithstanding, the eloquent recording that became the Drifters' first and only No. 1 single was not rushed into release, and even then Atlantic issued it as the b-side to a lesser Pomus-Shuman song, "Nobody but Me." According to Pomus, Dick Clark turned the record over and played "Save the Last Dance for Me." "On their own those schmucks would've never done it."

"This Magic Moment" and "Save the Last Dance for Me," both with lead vocals by Ben E. King, were produced and performed with extraordinary elegance and dignity. Leiber and Stoller, according to Drifter Charlie Thomas, "were just like brothers to us. . . . There was real prejudice back then, but these guys didn't believe in it, and we didn't believe in it, either. . . . They did the best that any producers ever could do for a black group back in those days. They were always respectful. They'd made sure that we were respectable and had that class. Mike was *down* on that class!"

Leiber and Stoller respected their writers, too, trusting them to rehearse the Drifters as well as backup singers, and sometimes even to choose the lead vocalist. "Mortie was with us mostly on the piano," Thomas said, although Leiber and Stoller were quick to intervene if they didn't approve what they overheard. "If someone was teaching us and it didn't sound right and Jerry was in another room, he'd stop what he was doing and come runnin' and say, 'No, no! We want Ben E. to do it this way and Charlie to do it that way. And I think that's the wrong key anyway.' Whoever was there—Carole King or Burt Bacharach— Mike and Jerry were on the top of what they did and 100 percent with the Drifters."

With Pomus and Shuman's abetment, the Drifters' music became ever more Latin as Leiber and Stoller pushed the *baion* beat as far as it could go and added Afro-Cuban and Mexican accents such as the Spanish guitar in "This Magic Moment" and the dramatic flamenco thrums that introduce Pomus-Shuman's "Room Full of Tears." Pomus had grown up within earshot of Puerto Ricans who lived down the block in Williamsburg. On summer nights he listened to them play music and praised it to his brother. Shuman would return from vacations in Mexico with ideas for songs which Pomus set to lyrics "that would sound something like a translation," he said, conjuring "the whole ambience of Spanish songs."

Shuman described himself as "a mambonik" who "wrote rock 'n' roll but lived, ate, drank and breathed Latino." He ingested it chiefly at the Palladium Ballroom, four blocks north of the Brill Building, at 1698 Broadway, where the bands of Frank "Machito" Grillo, Tito Puente, and Tito Rodríguez held court. Wednesday was Anglo night, when Killer Joe Piro taught celebrities like Kim Novak and Marlon Brando to mambo. "Stars of stage & screen danced and drank with cleaning ladies, seamstresses, pimps, pushers," Shuman wrote, "and M.S. was in the middle not only on Wednesday night but Friday, Saturday and Sunday too."

Mike Stoller shared Shuman's enthusiasm. As a teenager still living in New York, he had dated a Puerto Rican girl and dug Machito. In Los Angeles he was "the only Jewish pachuco" at his predominantly Chicano high school, and he sometimes sat in with a Latin band. In 1954, Leiber and Stoller had poked fun at the mambo in the Robins' "Loop-De-Loop Mambo":

> *Down in Puerto Rico and Havana, too*
> *This here is the dance that the people do.*
> *All you gotta do is to kick your feet.*
> *It's just Memphis boogie with a Latin beat.*

When they moved to New York, people were dancing the mambo on Broadway and in Brooklyn.

"*Everybody* danced to Latin music," recalled the boxer and writer José Torres. A newcomer noticed it right away. When Al Gorgoni, a session guitarist who played for Leiber and Stoller, Al Nevins, and many others, moved from Philadelphia to New York, he discovered a "completely different" musical scene. "The exciting stuff was the Latin thing. The Puerto Ricans, the Cubans, and whoever—the whole culture—were permeating the vibe. In Philadelphia it was more like Tony Bennett, Dean Martin, and stuff like that."

Charlie Thomas took it in stride when Pomus said he had "a little cha-cha song" for Thomas to sing. "Brought up in Harlem, you'd be around a lot of Puerto Ricans, so the Latin feel is part of your life. So when they presented it to us, it was already in our heart. Weekends and all night long, that's all you'd hear: the sound of Puerto Rican drums going through your head." "Sweets for My Sweet," on which Shuman played piano and added his lusty baritone to the chorus, featured Latin percussion and paid unabashed homage to what Tito Puente was performing at the Palladium. According to Jerry Wexler, the song's chord changes, appropriated from "Guantanamera," inspired "Twist and Shout," "You've Lost That Lovin' Feelin'," and many later rock songs with a Latin feel.

"Sweets for My Sweet," which reached No. 16 in October 1961, was the Drifters' most explicitly Afro-Cuban single to date and the last of seven hit songs that Pomus and Shuman wrote for the group. It was also the quintessence of the multicultural musical mix that prevailed at 1619 and 1650 Broadway: white writers producing black performers with a Latin beat.

Puerto Rican emigration to New York had peaked during the preceding decade when the city's Puerto Rican population more than doubled, from 254,880 to 612,574. As their numbers grew, so did the ubiquity of Afro-Cuban music and what Jack Kerouac, who yearned "to be vital, alive like a Negro or an Indian or . . . a New York Puerto Rican," called "that crazy out-of-this-world impossible-to-absorb mambo."

Although Jelly Roll Morton's dictum that jazz is not jazz without a "Spanish tinge" is deservedly famous, rock 'n' roll's relation to Latin music has received less attention. Yet the syncretic nature of Latin music—"neither black nor white, African nor European," in the words of one scholar, "but *negriblanca*"—modeled and mediated popular music's integration of black and white music. "The Palladium was the laboratory," another historian of Latin music observed. "The catalyst that brought [together] Afro-Americans, Irish, Italians, Jews. God, they danced the mambo. And because of the mambo, race relations started to improve in that era. What social scientists couldn't do on purpose, the mambo was able to accomplish by error."

"The Palladium opened the door," music historian Joe Conzo concurred, "and then, suddenly, there was no racism." Ernie Ensley, an African American who frequented the Palladium, confirmed that his fellow dancers "came from Brooklyn, the white guys and girls, and they could dance. . . . I used to go to these dance halls out in Brooklyn and be the only black guy there. But I always had someone to dance with. I never had any problem or discrimination. It was a dancing crowd."

Latin music had a musical as well as a sociocultural affinity with rock 'n' roll. However complex its clave rhythms, it still relied for the most part, like rock 'n' roll, on three chords. "Some of it was just one chord," according to Artie Butler, "built on a C-7 chord for the whole song. Basically, Latin music was simple, with a different kind of infectious beat. They were like Puerto Rican doo-wop records. We loved them, and we experimented—I know I did—with different kinds of Latin music." "Cuban music is based on repetition," said a veteran trumpeter in Latin bands, and repetition made it amenable to the short, simplified format of a rock 'n' roll single.

"Mambo and Latin started at the very same time as rock 'n' roll, and they were kind of neck and neck for a while," said Neil Sedaka, whose yearbook at Abraham Lincoln High School included among the highlights of his classmates' experiences "Exposure to Tschaikowsky, Stravinsky and cha-cha." Mort Shuman's graduating class a year earlier had memorialized "doing the mambo—that crazy new dance step."

According to Cynthia Weil, "The pulse of New York City, which is filled with Latin and African and every kind of music, was always there. That influenced everybody." The Latin influence seemed particularly pervasive among Jews. "If you were from Brooklyn and Jewish," said Tony Orlando, who was from Hell's Kitchen and Greek–Puerto Rican, "you loved Latin music." A lifelong friend of Sedaka remembered his own Grandma Becky at the Brighton Beach Baths dancing "in platform shoes and clunky jewelry" to "The Miami Beach Rhumba"—a hit that even survived translation into Yiddish. Bay Two, the three-block-long stretch of sand where the college crowd hung out in Brighton Beach, rang to the rhythms of La Playa Sextet and Joe Cuba. Machito entertained the Jewish clientele at the Concord before he performed at the Palladium, and Tito Puente recorded an early album at another famous Catskills resort: *Cha Cha Chá Live at Grossinger's*.

According to pianist Hilton Ruiz, "A lot of Jewish people were the greatest mambo dancers." They also conducted Latin orchestras. Bandleaders Al "Alfredito" Levy and Larry "El Judio Maravillosa" Harlow both hailed from Brooklyn. Arnold Friedman, the convicted pedophile in the documentary film *Capturing the Friedmans*, was Arnito Rey. Jews also championed Latin music on the radio. Dick "Ricardo" Sugar was New York's leading English-language Latin deejay, while Symphony Sid Torin eventually switched from jazz to an all-Latin format. And they committed it to record. Before he stumbled onto doo-wop, George Goldner, a zealous mambonik with a Puerto Rican wife, founded Tico, New York City's foremost independent Latin label, and recorded Tito Puente, Tito Rodríguez, Machito, "Alfredito" Levy, and other Latin artists. Even one of Goldner's R&B groups, the Crows, soldered the Latin-Jewish connection by recording a song (for which Morris Levy claimed a cowriter's credit): "Mambo Shevitz." Gerry Goffin told Doc Pomus years later how soulful and inspiring he had found the songs Pomus and Shuman had written for the Drifters. "Oh," Pomus replied, "it was just Jewish Latin."

When Ben E. King rebelled against George Treadwell's tightfisted control of the Drifters and set out on a solo career, he did not jettison Jewish Latin. He recorded Pomus-Shuman's "Souvenir of Mexico," with Ray Barretto on conga, and other songs that Pomus had written with Phil Spector as well as with Shuman. Paul Case had introduced Spector to Pomus, saying, "I want you to meet this character who's going to be a big, big star in the business." Pomus took an immediate liking to the nervous but ingratiating young man who carried an attaché case containing paper, a comb, and a loaf of bread, and who continually paced the floor, pausing before a mirror to fuss with his thinning hair. "Not only was he talented," Pomus said, "but he was very bright and very funny." Staying up all night in the Hotel Forrest, a seedy dive across Forty-ninth Street from the Brill Building, or spending the weekend by the pool at Pomus's Long Island home, the two started collaborating.

On October 27, 1960, when the Drifters' "Save the Last Dance for Me," with Ben E. King singing lead, was No. 1 in the nation, Leiber and Stoller went into Atlantic's new recording studio on Sixtieth Street and cut four songs with King. Two were by Pomus and Spector: "First Taste of Love," a workaday exercise in the Drifters' Latin manner, and "Young Boy Blues," which was interesting primarily because Pomus ended every line in the verses with a conjunction in order to create a run-on sentence. Both were overshadowed by a song that Spector had written with Leiber and another that Leiber and Stoller had coauthored with King.

Spector had been pestering Leiber to write with him. When Leiber acceded and invited Spector to the Upper West Side town house to which he had moved from Washington Square, Spector played a melody on guitar that reminded Stoller of "Valencia," the third and final port of call in Jacques Ibert's 1922 orchestral suite, *Escales*. (It would remind another Spector collaborator, Beverly Ross, with whom he had spent that afternoon, of a song *she* had written.) "It had that particular Spanish sound," Leiber said, "so I kept pushing him in that direction—building the chords, a third up, a third up. He wrote the tune, but I was pushing him. . . . While I was doing this I got the idea, which was literal. It was Spanish, 'Spanish Harlem,' and I wrote it . . . on the spot." Stoller, who was cooking a hamburger in the kitchen, joined in and added a figure of descending triplets (played on marimba in Stanley Applebaum's arrangement) that in Leiber's estimation merited a writing credit that the modest Stoller never claimed. Shortly thereafter, Artie Ripp invited Spector to share his room in the Hotel

Forrest and the company of "two maniac chicks." While Ripp was "getting sucked, fucked, and this and that and going crazy," Spector hunkered down on a credenza, strummed his guitar, and added finishing touches to "Spanish Harlem."

Although Ben E. King had lived in Spanish Harlem for a spell when his family moved to New York from Henderson, North Carolina, the song "frightened" him. "It's a great tune, but it's not a black song," he recalled. "It has nothing to do with R&B. And I said to myself when I finished, 'That's it. This won't make it.'" Truth be told, "Spanish Harlem" is also one of the few dumb lyrics Leiber ever wrote, betraying how uncomfortable a love song, even one that was ethnically adventurous, made him. How can you "pick that rose" *and* "watch her as she grows in my garden"? The recording's opening melody, castanets, and tambourine are indeed redolent of Ibert's "Valencia," but "Spanish Harlem" had contemporary currency, imbuing the Latin leanings of the Drifters' songs with geographic specificity. However exotic the song seemed to teenagers throughout much of the country, New Yorkers recognized a neighborhood and a realism that were unusual in popular music.

Atlantic Records was as dubious as King of the song's commercial prospects. Recalling its misjudgment of "Save the Last Dance for Me," the label released "Spanish Harlem" as the b-side of Pomus-Spector's "First Taste of Love." When the single was flipped over, "Spanish Harlem" reached No. 10 and made Ben E. King a solo star.

King's stardom was confirmed when the song that Leiber and Stoller produced at the tail end of that October 27, 1960, session, "Stand By Me," hit No. 4. With half an hour left, Leiber and Stoller asked King if he had a song they might squeeze in. He played one on piano that he had written for the Drifters but they had rejected. Just as Ray Charles and Sam Cooke had pioneered soul music by twisting gospel songs to secular ends, King had drawn on "the Baptist blues" of Charles A. Tindley, a founding father of gospel music, and on songs by the Reverend C. L. Franklin (Aretha's father) and the Soul Stirrers (Cooke's old gospel group) to compose "Stand By Me," which substitutes reliance on a woman's love for faith in God's. Leiber and Stoller concocted a head arrangement on the spot, added a modified *baion* bass line, and turned over a drum and scraped its underside to create a catchy scratching noise. "They were chance-takers," King said. "It's a nice song, but it's a great record," according to Leiber, who attributed its success to the bass line: "an insidious piece of work. It can put a hole through your head."

★

Burt Bacharach leapt at the chance to join Pomus and Shuman in the fold of songwriters supplying material for Leiber and Stoller and the Drifters. "I never saw anybody so terrific producing records as them," he recalled. "You can't help, if you're around greatness, to have some of it rub off on you. To go to a Leiber and Stoller recording session with the Drifters was an incredible learning experience."

Bacharach had a lot to learn, and he knew it. He had not had a record in the pop charts for nearly a year and a half, not since Jane Morgan's "With Open Arms," written with Hal David, peaked at No. 39 in August 1959. Much of the interval had been spent touring the world with Marlene Dietrich. "I was opening her in different places, trying to get there for important dates and having somebody else come and take my place," Bacharach said. "I didn't want to do it full-time, but it was a wonderful way to see the world, and she was awfully nice to me. She was kind of mean to everybody else who worked around or worked for her, but I always escaped that. It was a 'Burt can do no wrong' thing.'"

They met when Dietrich's arranger and director, Peter Matz, left her to work with Noel Coward two weeks before she was to open in Las Vegas and recommended Bacharach as his replacement. "Iz dot a cold?" she asked when Bacharach entered her suite at the Beverly Hills Hotel with a sniffle, and then stuffed him with vitamins. That evening Bacharach played her a song he had written with David. Dietrich telephoned Frank Sinatra and urged him to record it. When he declined, she warned him, "You'll be sorry." ("Warm and Tender" was eventually recorded by Johnny Mathis.)

Dietrich was smitten, and Bacharach became one of the last great loves, though unconsummated, of her life. Having divorced Paula Stewart (who went on to play Lucille Ball's crippled kid sister in the Broadway musical *Wildcat* and wed comedian Jack Carter), Bacharach was available but uninterested. "He was young, very young, and very handsome," Dietrich recounted in her autobiography, "and I have never seen such blue eyes." For the next four years she "lived only for the performances and for him." Harboring "no illusions about [her] voice," she relied on Bacharach's arrangements, accompaniment, and conducting to create them for audiences around the world. She depended and doted on Bacharach, even washing his shirts and socks. Comparing his role to the director Josef von Sternberg's in the 1930s, Kenneth Tynan called Bacharach Dietrich's "generalissimo."

Directing a sexagenarian's road show did not strike Bacharach as a terribly promising career path, however. Nor did writing more songs for the likes of Jane Morgan and Perry Como (who was pushing fifty). Their day had come and was going, while rock and soul were clearly the pop music of the future. Yet Bacharach, past thirty himself, felt locked out. For all his musical sophistication—*because* of his sophistication—he was fumbling for the key to contemporary commercial success.

Bacharach felt disdain for rock 'n' roll. "I never wrote a rock and roll song in my life," insisted the man who had contributed a song to *Don't Knock the Rock* yet repeatedly ignored its admonition. The feeling was mutual. When he played some of his compositions for Connie Francis, a friend of his father, she advised him to get a day job. Kenny Vance and other members of Jay and the Americans were unimpressed when he auditioned a song for them on Stoller's piano. "He couldn't really sing," Vance recalled, "and he wasn't cool. He was an Ivy League type of guy—maybe he had white bucks on, even." The group dismissed the song and Bacharach with a shrug (and did not enjoy success with two Bacharach-David songs they later recorded).

Although he was eight years Bacharach's senior, Hal David protested he "loved rock 'n' roll. I used to listen to other writers who were very establishment oriented . . . who would hate rock 'n' roll and thought it was a fad. I never could understand that kind of thinking. It's part of the environment; it's part of young people. I have two sons and I saw it happening before it necessarily became a big thing." Not only did Presley record one of Mack David's songs, but Hal contributed two trifles to an Elvis movie, *Kid Galahad,* in 1961.

Hal David was getting along without Burt Bacharach very well. During Bacharach's dry spell, David had four records in the pop charts that he had written with other people. One of these, "Broken-Hearted Melody," sung by George Treadwell's ex-wife and protégée, Sarah Vaughan, went Top Ten.

Burt Bacharach wasn't cool. No one was cooler, on the other hand, than Leiber and Stoller, and, given their success with Presley, the Coasters, and now the Drifters, no one was commercially hotter. Bacharach approached the pair and asked to become their apprentice. "You guys know how to make hits, and I want to learn how to do that." Leiber knew Bacharach as a writer of "chi-chi, East Side, red carpet–type songs." "He wasn't that knowledgeable about the pop forms," Stoller said. "He recognized them, but he employed kind of European cabaret-type forms in his music." Yet they made a deal: Bacharach would strive to write songs for Leiber and Stoller, and they would teach him what they knew about producing.

Bacharach had been introduced to Leiber and Stoller by another Famous Music writer with whom he sometimes collaborated. More than a decade older than Bacharach, Bob Hilliard had penned the lyrics for Sinatra's "The Coffee Song" and "In the Wee Small Hours of the Morning" and written Broadway musicals with Carl Sigman and Jule Styne. One of his most famous songs, "Civilization" ("Bongo, bongo, bongo, / I don't want to leave the Congo") had been a smash hit for Louis Prima in 1947. He was an odd choice of cowriter for someone eager to win a younger audience. (Facing a similar challenge, Pomus turned to the teenage Shuman.) But Hilliard, a big bumpkin of a man unanimously described by his colleagues as "offbeat," had an expansive sense of humor and hospitality, welcoming guests to the indoor pool in his suburban New Jersey home. Bacharach wrote with David three days a week and with Hilliard a couple of mornings. Hilliard often spent the afternoons following his sessions with Bacharach writing with David's frequent collaborator, Lee Pockriss; Paul Evans's hit, "(Seven Little Girls) Sitting in the Backseat," was a Hilliard-Pockriss ditty. Somehow both Bacharach and David also found time to write with the singer and actor Paul Hampton. At Famous as at Aldon, writers played musical chairs. "Cowriting was like Russian roulette," one songwriter explained. "You didn't write many songs with someone if it didn't click."

The two Bacharach-Hilliard songs that Leiber and Stoller produced for the Drifters between 1961 and 1963 are more memorable than the three Bacharach composed with David. Bacharach showed an easy expertise with the *baion* beat. Marlene Dietrich described how they "would climb the hills around Rio to listen to the drumbeats that rose from the city. He was tireless when he observed, when he learned, mastered, and arranged, and could refresh his memory with the sounds of the countries in which we had traveled."

Leiber and Stoller produced "Please Stay"—a collaboration with Hilliard that was Bacharach's first song to win their approval—at the same session that yielded Pomus and Shuman's "Sweets for My Sweet" and "Room Full of Tears." Rudy Lewis, recently recruited to replace the departed Ben E. King, sang lead on the song, a *baion* that begins with pleading bass interjections by Tommy Evans (another newcomer to the ever-changing group) and ends with stately strings echoing a Cuban *danzón.*

"Please Stay" reached No. 14. The next Bacharach-Hilliard song, "Mexican Divorce," although it never charted, is more remarkable. The theme is extraordinarily adult even for the Drifters, who seldom condescended to teenagers. Hilliard's lyrics are at once wry and moralistic, blending humor, pathos, and bitterness as they develop from the triple rhyme of "Down below El Paso lies Juarez / Mexico is different, yes / Like the travel folder says" to the pronouncement, "It's a sin for you to get / A Mexican divorce." As much as Bacharach wanted to reach a younger audience, he (and Leiber and Stoller) would not juvenilize his music, which is a sumptuous approximation, part tribute and part parody, of Mexican song.

"Mexican Divorce" was extraordinary on another account. While rehearsing the four young women who had been hired to sing backup vocals, Bacharach was captivated by one of them in pigtails and white sneakers whose voice was as high as her cheekbones. Twenty-year-old Marie Dionne Warrick's talent and Leiber and Stoller's tutelage sped Bacharach on his way.

★

A fourth song was recorded at the February 1, 1961, session that produced "Sweets for My Sweet," "Room Full of Tears," and "Please Stay." Carole King and Gerry Goffin, whose "Show Me the Way" had been diverted to Ben E. King, got their first Drifters cut with "Some Kind of Wonderful." "Carole and Gerry idolized" Leiber and Stoller, according to Tony Orlando, who sang lead on the demo of "Some Kind of Wonderful." "They talked about them as gods—and they were! Anything that happened to their lives in my time, it had to be off a map that was written by Leiber and Stoller and Stanley Applebaum and Pomus and Shuman. When you listen to the string lines on 'Will You Love Me Tomorrow' or my records, you're seeing them written sideways, upside down, and backwards from Stanley Applebaum and Leiber and Stoller. They were the Michelangelos."

"They were kind of like mythic figures," said Goffin, who was impressed by the intelligence of Leiber's lyrics, the duo's innovative use of strings, and their variations on the *baion* beat. "They have the copyright on it. . . . [S]oon everybody in the whole country was doing it." Everybody included Goffin, who wrote a song with Jack Keller entitled "Bione Rhythms." Who cared how you spelled it as long as you could dance to the beat? Recorded by Jimmy Beaumont, the lead singer of the Skyliners (famous for "Since I Don't Have You"), it began: "I guess the bione rhythms were to blame / 'Cause when I danced with you they set my soul aflame."

The arrangements of "Some Kind of Wonderful" and the next Goffin-King song the Drifters recorded, "When My Little Girl Is Smiling," are rather muscle-bound, encumbering King's melodies with steroid strings and overbearing background vocals. Goffin's lyrics are striking, however, for their vernacular directness, whether they draw on a common campus expression ("When I was in college, somebody always used to say, 'some kind of wonderful beer' or something") or, possibly, incipient tension within Goffin and King's own relationship ("Every time my baby and I have a quarrel / I swear I won't give in").

Goffin and King loved working with the Drifters. King rehearsed their songs with the group. "Carole used to hang in there with us tough," Charlie Thomas recalled. "She used to pound down. She wasn't no hard woman—a girl at her age—but Jesus, this woman couldn't sing at all! And she's going to give *me* the key? But she played the piano, and it was amazing the songs that she'd give us." Goffin popped his head in occasionally and played a more prominent role when they entered the studio to record.

The situation was so ideal that sometimes Goffin and King would circumvent Kirshner for fear that he might give someone else a song they had intended for the Drifters. According to Wexler, "We'd have the song without Donnie's authorization. Now, legally, he could stop us, because the copyright law is that the first recording has to be approved by the publisher . . . but he wasn't about to stop a record by the Drifters!"

On one such occasion Goffin and King completed a song in Leiber and Stoller's office in the Brill Building. As they were driving into Manhattan, Goffin said, "Carole came up with the melody in the car—an a cappella melody. I said, 'How about a place to be alone?' She says, 'My secret place.' So the song was originally called 'My Secret Place.' I said, 'No, that's no good. How about 'Up on the Roof'? It was imaginary—maybe something that I copped out of *West Side Story.*"

The setting of "Up on the Roof" and its luminous bridge—"At night the stars put on a show for free"—are indeed reminiscent of the original production of *West Side Story,* in which set designer Oliver Smith's tenement walls flew up to reveal a sky filled with stars. *West Side Story* was playing at the Winter Garden, doors down from 1650 Broadway and within sight of the Brill Building, when Goffin and King and other songwriters began making their music-business rounds. "I remember it was always there," Barry Mann recalled, "blinking on the marquee." The 1961 United Artists movie heightened interest in the score, so much so that Leiber and Stoller set Leonard Bernstein and Stephen Sondheim's "Tonight" to a *baion* beat and produced it as Jay and the Americans' first single, released, not coincidentally, by United Artists' record label. Neither Kenny Vance nor the group's lead singer, Jay Traynor, had ever heard the song or even seen a Broadway musical. "We were from the street," Vance said. "*West Side Story* was like from another planet." Leiber, having spent the formative years of his partnership with Mike Stoller light-years away from Broadway on L.A.'s Central Avenue, was too cool to be impressed by the musical, either, at least initially. Cynthia Weil recalled and Barry Mann confirmed that "Jerry Leiber hated it. He thought it was very pretentious and wasn't real." (For the record, Leiber denied this forty years later.)

King and Goffin's appreciation of *West Side Story,* which they shared with their stablemates at Aldon, Sedaka and Greenfield as well as Mann and Weil, enabled them to take a quantum musical leap with "On the Roof." Orlando observed that Goffin and King packed into the song everything that Leiber and Stoller had taught them and topped it off with *West Side Story,* "which had a great impact on them."

Although it represented a major advance for King and Goffin, "Up on the Roof" was entirely in keeping with the Drifters' Latin proclivities. Bernstein himself had not been inspired by the project for a musical, originally entitled *East Side Story,* until the *Romeo and Juliet* update was recast as a brawl between Anglo and Puerto Rican gangs. His "imagination caught fire," he said, "as the Latin-American rhythms began to pulse in his mind." One day Bernstein took a wrong turn off the Henry Hudson Parkway and ended up on or near 125th Street. "All around me Puerto Rican kids were playing, with those typical New York City shouts and the New York raucousness. . . . Suddenly I had the inspiration for the rhumba scene." Brooks Atkinson's *New York Times* review of *West Side Story* noted that Bernstein's score "capture[d] the shrill beat of life in the streets." This is precisely what Goffin and King, Mann and Weil, and other New York songwriters were attempting to do.

West Side Story was not the only source of inspiration for "Up on the Roof." Cynthia Weil had learned a great deal from Goffin and King; now they were learning from her. One day Weil saw a handsome African American pushing a hand truck in the Garment District. Downtown, she reflected, this black man was a nobody, but he enjoyed an identity and dignity uptown when he went home at the end of the working day. Using chords that Mann characterized as "very much like *West Side Story* or 'Soliloquy'" (from Rodgers and Hammerstein's *Carousel*), he and Weil composed what she called "one of the first sociological songs":

> *He gets up every morning and he goes downtown*
> *Where everyone's his boss*
> *And he's lost*
> *In an angry land*
> *He's a little man*
> *But then he comes uptown*
> *Each evening to my tenement*
> *Uptown where folks don't have to pay much rent.*

Weil owed her social consciousness to Woody Guthrie and hootenannies in Washington Square. The folk music scene gathering momentum in Greenwich Village attracted a college student rebelling against her conservative Republican upbringing. Mann's politics were pure Brooklyn. Like many Jews in the borough, where an estimated ten thousand mourners filed past the open coffins of Julius and Ethel Rosenberg when Mann was fourteen, the Imbermans were left-wing. "I always felt that political noise in the background," Mann said. "If you grew up in Brooklyn . . . coming from a Jewish background, you're not even conscious of it but it's always there." A "liberal heritage," he concluded, is "just part of your fiber." Mann was a sophomore at James Madison High School when one of its veteran teachers was threatened with dismissal for refusing to testify before the Senate Internal Security Subcommittee, occasioning Albert Einstein's famous call for intellectuals to refuse to testify before congressional investigating committees even at the risk of impoverishment and imprisonment. Growing up in Brooklyn, where Jackie Robinson broke the color line in major league baseball, also predisposed Mann to sympathize with the civil rights movement and its crusade against racial injustice in the "angry land" that "Uptown" described.

Artie Ripp was responsible for placing the song. George Goldner had squandered so much money at the track that he had to surrender his record labels, Gone and End, to Morris Levy. "I'll go to the grave for you," Ripp said he told Goldner, "but I'm not going to work for Morris." Ripp remained at 1650 Broadway, landing a job promoting songs for Aldon. When Phil Spector dropped by, seeking a song for the Crystals, a trio of young black women who were the first act Spector produced on Philles, the record label he had recently formed with Lester Sill, Ripp sang and played "Uptown" on the piano—"clumsily, because I'm not a pianist."

Spector, still very much under the influence of Leiber and Stoller's Latin productions, added castanets and Spanish guitar to "Uptown," suggesting that the song's protagonist was Puerto Rican rather than African-American. He also altered a few notes because the Crystals' Barbara Alston could not reach them. A disappointed Mann and Weil urged Spector to rerecord the vocal, and he obliged them by inviting Eva Boyd, who had not yet been transformed into Little Eva, into a New York studio for another try. As was his wont, Spector demanded take after take. "He would make her do it over and over again," Weil recalled, "and this poor, raw, undisciplined girl who had never been in a recording studio before didn't know what to make of it. She was totally pissed off, and she would sit there at the mic cursing, 'He's a bad man. This guy's a motherfucker. I hate him. What's he gonna do? Ask me to sing it again?'" Eventually giving up on Boyd, Spector released the version he had originally recorded.

"Uptown" became a hit the same year Michael Harrington's *The Other America: Poverty in the United States* popularized the term "underclass." Kirshner, who had always pressed Mann and Weil to write a catchy but innocuous song like "Little Darlin'," now urged Weil to "write another of those songs I don't understand." "Uptown" peaked at No. 13 in May 1962; in June, Goffin and King wrote "Up on the Roof," preserving Mann and Weil's urban setting but softening their social realism with a more romantic evocation of escape to an inner-city rooftop, "the only place I know / Where you just have to wish to make it so."

A magazine for songwriters noted that those lines "may be two of the finest . . . in pop history." That's stretching things, but "Up on the Roof" is a beautifully composed song, sweeping in scope yet sensitive and subtle in its details, as when it alludes with a wink and a held quarter note to the group that is singing: "And all my cares just *drift* right into space."

★

"Uptown" and "Up on the Roof" were New York City street scenes, vignettes from a New Yorker's point of view. That same year Mann and Weil wrote a song about the city as imagined by a small-town girl who would probably never see the street they walked down every day. Mann conceived "On Broadway" as "a Gershwinesque kind of melody," composing it with no particular artist in mind, and Weil "wrote a lyric about a girl wanting to come to Broadway," she said, "because Broadway was always my thing." Spector, eager for another "Uptown," cut a version by the Crystals but did not complete it to his satisfaction. Gerry Goffin produced and Carole King arranged a recording by the Cookies that was not terribly satisfying, either. The stiff, almost martial drumbeat was out of step with the song's naïve yearnings.

In January 1963, Mann and Weil played the song for Leiber and Stoller, who were looking for Drifters material. "They really loved it but said the perspective was wrong," Mann recalled. "They said, 'You can either go home and continue writing it yourself, or you could write it with us if you like.' We said, 'Sure!' We don't idolize many people, but we idolized them. We went to Jerry's apartment on Central Park West and wrote the song there. It was very exciting, especially with Jerry—the way he just kept throwing lines out, and then he'd take them back. 'Try this line!' Then he'd say, 'Let's go to the third verse or the second verse.' It was a totally different process from the way Cynthia writes." According to Weil, "It was like going to songwriters' school."

While Leiber tossed off lyrics, Stoller tinkered with the tune. "My melody originally had a piano in it and a minor note against a major chord," Mann explained. Stoller dispensed with these, gave the melody a bluesier feel, and suggested modulating three times—a key recommendation because the song consisted of a verse without a bridge or chorus, and otherwise the simple A-A-A format might not hold listeners' attention. Unquestionably, Leiber and Stoller earned their cowriters' credit and share of the song's publishing.

As they headed to the recording studio to cut the new, improved "On Broadway," Leiber and Stoller bumped into Spector. They invited him to join them, and Spector ended up playing a guitar solo on the song he had tried unsuccessfully to record. As reconceived for the Drifters, "On Broadway" is a song about disillusionment and determination. Although the way the melody repeatedly rises but returns to the middle C it starts from suggests that the singer will eventually "catch a Greyhound bus back home," his dream of stardom forever dashed by the big city's indifference to his talent on guitar, the lift to F at the end of the last verse and Rudy Lewis's improvised vows as the song fades hold out a glimmer of hope.

Two weeks before "On Broadway" reached No. 9 in the charts, the Drifters recorded a second four-way collaboration between Mann and Weil and Leiber and Stoller with drastically different results. Mann and Weil had originally composed another political song that Kirshner couldn't understand, a sarcastic indictment of racial discrimination that made Bob Dylan's "Blowin' in the Wind," written the previous year and shortly to become a hit single for Peter, Paul and Mary, seem circumspect. "Only in America," Weil had written (appropriating the title of Harry Golden's best-selling memoir of a Jew's experience in the American South), "where they preach the golden rule, do they start to march when kids try to go to school. Only in America, land of opportunity, do they save a seat in the back of the bus just for me."

Leiber and Stoller, according to Weil, "looked at us like, Are you crazy?" They said the song was too inflammatory ever to get airplay. "We were the rebel kids who wanted to stir stuff up, and they were the practical guys who were the producers and knew what they had to deal with." This may be underestimating Leiber and Stoller, who had always believed and proven in their songs for the Coasters that comedy could be more subversive than self-righteousness. "In the wildest hipster, there is no desire to shatter the 'square' society in which he lives, only to elude it," observed John Clellon Holmes, the writer who popularized the term "Beat Generation." "To get on a soapbox or to write a manifesto would seem to him absurd."

Leiber and Stoller persuaded Mann and Weil to turn the lyrics into a paean to upward mobility. "So we rewrote it from a WASP perspective," said Mann, still indignant thirty-eight years later. "Only in America," the new lyrics averred, "can a kid without a cent / Get a break and maybe grow up to be President!" (Jackie Robinson had concluded *The Jackie Robinson Story,* the 1950 biopic in which he starred as himself, by invoking an America "where every child has a chance to become President—or play for the Brooklyn Dodgers.") To Leiber and Stoller's way of thinking, such whitewashed lyrics, when sung by a black group, would have the same ironic effect as many Coasters songs. According to Leiber, the song was "a sendup, a black person talking about what a great place this country is for opportunity—an ironic, bitter statement. . . . We'd made what we thought was a hip track with the Drifters."

Jerry Wexler and Ahmet Ertegun did not agree. According to Charlie Thomas, who had no idea "Only in America" was ironically intended and "just wanted a hit song," the Atlantic executives sat the Drifters down and told them, " 'This is not the song for y'all 'cause there's too much prejudice happenin' out there.' They said we might get hurt or something if we do this song."

"I killed the record," Wexler said, "because it would seem to be a blatant piece of very smug hypocrisy to have these black people, all of whom came from poor backgrounds and still were subject to all the evils and misfortunes that this nation can bring, sing this song. . . ." Wouldn't listeners, at least black ones, get the joke? "That's fine. So I'll have a professor of semiotics at Harvard go around with each record and deconstruct it for the edification of the people whose sensibilities were too blunt to appreciate the irony."

Jerry Leiber, Kenny Vance said, "was able to look at the black situation and write about it in a way that no one else could possibly have written about it—from their perspective. If they wanted to laugh at things, they had to laugh at things that weren't that funny if they wanted to laugh at all." But the contentiousness over "Only in America" showed that by the spring of 1963, as Bull Connor turned water hoses and police dogs on civil rights demonstrators in Birmingham, Alabama, race was no longer a laughing matter. It had become next to impossible for Leiber and Stoller to express their sophisticated sense of racial humor without offending or embarrassing black as well as white Americans. The songwriters hadn't lost their touch; it had simply fallen behind the times. The Coasters' popularity had waned, and the virulent lyrics that Leiber wrote for unrecorded songs such as "Whitey!" demonstrated his own increasing frustration and anger.

Yet "Only in America" enjoyed a spectacular afterlife that was far more ironic than the Drifters' aborted single. Vance and Jay and the Americans' new lead singer, David Black (who adopted Jay as his stage name), heard the Drifters' record in Leiber and Stoller's office and begged to be allowed to cut the song. It certainly suited their name, which Leiber had given the group. (According to Vance, Leiber eyed an American Airlines ticket on his desk and suggested Binky Jones and the Americans. "We said, 'Who's Binky Jones?'" Leiber pointed to the group's original lead singer, John Traynor. "We said, 'No way!' It was so uncool." Since Traynor's nickname was Jay, they compromised on Jay and the Americans.)

Leiber and Stoller took Jay and the Americans into Atlantic's studio and recorded their vocals over the Drifters' unaltered instrumental track. Without telling the group, they subsequently sped up the tape, so that Jay Black, as he learned only when he heard the record on the radio, sounded like a castrato. Despite or because of the alteration, "Only in America" became a hit. When the group performed in Florida, they were astonished to find venues filled with Cubans. "They couldn't speak English," Vance said, "but they learned 'Only in America' phonetically."

Nothing illustrates more dramatically the racial and ethnic interplay of the music produced by the Brill Building and 1650 Broadway than the roundabout route by which a song that was pulled for fear of offending African Americans became, when sung by a Jewish group, an anthem for aspiring Cuban refugees.

Chapter Ten

BABY TALK

★

"Carole?" In the spring of 1962, Jerry Leiber heard a female voice in one of the cubicles in the offices of Trio Music and peered in to discover at the piano a strapping young woman wearing a college blazer over a prim blouse with a Peter Pan collar. Her hair teased into a platinum helmet, twenty-one-year-old Eleanor Louise Greenwich looked less like Carole King than comedienne Judy Holliday, who had recently starred in the stage and screen versions of *Bells Are Ringing*. She explained somewhat nervously that she was awaiting the return of John Gluck Jr., a friend of a friend with whom she had an appointment. Leiber urged her to continue playing her songs and was sufficiently impressed to invite her to return to Trio anytime, use the piano, hang out and write with whomever she pleased. All he asked in exchange was the right of first refusal to whatever she came up with.

Like Carole King, Ellie Greenwich was born in Brooklyn (on October 23, 1940), although she moved at age eleven from East Flatbush to a quarter-acre lot on the corner of Starlight and Springtime Lanes in the cookie-cutter development of Levittown, Long Island. "It was really embryonic there," Greenwich recalled. "There was no grass, and the trees were just planted. . . . You'd walk out in the backyard and sink into the mud up to here and laugh." Like King, Greenwich cut a few unsuccessful singles and went to Queens College to please her parents. But Greenwich stuck at it longer, transferring to Hofstra on Long Island, graduating, and teaching English to unruly high school seniors for less than a month before the principal and she agreed she was better suited to a career in music.

William Greenwich, a frustrated painter turned electrical engineer, was Catholic. His wife, Rose Baron, who managed the women's clothing department in a J. C. Penney store and later, after earning a nursing degree, a doctor's office, was Jewish. Both doted on the older of their two children, whom they named after Eleanor Roosevelt and raised as neither Jewish nor Catholic but "American," celebrating seder and Easter at different aunts' homes.

William Greenwich played the balalaika and mandolin. When friends returning from Germany gave the family an eighty-base Hohner accordion, Ellie took up the bulky instrument. With her mother's encouragement she took lessons and mastered "Lady of Spain" and "Carnival of Venice." "There was always music in the house," Greenwich said. "Singing and dancing went on constantly." When she was fourteen, she formed a group called the Jivettes that sang, mostly in unison, at schools, nursing homes, hospitals, and benefits. And when, as a high school freshman, she developed a crush on a senior, she started composing unrequited love songs on the accordion. "I would spend hours just getting stuff out." Listening to Alan Freed on her transistor radio when she should have been doing her homework, she fell in love with rock 'n' roll. She had admired the vocal harmonies of pre-rock "girl groups" such as the Andrews and the De Castro Sisters; now she switched allegiance to the Shirelles. Although race "was never discussed" in her home or racially exclusionary Levittown, she found herself unself-consciously preferring Fats Domino records to Pat Boone's cover versions, and LaVern Baker over Georgia Gibbs. "I'd go, 'Hmm, interesting: black, black, black.' It just felt like me."

Her mother, who "had balls," Greenwich said admiringly, wrote to Archie Bleyer and wangled an appointment with Arthur Godfrey's former music director. Bleyer headed Cadence Records, an independent label whose roster included the Chordettes and which released one of 1955's biggest hits, Bill Hayes's "The Ballad of Davy Crockett." Greenwich's obliging father put wheels on her accordion so she could maneuver it easily and drove her into Manhattan. But it was her mother who accompanied Greenwich into Bleyer's office. "He was wonderful," Greenwich recalled. "He listened to my songs and we talked and he gave me this advice: Please finish school, because the music business will always be here, but the opportunity to finish school won't."

Greenwich was still in high school when the owner of the Hicksville, Long Island, record store where she purchased "Earth Angel" and other treasured 45s put in a good word for her at RCA. Ed Heller, an executive there, listened to a couple of her songs and signed her. "I was absolutely a tax deduction," Greenwich said. "He goes, 'You give me $600.' I'm to pay *him*!" She balked, but RCA signed her anyway, recording and releasing a single, "Cha-Cha Charming" and "Silly Isn't It," in 1958. Greenwich wrote both songs and, fearing that teenagers wouldn't know whether to pronounce the "w" in her name, performed them as Ellie Gaye. Although the record went nowhere, Greenwich, chaperoned by her mother, lip-synched it as far away from home as Chicago and Baltimore. Opening for George Gobel, she towered over the diminutive comedian, who "would have a conversation with my breasts."

When the Manhattan School of Music rejected Greenwich because the conservatory did not accept accordion students, her parents purchased a piano and she entered Queens College. Greenwich brought her single to a music class and was devastated when her professor slapped it on the turntable and dragged his elbow across the record in disgust. She was happier at Hofstra, where she majored in English, joined a sorority, and reigned as Spring Queen.

Following her teaching fiasco at General Douglas MacArthur High School, Greenwich scouted the Brill Building and met Paul Case, who introduced her to Doc Pomus. They wrote a few obscure songs together, including "Who You Gonna Love This Winter, Mr. Lifeguard?" and Greenwich visited Pomus in Long Island. "He was almost like an older brother to me," Greenwich recalled. It was Trio Music on the ninth floor rather than Hill and Range in the eleventh-floor penthouse, however, that provided Greenwich a family nearly as supportive and protective as her own. Leiber was a nurturing mother, Stoller a brisk, businesslike father, and the men with whom she wrote—Ben Raleigh, Mark Barkan, and Tony Powers—the big brothers she never had. "She was bursting forth with music and ideas," Barkan recalled. "She would sit at the piano, and it would just jump out of her like an explosion. She was amazing. . . . Tony and I both knew right away, and that's why we vied to write with her."

Trio was not nearly as ambitious or extensive an operation as Aldon. It existed primarily to publish Leiber and Stoller's songs and to provide additional material for the many acts they produced. As Leiber and Stoller began to allocate more energy and imagination to production than composition, the extra material became increasingly important. When Leiber and Stoller didn't like or couldn't use what Greenwich and her cowriters came up with, they were free to pitch a song to Peer-Southern, Mills Music, and the scores of other publishers in the Brill Building. "Literally, it was songs for sale," Greenwich said. "We'd each get $25 or $35, and that paid for my commutation back and forth."

Greenwich drew attention for her singing as well as her songwriting. "I'd come in, play the piano, and bellow away like a street person." While Carole King was content to write for the Shirelles, Greenwich wanted to *be* a Shirelle. Her ardor and her ear for harmonies made her a much-sought-after backup and demo singer of songs that she had no hand in writing.

Greenwich's most productive writing partnership was with Tony Powers, who was principally a lyricist. "He was this big, bruising guy with dark hair and this very angular face, and he talked sometimes like *dis*," Greenwich recalled, "but what a doll!" Leiber and Stoller gave them the nod on two occasions that Greenwich was too naïve then to recognize as fool's errands: following up fluky first hits by groups whose modest talents made them unlikely ever to repeat their unexpected initial success. Jay and the Americans' second single, "She Cried," and the Exciters' first, "Tell Him," both produced by Leiber and Stoller, were enormous hits, but neither group had the gifts of the Drifters or Shirelles. Jay and the Americans' awkward rendition of Greenwich-Powers's "This Is It" missed the charts entirely, while the Exciters' frenetic "He's Got the Power" stalled at No. 57. The latter was culled from a marathon session at which Leiber and Stoller recorded nine songs, including one by Bacharach and David, for an album. Greenwich's father had driven her from Levittown to Manhattan's Bell Sound Studio. In the wee hours of the morning, Leiber and Stoller gave Greenwich the thumbs-up from the control room, indicating they had chosen her song as the Exciters' next single. Excitedly, she roused her snoring father, who drove her home, showered, and returned to the city for another day's work.

On the strength of these songs Leiber and Stoller put Greenwich and Powers on salary. Offered $50 a week, Greenwich held out for $100 and got it. Yet the team was most successful with material that Leiber and Stoller didn't care for. Greenwich had met Phil Spector at Trio and taken an instant dislike to him. While she played him a song

The Brill Building (1619 Broadway) *(above)* and 1650 Broadway *(left)*. "You might aspire to be able to get into the Brill Building, but if you were a kid from Brooklyn, 1650 Broadway was the cat's meow." *(© AD 1619 LLC, administered by Realty Group, Ltd.; Courtesy of United States Realty and Investment Co.)*

The original cool cats: Mike Stoller and Jerry Leiber *(above)* with Elvis, *(right)* in the recording studio, and *(below)* with their first mentor and partner, Lester Sill *(rear center)*, and Lou Krefetz *(front)*, later manager of the Clovers. *(© Michael Ochs Archives.com)*

First impression: Hank Medress, Cynthia Zolotin, Neil Sedaka, and Eddie Rapkin, a.k.a. the Tokens. *(Courtesy of Brian Gari)*

The magician and the mensch: Burt Bacharach and Hal David. *(© Charlie Gillett/Michael Ochs Archives.com)*

London welcomes Doc Pomus *(third from left)* and Mort Shuman *(far right)* in 1961. *(Courtesy of Sharyn Felder and Will Bratton)*

This magic moment: Pomus and his wife, Willi Burke. *(Courtesy of Sharyn Felder and Will Bratton)*

Kenny Rankin, Dion, and Shuman jamming at Pomus's Long Island home. *(Courtesy of Sharyn Felder and Will Bratton)*

Made for each other: Howard Greenfield, Neil Sedaka, Connie Francis. *(Courtesy of Neil Sedaka)*

The young lovers: Carole King *(left, at piano)* and Gerry Goffin *(far right)*, with Cynthia Weil and Barry Mann. *(Photo by William "PoPsie" Randolph. © 2005 Michael Randolph)*

All aboard: Don Kirshner, Al Nevins, Gerry Goffin, Carole King, and Little Eva *(front)*. *(© FDR/Michael Ochs Archive.com)*

No pop music songwriting team has
remained together, active, and successful
as long as Cynthia Weil and Barry Mann.
(© Charlie Gillett/Michael Ochs Archives.com)

Phil Spector, the "Tycoon of Teen."
(Photo by William "PoPsie" Randolph.
© 2005 Michael Randolph)

George Goldner (right) with
one of his first and youngest
hit makers, Frankie Lymon.
(© FDR/Michael Ochs
Archives.com)

Making movies for the ear:
Ellie Greenwich, Jeff Barry,
and "Shadow" Morton wrote
and produced most of the
Shangri-Las' *(below)* soap
operas with sound effects.
*(© BMI/Michael Ochs
Archives.com; © Michael Ochs
Archives.com)*

"If the name wasn't Neil
Diamond, it might have been
Jeff Barry": a Diamond in
the rough with producers
Barry, Ellie Greenwich, and
Bert Berns. *(Photo by William
"PoPsie" Randolph. © 2005
Michael Randolph)*

The exes: Goffin and King circa 1968 and 1971. *(© Russ Titelman; © Michael Ochs Archives.com)*

Içi on parle français: Jacques Brel and Mort Shuman. *(Courtesy of BMI)*

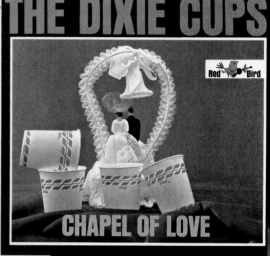

A potpourri of pop albums.
(Courtesy of Ken Emerson)

she thought would be perfect for the Paris Sisters, "the boy genius" primped before a mirror, muttered to himself, and wandered in and out of the room. According to Barkan, an exasperated Greenwich, who for all her sorority girl innocence had a mouth on her, finally said, "Listen to me, you little prick. Did you come to look at yourself or to hear my songs?" Greenwich recalled, "He never got to hear the song, and that was the end of it."

Months later, Greenwich learned that a song she and Powers had sold to Aaron Schroeder, a publisher at 1650 Broadway, had piqued Spector's interest and that he wanted to meet her. According to Greenwich, "He had no idea it was me." She arrived at his office for a two o'clock appointment, and he did not appear until six. She sat there all the while, scribbling lyrics, and when Spector finally showed up, she pointed angrily at her watch. Greenwich's songs plus her medley of spunk and passivity (after all, she had waited four hours for him) captivated Spector, who produced three Greenwich-Powers tunes and claimed a cowriter's credit for two of them. "Phil certainly did contribute," Greenwich said. "He *is* a writer." Spector recorded all three songs at Hollywood's Gold Star Sound Studios, where he was developing but had not yet fully realized his massive "Wall of Sound." Darlene Wright of the Blossoms, a Los Angeles trio that specialized in backing vocals, sang the leads.

"Why Do Lovers Break Each Other's Hearts?" a doo-wop descendant of "Why Do Fools Fall in Love," was ascribed to Bob B. Soxx and the Blue Jeans and reached No. 38 in March 1963. This was the first song Greenwich had written that she heard on the radio, and when she did, she was so thrilled that she slammed her Corvair into a toll booth. "(Today I Met) The Boy I'm Gonna Marry," by Darlene Love, as Spector rechristened Wright, finished close behind at No. 39 in May. Its echoing vocal chorale, reverberating instrumentation, and marital theme—"He smiled at me and, gee, the music started playing / 'Here Comes the Bride' when he walked through the door"—were auguries of many songs to come. But first Greenwich had to introduce Spector to her new writing partner—and fiancé.

★

They probably met as toddlers, since they were distantly related by marriage. Their paths might have crossed in 1958 when RCA released singles by both Ellie Gaye and Jeff Barry. But the first time Ellie

Greenwich and Jeff Barry met for certain was at Thanksgiving dinner in Valley Stream, Long Island, in 1960. Their hosts were Bill and Lola Baron—he was Greenwich's uncle; she was Barry's cousin. Greenwich brought her accordion, and Barry brought his wife. When they discovered their mutual interest in music, Greenwich said, "I went 'oooh,' he went 'mmmh,' and his wife went, 'I don't think I like this.'"

Barry's childhood had been as overcast as Greenwich's was sunny. Born Joel Adelberg on April 3, 1938, in Brooklyn, he moved to Plainfield, New Jersey, at age seven when his parents divorced. Blindness had not prevented his father from becoming a successful insurance broker, but his mother refused to accept alimony or child support. Instead, she squeezed her family—not only Joel but his mentally retarded sister and his maternal grandfather—into her mailman brother's attic. When they returned four years later to Brooklyn, the foursome shared a one-bedroom apartment in Flatbush. "We went from having stuff to no stuff," Barry said. "And that's the way it was until I earned my own stuff."

Roy Rogers and the Lone Ranger inspired a childhood fascination with cowboys that Joel Adelberg never entirely outgrew. He wore cowboy outfits and hats, packed a cap pistol, and at the age of seven or so made up a song whose words his mother preserved: "I got a gun and I got a saddle and I got a pony, too. / I even have a sweetheart, that sweetheart is you." "I've since dropped the cowboy part of songwriting," he said, "but it's still about love. Most songs are."

While attending Erasmus High School, Adelberg managed to find rodeos in Brooklyn, and he dated a girl who was wild about horses. He also formed a doo-wop group. "We'd stand on street corners and snap our fingers and tap on stuff. We would book little functions." Adelberg started making up songs for them to sing. This continued when, following a stint in the Army Reserves, he studied industrial design at City College. Fellow student Al Contrera, later of the Mystics, chanced upon a group that included Adelberg singing harmony in a hallway and joined in on bass, jamming for an hour. Initially Adelberg found engineering as engrossing as doo-wop. "I can't help looking at a refrigerator door and saying, 'The handle should be here' and 'This should be there,'" he explained. "As a teenager I would do that with car design— collapsible steering wheels, inventions. To this day I can't help inventing." But soon he decided he would rather tinker with music than with objects, and, like Barry Mann, another Brooklyn cowboy, Adelberg dropped out of college.

Marrying Lenore Kronstein "to get out of the house" and adopting the name Jeff Barry, he recorded several singles for RCA and then Decca but had better luck as a writer. Family connections won him an interview with Arnold Shaw, the general professional manager of Edward B. Marks Music Corporation. Shaw listened to him sing his songs. Although they were confined to C and G, the only chords Barry knew on the piano, which he was too impatient to master, Shaw detected more potential in him as a composer than as a performer, offered him $75 a week, and suggested that the tyro collaborate with an experienced E. B. Marks writer, Beverly Ross.

"I immediately had a great rapport with Jeff," recalled Ross, who wrote "Paper Crown," a b-side for Johnny Maestro and the Crests, with Barry. "He has got to be one of the kindest, wildest, and most creative personalities I have ever met. And he was so mechanically gifted, too. He seemed to be able to run machines. He was about six-five, and he would leap onto pianos and play the strings. You'd never know what he was going to do next. He was really a prankster." Their partnership was short-lived because Jean Aberbach wooed and won Ross for Hill and Range—"I was so young and so viciously ambitious"—and the publisher had no interest in an unproven writer like Barry.

On his own, Barry reduced Beethoven's "Moonlight Sonata" to "Teenage Sonata," a drudging ballad that became Sam Cooke's first and worst single on RCA. His fortunes improved when he teamed with Ben Raleigh (who would also collaborate with Greenwich) and composed "Tell Laura I Love Her," a Top Ten hit for Ray Peterson that raised Barry's salary to $125 a week. Ever the cowboy, Barry had originally set the song at a rodeo rather than a stock car race. The teenage protagonist uttered his dying words not from the wreckage of his hot rod but after being gored by a Brahma bull. "I didn't own a car," Barry said, "so I went with what I could relate to." When Arnold Shaw said he liked the song but not the setting and warned that kids would not identify with cowpokes, Barry rewrote the lyrics.

Barry was learning to write for kids, and kids were crazy about cars, so with Raleigh—a wizened older man who wore white sneakers, gobbled health food, had a laugh like a hacking cough, and maintained a voluminous list in alphabetical order of potential song titles—he penned

"Red Corvette." "My theory is that up until 1955, it was adults writing songs for adults," Barry said.

> Kids had Disney films, and that's writing for preschoolers, basically. Nobody was really creating music especially for teenagers, because they didn't have money. Then in the fifties they started to have disposable income. They had the buck, and they could buy the record. So then you got adults writing for kids, and you came up with "How Much Is That Doggie in the Window?"—what they *thought* were kiddie songs. And then young adults like myself—I was nineteen and starting to write—started to create music for young people. And that to me is the beginning of pop rock. I couldn't write for adults. I wasn't an adult. I had no experience.

In September 1959, Barry recorded a single, "Lenore," that paid tribute to his wife. The flip side was "Why Does the Feeling Go Away?" After Barry met Greenwich, the feeling dwindled and the marriage was annulled. "He'd come over to visit me in Levittown," said Greenwich, who was still a student at Hofstra, "and bring records and more records." They also made two records of their own: "Red Corvette" (with a song by Greenwich on the b-side), which Greenwich performed as Ellie Gee and the Jets, and "Big Hunky Baby," a song by Barry that she sang as Kellie Douglas.

Records and romance ran neck and neck, yet after she graduated, Greenwich initially retained her independence as a writer. She introduced Barry to an aspiring songwriter she had recently met, Barry Mann's childhood friend Artie Resnick. Together Barry and Resnick wrote a minor hit for Linda Scott ("I Left My Heart in the Balcony") and a major one with Cliff Crawford for Gene McDaniels ("Chip Chip"). "Jeff I consider my mentor," Resnick said. "I'd get an idea, and . . . if he liked the idea, he would basically shape and mold the song. I was a complete novice."

Greenwich and Barry were engaged in April and wed on October 28, 1962, one year almost to the day after Mann and Weil. "Jeff was crazy in love with her," Resnick said. "Between the two of them I don't have to tell you what an explosion of talent came together." Before they moved into a ground-floor apartment in Lefrak City, an immense housing development in Queens, Greenwich realized that if they lived together, ate together, slept together, and fought together, they would inevitably write together, too. She took Tony Powers to lunch at Lindy's and broke the news that their partnership was over. (So was his relationship with Barry, with whom he had also written several songs.)

Barry, meanwhile, had joined Greenwich in the Brill Building, moving from E. B. Marks on West Fifty-second Street to Trinity Music, whose offices were next door to Trio's. Bobby Darin acquired Trinity and summoned Barry to Los Angeles to sound him out about running T.M., as the publishing firm was renamed. Although hanging out with Darin and Hugh Hefner in Tony Curtis's cottage on a movie lot was heady stuff, Barry accepted another offer from Leiber and Stoller. (Stoller remembered his first impression of Barry: "He was tall and thin and dressed like the Marlboro Man.") Barry would earn much less at Trio, but he figured he could learn much more. Greenwich arrived at work one day to discover Barry there and their names inscribed on the door of a room containing a piano, a desk, and two chairs. "They were nice leather," she said, "not even Naugahyde!"

★

Jeff Barry and Phil Spector hit it off immediately and, with Greenwich, composed fifteen songs during 1963 and 1964 that cemented Spector's stature and his Wall of Sound while establishing Greenwich and Barry as major pop songwriters. Spector's production techniques were so innovative and overpowering, and so much has been written about them over the decades, that we tend to think of records such as the Crystals' "Da Doo Ron Ron" and the Ronettes' "Be My Baby" only incidentally as composed songs. Yet no one wrote more closely, consistently, or successfully with Spector than Barry and Greenwich.

After Mann and Weil had given Spector's Philles label its first major hit, the Crystals' "Uptown," Spector produced a weird trio of Goffin-King songs: "He Hit Me (and It Felt Like a Kiss)," "No One Ever Tells You," and "Please Hurt Me." Goffin said he was inspired to write the first of these lurid lyrics when Eva Boyd, shortly before she became Little Eva, showed up for work badly bruised, evidently by her jealous boyfriend. "But she sort of smiled before she went to her room," Goffin recalled, "and she said, 'He really loves me.'" (They would marry by year's end.) The masochism of all three songs, which the Crystals intoned with a glum fatalism, was bizarrely inappropriate for Top Forty airplay, and the recordings are unsettling even today. Spector quickly withdrew "He Hit Me" as a single to make way for the Crystals' rousing rendition of Gene Pitney's upbeat "He's a Rebel."

Spector turned once again to Mann and Weil for an even bigger hit than "Uptown": the rollicking "He's Sure the Boy I Love." Although the record bore the Crystals' name, Darlene Wright/Love and the rest of the Blossoms actually sang Weil's adroit lyric, which contrasted romantic dreams with erotic reality and opted for the latter. Who cares if the singer's sweetheart subsists on unemployment checks? "He sure ain't the boy I've been dreamin' of / But he sure is the boy I love." The single's success notwithstanding, Spector seemed to sour on Aldon writers, or at least to be searching for something, in addition to a songwriting co-credit and a share of the publishing, that they and Don Kirshner were not giving him. Although Barry, Greenwich, and Trio Music were more accommodating in such matters, Spector's new writing partnership was based on much more than business.

Barry and Greenwich were different from the Aldon writers—and from Pomus and Shuman, Bacharach and David, and Leiber and Stoller, for that matter. They had little interest in Broadway musicals or the Great American Songbook, and even less in classical music or jazz. Unburdened by the past and by the ambitions and doubts that the past can inspire, they took themselves and their music less seriously. This freed them to write entirely and unself-consciously in the present tense of teenage rock 'n' roll—which is why a 2004 *Rolling Stone* magazine listing of "The 500 Greatest Songs of All Time" included more by Greenwich and Barry (six, five of which they wrote with Spector) than by any of their songwriting peers.

Phil Spector, Doc Pomus once observed, "made the quintessential young record, because it had . . . to do with the wonderful pureness about adolescence. It almost didn't relate to some pimply kid. . . . It transcended. It was this great wall of enormous sound, and somehow through it all there was this lovely . . . romantic, sentimental innocence." Instead of Goffin-King's lockstep "He Hit Me (and It Felt Like a Kiss)," the newly wed Barry and Greenwich wrote with Spector the cantering "Then He Kissed Me": "Then he asked me to be his bride / And always be right by his side / I felt so happy I almost cried." Where Mann and Weil noted the difference between uptown and downtown, between small towns and Broadway, no distance divides desire from its object in Barry-Greenwich-Spector songs. Gratification is instant because yearning intensely makes it so in a world of little boys, little girls, babies, and baby talk where love is a full-time preoccupation and no one collects unemployment. "She was very into the teenage mind," Barkan said of Greenwich. To accentuate the adolescence of these songs, Spector replaced the womanly voices of Barbara Alston and Darlene Love on Crystals records with thinner, more girlish vocals by the group's newest and youngest member, La La Brooks, only fifteen when Spector erased Love's voice and substituted hers on "Da Doo Ron Ron."

"Then He Kissed Me" and "Da Doo Ron Ron" were the first songs Greenwich and Barry wrote with Spector. The nonsense syllables of "Da Doo Ron Ron" were placeholders that they meant to replace with lyrics, but Spector liked and retained them. In doing so he linked the song, through "Zip-A-Dee-Doo-Dah" (the ditty from Walt Disney's animated *Song of the South* that Spector had turned into a raunchy rumble for Bob B. Soxx and the Blue Jeans), to the ladies singing "doo-dah" in Stephen Foster's "Camptown Races," blackface minstrelsy, and the origins of American popular music more than a century earlier. Other Greenwich-Barry-Spector songs that the Crystals recorded included "Heartbreaker," "I Wonder," "Little Boy," "Girls Can Tell," and "All Grown Up," while Darlene Love cut "Wait 'Til My Bobby Gets Home," "A Fine, Fine Boy," "Christmas (Baby Please Come Home)," and, as Bob B. Soxx and the Blue Jeans, "Not Too Young to Get Married."

For the Ronettes, a trio that had previously recorded a Carole King song (cowritten with saxophone player Artie Kaplan) and courted celebrity by stuffing their bras with Kleenex and twisting the night away at the Peppermint Lounge, Barry, Greenwich, and Spector wrote not only "Be My Baby" but "Baby I Love You" and "Why Don't They Let Us Fall in Love?" While the Ronettes' lead singer, Veronica Bennett, was rehearsing the last of these songs, Spector kissed her for the first time. Eventually he would leave his wife and marry the half-white, quarter-black, and quarter-Cherokee singer who, performing with her sister and half-Spanish cousin, embodied the interracial allure of the era's pop music. Bennett was disappointed when Spector chose to release "Be My Baby" rather than "Why Don't They Let Us Fall in Love?" as the Ronettes' first single, and so, at first, was Greenwich. But the booming "Be My Baby" reached No. 2, while the stodgier "Why

Don't They Let Us Fall in Love?" issued under the name Veronica, missed the charts.

The discrepancy between Barry, Greenwich, and Spector's "silly little things," as Barry called the songs it took them a few hours at most to write in Manhattan, and the stupendous productions that required weeks if not months for Spector to complete in Los Angeles infuses these records with humor as well as power and a singular perspective. Spector had learned a great deal from Leiber and Stoller, and Barry and Greenwich were learning a lot from them, too. Barry cited as one example the *baion* drumbeat that famously kicks off "Be My Baby." But Leiber and Stoller, following Ertegun and Wexler, strove for a clean, clear sound in which every instrumental line was distinct. According to Stanley Applebaum, they continually sought to "thin out the palette": "There was always a give-and-take about what we should eliminate. Can we make it more sparse?" Spector, on the other hand, piled instrument upon instrument to raise an echoing Tower of Babel. "We had only one drummer and everybody else was on percussion," Stoller said. "Phil was the first to use multiple drum kits, three pianos and so on. We went for much more clarity in terms of instrumental colors, and he deliberately blended everything into a kind of mulch." This undifferentiated sound corresponded to the indiscriminate, infantile urgency of Greenwich, Barry, and Spector's short, singsong, nearly nursery-rhyme lines.

The three worked in Spector's office off the lobby of the building on East Sixty-second Street and York Avenue where he resided in the penthouse apartment. Usually Greenwich, Spector, or both of them sat at the piano while Barry pounded out a rhythm on its top or a file cabinet. One reason they collaborated so harmoniously is that they were able to slip in and out of roles. Leiber and Stoller, Pomus and Shuman, Bacharach and David, and the Aldon teams generally observed a division of labor between melodist and lyricist. Barry, on the other hand, frequently came up with a melody and lyric but depended heavily on Greenwich for chords. "The beauty of Jeff and me," Greenwich said, "was that we did do all things, and it became a total collaboration. Who did what? We just did it all, and, mushed together, we had something." The readiness with which they exchanged roles made it easier for them to welcome a third collaborator in Spector than it might have been for the more territorial King and Goffin or Weil and Mann—and also, perhaps, to tolerate his eccentricities.

Spector was "moldable" then, Greenwich reflected. "If he trusted you, I think he had the need to be mothered. I think Jeff and I offered that to him. There was a lot of stuff that went on." In the middle of a writing session, Spector might disappear without a word. "We'd be looking out the window and see him walking to a French lesson. But he'd come back and continue working. . . . There were the three of us doing it all."

★

Barry and Greenwich also enjoyed surprising success when just the two of them did it all. The first song Greenwich remembered writing with Barry was "What a Guy," a soundalike follow-up to the Sensations' "Let Me In" that they composed while riding the E train from Lefrak City to Manhattan. The demo they recorded intrigued Leiber and Stoller. "Listen, there's something about this," they told Greenwich. "About *what*?" she asked. "There was no artist, there was a piano and drum, that's all it was." Their bare-bones rendition was even sparser than King and Goffin's demo for "The Loco-Motion" and the polar opposite of Spector's elephantine productions. While Barry whacked a drum kit and interjected "di-dip's" in a bass voice, Greenwich played an almost inaudible piano and created a girl group of her very own with overdubbed vocals and harmonies. "Those were mono days," recalled Brooks Arthur, who engineered the demo. "We were going from tape machine to tape machine, and through the many generations, or the sounds I was adding to try to preserve the sounds, we *created* a sound."

"The difference between a demo and a master is the label," Barry said. Leiber and Stoller sold the "What a Guy" demo to Jubilee Records, which released it as is in the summer of 1963. Recapturing the playful spirit and street-corner simplicity of early doo-wop, it became a modest success for the Raindrops, as Greenwich and Barry dubbed themselves after Dee Clark's hit song "Raindrops." Hewing to the same less-is-more formula, they created a bigger stir in the fall with the delightful "The Kind of Boy You Can't Forget," a song originally intended, like "What a Guy," for the Sensations.

The Raindrops were strictly a studio confection, and Barry had no interest in going public. "I don't know whether it was an insecurity or I just didn't want to do it," he said, but he had lost much of his earlier drive to perform and "was having a great time creating." Although

Greenwich recruited her younger sister, another woman, and a man to join her in lip-synching the Raindrops' records at promotional appearances, subsequent singles yielded diminishing returns, with the exception of one unexpected dividend.

When Barry and Greenwich, always fast workers, completed a Raindrops session with an hour of studio time still to go, they called a break. According to Barry, they went in the hall, dashed off a song, returned, and recorded it, all in under sixty minutes. Differing in her recollection, Greenwich recalled composing the song with Barry while parked on Levittown's lovers' lane, inspired by the carryings-on in the automobiles around them. "Everybody else was making out but Jeff and I were making music." In either event, "Hanky Panky" consisted of little more than a slinky riff and an opportunity for Greenwich to toast their friends and Leiber and Stoller's franchises: "The Tokens do the hanky panky! The Drifters do the hanky panky! The Coasters do the hanky panky!" Released as the b-side of the Raindrops' third single, it was also recorded by two obscure girl groups, the Parlettes (whom the Tokens produced) and the Summits. None of these renditions won a hearing, and a fourth version, released regionally by a high-school band in Niles, Michigan, was also ignored for two years until a deejay in Pittsburgh stumbled across it and played it so frequently that it topped the local charts. In July 1966, more than two and a half years after the Raindrops' version appeared, Tommy James and the Shondells' "Hanky Panky," sung with a horny growl and howl that were far more sexually explicit than Greenwich's echoed and overdubbed harmonies, went No. 1 nationally.

"All songs are written in hours," Jeff Barry said. But a lucky few live on for decades. "I probably would have worked harder on all that stuff if I knew there was such a thing as classic rock 'n' roll coming down the pike. Certainly 'Hanky Panky' I would have made into a real song."

Chapter Eleven

AT WORK IN THE ELVIS ATELIER

★

A spacious office with a grand piano, art on the walls, and deep-pile carpet on the floor seemed an appropriate reward for Hill and Range's most successful pop songwriting team. In 1961, Doc Pomus and Mort Shuman were by at least one measure the most successful songwriters in all America, with thirteen singles in the pop charts. But their new quarters in the Brill Building were too deluxe for the drudgery of composition. "We never did a bit of work," Pomus recalled. "So we insisted that we had to get another office. There was one little room that no one else would use, that did not even have space for a couch—just a small piano and two upright chairs. It was so bad that we would desperately try to finish up just so that we could get out of that room."

"Those rooms were about six by seven," said Beverly Ross, who arrived at Hill and Range a couple of years after Pomus and Shuman. "They'd give us a piano, a table, and a couple of funky old chairs that needed reupholstering. We had a theory that there were no windows in those rooms because they wanted us to recirculate the creative energy and not let anything go out into the air—and that's how we could write smash hits."

In a cubicle to the far right of the receptionist's desk, past the corridor leading to Paul Case's office, then Freddy Bienstock's, and finally Jean and Julian Aberbach's, Pomus and Shuman labored over smash hit after hit for not only the Drifters but also Elvis Presley. They succeeded Leiber and Stoller as Presley's most-favored songwriting team, but the care and feeding of the King were not nearly so engaging in the 1960s as they had been in the 1950s. "I used to dread the couple of Elvis movies

I would handle a year," said Elaine Orlando, a secretary working for Paul Case who eventually married Tony Orlando.

"At one time he had a contract with MGM that called for him to make four pictures a year," Bienstock said.

> I had to find the scores. It was impossible to do that. We had it worked out like an assembly line. The producers would give me, like, eleven scripts with marks where a song would fit. Then I would give them out to various writing teams and ask them to try to write a song for these situations in the script. They would write the songs, and we would demo the ones we liked. And then eventually Elvis would decide which one he liked best for each section. But it was not the best material after a while. In the beginning, we used to screen songs for him very carefully and make suggestions and changes. And Elvis had some suggestions. But then when he had to do something like ten songs for a picture and we had to get forty songs in a year, it was impossible to do that. And on top of that, studios always insisted on having a title song, and it was difficult to write songs like "Wild in the Country" and "Harum Scarum."

Hill and Range was a much bigger operation than Aldon or Trio Music, with offices overseas. The ambience was inevitably less familial, and the intra-office rivalry for Presley records made it even more impersonal. "After all, we were competing," said Ben Weisman, who won the distinction of writing the most songs that Presley recorded, an astounding total of fifty-seven. "We're talking about an artist who had absolutely conquered the whole world. It was the pot of gold. It wasn't quite the right atmosphere for camaraderie when it came to Elvis."

Pomus and Shuman admired Presley. The first time he heard Presley, Pomus was reminded of "somebody who came out of the swamps," which he meant as high praise. "I couldn't believe it was a white guy," said Pomus, whose earlier career as a blues singer had provoked similar disbelief. Presley "was something wild, insane, like he was singing on the edge. . . . One of the secrets of people like Elvis [is] they sing within themselves but with great restraint and passion. . . . The great singers know how to do it." But Colonel Parker made Pomus and Shuman "well aware," in the words of Presley biographer Peter Guralnick, that they could "easily be replaced (and frequently were) if they ever got too big for their britches." Although Pomus and Shuman wrote sixteen songs together that Presley recorded, a few more separately, and some of his biggest hits, they never met him. Pomus never even saw him perform live. The one time he laid eyes on him, at a press conference in New York City, Colonel Parker prevented Pomus, whose songs helped sustain Presley's popularity well after the arrival of the Beatles and the British invasion, from speaking to him.

Given such disheartening circumstances, it's remarkable that Pomus and Shuman contributed so many memorable songs to the Presley catalog, beginning with the very first one he recorded. While Pomus and Shuman were in London following the success of "Teenager in Love," they met Lamar Fike, a portly Presley sidekick on his way to visit the GI in Germany. When Fike asked if they had any material suitable for Presley, Shuman went into a London studio and made a piano-voice demo of "Mess of Blues," a song they had composed in Pomus's Williamsburg apartment. They gave to it Fike and forgot about the song until Presley recorded it at his first session after his discharge.

Although Pomus said the material he and Shuman provided Presley "drifted by with everything else we were writing," he repeatedly singled out "Mess of Blues" as one of the few songs he had written for anyone that he remembered with fondness and pride (the others were "Lonely Avenue" and "Save the Last Dance for Me"). Released as the b-side of the No. 1 hit "It's Now or Never," "Mess of Blues" was overshadowed by the Americanization of *O Sole Mio* and only reached No. 32 in its own right. It is, however, one of Presley's most pleasurable performances. Far from being a formal blues, "Mess of Blues" is a pop song infused with a bluesy feel and set to a relaxed shuffle rhythm by Floyd Cramer's piano. Playfulness predominates in the lyric ("Oops, there goes a teardrop / Rollin' down my face") and in Presley's vocal, especially when he shudders in mock discombobulation as he sings, "I got to get myself together / Before I lose my mind." Presley was never more in command of his faculties and seldom seemed to have as much fun exercising them as here, while the Jordanaires urged him on with treble "whooh-whooh's" that would reappear eight years later in, of all unlikely places, the Rolling Stones' "Sympathy for the Devil."

Eager to repeat the success of "It's Now or Never," Hill and Range urged Pomus and Shuman to try their hands at translation. Mario Lanza,

Frank Sinatra, and Dean Martin had already sung *"Torna a Surriento,"* an Italian ballad dating back to 1911, as "Come Back to Sorrento." Pomus and Shuman turned it into "Surrender," their second No. 1 song (following "Save the Last Dance for Me"). Even as Concetta Franconero, Robert Cassotto, and so many other singers were changing their names, Mario Lanza and Dean Martin (who had changed his), both of whom were influential idols for Elvis, enjoyed hits with *"Arrivederci Roma"* and *"Volare."* American singers and songwriters frequently plundered Italian popular music. Leiber and Stoller wrote an English lyric for Carlo Donida and Mogol's *"Uno Dei Tanti"* that Ben E. King sang over the Italian record's instrumental track. "I (Who Have Nothing)" became a hit not only for King but, subsequently, for Terry Knight and the Pack, Tom Jones, and Sylvester. Americans also tended to lump together everything from Rio de Janeiro to Rome as "Latin." Much as an Italian movie had popularized the Brazilian *baion* beat, "It's Now or Never" and "Surrender" were a mishmash of mambo and Napoli.

Exaggerating the tempi and time shifts while amplifying the instrumentation and melodrama of the relatively restrained "It's Now or Never," "Surrender" was everything "Mess of Blues" was not: bloated, gaudy, forced, and false. Though sung with bravura, it initiated and epitomized many of the excrescences for which Elvis would become infamous. Fortunately, Pomus and Shuman had better songs in store for Presley that helped forestall his long, queasy decline.

On June 25, 1961, Presley recorded three Pomus-Shuman songs in Nashville. Although two of them would number among his best-remembered hits, none of them had been written with Presley in mind. Pomus and Shuman had originally intended "Kiss Me Quick" for the Flamingos, a doo-wop "bird" group most famous for its otherworldly rendition of "I Only Have Eyes for You." Presley's rendition of "Kiss Me Quick" was a knockoff of "Surrender" that benefited from being more concise and less histrionic.

Shuman and Pomus wrote "Little Sister" and "(Marie's the Name) His Latest Flame" for Bobby Vee. On his regular shopping trips to New York, Snuff Garrett befriended Pomus and visited him in Surrey Commons, where he remembered how a mechanical apparatus lowered Pomus into and hoisted him out of the swimming pool. Garrett also frequently played gin rummy with Paul Case, who told him that "the

biggest thing in Doc's life was the next step he took." Feeling sorry for
him and noting that the footloose Shuman was often out of town, leaving Pomus without the companionship of a collaborator, Garrett invited Pomus to spend a month in Los Angeles and paid for his plane
ticket. Every morning the boys in Liberty Records' mailroom would
carry Pomus up to Garrett's second-floor office.

Shuman joined Pomus in Los Angeles, where they wrote at least one
song that Vee recorded, but "All You've Got to Do Is Touch Me" was
a sweet nothing compared to "Little Sister" and "(Marie's the Name)
His Latest Flame." Garrett said he financed the demos even though he
recognized right off the bat that the material was too hard-charging for
the easygoing Vee. Freed to shop the songs elsewhere, Pomus and Shuman turned to their friend Bobby Darin. Married to Sandra Dee, settled
in Bel Air, and making it big in movies and nightclubs, Darin had put
away childish things like rock 'n' roll. He made a stab at recording the
songs, but to no one's satisfaction. Only then did Shuman and Pomus
send the demos to Presley.

And what demos they were! Shuman tore into "Latest Flame,"
pounding out a Bo Diddley beat on piano and hammering home a dramatic lyric about sexual betrayal. Mild-mannered Bobby Vee could
never have expressed such anger, and even Elvis turned down the heat
to a stoic simmer. According to Shuman, Presley loved the song so
much that he and his band played it for the better part of the evening in
the recording studio, and Shuman received a telephone call inquiring
how he had recorded the piano. Pomus got a ring in Long Island, too,
asking about a lyric they couldn't decipher. Only after he hung up did
Pomus learn that his caller had been Presley himself. The one and only
conversation he ever had with Elvis was unwitting.

Presley was equally enthusiastic about "Little Sister," which Shuman composed on guitar, for a change, in Hollywood's Roosevelt Hotel. "I started fooling around with a riff which had nothing to do with
the rhythm on Elvis's record. I had a very fast, driving guitar thing going and Elvis slowed it down by half." Even at half speed, "Little Sister"
rocks powerfully as Hank Garland's snaky guitar twines around Presley's vocal in bluesy call-and-response. As in "Latest Flame," the song's
impetus is betrayal, this time by an older sister who is the target of three
verses ("She's mean and she's evil / Like that little old boll weevil")

while the little sister of the title, whose "turned-up nose" the singer used to pinch, is the subject of only one. "Little sister, don't you do what your big sister done" isn't a plea but a threat.

Shuman and Pomus wrote other songs that were as rich as "His Latest Flame" and "Little Sister," but they never wrote greater rock 'n' roll songs, and these brought out the best in Elvis and his band. Released on the same single and competing with each other, "Latest Flame" reached No. 4 in the charts the same week in September 1961 that Vee's "Take Good Care of My Baby" by King and Goffin topped them. Two weeks later, "Little Sister" peaked at No. 5. To capitalize on its success, Pomus and Shuman altered a few words and created an answer song, "Hey Memphis," in which LaVern Baker growled that she'd never treat Presley like *her* big sister done. The songwriters were returning a favor, since the "Jim Dandy" who made a cameo appearance in the lyrics of "Little Sister" had had star billing in one of Baker's biggest hits, "Jim Dandy." "Hey Memphis," produced by Phil Spector when he was apprenticing at Atlantic Records, did not dent the pop charts.

Pomus and Shuman's ascendancy in the Elvis atelier was confirmed in March 1962 when, over two days, Presley recorded three of their songs, a fourth that Pomus had written with an occasional collaborator at Hill and Range, Alan Jeffreys, and a fifth that Pomus had composed with Leiber and Stoller, as well as the first song in more than four years that Leiber and Stoller had written by themselves expressly for Presley—which would also be their last. Leiber and Stoller visited Pomus's office when Shuman was trotting the globe. Pomus suggested that together they write a song for Presley. "It didn't take long," Leiber and Stoller recalled, to compose the country-and-western ballad, "She's Not You." On their own, Leiber and Stoller wrote another country song, "Just Tell Her Jim Said Hello." Pomus's prestige by then was such that "She's Not You" was released as the a-side of a single and reached No. 5, while "Just Tell Her Jim Said Hello" was relegated to its b-side and made it only to No. 55.

The biggest hit Presley recorded at the March 18–19 session was the one that got away. Pomus and Shuman's "Suspicion" continues the theme of betrayal sounded in "His Latest Flame" and "Little Sister," only this time infidelity may be a figment of the singer's mistrustful imagination. Elvis plays Othello with desperation yet delicacy, while

Shuman's music sets the long, fluent vocal line against a snappy rhythm that almost constitutes a counter-melody. The song appeared on an album and attracted little attention until Terry Stafford, an unknown singer who had moved from Texas to Hollywood, covered it a couple of years later. "Suspicion" was Stafford's first record, released on an obscure independent label, yet it went all the way to No. 3. Although RCA released Presley's original as a single too belatedly to enter *Billboard*'s charts, "Suspicion" provided the template for Presley's only No. 1 hit in years to come: Mark James's "Suspicious Minds."

When Pomus and Shuman wrote "Viva Las Vegas," they knew the setting of the Presley movie for which it was intended, but they had not read the script. Presley's recording quickened the tempo of Shuman and Pomus's demo, heightening the song's jittery energy and evoking the exhilaration and desperation of high-stakes gambling so vividly that MGM substituted it for the film's original title, *The Only Girl in Town*. Although "Viva Las Vegas" is widely recognized today as classic Presley, it was released as the b-side of Elvis's version of Ray Charles's "What'd I Say" and made it only to No. 29. After four extraordinarily rewarding years, Pomus and Shuman's relationship with Elvis, so intimate musically yet utterly impersonal, was, like Presley's career, beginning to falter.

When Pomus and Shuman were at the peak of their powers in the early 1960s, their versatility extended beyond the rock 'n' roll they wrote for Presley and the romantic ballads they composed for the Drifters. Gary "U.S." Bonds had some success with "Seven-Day Weekend," which emulated the raucous ebullience of the singer's earlier hits, "New Orleans" and "Quarter to Three." Nearly four years after "Teenager in Love," Dion recorded the doleful "Troubled Mind." Seven years after "Lonely Avenue," Ray Charles had a hit with Gerald Wilson's swaggering big-band arrangement of "No One," which had been the b-side of Connie Francis's "Where the Boys Are." But the biggest hit Shuman and Pomus wrote for another artist was for the least likely.

Andy Williams had scored five Top Ten singles on Archie Bleyer's Cadence Records when Columbia signed Steve Lawrence's predecessor as the resident crooner on Steve Allen's *Tonight Show*. Williams recorded a formulaic ballad by Mann and Weil and Burt Bacharach and Bob Hilliard's somnolent "Don't You Believe It" before registering a very minor hit. It looked as though Columbia was not going to recoup its investment in the bland tenor from Wall Lake, Iowa. To the rescue came Paul Case, Pomus, and Shuman, for whom Williams's producer, Robert Mersey, had arranged "Go Jimmy Go" before joining Columbia. They gave Williams "Can't Get Used to Losing You," a beguiling song that juxtaposes, somewhat in the manner of "Suspicion," a legato vocal line and a rhythmic counter-melody, daring listeners to decide which to heed more closely. Mersey wrote a striking arrangement to complementary effect, alternating percussive pizzicato violins on the verses with bowed strings on the choruses, and he elicited an uncharacteristically robust performance from Williams. Going all the way to No. 2, "Can't Get Used to Losing You" easily outperformed its b-side, Johnny Mercer and Henry Mancini's theme to the film *Days of Wine and Roses,* which was far more familiar Williams fare. The singer did not have a bigger pop hit in his career.

Williams followed "Can't Get Used to Losing You" with "Hopeless," a countryish ballad that Pomus wrote with Alan Jeffreys, a jazz trumpet player turned writer of revues, sketches, and special material. Jeffreys had little regard for pop music, and the dozen songs he wrote with Pomus (and two more with Pomus *and* Shuman) were indifferent. "Helpless" even stooped to stealing a line Howard Greenfield had written for Connie Francis: "'Cause my heart has a mind of its own." A year later Pomus and Shuman furnished Williams with "Wrong for Each Other," an account of a failing relationship that accelerates from a deadbeat 3/4 time to a manic waltz on the choruses. "You go on your way / I'll go on mine," runs the lyric. "I'll be better off now with somebody new / And you should find someone more suited to you." The song may have been autobiographical in more ways than one.

★

Doc Pomus and Willi Burke had at least one thing in common when they married: Neither had a career. Pomus had abandoned his as a blues singer, and Burke had yet to launch hers as a Broadway actress and singer. "We had no money, zilch," Burke recalled. "I didn't marry a famous songwriter. He started applying himself." So did Burke, who, despite her unfamiliarity with rhythm and blues and pop music, drew on her classical training to compose a few songs with Pomus—Mickey and Sylvia recorded one of them—and played piano on some demos. Getting out and about was difficult for Pomus, so they often entertained.

Paul Case, Bobby Darin, Neil Sedaka, Phil Spector, and Dion were among the guests who enjoyed Burke's cooking and the pool at Surrey Commons.

Their most frequent visitor was Shuman. "They could go into a room and come out with a song after a couple of hours," said Burke, who often served them dinner afterward. "Doc would come up with melodies all the time. Mortie provided the rhythm with the piano. Once in a while Mortie would come up with a melody from his chord changes. It was back and forth. . . . Sometimes they would sit there and woodshed, but more often than not Doc had the idea." Many of these ideas came from paperback novels and mysteries, which Pomus bought by the dozens, devouring at least one a night. He would scrawl a phrase or saying that struck him on a matchbook or napkin, and when Burke tried to clean up, he would protest, "Don't touch it! That's my song! That's my idea!"

Burke did not give up her dreams of Broadway, which came true when she replaced the lead actress in *Fiorello!* and starred opposite Tom Bosley. The musical had not ended its run when she became pregnant with her second child, Geoffrey. Her water broke while Pomus and Shuman were at work in the music room, and Shuman drove her to Doctors Hospital. To accommodate her children's school schedules, Burke restricted herself to summer stock for a while, but she felt unfulfilled. "I was starting to bloom as a person and find out who I was. I was no longer the little girl. I wanted to stretch myself in certain areas, and there were problems about that." According to Burke, an interfering mother-in-law and Pomus himself posed the problems.

"My experience has been," Pomus once admitted, "it's always tougher for me to take success because most of my life has been filled with failure and I found it very easy to live with. It was only when I started getting successful . . . that I found it impossible. I must have blown half a million dollars, all because of one thing—I couldn't cope with success. It's a madness. You know, up until the time I was thirty-two years old my good years were when I was able to buy a suit. . . . Then suddenly you're going into a store and having ten made to order."

Success, good eating, and increasing immobility put pounds on Pomus. As it grew harder to support his weight on crutches, he resorted more frequently to a wheelchair. As Pomus became more dependent, he became more demanding and insecure. "Doc felt he was someone who was always on the outside," said his closest companion in later years, Shirlee Hauser. "Even though he had the key to go in, when he went in, he didn't feel comfortable." According to Hauser, Pomus and Burke "had very different prisms with which they looked at the world. . . . Now he was a father, he was living in the suburbs, and of course that wasn't who he was at all."

Pomus kept a room across the street from the Brill Building in the Forrest Hotel. At first, given the unpredictable hours and late nights of the music business, it was a matter of convenience and not at all unusual. Ahmet Ertegun remembered the Forrest as "a dumpy little place" as far back as the early 1940s. Its location just off Broadway attracted a musical and show business clientele: Ray Charles, Eddie Fisher, Steve Lawrence and Eydie Gorme, Tony Orlando, Richard Pryor, and Rodney Dangerfield, plus an assortment of Runyonesque characters that included Damon Runyon Jr., who lived in the penthouse and was a friend of Pomus.

Gradually Pomus began to feel more at ease in these seedy but stimulating surroundings than on Long Island. It was a homecoming of sorts to the bohemian environment in which he had lived before his marriage. The buzz of round-the-clock action in the Forrest Hotel made it easier to bear his own physical inactivity. Pomus became a familiar sight, holding court in the lobby, where engineer Brooks Arthur remembered him "surrounded by these babes and telling great stories in his bellowing voice" or overtipping the waiter for a well-done steak in the hotel's Spindletop Restaurant. According to Phil Spector, a mob hit once interrupted their dinner there. "[A] guy in a raincoat walks in with a hat," Spector recalled, "and goes up to a guy and *boom boom boom,* three booms in the head and the guy slumps over dead, just like that." Pomus couldn't understand why Spector, barely twenty and still a stranger to gunplay, was reluctant to return to the Spindletop: "The place is incredible, right, the salads, I mean how about the service in that restaurant? You have to look at the up side."

Pomus's marriage was not his only relationship that became strained. His junior partner in songwriting was also growing restive. "Sometimes Mortie wouldn't show up, and Doc was furious," Burke said. "He had this twinkle in his eye like he was going to play some kind of trick. If he were late or something, he'd give Doc some cock-and-bull story why he wasn't there. Doc would say, 'Come off it. Just get here. Let's work.'"

Sometimes the twinkle in Shuman's eye was put there by the pot he smoked openly in the Hill and Range office, dangling a joint over a secretary's desk. "He was always stoned on something," Beverly Ross recalled. Pomus, on the other hand, had become abstemious with age and responsibility.

Polio and eleven years in age contributed to fundamental differences in temperament and experience that divided Shuman and Pomus. Shuman was someone to whom everything—music, languages, women— seemed to come easily, while for Pomus everything was hard. Shuman loved to travel and ventured to Mexico, Europe, and, with his mother in tow, to Israel, where he performed in a Jaffa nightclub and bedded a kibbutznik who "taught him the modern version of the Psalms of Solomon." Pomus had difficulty making it to the bathroom.

Shuman returned to Manhattan from Israel reluctantly. Out of curiosity and homesickness for a land where he had felt welcome and loved, he dropped by the Café Sahbra, which advertised itself as "the only Israeli Café in America." In April 1963, the nightclub in the Hotel Westover on West Seventy-second Street presented "the Glamorous Esther Thobi, Israel's Latest Singing Sensation." Freudians might note that the diminutive, dark-haired Tohbi (as her surname appeared elsewhere) shared her first name with Shuman's mother. "She was sultry, smoky, with a great body," Shuman wrote decades later, "and she knew how to use all of it to great advantage." On May 5, nightlife columnist Earl Wilson reported their marriage, which they repeated in Jerusalem.

A magic moment turned into a nightmare. "She was a shrew," Shuman wrote. The two of them "were always fighting and making up and fighting," to such an extreme that he "almost killed her twice, literally." Pomus's brother, Raoul Felder, soon represented Shuman in the first of his many divorce cases to make tabloid headlines. "Waiter Spills a Piping Dish," declared the *Daily News,* recounting testimony by a Dutch waiter that he had had sex with "the international chanteuse" both before and after her wedding, at which he had been best man. "Daubing at her eyes, Esther said that she and her husband had very little sex life." She sought $700 a week in alimony from Shuman (who was reported to be making $45,000 a year), but Felder stage-managed the revelation of her infidelity to reduce this to $150. Their divorce became final on March 23, 1964.

"Poor Mortie! He was the first *scandale* that I knew in our business," said Paul Evans, describing how Shuman would dart into the Brill Building's elevator to avoid public recognition. "He was humiliated," Brooks Arthur recalled, "and pissed off, too." A liberated Shuman "discovered model girls," as he related in his autobiographical sketch. "Beautiful ladies were available to him," a close friend and collaborator recalled.

While Shuman ranged widely in his musical as well as his amatory pursuits, Pomus remained wedded to blues-based jazz and rock 'n' roll. One moment Shuman was a "mambonik" at the Palladium; the next he was hanging outside Birdland to meet Duke Jordan and take a jazz lesson from the bop pianist. "During the day M.S. was a white rock 'n' roll songwriter," Shuman wrote. "At night he was a black soul musician. Talk about schizophrenia!"

As early as 1959 or '60, Shuman warned Barry Mann, "Those four-chord songs are not going to last a long time." Meanwhile, Pomus, repeating his words as if they were a mantra and pushing the wheels of his chair in time to his chant, assured the Drifters' Charlie Thomas, "Rock 'n' roll will never die. Rock 'n' roll will never die."

"It's just a song," Thomas said.

"No, it's not a song, Charlie. It's a place in your heart."

Chapter Twelve

THE MAGICIAN AND THE MENSCH

★

When Burt Bacharach encountered Marie Dionne Warrick at the August 13, 1961, session where Leiber and Stoller produced the Drifters singing Bacharach and Bob Hilliard's "Mexican Divorce," he recognized that even in pigtails and sneakers the backup vocalist possessed, in addition to a grin as toothy as his own, "a kind of regal elegance." The twenty-one-year-old music major at Hartt College in West Hartford, Connecticut, hailed from East Orange, New Jersey, and a deep gospel background. Her mother sang with and managed a gospel group, her father promoted gospel music for Chess Records, and Warrick was a member, with her sister Dee Dee and their aunt, Cissy Houston, of the Gospelaires, who sang background vocals at the Apollo Theater and recording sessions.

Although Leiber felt that Warrick's "piping voice" was too "high-pitched" to carry a pop song, Bacharach was captivated. Yet it was Warrick who made the first move, approaching him at the session in search of work as a demo singer. Later she auditioned for Bacharach and David in their Brill Building office. "After two or three songs," David recalled, "Burt and I were impressed. We told her that the next time we wrote a song that was right for her we would ask her to make the 'demo.'"

It would be well over a year before Warrick released her first single. In the interim, Bacharach, writing with David, Hilliard, and others, had four Top Ten singles, seven more in the pop charts, and at least two other records worthy of becoming hits. During these months David also wrote two minor and two major hits apart from Bacharach, most notably Don Gibson's country ballad "Sea of Heartbreak" with Paul Hampton and, with Sherman Edwards, Joanie Sommers's pert "Johnny Get Angry." In other words, as fortunate as Bacharach and David were to find, in Warrick, their muse, they were already extremely accomplished songwriters when they consummated one of pop music's most memorable ménages à trois.

For Bacharach the hits had begun with Gene McDaniels's "Tower of Strength." Born in Kansas City, raised in Omaha, and discovered in L.A., McDaniels was steeped in gospel and jazz. He had performed with jazz pianist Les McCann and cared little for the pop music he recorded for Liberty Records, beginning with a Bacharach-David song, "In Times Like These," that sank like a stone. Although "A Hundred Pounds of Clay" made a big splash six months later, he loathed the genial update of Genesis by Bob Elgin, Eddie Snyder, and Luther Dixon, as he did Jeff Barry, Artie Resnick, and Cliff Crawford's "Chip Chip." A nimble tenor who could turn on a dime from a growl to a falsetto, McDaniels felt more kindly toward Bacharach and Hilliard's "Tower of Strength," appreciating its humor and hammy trombone solo. Bacharach felt that producer Snuff Garrett rushed the tempo, which may explain why the lead sheet for the next song of his that McDaniels recorded, "Another Tear Falls," with a Hal David lyric, dictated the arrangement with penciled instructions such as "use Bass & Drums with or without Elect. Guitar" and "add piano over girls."

Garrett enlisted the Brill Building and 1650 Broadway's best songwriters for McDaniels as he did for Bobby Vee. McDaniels recorded songs by Gerry Goffin (writing with Jack Keller and with Carole King), and by Doc Pomus (writing with Phil Spector and with Mort Shuman), but the would-be jazz singer regarded much of the material he recorded as "mickey-mouse."

Providing fodder for Snuff Garrett's stable of singers in Los Angeles was less important to Bacharach's development as a songwriter than the hands-on experience he acquired working with Scepter Records, headquartered at 1650 Broadway and then at West Fifty-fourth Street. Don Kirshner claimed credit for putting the independent label on the map with "Will You Love Me Tomorrow," but it was Bacharach and David who kept it in the money for more than a decade.

Florence Greenberg, Scepter's founder, was "just about the unlikeliest head of a record company" Ruth Brown ever saw. "In her blue knitted suit with a double rope of pearls," the singer recalled, "she looked like Barbara Cook crossed with Molly Goldberg, a real four-star ash-blonde Jewish mama." Boredom had driven Greenberg, the middle-aged wife of a potato chip company executive, out of her house in Passaic, New Jersey, and into the record business. Freddy Bienstock, who had cousins in Passaic, introduced her to Hill and Range and the Turf. "It was there," Greenberg said, "that I got interested in colored music." There and at her daughter's high school, where four girls formed a singing group called the Poquellos that Greenberg shepherded to stardom as the Shirelles.

"She was a brave woman," said another Scepter artist, Maxine Brown (unrelated to Ruth), "to be the only woman to own a record label in this business, competing with men and standing in there toe to toe with male producers and record owners." All of Greenberg's artists were "her babies—her *bubbela,* as she used to call us. And she'd fight tooth and nail for us." She could fight tooth and nail against her artists, too, over money. "People would be afraid to deal with her," recalled Steve Tyrell, who joined the label as a promoter and producer. "It would be like getting your mother mad at you."

As unconventional as it was for a woman to head a record label, it was equally if not more extraordinary in the early 1960s for a Jewish matron to have an affair with a young black man. Many people who worked with them confirmed the gossip that Greenberg became more than just good friends with Luther Dixon after she met him in an elevator and hired him to produce Scepter's acts. The couple "did not venture outside the recording industry," Maxine Brown said, "which was more liberal" than society at large.

Dixon cut two Bacharach-David songs in 1961 with Chuck Jackson, a gruff baritone who had sung with the Del-Vikings, an integrated doo-wop group, before striking out on his own and becoming the first artist on Scepter's subsidiary label, Wand. "I Wake Up Crying," a haunting ballad, and the frenetic "The Breaking Point" were eclipsed the following year by Bacharach's last collaboration of consequence with Hilliard, "Any Day Now." Kicking off with a *baion* beat straight out of the Leiber-Stoller songbook, the song introduces itself with a shrill figure played on the Hammond organ that is as indelible as the vocal melody and as nagging as the singer's dread that his "wild, beautiful bird" of a lover will desert him. Shifting from major to minor chords, doubling and halving the tempo, leaping an octave, the music embodies both the

singer's agitation and the flightiness he fears in his lover. Jackson also
recorded songs by Goffin and King and a marvelous single produced
and written by Leiber and Stoller. "I Keep Forgettin'" sported one of
Leiber's punchiest lyrics ("And this stubborn old fist / At the end of my
wrist / Keeps knockin' on your front door"), tricky time-keeping, and
complex, clattering percussion. After cutting the song Leiber returned
to his office and cavorted around it, Kenny Vance recalled, "doing that
dance that he would do, picking his knees up to his chin, almost." But
Smokey Robinson of Motown's Miracles warned Jackson that "I Keep
Forgettin'" was too far ahead of its time to become a hit, and he was
right.

Bacharach worked closely with Dixon and various arrangers on
Jackson's Scepter singles. The singer recalled that "I Wake Up Crying"
was recorded "as if Burt was producing it." It was a song Florence
Greenberg rejected, however, that gave Bacharach control of the finished product. When Greenberg dismissed the demo of "Make It Easy
on Yourself," performed by Dionne Warrick, Bacharach and David
brought the ballad to Vee Jay Records, whose vice president for A&R
and publishing, Calvin Carter, snapped it up for Jerry Butler, an original
member of the Impressions who was now a solo star on the Chicago-
based label.

Carter gave Bacharach free rein in the recording studio, allowing him
to conduct the orchestra playing his own arrangement, while Carter
presided passively in the control booth. Butler recalled that Bacharach,
always the ladies' man, showed up at the recording session with a beautiful, deeply tanned woman in an orange dress who turned out to be
Angie Dickinson, Frank Sinatra's friend and costar in *Ocean's 11,* whom
Bacharach had begun dating.

"I've always been grateful to Calvin Carter," Bacharach said, "because he let me go in and make my first record where I could actually
be in the studio and write the arrangement. That gave me the confidence and enough of a story so that other people would let me do the
same." "Make It Easy on Yourself" distilled everything Bacharach had
learned from Leiber and Stoller and his years of experience arranging
and conducting for Dietrich and dozens of other singers. "Many of the
flourishes that one might think characterize Bacharach as a songwriter
turn out on closer inspection to be evidence of his skills as an orches-
trator," the critic Francis Davis observed in a perceptive appreciation of

Bacharach. "Bacharach himself might not see the point of such a distinction." The songwriting is inseparable from the sweep of the strings
on "Make It Easy on Yourself" and the delicate clarity of its instrumental details. "All these years later what's remarkable about the song
is how grown-up it sounds," Davis continued. It's all the more remarkable because the self-sacrificing sentiment of Hal David's lyric might
have lent itself to Bobby Vee's juvenile mewl just as easily as to the sto-
icism of Butler's magisterial baritone.

The success of "Make It Easy on Yourself" strengthened Bacharach's
hand. He no longer had to fold when an A&R man told him, "Burt, I like
that song, but it's in 3/4 time. If you put it in 4/4 time, we'd record it."
"That's how I started in this business," Bacharach said, "with somebody
putting their two cents in and kind of ruining the song . . . obscuring
what it was that I had really intended." Once Bacharach assumed control
as arranger and conductor, if not always producer of record, he occasionally intimidated an artist. "I was never so nervous as when Burt Bacharach was in the studio," recalled the Shirelles' Shirley Owens. "I told
Florence, I just can't sing with him in the room. He's a perfectionist,
and . . . I thought if I sing one little note that's flat he's going to know it.
But he said, 'I'm not going anyplace,' so that was that."

Bacharach inspired two of Owens's finest performances. "Baby It's
You," written with Hal David's brother, Mack, and Luther Dixon (un-
der the ASCAP pseudonym of Barney Williams), was "I'll Cherish
You" until Dixon requested new lyrics. The only Shirelle on the record,
Owens added her lead vocal to the demo. (Bacharach can be heard in
the chorus of "Sha la la la la's.") Her solitariness enhances the song's
starkness (no strings) and hushed intimacy. Although "Baby It's You"
reached No. 8 in February 1962, the Shirelles' charming rendition of
Bacharach and Hal David's "It's Love That Really Counts (in the Long
Run)," released as a b-side six months later, never charted. Yet the
record remains magical as Owens's girlish whisper, floating above an
ethereal chorus of "loo loo loo's," breaks with vulnerability at the top
of its range.

Leiber and Stoller claimed credit for producing "It's Love That Really
Counts" and another Bacharach-David song on Scepter that should have
been a contender in the latter half of 1962. ("I Keep Forgettin'" dates
to the same period, when Capitol Records wooed Luther Dixon away
from Scepter and Florence Greenberg.) Sung by Tommy Hunt, a former

Flamingo, "I Just Don't Know What to Do with Myself" was almost as eloquent as "Make It Easy on Yourself." Bacharach arranged the song with nearly identical tremulous guitar chords and rat-a-tat-tat brush-work on the drums, while introducing a treble figure on piano that owed more than is commonly recognized to Nashville pianist Floyd Cramer and became one of Bacharach's trademarks. Greenberg disliked Hunt and had signed him only at Dixon's urging. Quite possibly the single fizzled because Scepter declined to promote it when Dixon spurned the company and its founder.

Bacharach's commercial failures and successes with Greenberg's *bubbela* grounded him in popular music, particularly the black music compounded of R&B and gospel that was not yet commonly called soul. Yet he continued to work in the early 1960s with white artists of the preceding generation such as Perry Como and Andy Williams as well as with up-and-coming kids. Under the aegis of Leiber-Stoller Productions he helped produce two Bacharach-David songs performed by Jay and the Americans, and he produced and wrote (with David and with Hilliard) bouncy singles for Babs Tino. On one of these, "Forgive Me (for Giving You Such a Bad Time)," Tino sounded like Lesley Gore before Lesley Gore did. Although she bubbled under the pop charts in 1961 and '62, Tino never burst into them.

Because of Famous Music's ties to Paramount Pictures, "motion pictures surrounded us," David recalled. This created many more wide-screen opportunities than were available at Aldon or Hill and Range (apart from Presley movies). Separately and together, David and Bacharach wrote dozens of songs that appeared in films or promoted them, including "The Blob," Bernie Nee's "Country Music Holiday," Tommy Sands's "Love in a Goldfish Bowl," and Linda Scott's "Who's Been Sleeping in My Bed?" *The Man Who Shot Liberty Valance* was a Paramount property, so Bacharach and David wrote a theme song for John Ford's latest Western. Since his rendition of "Town Without Pity" had recently won an Oscar nomination for Best Song, Gene Pitney was an obvious choice to sing it. Pitney's manager, Aaron Schroeder, oversaw production, and Chuck Sagle arranged "(The Man Who Shot) Liberty Valance," which pays homage to the Hollywood-on-the-range ballads sung by the likes of Frankie Laine in the 1950s while it gently pokes fun at them with a wheezy country fiddle and gunplay on the snare drum. David's lyric is a neat feat of narration, encapsulating the film's entire plot without giving it away. Although the single (with Leiber and Stoller's "Take It Like a Man," one of Pitney's favorite songs, on the b-side) went all the way to No. 4, it did not appear in the film. Either the seventy-seven-year-old Ford failed to appreciate the song's humor, or he didn't cotton to greenhorns.

Bacharach, David, and Pitney followed up "Liberty Valance" with three more hits. All that prevented their next single, the swooning ballad "Only Love Can Break a Heart," from reaching No. 1 was a song that Pitney, who led a double life as a performer and composer, had written and Phil Spector produced: the Crystals' "He's a Rebel." Pitney's piercing tenor was perfectly suited to Bacharach's increasingly sophisticated melodies. He deftly negotiated half steps and wide intervals that few other pop songwriters used for fear that most pop singers would fall flat. Pitney could even whistle, as he proved on "Only Love Can Break a Heart," reviving for reasons best known to Bacharach and David fading memories of "Magic Moments" and "The Story of My Life."

Pitney once said that having Bacharach as an arranger and conductor "was better than having a producer." Schroeder and Wally Gold were only nominally in charge when Bacharach arranged and conducted "Only Love Can Break a Heart," "True Love Never Runs Smooth," and "Twenty-four Hours from Tulsa," one of Bacharach and David's greatest records. Having written so much for the movies, Bacharach composed a song for Pitney that sounded like a score. Instead of reflecting or recapitulating a film's plot, David made up a story line out of whole cloth this time, fabricating a yarn of adultery that made Bacharach-Hilliard's "Mexican Divorce" seem like child's play. Suspense mounts from the opening measures as trumpets, an electric guitar, and finally Pitney himself in turn repeat a two-note figure so catchy that no one complained when it reappeared two years later in Billy Joe Royal's "Down in the Boondocks." The *baion* beat seems out of place on the Great Plains, but so is the singer, who will never make it home to Tulsa, as it turns out. When he succumbs to a roadside woman's attractions, the tempo races and the trumpets flutter deliriously, sweeping listeners up into the singer's sexual abandon. After this thrill comes the chill of the concluding decrescendo as the opening riff returns, tolling faintly now like a distant death knell, and the singer realizes, "I can never, never, never go home again."

Pitney recorded a few other Bacharach-David songs, including "Little Betty Falling Star," which Jay and the Americans rejected, and the exotic "Fool Killer," written for a film that was never made. But their relationship ended when Bacharach and David fell out with Aaron Schroeder, whose aggressiveness was extreme even for the music business and earned him few lasting friends. By then Bacharach and David had found another singer who could meet their every musical demand.

When Florence Greenberg heard the demo of "Make It Easy on Yourself," she was excited by the singer, not the song. (She also turned down "He's a Rebel" for fear it might lose the Shirelles airplay and bookings in a South that did not take kindly to uppity black girls.) "To hell with the song," Greenberg said. "Who's the girl?" She was Dionne Warrick, and Greenberg not only signed her to Scepter but also engaged Bacharach and David in a package deal to produce her, even though David had not played a credited role in Bacharach's previous productions. When a single did not quickly ensue, Warrick, singing demos and backups for Bacharach and David and filling in for an indisposed Shirelle at live performances, gave vent to her increasing frustration. "I felt Burt and Hal had given my songs away and they felt they hadn't and that maybe I was being a bit unreasonable. Well, one word led to another . . . and finally I said, 'Don't make me over, man!' and I walked out. About a week later I walked back in. The mad was gone—and they had written 'Don't Make Me Over.'"

Although Greenberg was not initially enthusiastic about the song, Warrick's recording of the ballad established her career and, thanks to a misprint on the single's label, her name: Dionne Warwick. She took in stride not only the melody's daunting range ("She had to sing an octave and a sixth," Bacharach marveled, "and she did it with her eyes closed") but also the rhythm's highly irregular vacillation between 12/8 and 6/8. Moreover, she infused the song, which escalates from a lover's plea to a proto-feminist demand ("Accept me for what I am / Accept me for the things that I do") with a gospel fervor that Bacharach and David could never have notated.

"Don't Make Me Over" peaked at No. 21 in January 1963. Instead of capitalizing on this auspicious debut, however, Warwick's next two singles scarcely nudged into the charts. This was especially dismaying because in 1963 Bacharach and David enjoyed enormous success not only with Pitney but with far less talented singers.

After writing for Gene McDaniels, Bacharach and David tried their hand with his label mate, Bobby Vee. Although one song, "Anonymous Phone Call," went nowhere, the story of its recording illustrates Bacharach's strenuous perfectionism. He played piano on the session and insisted on take after take until there was little time left to record the other song scheduled for the date, "The Night Has a Thousand Eyes" by Ben Weisman, Dorothy Wayne, and Snuff Garrett himself. Weisman pleaded with Garrett to make Bacharach call it quits and give *his* song its due. With less than half an hour remaining, they raced through "The Night Has a Thousand Eyes." Bacharach and David's pop waltz was released as an a-side and found few takers. When the single was flipped over, "The Night Has a Thousand Eyes," recorded in an eighth of the time lavished on "Anonymous Phone Call," became one of Vee's biggest hits.

Vee had better luck with Bacharach-David's cheery "Be True to Yourself," No. 34 in July 1963, the same month Bobby Vinton reached No. 3 with their treacly ballad "Blue on Blue." Even television's Dr. Kildare, Richard Chamberlain, scored a minor hit with Bacharach-David's somber "Blue Guitar," and Jack Jones capped the year with "Wives and Lovers." Bacharach and David touted the film of the same name with a jazz waltz for swingers for whom all women are girls and "men will always be men." These are the kinds of empty-headed songs, which Bacharach and David wrote throughout their careers, that make some people wince and caused surveys such as the original *Rolling Stone Illustrated History of Rock & Roll* to all but ignore their contributions to popular music. Take away the zest of R&B and gospel or the tang of rock 'n' roll, and their music tended toward the insipid. Artificial sweetening came as naturally to Bacharach and David as saltiness did to Leiber and Stoller and the sap of youth did to the writers at Aldon. Bacharach and David weren't white Negroes; they were white bread. They weren't adolescents; they were middle-aged.

That's why, for artistic far more than for commercial reasons, Bacharach and David needed Dionne Warwick as much as she needed them. Bacharach once said that Warwick's voice had "the delicacy and mystery of sailing ships in bottles." It's a disconcerting image, suggesting music that is hermetically sealed and, no matter how artfully contrived, devoid of emotional affect. Fortunately for everyone, Warwick refused to be bottled.

Warwick listened to Bacharach play a sketch of a song in his apartment on East Sixty-first Street. "What are you waiting for?" she said. "Finish it!" David completed the lyric for "Anyone Who Had a Heart" in the bedroom while Bacharach and Warwick rehearsed another song on the piano in the living room. As painstaking as Bacharach, David always regretted that an accent in the fourth measure fell on the preposition "of" rather than on the noun "dream." "Hal is so intense," Bacharach recalled decades later, acknowledging that he liked people "who torture themselves, just like me." Setting lyrics to a song that shuttled between 5/4 and 4/4 and threw in a bar of 7/8 for good measure certainly posed a challenge. So did playing it. When the house band at the Apollo balked at the score of "Anyone Who Had a Heart," Bacharach insisted, "*Feel* it rather than read it."

When Ben Weisman first heard Bacharach's music, he thought his songs would never make it because they were too complicated. But the time changes and chord changes in "Anyone Who Had a Heart" do not register consciously with most listeners; instead we hear a reassuring pulse of rock 'n' roll triplets and Warwick's devastated cri de coeur. A dynamic tension between the complexity of Bacharach and David's musical demands and the emotional intensity of Warwick's vocal, between form and content, galvanizes this and many of their other early collaborations.

"Anyone Who Had a Heart" peaked at No. 8 in February 1964, and "Walk On By" came close on its heels. Greenberg preferred another song, "Any Old Time of Day," and released "Walk On By" as its b-side, but when New York deejay Murray the K played both songs and asked his listeners to pick their favorite, they flipped for "Walk On By." Here the *baion* beat had evolved into the gentler sway of the bossa nova, which jazz guitarist Charlie Byrd and tenor saxophonist Stan Getz had popularized in the United States with their 1962 hit recording of Antonio Carlos Jobim's "*Desafinado.*" According to Artie Butler, "the semi–bossa nova feel" of "Walk On By" and many other Bacharach-David productions owed greatly to the subtle drumming of Gary Chester, who played with a stick in his right hand and a brush in his left. "It wasn't just 'boom, boom-boom,'" Butler said. "It was 'sh-shook, sh-shook.'" In much the same way, the flügelhorn Bacharach used on "Walk On By," which became one of his signature instruments, produced a softer sound than a trumpet.

"Walk On By" reached No. 6 and was followed by an embarrassment of riches. Before the year was out, Warwick released "You'll Never
Get to Heaven (if You Break My Heart)," "A House Is Not a Home,"
and "Reach Out for Me." While the enchanting "You'll Never Get to
Heaven" was another Bacharach-David-Warwick original, sprinkling
the light fantastic on the bossa nova of "Walk On By," the other songs
had previously been recorded. Warwick had become such a star that her
version of "A House Is Not a Home" outsold Brook Benton's rendition of the theme song for the film based on madam Polly Adler's memoirs. David wrote the lyric first in this instance and did so quite
cunningly. You'd never guess that the house in question is a brothel
from David's wrenching romantic plea: "I'm not meant to live alone /
Turn this house into a home." "Reach Out for Me" had been released
earlier by Lou Johnson, an eloquent and subtle tenor, though not nearly
as distinctive a singer as Warwick. Hired by Hill and Range to produce
Johnson on its Big Top and Big Hill record labels, Bacharach wrote
several superb songs with David for Johnson and arranged and conducted them with imagination and energy. Yet two of these became
much bigger hits for Warwick, and Johnson's performance of a third,
"(There's) Always Something There to Remind Me," made it only to
No. 49 in 1964.

Bacharach, David, and Warwick were such a formidable team that
year that the songwriters felt little need to collaborate with anyone else.
"There was nothing that Burt could write musically, or I could write
lyrically," David said, "that she couldn't do." "The more that Hal and
I wrote with Dionne, the more we could see what she could do,"
Bacharach explained. "She can go that high, and she can sing that low.
She is that flexible. She can sing that strong and that loud, and be so delicate and soft, too. . . . The more that I was exposed to that musically,
the more risks, the more chances, I could take."

Bacharach credited his study of classical composition with enabling
him to "move beyond the boundaries" of pop songwriting. Instead of
composing at the piano, he wrote music in his head and then wrote it
down on paper. Elaine Orlando remembered when Bacharach rushed
into Hill and Range's offices frantically seeking a pencil and paper.
"What's wrong?" she asked. "I wrote something on a fence," Bacharach
said, "and I have to go back and copy it."

Decades later Bacharach reflected, "When you're sitting at the piano, you tend to go to what's familiar and you can get trapped by pretty chords. And you go by the step, by the beat. . . . When you get away from the piano and hear the melodic contour as well as the harmonization in your head, you're hearing a long vertical line. I like to take a long look at the song."

Bacharach elaborated elsewhere: "My nonsymmetrical phrasing has never been a conscious effort to break the rules or even a reflection of Hal's lyrics. In fact I never realized anything was complicated until I wrote it down and looked at it. 'Look at that—that's a five-bar phrase!' or 'That's a 7/8 bar.' In other words the music sounded good to me, not strange, you know?"

It seldom seemed strange to David, either. "I never felt his music was quirky," David said. "Rarely did I ever find his music unnatural." Bacharach was so absorbed in his music that he often took David's lyrics for granted, but they followed the twists and turns of Bacharach's writing as dexterously as Warwick's voice. Bacharach recorded a couple of songs written with Bob Hilliard in 1963, when at least three by David and Sherman Edwards appeared. By 1964 they were writing together exclusively. "I don't think we ever said anything to each other," David recalled. "It just happened." The parting was friendly with Hilliard, who promptly wrote a No. 1 hit with Mort Garson: Ruby and the Romantics' "Our Day Will Come." The singer on their demo was Dionne Warwick, who would not have a No. 1 record for eleven years, and then she shared billing with the Spinners on "Then Came You."

The devoted husband, father, and chain-smoker who commuted from Long Island and the boyish lady-killer with a bachelor pad on the East Side—songwriter Mark Barkan called him with admiration and envy "the playboy of the Western world"—whom cigarette smoke nauseated continued to be an odd couple. They shared little in common but workaholism. The only thing casual about Bacharach were the sweaters and turtlenecks that the son of the menswear authority favored. Otherwise he was as compulsive as the button-downed David. Perhaps it was partly the achievements and examples of Bacharach's father and David's brother that drove both men to compete and succeed. "All my stuff was piled on the desk like a W. C. Fields comedy," David recalled. "If we weren't finishing a song, we'd be starting a song. Burt would have part of a melody and I would have part of a lyric, and we'd start with one or the other. At night I'd go home and work on a lyric to one of his tunes, and he'd do just the reverse. We'd be working on three songs at the same time. It seemed to me we were working seven days a week."

In their Brill Building office they were equals. In the recording studio Bacharach inevitably predominated in his roles as conductor and arranger. Al Gorgoni, who played guitar on many sessions, recalled that even when recording a demo, Bacharach "had everything written out." Despite or because of this meticulousness, he would sweat profusely and become so wrapped up in his music that he bobbed and weaved and jerked his head and shoulders like Stevie Wonder. If something wasn't working, he called a break and retreated to the men's room, where in silence he tried to recapture the music in his head.

"I used to watch the arc of Burt's sessions," Steve Tyrell recalled, "and how he would push the envelope and push the musicians to play as well as they could possibly play. He did it instinctively. If somebody played one wrong note, he'd start all over. He didn't compromise his vision." Although Paul Griffin played keyboards on most sessions, a second instrument was usually on hand. "Burt would conduct the band and be like Leonard Bernstein," Tyrell said, "but there would always be one of those signature keyboard licks that he'd walk over and play, and then he'd go back and conduct." Frequently he did so under the adoring eyes of his parents and/or Angie Dickinson. Bacharach's mother dressed for a recording session as if she were attending a Broadway show.

Because he had not played a significant role in the studio prior to their arrangement with Scepter and Warwick, it took a while for David to discover and assert his authority. "I was coproducer," he insisted. "We made the decisions together." Tyrell confirmed, "Hal sat in the studio with the engineer and really had the overview of everything. He was listening to the lyrics, number one, if they were moving, but he was listening to everything. He would sit in there and absorb the entire fabric."

Their priorities differed slightly. For David, writing songs was more important than making records. "Producing records was a means of protecting the song," he said. "The song was always the thing." Bacharach, on the other hand, said he got "a greater kick out of making the record. . . . You can have a hell of a song and have it spoiled by a bad arrangement or production."

Tony Orlando, who by 1964 could no longer rely on his friends at Aldon for hit songs and recorded Bacharach-David's "To Wait for Love" with no better luck, said that "Hal was very much in the studio, very much a part of the phrasing of the lyric, and more musical than you'd think." According to Orlando,

> Burt had a kind of genius quality about him. I don't mean to imply there was an insanity around him, but the way geniuses are supposed to act, he was acting. He was completely into his music and his moment, while Hal had not only the abstract but the concrete side of him. . . . Hal had a regular Joe way about him, although he was probably the most brilliant lyricist of all time. They really complemented each other.

Dionne Warwick agreed. Bacharach is "a very, very tense and hyper type of personality," she told an interviewer, and had "a little boy quality about him that endears him to the opposite sex." David, according to Warwick, "was more the stabilizing force" for the trio and "kind of the father image. A very stable person, the one who thought things out and the one who really got the things done for us." Bacharach worked the magic; David was the mensch.

By now the magician and the mensch had loosened their ties to Famous Music. Although they continued to offer some songs to Eddie Wolpin, the man who had suggested they collaborate, "we weren't so interested in sharing the publishing with anybody," Bacharach said. Hill and Range briefly handled their foreign rights while they formed their own publishing companies, Jac Music and Blues Seas, and, against David's better judgment, teamed up with Leiber and Stoller in U.S. Songs. This joint publishing venture dissolved after Bacharach and David realized that their mentors' songwriting days were winding down while their own had not yet reached their zenith.

Striking out on their own gave Bacharach and David a creative freedom that Pomus and Shuman did not enjoy at Hill and Range and no one did at Aldon. Kirshner's writers did not show up for work in the morning saying, "Well, I'm going to write a great song today," Richard Gottehrer explained. "It was 'I'm going to write a song for the Shirelles,' and you'd have five groups of people writing songs for the Shirelles.

They would go in and make the demos, Donnie would screen them, pick the ones he wanted to present, and that was it."

No one was looking over Bacharach's and David's shoulders. The only competition Bacharach felt, he said, was "maybe with myself, competing with the last hit." In 1964, Maxine Brown recorded a ballad, "I Cry Alone," that Bacharach and David had written for Dionne Warwick but abandoned. Brown felt awkward singing in Warwick's key and almost ran out of breath. Brown approached Bacharach and begged him to write a hit song for her as he had for so many other Scepter artists. "Maxine, I'm so sorry," he said. "I don't play your style. Most people, when they sing, they have to sing *me*."

Chapter Thirteen

SELLING OUT

★

Carole King, Gerry Goffin, Cynthia Weil, and Barry Mann had the world on a string of hits when spring arrived in 1963. Goffin and King had just scored their fourth No. 1 record in two years with Steve Lawrence's "Go Away Little Girl." Mann and Weil enjoyed almost as much luck with Lawrence's wife, Eydie Gorme, who sang their "Blame It on the Bossa Nova" (originally intended for Bobby Rydell), and with Paul Petersen, who introduced their syrupy "My Dad" on *The Donna Reed Show*.

Steve and Eydie were close friends of Kirshner. The staid show-biz sweethearts did not bring out the best in Aldon's youthful songs, yet these were the biggest hits the couple ever had. (Between them the Lawrences released at least five more songs by Goffin-King, two by Mann-Weil, and one by Goffin and Jack Keller in 1963, though none was nearly so successful.) Even double-tracked, Lawrence's demure vocal diminished sexual temptation in "Go Away Little Girl" to goody two-shoes. "Blame It on the Bossa Nova" bore scant resemblance to the latest twist on the samba and Gorme groped for several notes, but enlivened by Mann's presence in the band (playing organ) and the Cookies' backup vocals, it showed a bit of pizzazz.

Paul Petersen was a decade younger than Steve and Eydie, but like them he had made his career in television, a more broadly based and therefore blander medium than radio and records. The Oedipal rebelliousness that gave rock 'n' roll its aggressive edge was absent from Petersen's mawkish tribute to a father who "understands when I bring him troubles to share." Rock 'n' roll thrived on the inability of fathers (not to mention mothers) to understand, often going out of its way to provoke parental *mis*understanding, but most teenagers did not have Carl Betz, playing Dr. Alex Stone, as their on-screen father.

Goffin, King, Mann, and Weil were not proud of such pabulum. "Some great American work of literature," Goffin said contemptuously of "Go Away Little Girl." "I was never happy with the song." But both couples took justifiable pride in other compositions. Goffin-King's "Up on the Roof" reached No. 5 in February 1963. The Drifters followed it up with Mann and Weil's "On Broadway" (written with Leiber and Stoller), and the Crystals reached No. 11 with Mann-Weil's "He's Sure the Boy I Love."

Aldon seemed one big happy family, with nearly every youngster on the honor roll of hits that adorned the wall of Don Kirshner's office, when the writers read in the trade papers that their daddy had decided to divorce and remarry. *Billboard* reported on its March 23 front page that Kirshner and Nevins were negotiating with both Columbia Pictures and United Artists to sell Aldon Music, Dimension Records, and their production company for "between $3 million and $4 million." By the following week United Artists had dropped out of the bidding and the price had fallen to $2.5 million. When *Billboard* confirmed the sale to Screen Gems, Columbia Pictures' recording and publishing subsidiary, in April, it was a "$2 million deal" that included "a substantial amount of cash plus Columbia Pictures stock." While Nevins became a consultant to Columbia Pictures, Kirshner was named "executive vice-president in charge of all Columbia Pictures–Screen Gems publishing and recording activities" with a contract "reported to be for five years, at a salary of close to $75,000 a year." According to one of Kirshner and Nevins's attorneys, putting a precise dollar figure on the deal was complex and depended on the value assigned to Columbia stock and the contracts for Nevins and Kirshner's services, but the total was somewhere between $2 and $3 million. Splitting roughly fifty-fifty with Nevins the proceeds from the sale of the joint venture they had launched five years earlier, Kirshner, just turned twenty-nine, became a millionaire.

And what about Aldon's anonymous "twoscore writers," by *Billboard*'s head count? "Kirshner will concentrate not only on coming up with the same hot material from his writers as they have produced over the last three years for Aldon, but will also groom his writers for Broadway musical scores, Hollywood picture scores and music for TV shows.

"The tie-up here between Aldon Music and Columbia Pictures and Screen Gems TV shows is obvious."

However bright and expanded their prospects, Aldon's writers, whose contracts had been sold without warning to a major media corporation, felt betrayed. "We were in the Garden of Eden," Jack Keller said, "and nobody bit the apple until they sold the company."

Kirshner was ridiculed decades later in hindsight for having sold too soon for too little. A million dollars was not chump change in 1963, however, especially for a Harlem tailor's son still under thirty. "At that time, that was a fortune," Dick Asher, one of Nevins and Kirshner's attorneys, recalled. "To all of us it seemed like a lot of money." And although Kirshner was starstruck by Hollywood (meeting Joan Crawford! dining with Anthony Quinn!), he was sharp-eyed enough to appreciate the convergence of the recording, motion picture, and television industries decades before "cross-marketing" and "multiple platforms" became buzzwords. In all, Richard Gottehrer concluded, "he probably did the smart thing."

Kirshner's "cardinal sin," by his own admission, was to have sold the copyrights of all Aldon's songs. "It's like a piece of real estate," he said. "It's like a fine wine. It will only get better and increase" in value. Yet it must be remembered that most pop songwriters in those days thought their songs were as short-lived as their initial stint on the charts. Few if any suspected that some of their work would outlast the puberty of the teenagers who bought it and become standards like the best songs of the previous generation, replayed and revived and accruing value as surely as "Smoke Gets in Your Eyes" or "My Funny Valentine." "We never, ever, ever—any of us—thought that this music would be on the radio thirty-five years later," Artie Butler said. "We thought it would be like calypso—in and out." That's why Barry Mann couldn't stop and chat with Paul Evans on Broadway. His records were slipping down the charts into oblivion, and he had to write some more, fast!

Columbia Pictures–Screen Gems' new employees moved from 1650 Broadway to the company's offices at 711 Fifth Avenue, next door to Tiffany's. The address was tony and the accommodations, which Kirshner redecorated, garish. He installed cubicles to make his writers feel at home, but these only added to their sense of estrangement. "They looked like concentration camps," Weil said, "like we were automatons who were supposed to go in there and write." Cultivating relationships with the corporate hierarchy at Columbia–Screen Gems and courting film and television producers and directors left Kirshner little time for the writers who had vied for and depended on his paternalistic attention. Herb Moelis, an Aldon attorney who followed Kirshner to Columbia–Screen Gems, recalled, "Donnie built beautiful offices for the writers, but the big writers never came. They felt that they had lost their connection and intimacy with Donnie. His office was huge, meant to impress—but it didn't impress the writers."

Negotiating contracts became more contentious when writers used to dealing with Kirshner and Nevins personally, now made more aware of their worth by the sale, confronted a corporation. Previously, Kirshner had played skillfully on their innocence and insecurity, renegotiating and extending five-year contracts every couple of years. "I have to know if you're with me," he would intimate to Mann and Weil, "because if you're *not* with me, Carole and Gerry are." "We always got the feeling that if we didn't [extend our contracts]," Weil said, "we'd be signed to him for three more years and he wouldn't work our stuff. And then we'd starve to death."

The writers grew restless. Shortly after earning a pilot's license, Goffin refused to re-sign unless Kirshner, who was notoriously afraid of flying, joined him for a spin. When Goffin flew over a garbage dump, the heat from decomposition created updrafts that rocked the rented Cessna. As Kirshner begged him to return to the airstrip, Goffin demanded a million-dollar guarantee for eight years. "I'll give you anything you want," Kirshner pleaded. "Just get me down!" "And it wasn't even a good deal," Goffin recalled, "because we had earned much more money than that."

Yet Goffin and King's dependence on Kirshner was so great, Goffin admitted, that "we wanted to stay with Donnie just as much as Donnie wanted us." This gave Kirshner the upper hand even when King, Goffin, Weil, and Mann formed a common front and hired the predatory music business accountant Allen Klein. Knowing that Kirshner disliked animals, Mann and Weil brought their German shepherd to one meeting in his office. When Kirshner named a figure they thought was preposterously low, Jody vomited and brought the bargaining session to an end.

Early in the negotiations, Kirshner called Lester Sill, the former mentor and partner of Leiber, Stoller, and Spector, and told him "his writers [were] upset. They never knew he was going to sell the company, and they resented him treating them, in their words, like meat." Kirshner hired Sill to help bring them around, and he played a role in persuading them not to bolt. "They were all pissed off at Donnie, and now they were deciding to stay with him because of me."

The contracts Columbia–Screen Gems negotiated with Mann and Weil and Goffin and King were among the last major deals in music publishing that gave the writers 50 percent of the profits from their songs rather than the 75 percent that became standard as the 1960s progressed. In retrospect, the writers regretted allowing Columbia–Screen Gems and its successors to renew their songs' copyrights as long as the law permitted, but such an agreement "was not an aberration at the time," Moelis insisted. "How much would you pay Ted Williams if he were playing today?" he asked by way of illustration. "His timing was bad."

At Columbia–Screen Gems, Kirshner had less time to spend not only with his writers, but also with the record producers to whom he had peddled their songs so effectively at Aldon. Although his writers had ten Top Ten singles in 1963, at least seven of these were in the can before the sale. They scored only two in all of 1964. This was, of course, the year of the Beatles, but Bacharach and David and Jeff Barry and Ellie Greenwich braved the British Invasion and enjoyed tremendous success. Distracted by his new responsibilities and dizzied by the opportunities and celebrities suddenly available to him, Kirshner was no longer minding the store that had made his fortune.

The first person Kirshner signed was the first to suffer. As independent producers, Nevins and Kirshner had proven more adept at making records than stars. Tony Orlando had only two major hits, Barry Mann just one, and other Nevins-Kirshner acts such as Tina Robin (signed to Mercury) and Kenny Karen (on Columbia) never made it out of the gate. Only Neil Sedaka, through his drive, talent, and collaboration with Howard Greenfield, sustained a successful recording career, yet in 1963 it began ineluctably to wane.

A disgruntled Sedaka wrote some songs under the pseudonym Ronnie Grossman, his sister's married name, in order to keep the publishing from Screen Gems. With the dissolution of Nevins-Kirshner Productions, responsibility for producing his records fell to RCA staff producers with whom he did not have the rapport he had enjoyed with Nevins. He started repeating himself, and his singles, always sugary, turned hyperglycemic. When imitating himself yielded steeply diminishing returns, he and Greenfield tried to imitate others: the Four Seasons' "Sherry" on "Sunny" and, with "Bad Girl," the hit that Helen Miller and Greenfield himself had written for the Shirelles, "Foolish Little Girl."

Orlando heard Miller play another song that she had written with Greenfield, a ballad entitled "It Hurts to Be in Love," and urged them to speed it up to a rock 'n' roll 4/4. When they followed his suggestion and made a demo at a stomping tempo, Sedaka was eager to cut the song even though it had been promised to Gene Pitney. Sedaka recorded his voice "right over their demo," he recalled. His wife, Leba, and a teenage writer, Toni Wine, whom Kirshner had recently signed, added hand claps. But Sedaka's contract with RCA stipulated that he record in RCA's studios, where he was unable to recapture the demo's excitement. Singing over the same track, Pitney had a hit in 1964 that kept him in the charts after his parting with Bacharach and David, while Sedaka, in his view, missed a chance at a comeback.

Sedaka found Columbia–Screen Gems' Fifth Avenue offices "very staid, very tight." The creative atmosphere had "lost its magic" as surely as his own career had. Sedaka realized his star was fading when his brother-in-law, Eddie Grossman, told him, "Neil, you know this doesn't last forever." Sedaka replied in befuddlement, "It doesn't?"

The fault for Sedaka's precipitous decline lay in his management as well as in his music. Nevins and Kirshner handled his performing career at the outset but did little to nurture it. Sedaka bought out his management contract for $25,000, but instead of securing professional representation as Bobby Darin, who had dismissed Kirshner years earlier, urged, Sedaka, ever the mama's boy, entrusted his career to his mother. The next thing he knew, his manager was Ben Sutter, an air-conditioning salesman with whom Eleanor Sedaka was carrying on an affair. "My father accepted it," Sedaka said, maintaining that his mother and father, who became his road manager, "remained very much in love and very happy together."

Sedaka was less accepting. "My money, my entire life was being run by Donnie Kirshner, Al Nevins, my mother, and my mother's friend."

When Neil and Leba had their first child, Dara, in June 1963, it became difficult to subsist on their weekly allowance of $275 a week, $25 of which went directly into a savings account. When they had a son, Marc Charles, it became insupportable. "My God, Leba," Sedaka complained, "we can't buy a roll of toilet paper without getting approval." Relations were strained all around. Ben Sutter and Kirshner even traded punches at a recording session. When Sedaka tried to wrest back control of his bank account and his career, his mother retaliated by swallowing a bottle of pills. "I picked up my mother off the kitchen floor and got her into an ambulance [and to] Coney Island Hospital," Sedaka said in 2002. "They had to pump her stomach. I didn't talk to her for a few months, but we're closer than ever."

By the time RCA Records dropped Sedaka in 1966, he had lost much of his confidence in Greenfield and was casting about for new collaborators. These included Carole Bayer, a lyricist recently hired by Screen Gems who had better luck composing "Groovy Kind of Love" with Toni Wine. Sedaka also issued two unsuccessful singles written by Peter Allen with Chris Bell and Dick Everitt. The obscure Australian, engaged but not yet wed to Liza Minnelli, was still playing nightclubs with Bell as the Allen Brothers.

Except for an occasional tour of Australia, where Sedaka remained popular, he quit performing as well as recording. He eked out $30,000 a year as a staff writer at Screen Gems, but his continuing collaborations with Greenfield found fewer takers than the television sitcom themes Greenfield wrote with Jack Keller ("Bewitched," "My Gidget") and Helen Miller ("Hazel"). "In those days people would come up to me and say, 'Didn't you used to be Neil Sedaka?'"

The Aldon writers who profited most from the sale to Columbia–Screen Gems were not the stars but the second, slightly senior tier. Greenfield and Keller were three years older than Sedaka, Goffin, and Mann; Helen Miller was older still; and none was a card-carrying member of the rock 'n' roll generation. "Howie and I wrote vanilla," Keller said, "while Gerry and Carole wrote R&B." That's not entirely fair, but Greenfield, Keller, and Miller were more comfortable and less conscience-stricken than Goffin, King, Mann, and Weil when it came to fulfilling the insipid film and television assignments that Columbia–Screen Gems secured for them.

Greenfield and Keller visited Los Angeles for the first time in 1965, renting a suite at the Chateau Marmont on Sunset Strip for a few weeks while they shopped songs. Among the producers they called on was Jimmy Bowen, whom they had met in the Brill Building when Bowen and Buddy Knox had hits ("I'm Stickin' with You" and "Party Doll") on Roulette Records. Now Bowen was heading A&R for Frank Sinatra's record label, Reprise. Keller and Greenfield played a song for him that they had written for *The Donna Reed Show* and revised for a Lana Turner movie but failed to sell in both instances. "That's Sinatra's next song," Bowen said. "Change the lyrics."

As Keller recalled, "Howie came up with 'When somebody loves you,' which was questionable because it's the opening line of 'All the Way.' It didn't stop us, but Howie ran into a writer's block. The man who wrote a million songs couldn't write a lyric! My guess is he froze because it was The Man, the Chairman of the Board. This ain't Neil Sedaka, this ain't Connie Francis. You can't write 'puppets' and 'hearts.' This is Sinatra! You gotta write classy lyrics." Weeks went by and they returned to New York, where Greenfield was still stymied. Finally, Bowen telephoned Keller and asked him to play the melody with one finger on the piano, tape it, and send it express to Los Angeles. Keller complied and the singer Keely Smith, Bowen's wife at the time, completed the lyric to "When Somebody Loves You." It was not one of Sinatra's better performances and far from one of Greenfield and Keller's best efforts, but the "cretinous goons" had sold a song to Sinatra.

The following year Greenfield moved with Tory Damon to Los Angeles, becoming the first of the major pop songwriters who figure in this book (apart from Leiber and Stoller in childhood) to do so. When Artie Butler followed in 1967, he bumped into Greenfield in the airport and, sitting on a suitcase amid a mound of luggage, Connie Francis. "What are *you* doing here?" Greenfield asked.

"I just moved here," Butler explained.

"You'll hate it," Greenfield warned. "You can't get a good bagel."

Although Columbia–Screen Gems' headquarters in New York was not as conducive as Aldon's offices at 1650 Broadway, the writers continued to compose stirring records. The Chiffons' "One Fine Day," propelled by Carole King's clarion piano and the group's echoing "shooby dooby dooby dooby dooby doo wah wah's," was scintillating. King and Goffin had written the song to follow up Little Eva's "Loco-

Motion," but "we couldn't get it to work," Goffin said. "It started out like ten men with that piano lick of Carole's, and then once the song started, the whole rhythm track fell apart."

Enter the Tokens. Neil Sedaka's reconstituted high school group had had an enormous hit in 1961, "The Lion Sleeps Tonight." They were not nearly as talented as Sedaka and knew it, but they were shrewder. Recognizing their days on the top of the charts were numbered, they formed a production company, Bright Tunes, and signed four teenage girls from the Bronx called the Chiffons. Their first single, "He's So Fine," went all the way to No. 1. Unfortunately, the man who had discovered the group and written the song, Ronnie Mack, died shortly thereafter of Hodgkin's disease. The Tokens turned to Aldon for material and "flipped," Hank Medress recalled, over "One Fine Day." The recurrence of the word "fine" added to the unused song's appeal. The Tokens erased King's vocal (but not her piano) from the demo of "One Fine Day," tweaked the instrumental track, added the Chiffons' voices, and came up with a second big hit for the group. According to Medress and Jay Siegal, they made only minor changes, yet Goffin credited them with turning the song around entirely. "They really earned their production on that."

One of his own productions in which Goffin took special pride was "Hey Girl" by Freddie Scott. Originally hired as Helen Miller's writing partner, Scott was an African American and an anomaly at Aldon, which employed even fewer blacks proportionately than many other publishing companies in what was still a highly segregated business. In addition to writing songs with Miller for Paul Anka and Gene Chandler, Scott sang on some demos. One of these, Goffin-King's "Hey Girl," was submitted to Chuck Jackson. Not only did Scott perform the ballad in Jackson's husky, impassioned style, but Goffin and King evoked the impending loss and doom that had made Jackson's recording of Bacharach and Hilliard's "Any Day Now" so gripping. When Jackson rejected the song, perhaps because it sounded too familiar, Goffin, King, and Scott returned to the studio and rerecorded the song, which became a Top Ten hit on Colpix Records.

By then King and Goffin were living in a boxy house in a new development on a treeless hillside in West Orange, New Jersey. The front doorbell chimed "Will You Love Me Tomorrow," while out back were a pool and barbecue. Although this was several steps up in the world from their ground-floor apartment in Sheepshead Bay, suburban blandeur left them isolated and unstimulated. They had moved there at Kirshner's urging, to be at his beck and call from his new fifteen-room estate in nearby South Orange. "He would call us at the most fantastic hours," Goffin said. "Anytime he wanted his spirits lifted up, he would come over." Or Kirshner's chauffeur would drive by to pick up demos and tapes.

Another frequent visitor was nineteen-year-old Russ Titelman, a young writer and producer. Initially a protégé of Phil Spector, who appropriated and married his girlfriend, Titelman had been working for Screen Gems in Los Angeles. Barry Mann met him there and urged Titelman to come to New York. He arrived in December 1963 and stayed for the better part of the following year, working with King and Goffin as well as Weil and Mann.

When Goffin and King finished a sultry ballad they were eager to pitch, Titelman drove into Manhattan with them. First stop was the Brill Building, where Jerry Leiber listened to King perform "Oh No Not My Baby." Leiber said he liked it but could think of no one he was working with at the moment for whom it was right. On to 1650 Broadway and Scepter Records. The Shirelles loved the song, but it turned out to be not quite right for them, either, because months later Stan Green, Florence Greenberg's son, yelled out the window of Scepter's new offices on West Fifty-fourth Street to Maxine Brown: "Maxine, is that you down there?" shouted Green (who was blind). "Get up here! We've got a hit. But you have to figure out the melody, all right?"

The tune on the acetate that Green played for Brown was indeed elusive, because the Shirelles, according to Brown, "were competing with each other to sing lead and each sang a line, scrambling the melody." Brown took the recording home to Queens and played it over and over on her porch, trying to unravel the tune. Suddenly, two girls skipping rope nearby piped up, "Oh no not my baby!" "They were singing the hook," Brown recalled. "I was smart enough to know that when the public can handle a hook, then you've got something."

"Oh No Not My Baby," like "Hey Girl," revealed a maturity and soulfulness that seldom surfaced in the material King and Goffin wrote for Bobby Vee and Steve and Eydie. The slight stiffness that had prompted many black performers to call their music, especially on first hearing, "country" was melting into an easier rhythmic and melodic flow. Goffin and King were growing up.

They were also growing further apart from Kirshner. Despite his proximity in New Jersey and the fear of flying that held his visits to Hollywood to a minimum, Kirshner was neglecting his writers and the record label he had created for them. When announcing the sale to Columbia–Screen Gems, *Billboard* cited reports that Dimension Records would continue as "a separate subsidiary label" and not be subsumed under the company's Colpix label. But Dimension had already begun to dwindle.

Goffin and King followed up Little Eva's "The Loco-Motion" with the tough-talking "Keep Your Hands Off My Baby," but after that they frittered away her career with trivial dance records whose very titles vouched for their inanity: "Old Smokey Locomotion," for instance, and "Makin' with the Magilla" (tying in with the Hanna-Barbera cartoon series *Magilla Gorilla*). Goffin and Jack Keller wrote "Let's Turkey Trot" ("My grandma taught this dance to me / She did it at the turn of the century") on a Sunday and recorded it on Monday, not even bothering to come up with an original melody. The tune was taken from "Little Girl of Mine," a hit in 1956 for the Cleftones, doo-woppers whom George Goldner had discovered and recorded. Goldner claimed to have coauthored "Little Girl of Mine" with the Cleftones' lead singer, Herb Cox, but when he surrendered his record companies to Morris Levy, he evidently signed over his interest in the publishing as well. It took courage to stand up to Levy under the best of circumstances; it was crazy when he had you dead to rights. Levy demanded that his name (and Cox's) be added to "Let's Turkey Trot," and it remains there to this day, making him Goffin's most unlikely collaborator.

The second hit on the Dimension label had been "It Might as Well Rain Until September." According to Herb Moelis, King did not capitalize on its success because "Gerry didn't want her to be an artist at that time." But the lack of consistency and quality control that undermined King's follow-up records cannot be blamed entirely on her husband's insecurity or sexism. King sang excruciatingly flat on one side of her next single (the trudging "I Didn't Have Any Summer Romance") and with an inexplicable Jamaican accent on the other ("School Bells Are Ringing"). She assumed a country twang on the b-side of her third single, which might have been a Nashville-bound demo for Brenda Lee (who had recorded Goffin and Keller's larky "It Started All Over Again") or Skeeter Davis (who had a hit with Goffin and King's Sedaka soundalike "I Can't Stay Mad at You"). The a-side, "He's a Bad Boy," was a charming song unlike any other King and Goffin had written or produced. A revolving riff played on acoustic guitar and accompanied by a wheezing harmonica gave it a folky feel and seemed almost to anticipate George Harrison's "Here Comes the Sun." By then it was too late to revive popular interest in King as a performer, especially since she showed little interest herself. These were not the records of a woman who cared about pursuing a singing career, and she had many reasons not to care. She was the mother of two young children. She was not by conventional standards pretty, and her scrawny voice wasn't, either. She was making more money as a writer than she had ever dreamed of, and a writer's career was not only more lucrative but more secure than a performer's. Or so it seemed in 1963.

The best records that appeared on Dimension were by the Cookies, Aldon's in-house backup singers. King and Goffin put them in the fore-front on "Chains" and "Don't Say Nothin' (Bad About My Baby)," hit singles that grooved to a hand-clapping beat that was at once rock-hard and relaxed. Earl-Jean McCrea's stolid alto stood out, while Little Eva frequently joined the chorus to give it an extra edge. "Girls Grow Up Faster Than Boys," written by Goffin and Keller, added a leering lyric ("I'm everything a girl can be now: 36-21-35") to music that echoed Maurice Williams and the Zodiacs' "Stay." Devoting a day or so to a record on which Spector might lavish months, Goffin "really had something when it came to producing," Barry Mann said admiringly.

The Cookies turned more romantic under the influence of Russ Titelman, who wrote and produced the gorgeous "I Never Dreamed" with Goffin. "I haven't really made a record better than that record," said Titelman, giving much of the credit to King. While King and Goffin introduced Titelman to Aaron Copland's *Appalachian Spring* in their rec room, he played Bach for them. Picking up on this, King arranged "I Never Dreamed" with "interweaving counterpoint, like this little teenage Bach piece."

Titelman wrote two songs with Cynthia Weil that he produced with Barry Mann for the Cinderellas, a nonce group consisting of the Cook-ies' Margaret Ross and "a couple of girls from New Jersey." Mann played piano, and Weil joined them in the studio, offering advice to "Beanie," as she sometimes called her husband. "She was a great critic," Titelman said. One of these songs, "Please Don't Wake Me," was an homage to Phil Spector that evoked the Crystals and Ronettes. But the Dimension records by the Cookies and their spin-offs were more spontaneous and informal than Spector's productions. No Wall of Sound divided the singers, who seemed to be having fun, from listeners, whom they invited to share their amusement.

The Cookies, like every other Dimension act, suffered declining sales, though in their case it was through no fault of their own, Goffin's, or King's. Motown was muscling in on the market for dance music. Streamlined, turbo-charged singles by the Marvelettes, Martha and the Vandellas, and the Supremes rolled off the Detroit assembly line and over King and Goffin's mom-and-pop product. Berry Gordy's "Sound of Young America" challenged the Brill Building, 1650 Broadway, and 711 Fifth Avenue as severely as the British Invasion because it proved that black artists did not need white writers to reach a broad pop audience.

Promoting Dimension was not a high priority at Columbia–Screen Gems, which had its own record imprint to push. When Goffin and King wrote a song for Earl-Jean McCrea as a solo artist, "I'm Into Something Good" was released, like Freddie Scott's "Hey Girl," on the Colpix label. A few weeks after it peaked at No. 38, Kirshner was promoted from executive vice president to president of Columbia–Screen Gems' music division.

Nominated by the Junior Chamber of Commerce as "one of America's ten outstanding young men of 1964," Kirshner moved in high circles. On October 29 of the previous year, accompanied by British ambassador Sir David Ormsby Gore, he had presented a specially bound Colpix album of Winston Churchill's speeches to President Kennedy. (Kirshner told Snuff Garrett that the president glanced at Kirshner's feet and pointed out that his shoes and socks didn't match.) Less than a month later, the president was dead in Dallas. The news reached Goffin and King while they were in the recording studio with Little Eva. Paul Case broke the mournful silence in Hill and Range's offices by playing Pomus-Shuman songs at full volume. "The only way he knew how to deal with the grief of the moment," his secretary said, "was to go to the tried-and-true."

Chapter Fourteen

SEESAW

★

As Gerry Goffin, Carole King, and Russ Titelman neared the Lincoln Tunnel on their way to New York to see *A Hard Day's Night*, King insisted they turn the car around and head back to West Orange. "She was afraid," according to Goffin, and it was all they could do to convince her to continue on and see the Beatles' first film. An American songwriter, especially one still reeling from the sale of Aldon to Columbia–Screen Gems, had good reason to balk.

The Beatles' arrival on the heels of John F. Kennedy's assassination lifted the dazed spirits of young Americans but alarmed many of the performers and songwriters who entertained them, as British groups commanded the pop charts. "You couldn't get a record played unless you had an English accent," the Tokens' Jay Siegal complained. The Beatles and the British groups whose invasion they spearheaded admired and exploited the songcraft of the Brill Building and 1650 Broadway. John Lennon and Paul McCartney proclaimed King and Goffin their favorite songwriters. The Beatles covered Goffin-King's "Chains" on their first American album (as well as Bacharach, Mack David, and Luther Dixon's "Baby It's You" and another Shirelles song, Dixon and Wes Farrell's "Boys"). *New York Post* rock columnist Al Aronowitz orchestrated a summit meeting at the Warwick Hotel during the group's tumultuous first visit to New York City. "John Lennon made come-ons to Carole," Goffin said, "but he did it in a kidding way."

When Snuff Garrett made his regular rounds of New York publishers and found the pickings unusually slim, he would ask whether Mickie Most, the spectacularly successful British producer of the Animals, Herman's Hermits, and Donovan, among others, had been in town recently. If so, he would rearrange his schedule to let more time elapse and an inventory accumulate, provoking Most, on *his* next visit, to inquire when his good friend Garrett had last dropped by. "We were vying for what was new and fresh," Garrett said.

Herman's Hermits' first single was Goffin-King's "I'm Into Something Good," which reached No. 13 in the States four months after Earl-Jean McCrea's original version stalled at No. 38. The chirpy quintet also covered King-Goffin's "Walking with My Angel." Although lead singer Eric Burdon derided "Take Good Care of My Baby" in a talking-blues tribute to Bo Diddley that contrasted the manly authenticity of R&B to the effeminacy of Brill Building and 1650 pop, the Animals could not have evolved without Mann and Weil's "We Gotta Get Out of This Place" or Goffin and King's "Don't Bring Me Down." After Jeff Barry and Ellie Greenwich's "Do Wah Diddy Diddy" broke Manfred Mann internationally, the group scored a U.K. hit with King-Goffin's "Oh No Not My Baby." Shortly after seeing *A Hard Day's Night,* Goffin and Titelman wrote and King sang on the demo of "I'll Be True to You (Yes I Will)," a ballad emulating the Beatles' "If I Fell" that was recorded by the Hollies, who had kicked off their career with two covers of Coasters songs.

However much the British bands honored and relied on New York City songwriters, their stateside success was also a rebuke. Their music was a blast of fresh sound and testosterone blowing over the Atlantic after too many perfunctory singles by Steve and Eydie and sitcom simps. At twenty-two and twenty-five, respectively, King and Goffin as well as their colleagues were in danger of becoming has-beens as their own entropy and the novelty of the British Invasion threatened to consign them to the nostalgia bin.

In the spring of 1963, Morris Levy and George Goldner introduced the notion of "Golden Oldies" to a youth market that had previously lived for the moment. Roulette Records issued a series of albums consisting of licensed hits from only yesterday by the likes of Dion and the Drifters. After Leiber and Stoller ceased producing them that year, the Drifters had an immense hit with Artie Resnick and Kenny Young's vivid "On the Boardwalk" (which the Rolling Stones covered) and then began to skid. King and Goffin and Weil and Mann continued to furnish the group with songs, but they were minor pleasures (Mann-Weil's slick "Saturday Night at the Movies," Goffin-King's Afro-Cuban stomp "At the Club") rather than major accomplishments like "Up on the Roof" or "On Broadway." Meanwhile, Dion had greater success reviving "Ruby Baby" and "Drip Drop," songs that Leiber and Stoller had written for the Drifters in the '50s, than he did recording new material by Pomus and Shuman (the plaintive "Troubled Mind") or Goffin and King (whose "This Little Girl" reduced the swagger of Dion's "The Wanderer" to a saunter).

The English onslaught was "traumatic" for everyone, according to Weil. Yet it was Bob Dylan far more than the Beatles who devastated Goffin, especially when the folksinger plugged in and started playing rock 'n' roll in 1965. While the Beatles paid obeisance to the Brill Building and 1650, Dylan dismissed the music spawned there as "I'm hot for you and you're hot for me—ooka dooka dicka dee." "Tin Pan Alley is gone," he bragged with a Greenwich Villager's disdain for uptown. "I put an end to it." (Dylan wrote more diplomatically in his 2004 memoir that the Brill Building "was only a few blocks away," but he "never crossed paths with any of those people because none of the popular songs were connected to folk music or the downtown scene.")

Goffin, King, and Dylan crossed paths at Carnegie Hall when Dylan performed there in October 1965. Hearing, as he recalled, "Maggie's Farm," "Leopard-Skin Pill-Box Hat," and "Ballad of a Thin Man" for the first time, Goffin was "amazed at the lyrics, at the poetry." Something was happening here, and it made Goffin feel, he said decades later, "like a dwarf." Dylan crammed more words into a verse than Goffin expended in an entire song, and they were wide-ranging, in-your-face, and adult (or at least collegiate). "Tax-deductible charity organizations" and "all of F. Scott Fitzgerald's books" expanded the lexicon of popular music far beyond the adolescent love to which Goffin and King and their colleagues—and the Beatles at their outset—had confined themselves. And the music, played with ferocity by the Hawks (eventually to become the Band), ran roughshod over the verse-chorus-bridge structure and three-minute running time that fenced in King, Goffin, and their confreres (including once again, in the beginning, the Beatles).

Going backstage to congratulate Dylan, Goffin shook his hand and said, "You've got a right to be very proud of yourself." "I do?" Dylan deadpanned. Meanwhile, King picked up Dylan's guitar and started to strum. Her presumption, Goffin recalled, incensed Bob Neuwirth, one of Dylan's most rabid acolytes, "so I had to rush to her defense."

(Neuwirth was "a bulldog," according to Dylan. "With his tongue, he ripped and slashed and could make anybody uneasy.")

Goffin's self-esteem did not rebound when his friend Al Aronowitz hailed Dylan as "the new Messiah." "I was trying to achieve something," Goffin explained, "to make some good music and some good songs. When I heard Dylan, I said, 'We're not even close.'" King and Goffin piled up some old demos, broke them in half, and vowed to "grow up." But Goffin felt outgunned by Dylan's word-slinging and overawed by the "big difference between being a pop lyricist and being a poet. . . . Being a poet is a lot harder, it's really work. I had a desire to write that kind of song—to be a poet—but I wasn't able to."

The self-sufficiency of Dylan and the Beatles, who soon stopped recording songs other than their own, made Goffin feel irrelevant as well as inadequate. What good were songwriters anyway? The question had seldom occurred to Irving Berlin or Sammy Cahn, but the premium that the 1960s placed on self-expression was a sea change that plunged their successors into self-doubt. "After the Beatles started to grow and get real good," Goffin said, "it suddenly didn't appear that going in and writing songs for whoever you were writing songs for was the way anymore."

Frustration and futility exacerbated tensions between Goffin and King. More than one friend likened their turmoil in the recording studio to World War III. Goffin was "not only a nonmusician but a nonsinger," Tony Orlando explained. "That frustrated him more than anything else. He wasn't able to sing what he heard, and he was too shy a man to go 'la-la.' . . . Carole would go, 'So explain it to me! What do you mean?' 'I can't say it, Carole!' He couldn't get it out."

King, according to recording engineer Brooks Arthur, would enter the studio with

> a clear plan in mind. Gerry had some more visceral things he wanted to see in these songs, and he would battle for them. . . . Be it the Cookies or Freddie Scott, he would want a song or a phrase sung a certain way, and Carole would say, "Well, no, it's good that way." He'd say, "No, no, it's bullshit! It's jive! It's too white! It's too black!" Whatever it was, he was not happy with it. They would fight over that. Or Carole might get a little flowery in a certain piano

passage, and he'd say, "Carole, don't do that!" And he'd slam
his fist down.

Goffin's stammer, Arthur continued, made matters worse. "He
stayed on the word 'uh-uh-uh-uh' too long, and by that time things
were moving very fast. He got so frustrated that he would blow his
stack and run out. It wasn't that they were in disagreement with each
other. They just couldn't articulate it."

Goffin was one among the millions of young Americans who started
doing drugs in the mid-1960s. While Dion was buying heroin and am-
phetamines from a neighbor and the parking valet in the East Side
apartment building where he, Mann, and Weil lived, Goffin was trying
marijuana and psychedelics. "I feel a bit guilty," Mann said. "I think I
turned [Gerry] on to grass. . . . The first time he did it, he got very para-
noid. He started looking in closets because there was something in
there."

According to Goffin, Aronowitz introduced him to acid, and he
"liked the effects." (Aronowitz denied ever having given Goffin LSD,
though he said he had shared marijuana with him and that it affected
Goffin, who had always been "a little loony," powerfully. "His reaction
was very heightened.") Goffin said he was with King on Fire Island
when he dropped acid for the first time. "I got into this little romantic
interlude with a girl under the influence of LSD, and I came home three
days later. This was the beginning of my fallings-out with Carole."

Goffin's involvement with drugs was more than a sign of the times.
Fearful of being left behind, he wanted to catch up with the times and
latch on to some of the creativity that he envied in the Beatles and Dylan. "He didn't just take [drugs] for the fuck of it," Steve Tyrell said.
"He was trying to expand his mind, like a lot of people were. . . . He
thought he was going to become a better lyricist. He thought he was
going to be smarter, more intuitive."

The psychedelic experience yielded several extraordinary songs.
"Goin' Back," for instance, a warm bath of a ballad, washed away the
anxiety of aging: "But thinking young and growing older is no sin /
And I can play the game of life to win." The lyrics are Goffin at his
characteristic best: natural, direct, transparent, and touching. Their art-
ful simplicity draws on a self-awareness no less hard-won for having
been drug-induced.

Dusty Springfield's rendition of "Goin' Back" was a Top Ten single in England in 1966 but unreleased in America, where the Byrds recorded it the following year. David Crosby left the session in a huff because the group preferred "Goin' Back" to a song he had written about a ménage à trois that the Jefferson Airplane would eventually cut. Crosby was fired from the band, and "Goin' Back" became a luminous track on the album, *The Notorious Byrd Brothers,* its delicate arrangement and gorgeous harmonies easily outshining Springfield's rather overblown version. Crosby was not alone in considering Goffin and King hopelessly unhip, however. Why record hack work when you could do your own thing? As the sixties marched on, King and Goffin fought a losing battle against this mind-set.

Goffin also fought a losing battle against drugs. "Gerry should never have tried acid," said Barry Mann, speculating that his friend "was probably manic-depressive." Goffin "wasn't ready for it," Jack Keller said. "We're not sure what Gerry's brain thing was at the time he was just Gerry, writing all the songs. He was very intense, he was very, very sensitive, he was very deep. You always felt Gerry was on the edge. . . . *That* would put him over."

Goffin "was out there before it was hip to be out there," said Hank Medress. When the Tokens visited West Orange to rehearse a song, King welcomed them and grilled filet mignon while Goffin floated throughout the day on a raft in the pool, speaking to no one. "He was nuts," Medress said. Yet the song King and Goffin had written for the Tokens, "He's in Town," turned out to be one of the group's finest singles. A moody ballad accented by Spanish guitar and steeped in stately harmonies, it featured Titelman on an unorthodox rhythm instrument that typified the try-anything innovativeness Leiber and Stoller had encouraged and their progeny embraced. Titelman played—you can hear it distinctly on the record—a Slinky.

The Tokens recorded "He's in Town" in the summer of 1964. In 1965, according to Barry Mann, King and Goffin asked if Weil and he could recommend a therapist. A couple of weeks later, Goffin telephoned in the middle of the night and started babbling about Bob Dylan. "He was wigged out, saying stuff, but he sounded brilliant. It was kind of like a schizophrenic tirade. . . . He was going to speak to Dylan and then we'd cut this song. . . . Part of me thought, 'This guy's crazy.' But also, 'This guy may be on to something really great.'"

"And he said he would only share this with the people he loved," Weil added, "that he wanted to save us because he loved us."

Things grew worse and Mann and Weil grew more alarmed until Mann finally telephoned Kirshner. In Weil's telling phrase, "We needed an adult. Donnie lived right near there, and we were in New York. We had no car then, and we didn't know how to get out there." By then Goffin had climbed onto the roof of his house, according to Mann. "Finally Donnie came over with a doctor, and they got him and took him to a hospital," Mann said. "When I found out about it, I started to cry, I was so relieved."

"He called me before they took him away," Weil recalled, "and he was saying, 'How could you do this to me?' Our whole world was shattered."

King and Goffin wrote and King recorded a bleak song that confronted their collapsing marriage with brutal candor. After the demise of Dimension Records, they had started another label, Tomorrow Records, to be distributed by Atlantic. Aronowitz brought to them a group of teenagers from suburban New Jersey, where Aronowitz as well as Goffin and King resided. He managed the band, which he had renamed the Myddle Class, and convinced King and Goffin to write for and produce his charges. The Velvet Underground was the opening act for the Myddle Class at Summit, New Jersey's public high school, and the group never got closer to celebrity. Its two singles on Tomorrow (one featuring a version of Dylan's "Gates of Eden" on its b-side) failed miserably. "What are you going to sell me now?" demanded King, according to Aronowitz. "The Brooklyn Bridge?"

Yet King fared no better with her own Tomorrow single. Set to droning guitars and vaguely Oriental percussion that clinked like a chain, "A Road to Nowhere" did not mince words: "Our love it has rotted right down to the core. / Whatever we had, we don't have it anymore." In 1967, King and Goffin moved separately from West Orange to Los Angeles and filed for divorce.

Although the sound of 1650 and the Brill Building survived the British Invasion, it became, Barry Mann said, "part of the underbrush." King and Goffin certainly suffered a setback, but as the popularity of their music waned, Weil and Mann's rose to new prominence. With four No. 1 singles to Mann and Weil's none, Goffin and King had far surpassed their friendly rivals in the early '60s. It was King and Goffin whom Kirshner coddled and wanted to live nearby, Goffin and King whom the Beatles were eager to meet. By 1965, however, the couples had reversed roles.

At the tail end of 1964, Gene Pitney followed up Howie Greenfield and Helen Miller's "It Hurts to Be in Love" with Mann and Weil's "I'm Gonna Be Strong," the only other single written by former Aldon staffers to crack the Top Ten that year. That Pitney sang both songs demonstrated his star power and Kirshner's faltering management of his demoralized writers. A dramatic ballad that built to a bravura climax, "I'm Gonna Be Strong" led to a second, lesser hit for Pitney by Weil and Mann, "Looking Through the Eyes of Love."

Another single released toward the close of 1964 marked Mann and Weil's reunion with Phil Spector, with whom they had not worked since "He's Sure the Boy I Love" a year and a half earlier. In the interim, Spector's collaborations with Jeff Barry and Ellie Greenwich had met with phenomenal success, but a chill in their relationship and Greenwich and Barry's engagement in other projects (as related in Chapter 16) led Spector to call once again on Weil and Mann. Together they wrote a single for the Ronettes that Mann and Weil later belittled as an imitation of Barry and Greenwich. "I was just trying to sound adolescent," said Weil, acknowledging with a mixture of admiration and condescension that girl group songs came more naturally to Greenwich and Barry than to socially conscious Broadway sophisticates such as Mann and herself. The wistful "Walking in the Rain" was more sentimental and less street-sexy than Barry-Greenwich-Spector's hits for the Ronettes. Its slower tempo exposed the wobble in the vibrato of Veronica Bennett, who recorded the lead vocal in a single take. But the chorus rose above the sound effects of thunder and rain like a benedictory rainbow, and Spector's elaborate production would reverberate in many a single that Brian Wilson wrote and produced for the Beach Boys. ("Listen to Phil Spector's records," Wilson once advised aspiring rock musicians, "and get the beat, and then go on from there.")

"Walking in the Rain" was not a major hit, and a second Ronettes single by Mann-Weil-Spector fell on deaf ears. Spector's Wall of Sound was beginning to crumble, and the rubble smothered the melody of "Born to Be Together." Redundancy, overkill, and Spector's mounting capriciousness were diminishing the allure of the girl groups that had made him famous and his Philles record label a success. During the recording of "Born to Be Together," Spector turned to his arranger, Jack Nitzsche, and said, "It's over. It's over. It's just not there anymore." Desperate to diversify his portfolio, Spector leased from another independent label, Moonglow Records, the right to record and release on Philles in the United States, the United Kingdom, and Canada a male duo that had made a bit of a stir in California.

Two white boys had seldom sounded as black as Bill Medley and Bobby Hatfield, whose fervent performances had inspired African Americans from Orange County's El Toro Marine base to dub them the Righteous Brothers. Working with them was a change and a challenge for Spector because the Righteous Brothers were white, they were men, and they owned their name. Each factor made them less subject than Darlene Love, the Crystals, and the Ronettes to Spector's control and whim. To assist him in this sensitive undertaking and write the perfect song to launch it, Spector called on Weil and Mann.

At Kirshner's begrudged expense, Mann, Weil, and their German shepherd flew to Los Angeles and settled in the Chateau Marmont, the only hotel that would accommodate Jody and a piano. When Spector played them the Righteous Brothers' Moonglow singles, they could not believe the group was white. Although those songs were feverish rockers, Weil and Mann composed a ballad suffused with the passion and urgency of the Four Tops' recent Motown hit, "Baby I Need Your Loving," one of their favorite songs.

Unusually, it was Mann who came up with the opening line: "You never close your eyes anymore when I kiss your lips." In doing so he echoed and updated Larry Kolber's opener to the first song by Mann that Spector had produced, the Paris Sisters' "I Love How You Love Me." Three years later Mann and Weil had matured into dramatists of adult emotion. The singer notices that his lover no longer closes her eyes because his eyes are wide open, too, searching for signs of boredom or betrayal. "[W]e are eavesdroppers on this conversation," observed the songwriter Jimmy Webb, adding that this was the first song that ever "blindsided" him, forcing him to pull "to the curb, windshield wipers flapping at top speed, to clear away the tears while listening to the radio." Weil wrote the rest of the lyrics, including a chorus line they didn't particularly care for and intended eventually to replace. But when they played the song for Spector over the telephone, he assured them the dummy line would make a great title and said they were crazy to think of changing "you've lost that lovin' feelin'."

Mann's music is even more moving than the lyrics. The verses climb the scale in hope and anxiety while the end of each chorus falls off a cliff in despair. It was Spector's idea to add a third section in the form of an extended Latin break that reappears briefly before the final chorus, giving the song an unorthodox structure of ABABCBcB.

When Mann and Spector sang the song for the Righteous Brothers, their "little high thin voices" misled Medley into thinking that "Lovin' Feelin'" was more suitable for the Everly than the Righteous Brothers. Hatfield fretted that he didn't enter until the first chorus. "What am I supposed to do while the big guy's singing?" Medley, by this time convinced of the song's hit potential, told Hatfield, "You can go to the bank."

Barney Kessel, one of three guitarists at the recording sessions (which featured three keyboards as well), said that Spector "was working on a strategy, like he was going to invade Moscow." From Medley's cavernous baritone (so low that when Weil and Mann first heard the record, they thought it was played at the wrong speed) to Hatfield's falsetto squeals, the Righteous Brothers spanned octaves. So did Spector's monumental production, which expanded his Wall of Sound into an echoing cathedral and extended the playing time to 3:50 (which Spector blithely altered to 3:05 on the single's label so as not to alarm disc jockeys pressed for time).

Over the next four decades "You've Lost That Lovin' Feelin'" was broadcast more than ten million times in the United States, more frequently than any other song in the BMI catalog, even those by the Beatles. It was an impossible act for Spector or the Righteous Brothers to follow, although Weil and Mann would come close with "(You're My) Soul and Inspiration." They wrote this song to follow up "Lovin' Feelin'" and were dismayed when Spector, untrustworthy as ever, spurned them for King and Goffin. King went to Los Angeles and worked with Spector and the Righteous Brothers on "Just Once in My Life." Medley was impressed and amused that a woman with girlish braces on her teeth and "little teeny children" possessed so prodigious a talent. But "Just Once in My Life" was a jumble. Although any song that came after "Lovin' Feelin'" would have been anticlimactic, "Just

Once in My Life" compounded the problem by trying too frantically to sound like its predecessor. Goffin and King wrote a second song for the Righteous Brothers, "Hung on You," which was overshadowed by the single's original b-side, Hatfield's histrionic rendition of "Unchained Melody," the standard by Alex North and Hy Zaret. During this period, still a couple of years before their divorce, King and Goffin also collaborated with Spector on an unreleased song by Darlene Love and an unsuccessful one for the Ronettes, the murky "Is This What I Get for Loving You?"

A rupture between the domineering Spector and the headstrong Righteous Brothers was inevitable. When it occurred in late 1965, the duo departed to MGM Records, and Medley called Weil and Mann to inquire about "Soul and Inspiration." Mann and Weil, who considered the song little more than a sketch, insisted they had better material and sent it to Medley, but he insisted on "Soul and Inspiration." Taking command of the recording, he "produced it the way I thought Phil would have." Although it was as imitative of "Lovin' Feelin'" as "Just Once in My Life," the song was more focused and melodic. It was vindication if not revenge for the group and the songwriters when "Soul and Inspiration" became the Righteous Brothers' second No. 1 single in April 1966.

Later that year, King and Goffin provided the Righteous Brothers with both sides of an appealing single. While "On This Side of Goodbye" juxtaposed forlorn lyrics with a jaunty chorus, "A Man Without a Dream" suggested that Goffin and King had been listening to the sweet Chicago soul music of Curtis Mayfield and the Impressions. Both songs regretted a failed relationship and yearned for reconciliation. By then the Righteous Brothers' career, like King and Goffin's marriage, was disintegrating.

Medley's relationship with Weil and Mann endured, however. In 1968, while Medley was pursuing a solo career and a romance with Darlene Love, who had sung backup vocals on "Lovin' Feelin'" and other Righteous Brothers songs, Mann wrote with Weil and produced with Medley a powerful, disturbing ballad about an interracial love affair. Medley recorded the song with Love in the studio and sang it directly to her. "Brown-Eyed Woman" is anything but a feel-good, we-are-family anthem. Despite the blue-eyed singer's ostensibly well-intentioned liberalism, he lays the blame for a black woman's resistance to his advances entirely on her heart, which has been "twisted" by "All of the years / All of the hate and the fears." Throughout the song a chorus of female voices that sound black warn the woman, "Stay away, baby." At the end of a song that may be more provocative than Weil, Mann, and Medley intended, the white man and black woman, the verses and the chorus, remain at an impasse. Expressing, however inadvertently, a racial realism few people wanted to hear, "Brown-Eyed Woman" made it only to No. 43 on the pop charts. It was not long before Medley and Love ended their affair.

Demonstrating their mastery of rock 'n' roll and adaptability to its trends, Weil and Mann sent to Medley along with "Soul and Inspiration" two other songs that became hits for other groups: "We Gotta Get Out of This Place" and "Kicks." "Barry is probably the most insecure, self-absorbed human being I've ever known," Hank Medress said, "and I think that's helped his songwriting. He's so concerned in every era of doing it within that era that he never looks back." The mother of invention was panic. "Every time something new happened," Weil explained, "we were sure this was the end." Like his peers, Mann composed on the piano, but having strummed the ukulele as a kid, he adjusted with greater alacrity than others to the shift that occurred with the Beatles to pop music in which guitars rather than keyboards predominated. According to Al Gorgoni, who played guitar on the demos of both "We Gotta Get Out of This Place" and "Kicks," Mann "would make up the licks on the piano. The left-hand parts were often guitar-bass kinds of things. He's great at making up instrumental kind of hooks."

The guitar and bass galloped on "Kicks," a vehement antidrug song recorded by Paul Revere and the Raiders that Mann and Weil composed with Gerry Goffin in mind. "We saw him deteriorate and thought if we wrote it for him, maybe he'd listen to that," Weil recalled. "He still didn't." Revere and the Raiders, a countercharge to the British Invasion absurdly costumed in breeches and tricorns, had a second Top Ten hit with Weil-Mann's lustful "Hungry." Both songs adroitly married crudeness to craft, dressing up the whomp, stomp, and cheesiness of garage rock with cunning choruses and anthemic harmonies.

The demo for "We Gotta Get Out of This Place," with Mann singing lead, was so strong that it was scheduled for release as a single in an attempt to revive the singing career that had collapsed after "Who Put the

Bomp." But Weil and Mann had given a copy of the demo to Allen Klein, who passed it on to Mickie Most. Knowing a hit song when he heard one, Most produced a version by the Animals. For Mann, "this place" might well have been stultifying Brooklyn, where people, in Weil's lyric, grew old before their time. The Animals shifted the setting to the gritty coal mines of northern England and intensified the danger to *dying* before one's time. Kirshner summoned Weil and Mann to his office. The bad news, he said, was that Mann's record would not be coming out. The good news was that in a single week the Animals' version had leapt to No. 2 in England. "We were crushed," Weil said—Weil because "they had changed the lyric and compromised the song" and Mann because, in the words of Bill Medley, he "would give every one of his songs away if he could just get a couple of hit records."

The following year, the Animals had yet another hit with Goffin and King's thumping "Don't Bring Me Down," a more personal and less political song than Mann and Weil's (King and Goffin's songs usually were) in which the singer assails the woman who undermines him rather than the social structure that oppresses them both. By then Goffin and King were following Weil and Mann more frequently than they led, and Mann and Weil's marriage as well as their music had come out ahead.

Chapter Fifteen

DOUBLE TROUBLE

★

Lolling in St. Tropez, lunching with the likes of Charles Aznavour, Alain Delon, and Jean-Paul Belmondo, Mort Shuman was enjoying his summer vacation when he was struck by a bolt out of the azure that marked him as indelibly as Dylan did Gerry Goffin. Someone played a record by Jacques Brel, the gruff Belgian *chansonnier* who rolled his "r's" theatrically around lyrics that were as literary and sentimental as they were cinematic and mordant, and Shuman "saw the light," he later wrote. "All became clear + clean and bright once again. And he knew what he had to do."

Shuman was weathering the British Invasion quite well, for the most part without Doc Pomus. Shuman "found making transitions easier," Elaine Orlando said. "Doc basically just wanted to sing the blues." Decades afterward, Shuman could scarcely recall some of the songs they contributed to the Presley films that followed *Viva Las Vegas.* The music was as negligible as the movies. Yet Pomus clung to the King well after the Beatles deposed him. Paul Case urged Jerry Ragovoy, a songwriter and producer from Philadelphia (where he had conducted the orchestra and chorus on Frankie Avalon's "Gotta Get a Girl," by Bacharach and David), to collaborate with Pomus during Shuman's lengthening absences. They were in Pomus's office at Hill and Range when word came that Pomus and Shuman's submission for the title song to Presley's next picture had been rejected—along with every other entry. In little more than an hour, Ragovoy and Pomus concocted "Girl Happy," which made the movie but not the charts.

The same week in 1964 that "Viva Las Vegas" peaked at No. 29, Shuman topped Presley and even beat out the Beatles when "Little Children" by Billy J. Kramer and the Dakotas, one of several British acts that manager Brian Epstein added to his stable after his astonishing success with the Beatles, hit No. 7. (The single's flip side, Lennon and McCartney's "Bad to Me," trailed at No. 9.) Shuman composed the song with a minor writer, John Leslie McFarland, at Hill and Range. Elaine Orlando's son by her first marriage (to folksinger and songwriter Fred Neil, best known for "Everybody's Talkin'" in the film *Midnight Cowboy*) made a nuisance of himself by continually knocking on their cubicle's door, inspiring the charming song's lyric about a beau bent on necking who is inconvenienced by his girlfriend's younger siblings.

Shuman also visited Hill and Range's office in London, where he wrote with Welsh-born Clive Westlake the ebullient, Beatlish "Here I Go Again," a success for the Hollies in England and their first single that was not a cover version of an American R&B song. With Cockney comedian and singer Kenny Lynch he later wrote "Sha La La La Lee," a lively rocker that became the Small Faces' first British Top Ten single. Shuman and Lynch also provided the Drifters with one of their last songs to make the charts, "Follow Me." On a rare occasion when he wrote lyrics as well as music, Shuman took sole credit for Manfred Mann's "Machines." The catchy denunciation of mechanization, driven by comically clockwork percussion, miniaturized the madcap factory scenes in Charlie Chaplin's *Modern Times*.

Shuman's travels and dalliances with other writers inconvenienced and angered Pomus. "Doc would be beside himself," recalled Willi Burke. "He said he had to rethink things because Mort wasn't available to him." "Mortie was like a kid," said Shirlee Hauser. "He needed to rebel, and I can see Mortie at times finding Doc oppressive in terms of wanting him to be disciplined. . . . Mortie had a right to go out and explore who he was quite apart from Doc."

"Mortie was a free spirit," Freddy Bienstock observed, "and he couldn't be tied down to Doc. He wanted to explore the world and traveled all over, and working with Doc would inhibit that." One evening Shuman and Burke went out to dinner together, apart from Pomus. Burke talked candidly about her increasingly unhappy marriage. Shuman listened and replied, "I'm divorcing him, too."

Before either of them made the break, Pomus took a bad spill from the wheelchair to which he frequently resorted in order to navigate midtown traffic. "He was like a slow beetle crossing the street in the middle of New York City," Snuff Garrett said. A young attendant pushing Pomus's chair accidentally dumped him onto the street, severely damaging the ligaments in his knees. Pomus was admitted to Doctors Hospital, where, on another floor, his father was recovering from a heart attack. Soon they were joined by Millie Felder, who injured her hand in a minor traffic accident while returning home in a taxi from a visit with her husband and son.

While Pomus was recuperating in the hospital, Burke announced—not for the first time—that she wanted a divorce, and Shuman told him he wanted his freedom as well. "I was in a state of shock from all the shit that happened at once," Pomus recalled. On June 29, 1966, Elvis Presley recorded the last song that Pomus and Shuman copyrighted. Its title was "Double Trouble." Four months later, Burke and Pomus legally separated. On July 8, 1967, a week and a half after their tenth wedding anniversary, Burke obtained a Mexican divorce on grounds of "incompatibility of character."

Pomus was devastated by the loss of his wife and his writing partner, yet he also confessed to an odd sort of relief. At least he no longer had to pretend to be a suburban husband and provider. He no longer had to write teenage love songs. Indeed, although Don Kirshner signed Pomus to Screen Gems after he parted company with Hill and Range, he seldom wrote at all. Neil Sedaka tried briefly to collaborate with him, but Pomus was sick and fell asleep during songwriting sessions. And he no longer had to hoist himself laboriously and walk upright on crutches.

"I'm not going to do this anymore," he told a friend.

"I think you should always be able to face the world standing up at least some of the time," Shirlee Hauser remonstrated.

"It makes me too nervous," Pomus said. "It's just too hard."

"And that," Hauser recalled, "was that."

Mort Shuman did not give up rock 'n' roll altogether. Taking up where Pomus left off writing with Jerry Ragovoy, Shuman collaborated with him on several songs in the soulful style that Ragovoy refined as a writer and producer. These included Dusty Springfield's "What's It Gonna Be," Howard Tate's "Look at Granny Run, Run," "Stop," and a song that Tate, an eloquent and elusive soul singer, recorded originally but that became famous only later as Janis Joplin's fierce epitaph. "Get It While You Can" appeared on her posthumously released album *Pearl.* For old times' sake and no doubt for the money, Shuman also wrote, by himself, one last song for Presley that was defiled by a gim-crack electric sitar which was typical of the time (1969) and also of Presley's increasingly futile attempts to sound trendy. Lines such as "You'll see me comin' / You'll see me goin'" and "I know you'd follow me across that anguished sea" suggested that "You'll Think of Me" was Shuman's semi-autobiographical kiss-off.

Jacques Brel distilled and directed Shuman's dissatisfaction with "those four-chord songs" that he had warned Barry Mann would never last. "It closed the book on writing rock 'n' roll music," he told a friend. "When he heard Brel, he just was blown away by what was possible in popular songs." After his epiphany in St. Tropez, Shuman saw Brel perform and followed and befriended him on tour in Europe, becoming, he later wrote, "his number one groupie." He returned to America determined to translate and popularize his new idol. Like Dylan, Brel wrote about a world of adult experience that most pop music shunned. Instead of thanking heaven for little girls, Brel sang about spinsters and whores, drunkenness and death, "and wars and the human condition," Shuman noted enthusiastically. His music as well as his lyrics could not have been further removed from rock 'n' roll. Performed in concert or a cabaret, it was meant for listening, not dancing. And Brel's French offered Shuman—who had spoken Yiddish as a toddler and had become a "white Negro" and "mambonik" in his teens and early twenties—yet another language to master and another identity to assume.

Shuman had such a flair for self-transformation that his French soon excelled Eric Blau's. Although Blau had translated Aragon, Eluard, and other French poets before rendering some Brel lyrics into English at the urging of his wife, the singer Elly Stone, he readily acknowledged Shuman's superior command of the language. "Not only was French beautiful on his tongue, he knew Paris so well he could direct errant French taxi drivers." On his thirtieth birthday Shuman was introduced to Blau and Stone at Julius Monk's Plaza 9, where Stone sang several Brel songs and Shuman applauded her performance and Blau's translations. Shuman threw a party at his Riverside Drive apartment later that evening. Bald and wearing a suit, Blau felt out of place "[a]mid the maxis and the minis, the beads and open breasts." But he sensed that Shuman did, too. "Although he said 'Hiya, Baby!' to everyone who got to his ear or tugged at his pale blue velvet-corduroy coat, it didn't seem that he was really with it that night. He was making his party go, but he was not enjoying it. Broad finger-wide strokes of sweat came out of the curly hair and washed slowly down his face."

Blau and Shuman soon set to work translating Brel songs. When they completed one, Shuman sometimes called Brel in Paris or Brussels and sang it over the phone. Blau later described how he "would sit by anxiously, not being able to follow Mort's fast French." He had yet to meet Brel, but Shuman reassured him, "Jacques trusts me. And I trust you. And what else is there, man?" Gradually, they formed the idea of presenting Brel's music in a revue starring Stone, Brel's earliest American champion and the first to sing his songs in English. Eventually, it was agreed that her costar would be Shuman.

Jacques Brel Is Alive and Well and Living in Paris opened at the Village Gate on January 22, 1968, and didn't depart the Greenwich Village club for seven years. The *New York Times* panned the first of its 1,847 performances, but lead critic Clive Barnes made amends with a rave review on WQXR. An exuberantly mustached and muttonchopped Shuman towered physically over Stone and the two younger actor-singers who completed the cast. Many critics also singled him out for his talent and gusto. Barnes called him "a huge tragic-comedian of a singer," and Mike Gross in *Billboard* hailed him as "the leader of the pack" and "a virtuoso performer."

Not only Shuman's performance but his musical direction and the production conception, translations, and additional material for which he shared credit with Blau were a personal triumph. He even slipped a little autobiography into his translation and fierce rendition of Brel's "Jackie," conjuring up a time when he was "cute, cute, cute in a stupid-ass way" and "My record would be number one / And I'd sell records by the ton / All sung by many other fellows." Now Shuman was singing for himself, although, ironically, someone else had written the music and original lyrics.

Shuman was a dynamo. The revue was already running when Blau raised a question about "My Death," a melodramatic tour de force for Stone that Shuman would also record, produced by Ragovoy. Shuman agreed that the music did not quite work, telephoned Brel in Paris, and persuaded the composer to allow him to adjust the song.

Yet even at the height of his success, Blau and Stone detected and deplored the erratic and undisciplined behavior that had irritated Doc Pomus. "He was a mess, but he was adorable," said Stone, who believed that Shuman "could have been a successor to Kurt Weill" or "a great performer had he worked at it. He had it all, and he pissed it away." Some people who knew Shuman well in the 1960s alluded to his indulgence in drugs, others to his fondness for alcohol. Stone was emphatic: "He was a wino."

In the fall of 1968, Jay and the Americans recorded two Shuman and Pomus songs. While "This Magic Moment" turned out to be an even bigger (though far less memorable) hit for them than it had been for the Drifters, their version of "Hushabye" did not enjoy the success of the Mystics' original a decade earlier. Instead of reviving Pomus and Shuman's songs, Jay and the Americans' renditions embalmed them as oldies. Neither writer would ever again see his name on a new song that nudged higher than No. 78 in the American pop charts.

Chapter Sixteen

GOLDEN GIRLS

★

Like a tornado that demolishes some houses yet leaves their next-door neighbors unscathed, the onslaught of the Beatles, Motown, and an electrified Bob Dylan bowled over some New York songwriters, while others in nearby offices and cubicles survived and even thrived. Jerry Leiber and Mike Stoller dislodged the Beatles' "Love Me Do" from the No. 1 spot with one single on their new record label, Red Bird, in 1964, and the Supremes' "Baby Love" with a second. In an unprecedented showing for an independent record company during its very first year, Red Bird released four Top Ten records and five more that made the Hot Hundred. All but two of these were written or cowritten by Jeff Barry and Ellie Greenwich, who had an astounding total of seventeen singles on the pop charts in 1964. The only songwriting teams who ever surpassed this record were Lennon and McCartney, and Motown's Eddie and Brian Holland and Lamont Dozier.

The same frustration and determination to reap the profits of their labors that had provoked Stoller and Leiber to launch Spark Records nearly a decade earlier when they were shortchanged on royalties for Big Mama Thornton's "Hound Dog" caused them to try their luck as label owners once again. An audit they had requested of their dealings with Atlantic Records had strained their relationship with Ertegun and Wexler. The accounting revealed that Atlantic owed them $18,000. Wexler, who called Leiber and Stoller "Mister Greed and Mister Avarice" only half in jest, could not understand why they were upset about "chump change." The money was theirs if they insisted, but the Coasters, the Drifters, and other performers they produced for Atlantic were signed to the label, he warned, not to Leiber and Stoller. Atlantic,

Wexler recalled decades later, "had no contract . . . that obligated us to use them. It was all by mutual agreement." Over a barrel, Leiber and Stoller forwent the $18,000. Still, as if to make sure they got the message, Ertegun cowrote and produced a hit single by Ben E. King, "Don't Play That Song," and rubbed it in by borrowing the bass line from Leiber, Stoller, and King's "Stand By Me."

Leiber and Stoller got the message. Although they continued to work for Atlantic, they poured more time and energy into producing acts for United Artists—not only the Exciters and Jay and the Americans but also would-be teen heartthrob Mike Clifford, R&B veteran Marv Johnson, country singer Billy Edd Wheeler, the pop-classical piano duo of Ferrante & Teicher, and even Jeff Barry. Barry's single disappeared without a trace, but Leiber and Stoller produced so many other hits for United Artists that they asked each other, according to Leiber, "Why are we making all these record companies rich? Why don't we go into the record business again and do what we want to do, and not have to call upstairs for budgets, etc.?"

Taking its name from the joint publishing venture they had formed in the fifties with Atlantic, Leiber and Stoller started Tiger Records in the fall of 1962. Hoping to cash in on the bossa nova craze, they wrote "Bossa Nova Baby" in a humorous Coasters vein and recruited Roosevelt "Tippie" Hubbard and three members of the Clovers to sing it. They composed the somewhat more romantic flip side, "The Bossa Nova (My Heart Said)," with Weil and Mann, although a few lines are quintessential Leiber in their comic concision: "My heart said, 'What can you lose? / You've got feet, you've got shoes / And the bossa nova.'" While Mann and Weil would soon have a major hit on their own with Eydie Gorme's "Blame It on the Bossa Nova," Tippie and the Clovers' single did not even enter the charts, and Tiger Records suspended operations (although "Bossa Nova Baby" would be a hit for Elvis Presley the following year).

Leiber and Stoller continued to collaborate with Weil and Mann in 1963 and produced "On Broadway" and "Only in America," as well as a Barry-Greenwich song for the Exciters, "Do Wah Diddy Diddy." Although it reveled in the kind of nonsense syllables that had been so successful on the Crystals' "Da Doo Ron Ron," "Do Wah Diddy Diddy" reached only No. 78 on the pop charts. In November, a year after Tiger's demise, *Billboard* announced that Leiber and Stoller were reviving the label and creating a second one, Daisy. The "writer-producers" expected to be involved in the "diskery" included not only Barry and Greenwich but Bacharach and David.

Tiger (and Daisy) failed just as ignominiously the second time around, not even achieving the brief success that Don Kirshner's Dimension Records had enjoyed in 1962. Only one of ten singles, Alvin Robinson's slow-as-molasses "Something You Got," made the charts, peaking at a lowly No. 52, while their greatest release, Bessie Banks's "Go Now," was utterly ignored. Leiber and Stoller produced "Go Now," a searing ballad written by Milton Bennett and the singer's husband, Larry Banks, and its funky flip side, "It Sounds Like My Baby." The drama of "Go Now," as Banks fights for and loses her composure, lurching from self-sacrificing denial to angry denunciation to pleading desperation, is nearly operatic. Descending piano chords doom the singer while Stoller's light, tight horn arrangement makes her fate seem even crueler by sounding indifferent to her cries. Like the contemporaneous recordings of Otis Redding, Solomon Burke, Howard Tate, and Garnet Mimms, this single may have been too black and too adult for a teenage audience not yet initiated by Aretha Franklin (or Rolling Stones cover versions) into the mysteries of soul. When the Moody Blues released "Go Now" a year later, few Americans realized that the British group's first hit single was the song's second time around.

Barry and Greenwich, who wrote and/or produced as many Tiger/Daisy singles as Leiber and Stoller (Bacharach and David never materialized), had their fingers closer to the teenage pulse with the dance-party tempos of Moody and the Deltas' raucous "Everybody Clap Your Hands" and Leola and the Lovejoys' wailing "He Ain't No Angel" ("Well, I don't want a lover with a halo 'round his head / My sugar baby wears big dark shades instead").

Apart from "Go Now," however, the most positive result of the Tiger/Daisy debacle was that it involved Leiber, Stoller, Barry, and Greenwich with Joe Jones. A New Orleans bandleader and singer who had had a hit in 1960 with "You Talk Too Much," Jones introduced the New Yorkers to Alvin Robinson, originally the guitarist in Jones's band and, in Stoller's estimation, "a stone soul blues singer," to Moody and the Deltas, and to two sisters from New Orleans's Calliope housing projects and their cousin. Heavily influenced by the Shirelles, the trio called themselves the Mel-Tones.

"We were about to go out of business," Leiber said, when he bumped into George Goldner at Al & Dick's, a steakhouse on Fifty-fourth Street. Goldner was dining with Hy Weiss, the proprietor of Old Town Records, who had grown up with Morris Levy in the Bronx and was reputed to have invented the fifty-dollar handshake. "Why waste time going out with someone you don't like, and sit down and feast with them when you can't stand them?" Weiss explained. "Just give them the money and let them play the fucking record."

Goldner was dressed as impeccably as ever, but his clothes, Leiber recalled, were "a bit frayed." He had left Levy's employ at Roulette Records to launch yet another label of his own, but nothing had come of it. According to Leiber, "Weiss was blowing cigar smoke in his face, calling him a schmuck, and telling him what kind of fool he was, and trying to get [Goldner] to work for him for like $200 a week." Goldner protested that he "couldn't get his shirts done for that kind of money."

Inspiration seized Leiber. As Stoller acknowledged and as their lack of success with Spark and now Tiger and Daisy confirmed, the two of them knew how to make records but not how to sell them. Goldner, on the other hand, was "the best salesman ever." Leiber invited Goldner to go into business with them, whereupon Goldner, according to Leiber, opened a Tiffany cigarette case, lit a Pall Mall, and blew smoke into Weiss's face, saying, "Hy, we're going to see who the schmuck is."

When Leiber mentioned some demos in his office, Goldner insisted on listening to them that very evening. " 'Are you going to stay there all night?' He said, 'I might.' I gave him the keys and I came in at eleven o'clock the next morning and he was sitting behind my desk, not a hair out of place. . . . He held up this acetate and said, 'On my life. On my life.' . . . He put it on, and I hated the fucking record."

It was the Mel-Tones singing a song that Barry and Greenwich had originally written with Phil Spector. Although Spector had cut "Chapel of Love" with both the Crystals and the Ronettes, he had released nei-ther version. (Darlene Love complained that Spector belabored the Crys-tals' recording until its "lugubrious tempo . . . made my walk down the aisle sound more like the march to Bataan.") Convinced that the song had hit potential, Greenwich and Barry played it for the Mel-Tones, who disliked it for the same reason the Shirelles had originally dis-missed "Will You Love Me Tomorrow": They thought it sounded country-western. The young women came around, but Leiber, who found the song's fantasy of eternal marital bliss horrifically sappy, steered clear of the recording session. The New Orleans lilt in the rhythm section and Stoller's breezy horn arrangement added savor to the sentimentality, and Greenwich ran out of the control booth to augment the trio's wispy voices with a few extra "yeah-yeah's."

The Mel-Tones were rechristened the Dixie Cups, Leiber and Stoller's record label was renamed Red Bird, and "Chapel of Love" went to No. 1 in June 1964, bucking the Beatles and establishing Goldner as a full partner in the enterprise and Red Bird as a purveyor of girl groups. It also created a rift between Barry and Greenwich, and Spector, who had not objected when they recorded the song but felt embarrassed and outraged when its success called into question his reputation as a producer and picker of hits. The light touch and offhand charm of the Dixie Cups' "Chapel of Love" were diametrically opposed to Spector's big bang.

Greenwich and Barry wrote a few more hits for the Dixie Cups that hewed to the "Chapel of Love" formula. The incessant reinventions of the Beatles and Dylan did not deter the Brill Building and 1650 Broadway from continually rewriting the same song (or Motown from emulating them), usually with diminishing returns. "The first song was a labor of love," Greenwich said, "and the second song was usually labor." "Iko Iko" proved an exception, however, and showed the improvisatory freedom with which an increasingly confident Barry and Greenwich approached recording.

Some studio time remained after putting the finishing touches on the group's second single, "People Say." Most of the band had already departed when the Dixie Cups began singing in English and Creole a ditty that they knew from New Orleans playgrounds, Mardi Gras parades, and the radio, on which James "Sugar Boy" Crawford and His Cane Cutters' "Jock-o-mo" had been a local hit when they were in grade school. According to Brooks Arthur, the engineer on the session, "The kids were kind of screwing around on the other side of the glass, and Jeff said, 'What is that?'" Barry urged everyone to grab whatever was at hand and bang on it, demonstrating by tapping an ashtray with a screwdriver. *Chick-chick-chick-chick.* "He gave everybody a little part," Arthur remembered. "We were engineers, we were percussionists, we were background vocalists." A Caribbean curio that Barry and Greenwich had brought home from their honeymoon in Jamaica filled in for a bass. "It was a little wooden box with a hole in the front and four or five prongs over the hole," Barry said. "You'd tweak them, and it would go *doing doing doing doing.* It was a very handmade record, which is the kind of record I love to make."

"The most important thing I learned from Jeff Barry was to throw out the rules," Artie Butler said, recalling a time when they were recording a song Barry and Greenwich had written for Connie Francis. Unhappy with the drum sound, Barry hauled in a plastic garbage can and told the drummer, Gary Chester, to pound it with a mallet. "As trivial as that might seem, (a) it was the right sound; and (b) it was groundbreaking, profound, for guys like me because you could make music out of anything. You could bang on a garbage can and it's music."

"He just loved sounds," Arthur agreed, noting that it made little difference whether a guitar, a garbage can, or an electric fan produced them. Barry himself likened the recording studio to "a musical Erector set." The industrial design major delighted in tinkering during what he later called "the Wright Brothers days of rock and pop." Less laborious than Spector, less meticulous than Leiber and Stoller and Bacharach and David, Barry worked fast. "Jeff came to leave," Arthur said.

> He couldn't wait to get in and get out. Ellie was a little more detail-oriented and worried about piano notes and changes and fixing the background parts and getting the correct lead vocal. Jeff would worry more about feel. He and especially *they*—Jeff and Ellie—would not let the record get out the door unless the feel was right. . . . They were like, literally, teenagers in love—with each other, with their songs, and with their artists.

"Jeff seemed to be more in charge of the console, and Ellie seemed to be more in charge of the songs themselves," recalled the Tokens' Jay Siegal, contrasting their harmonious working relationship in the studio to the "screaming and yelling" of Goffin and King. If their marriage appeared idyllic, however, it was so consumed by music that the couple had little opportunity to develop other bonds.

Shortly after "Iko Iko," Joe Jones took the Dixie Cups to ABC-Paramount, where their career crumpled. Their departure did not make a great difference to Red Bird, which was awash in girl groups. The Jelly

Beans, who included one scarcely audible man, had hits with Greenwich-Barry's buoyant "I Want to Love Him So Bad" (pronounced "bed" with what Stoller insisted was a Long Island accent despite the group's Jersey City provenance) and tender "Baby Be Mine" (written and produced with Steve Venet, another Trio Music/Red Bird staffer). The Butterflies, featuring an original member of the Crystals, scored with "Goodnight Baby," another Greenwich-Barry-Venet collaboration, which fended off an importunate boyfriend with an angelic lullaby.

"When a label starts to happen so quickly," Greenwich said, "you become kind of a factory." As one Red Bird record after another hit the charts, she recalled, the songs and their singers blurred together: "Hello, you're with the—? Oh, fine." Barry and Greenwich were so prolific in 1964 that not even Red Bird could contain their energy or their success. When the Exciters' original rendition of "Do Wah Diddy Diddy" faltered, Greenwich and Barry decided to record the song themselves as the Raindrops, only to be beaten to the punch by Manfred Mann, whose manager had pressed the British band to cover the Exciters' single. Most of the group disliked the song, but it went all the way to No. 1 in the United States as well as in England.

It is easy but unfair to dismiss Manfred Mann's recording of "Do Wah Diddy Diddy" or the Moody Blues' cover of "Go Now" as yet two more examples of the racism endemic to rock music—no better than Pat Boone's and Georgia Gibbs's pallid imitations of Little Richard and LaVern Baker in the 1950s. Pasty-faced Englishmen trumping African-American women—so what else is new? But apartheid no longer rigidly segregated pop from rhythm and blues. Black artists, including the Dixie Cups, had six No. 1 records in the American pop charts in 1964. The original versions of "Do Wah Diddy Diddy" and "Go Now" had already failed commercially when Manfred Mann and the Moody Blues covered them, and the British bands did not water down Leiber and Stoller's productions so much as they stripped them down, making records that were derivative, to be sure, yet dramatically different from the originals. Manfred Mann's insistent organ and Paul Jones's guttural lead vocal transformed the Exciters' rather cluttered original into a catchy sing-along. The Moody Blues could not improve on Bessie Banks's wrenching rendition of "Go Now," but Mike Pinder's pounding piano and the group's shrill, echoing harmonies created a distinctive and indelible aural impression. The distance and detachment of the best British groups, including the Beatles, and an appreciation that surpassed their understanding of American R&B enabled them to make it new. (To be sure, many British cover versions, such as the Searchers' hit recording of Leiber and Stoller's "Love Potion Number Nine," were rote imitations.)

In addition to writing and producing "Don't Ever Leave Me" for the fading Connie Francis, Barry and Greenwich wrote two hits for her successor as America's sweetheart, Lesley Gore. Since their friends and former collaborators—John Gluck Jr., Beverly Ross, Mark Barkan, and Ben Raleigh—had had a hand in three of Gore's four Top Ten records and Greenwich had sung backup on several demos and one of her singles, "That's the Way Boys Are," Greenwich felt "a camaraderie right away" with the singer whom "It's My Party" had turned into a star at age seventeen. Gore's family, like Greenwich's, had climbed the social ladder from Brooklyn to the suburbs (in Gore's case to Tenafly, New Jersey), and Gore was about to jeopardize her musical career by attending college, as Greenwich had done. The two of them could easily have worn matching sweater sets.

Quincy Jones and Claus Ogerman produced Gore's records, but when Greenwich sang backup vocals on the songs she and Barry had written for her, she felt as if she had her "own little girls' group." Unlike most of the girl groups she worked with, Gore was middle-class, suburban, and white—although, in one of the racial ironies in which pop music by definition abounds, it took the first black vice president of a major American record label, Quincy Jones, to imbue the girl-group sound with upscale social and production values. Greenwich came up with the title, melody, and chorus of "Maybe I Know" in a taxi and wrote the bridge and the words with Barry that evening. The song sets a fretful lyric to a cheerful melody, juggling tempos and major and minor keys. It is a study in ambivalence as the singer tries to persuade herself that "deep down inside" her boyfriend, who she can barely bring herself to admit is unfaithful, really loves her. A second single by Barry and Greenwich, "Look of Love," added a dash of Motown to Gore's sound.

Gore also recorded a Goffin-King song and another by Goffin and Titelman. Greenwich and Barry occasionally dined with Goffin and King (though not with Mann and Weil, who Greenwich felt were "stand-offish"). Competition made conversation difficult. When King mentioned artists they were working with, Goffin grew nervous, as if she were betraying a trade secret, and he began to stammer. Since they had little in common but music, what else could they talk about? Barry and Greenwich had little more to talk about even when they were alone.

Leiber and Stoller rewarded Barry and Greenwich for their labors with generous Christmas bonuses and a piece of the action. Barry said they were given 10 percent of Red Bird, although Leiber and Stoller preferred to characterize it as "a profit participation." The money was good enough that Barry, Artie Butler, and Brooks Arthur visited the Lincoln dealership that Goldner patronized. "We were probably looking scruffy, in jeans or whatever," Barry recalled, and "we just couldn't get anyone's attention, to the point where we went out and bought Cadillacs. As history has it, we parked them all alongside the Lincoln showroom and knocked on the window until they looked out. We showed them the three new cars we had bought. I think Artie did end up with a Lincoln, actually."

Barry and Greenwich were grateful for the free rein Leiber and Stoller gave them. "The beauty of working for Leiber and Stoller as opposed to just somebody who was running a business is that, God knows, they're wonderful songwriters and producers," Greenwich said.

> Whenever we played them something, they'd say, "You know that bridge? Maybe you should rethink it." Talk about constructive criticism! We're listening to what they say, because we know it's coming from an educated, talented mind. The freedom was wonderful, and they never criticized. Just every now and then they'd say, "Maybe it should be a little less flirty. Just sit with it for a while." Even in that they were very tactful. We really wanted to make them happy and deliver for them because they were so good to us and we had so much respect for them.

"We only edited those records," Leiber said of Red Bird's girl group releases. "We executive-produced them." "They'd gotten too old for the market," Meryl Stoller said. "They came out of rhythm and blues, and the kids later on were definitely rock 'n' roll. It was no longer their music. Even when it was good, it wasn't their music."

"I didn't dig it, I didn't understand it," Leiber said. "It was the forerunner of bubblegum music—teenage ballads. Jeff and Ellie wrote most of it. They were like super-aces at making this type of material."

Leiber and Stoller created a subsidiary of Red Bird, Blue Cat, which issued many of the more R&B–oriented records in which they were involved. Only one of these, the Ad Libs' "The Boy from New York City," rivaled Red Bird's releases in popularity. Written by the Newark, New Jersey–based quintet's manager, John Taylor, "The Boy from New York City" kicked off with a lip-smacking imitation of a string bass— *boo-oom bim bim bim bim bim bim bim bim*—and strutted straight into the Top Ten. Although the group's only female member, Mary Ann Thomas, sang the sassy lead, the song's jazzy feel distinguished it sharply from Barry and Greenwich's girl-group productions, and when the Ad Libs recorded a Greenwich-Barry song as their follow-up single, they stumbled badly.

The kind of music that Leiber and Stoller preferred to produce was indicated by the name of one of their groups, the Soul Brothers, and the title of one of their songs, "Bottom of My Soul," sung by Alvin Robinson. Although Blue Cat never found a following in the United States, its very lack of commercial success made it an invaluable resource for British groups seeking little-known material. In addition to "Go Now," the Moody Blues recorded a version of the Soul Brothers' novel mixture of flutes and funk, "I Got a Dream," written by Barry and Greenwich and produced by Leiber and Stoller. The Rolling Stones covered Alvin Robinson's comic-erotic "Down Home Girl," which Leiber wrote with Artie Butler. And the Hollies turned Evie Sands's captivating "I Can't Let Go," written by Al Gorgoni and Chip Taylor, into an even more scintillating hit single.

Red Bird and Blue Cat released a fairly wide cross-section of records, including Latin, surf music, and even an icky ballad, "Amy," sung by Barry Mann. Had it not been for the Animals, Mann's original rendition of "We Gotta Get Out of This Place" would have been a Red Bird single as well. But Red Bird became best known as "an assembly line," in Jeff Barry's words, "cranking out songs for nine-year-old girls."

George Goldner brought more gusto to this task than Leiber and Stoller. Pondering why Goldner and Don Kirshner were the best record pickers of their generation, Leiber concluded, "They both had the soul, temperament, and minds of twelve-year-old girls. And those are the people that buy pop records. They never missed." Goldner's energy and enthusiasm could be overpowering. "Goddamn it, relax," he would tell an artist, "or I'll kill you." He got so excited in the recording studio when he heard what he hoped was a hit that he would bellow, "That's a *smash*!" and hurl a chair, gouging the control booth's wall.

From the moment he championed "Chapel of Love," Goldner worked closely with Barry and Greenwich. When Goldner's protégé Artie Ripp and a friend from Greenwich's high school days named George Morton got in on the act, Red Bird soared to new heights of success.

Chapter Seventeen

"SOMETHIN' DIED"

★

The Shangri-Las were elusive, as if they didn't come from Queens, which their accents announced, but from the lamasery in *Lost Horizon*, the James Hilton novel from which they took their name. Were there three of them or four? Some record jacket covers displayed a quartet, but promotional pictures and concerts frequently featured a single blonde flanked by two brunettes. James Brown was startled to discover they were white. Who brought them to Red Bird Records? Artie Ripp and George Morton each took credit. Both of them also claimed to have produced the group's first hit single, the keening "Remember (Walkin' in the Sand)," but so did Jeff Barry and Leiber and Stoller. And who pinned George Francis Morton with the nickname "Shadow," tantalizing readers of small print on record sleeves? Again, Barry and Leiber each said he did, though Morton himself wondered whether it might have been George Goldner.

Relating the rise and fall of Red Bird's most legendary act is a challenge because Leiber and Morton, as their records demonstrate, and the rapscallion Ripp as well, have taken more delight in telling stories than in telling the truth. When Jerry Wexler called Leiber "a genius-level fabulist," he could have been describing all three of them. Litigation poisoned some participants' memories and sealed others' lips. Mary Weiss, the Shangri-Las' lead singer, was so embittered by her career that she spoke only guardedly about it. "Everybody's recollection is revisionist history," Ripp acknowledged.

Mary Weiss and her older sister, Betty, were from Cambria Heights. Their father died when Mary was an infant, and she described scuffling to make ends meet in a single-parent household as "a hell of a way to grow up." At Andrew Jackson High School they teamed with twin sisters Marge and Mary Ann Ganser, forming a group that eventually signed with Kama Sutra, a production and publishing company operating out of 1650 Broadway. Ripp, no longer working for Don Kirshner, was one of Kama Sutra's three principals—or four if one includes, as some accounts do, organized crime. Dubbed the Shangri-Las, the group released a single that fizzled and soon fell in with George Morton, a young hustler eager to get into the music business. Born in Brooklyn, Morton had moved as a teenager to Hicksville, Long Island, where he met Ellie Greenwich at a record store.

Now Morton made a demo in a Hicksville recording studio of the Shangri-Las singing a seven-minute soap operetta that he had composed in his head; it was inspired in part by the dramatic chords and finger-snapping rhythms of the Modern Jazz Quartet's "Sketch," a 1959 John Lewis composition that the group recorded with the Beaux-Arts String Quartet. There was nothing artsy about the Shangri-Las' nasal "squelp," as the sociologist and writer Donna Gaines aptly characterized girl groups' "combination squeal and yelp," the sound of "a real teenage girl declaring her love"—in this instance for a boy who had "found someone new" and stranded the singer on a desolate beach with only erotic memories and the cries of gulls to keep her company.

According to Morton, he presumed on his lapsed acquaintance with Greenwich to approach Red Bird with "Remember (Walkin' in the Sand)." Although Greenwich confirmed this, Ripp claimed to have brought the song to his old mentor Goldner. In either event, when Morton, Ripp, Barry, Greenwich, Artie Butler, and session musicians went into Manhattan's Mirasound Studio to flesh out the demo, "it became a whole other record," recalled Brooks Arthur, the engineer on the date—as well as a much shorter one suitable for radio play. "The guy with the palette and the colors was Shadow Morton," Arthur said, but the finished product was "a cross-pollination" to which everyone contributed.

"Remember" reached No. 5 in the charts and introduced most of the elements of the Shangri-Las' (and George Morton's) style: a melodramatic story line embellished with sound effects, spoken words, and swirling harmonies that created what Barry called "a movie for the ear." Barry said, "We were conscious that we were making little soap operas with sound effects. . . . It was all to evoke the imagination that MTV has eliminated today. This was radio. . . . Songs sound better with your eyes closed. My father was blind, so I know about these things." As the Shangri-Las sang on their next single, "Leader of the Pack": "I met him in a candy store / He turned around and smiled at me / You get the picture? (Yes, we see)."

Although Morton said that he alone wrote "Leader of the Pack"—a claim supported by engineer Rod McBrien, with whom Morton once again made the basic demo in Hicksville—Barry and Greenwich insisted they deserved the credit they received as coauthors of the song, which added another ingredient that became a Shangri-Las staple: death. As cowriter of the morbid "Tell Laura I Love Her," Barry knew something about that, too. Leiber and Stoller were also familiar with the tale of a motorcyclist who skids to his death after parting with his girlfriend. They had written it themselves nine years earlier for the Cheers. But while "Black Denim Trousers and Motorcycle Boots" had been played strictly for laughs, "Leader of the Pack" teeters between parody and pathos. If it is intended entirely as a joke, the Shangri-Las sing with such conviction that one wonders whether they were in on it. "I remember sitting opposite [Mary Weiss] when she sang it," Barry said,

> me on one side of the hanging microphone and she on the other, my side dead. I directed her in it, saying, "Look what happened to this guy. Here he is, he loves this girl. And just think about her: She stands there and sees him pull away on his motorcycle." I got her all psyched up, and she was crying. When she sang, "Look out! Look out! Look out!" you can hear it. Her performance is a big part of the success of that record. It's genuine.

"I'm kind of a shy person," Weiss said, "but I felt that the recording studio was the place that you could really release what you're feeling without everybody looking at you. . . . I had enough pain in me at the time to pull off anything and get into it and sound believable."

A real motorcycle revved up in the recording studio to create the roar in "Leader of the Pack," and after the single went to No. 1, Morton bought Barry his first bike, a little white Honda. By then Morton had acquired the nickname of Shadow because of the vanishing act he frequently pulled. "He'd always go to some saloon and have a brew with some of his buddies and a couple of chickaroos," Brooks Arthur recalled. "He'd disappear like the Shadow." His erratic behavior may have led to Barry and Greenwich's increasing involvement with the Shangri-Las, who recorded several Greenwich-Barry songs that Morton had no share in writing. They recycled "Give Us Your Blessing," previously recorded by Ray Peterson, the singer of "Tell Laura I Love Her." This maudlin ditty, in which a car crash kills eloping teenagers after their folks forbid them to wed, reiterated a persistent theme of the Shangri-Las with which many a frustrated adolescent could easily identify: Defy it or defer to it, parental disapproval is deadly.

The Shangri-Las cultivated a spirit of rebellion in their dress as well as their songs, wearing leather vests and boots when even the Ronettes performed in frocks and high heels. "The Shangri-Las were tough girls," Greenwich said, "and I was somewhat afraid of them. They had an attitude *before* they made it. One day during rehearsal, while popping gum and carrying on, they yelled something at me, and we had it out in the ladies' room. From then on, things were fine." Their songs captured how many teenagers talked and felt or, more precisely, how they *wished* they talked and felt, mixing trash and tragedy. Morton showed his mastery of this titillating idiom in "Give Him a Great Big Kiss," which he originally intended for another group, the Goodies. "Mmmm, he's good-bad, but he's not evil," Mary Weiss says of her boyfriend with "dirty fingernails." Here, too, Morton recalled Leiber and Stoller's motorcyclist who had "axle-grease embedded underneath his fingernails."

Although it was one of the Shangri-Las' less successful singles, Barry and Greenwich's "Out in the Streets" was one of their most haunting and a favorite of Mary Weiss, who especially enjoyed working with Barry. The production, credited to Barry and Morton, and Artie Butler's arrangement are unusually sumptuous, with pizzicato strings and whorls of vocal harmony. Subtler and far sadder than most of the group's songs, "Out in the Streets" does not indict the deadliness of parental authority but the living death of conforming to and, worse, internalizing adult standards of respectability. The Shangri-Las' rough, tough boyfriend with dirty boots and greasy hair has cleaned up his act at their insistence, but domestication has emasculated him:

He's not the same,
There's somethin' in his kissin'
That tells me he's changed
I know that somethin's missin' inside
Somethin' died.

It's not entirely far-fetched to detect in the elegiac solemnity of "Out in the Streets" an apprehension that perhaps rock 'n' roll, cleaned up and commodified for the pop charts and young white consumers, was suffering a similar fate. Leiber and Stoller certainly felt such misgivings.

★

At the height of the Shangri-Las' and Red Bird's success, Leiber, Stoller, Goldner, and Red Bird's lawyer, music attorney Lee Eastman (whose daughter would marry Paul McCartney), met with Ahmet Ertegun, his brother Nesuhi, and Jerry Wexler in the Oak Room of the Plaza Hotel and discussed the possibility of merging Red Bird with Atlantic Records, which was not faring nearly so well in the charts at the time. Ahmet was angered by the suggestion and convinced that Wexler was conniving with Leiber and Stoller. Goldner and Eastman also opposed the idea, which went no further. Leiber and Stoller had proposed it because they were feeling increasingly estranged not only from the music that Red Bird was releasing but also from their partner, whom they suspected of cheating them. "We were trying to use Atlantic," Leiber explained, "to drive George out. Goldner was involving us with guys with faces you'd see only at fights at the old Madison Square Garden. We were afraid of George and thought of Ahmet and Jerry as executives strong enough to control him. We thought of Goldner as crass and Atlantic as class."

If Goldner was indulging in skullduggery at the company that Leiber and Stoller had established—pressing, shipping, and selling records off the books for personal profit, according to Leiber—their claim to be shocked strains credulity. "At the time George Goldner was invited to be a partner in Red Bird Records," Stoller insisted, "the only thing we knew about him was that he was a great record man." If so, they had not done due diligence and checked Goldner's bona fides with Sam Weiss, Hy's brother, who had been involved in Tiger and Daisy Records, or Norm Rubin, who had worked for Goldner and Morris

Levy before Leiber and Stoller hired him to head sales and promotion for those ill-fated labels. "Jerry Leiber and Mike Stoller were caught up in the Damon Runyon–esque atmosphere," recalled Jay and the Americans' Kenny Vance. "There were all kinds of characters coming through that door all the time—not just songwriters and singers but gangster wannabes who wanted to be in the music business and all kinds of Broadway shady types. That was part of the color of it." Leiber and Stoller may have been naïve when they enlisted Goldner to win radio play for their records, but their naïveté consisted chiefly in their confidence that they could control him.

Leiber and Stoller began to disengage from Red Bird, and so did Barry and Greenwich. Hired to sing backup on a demo by an obscure Brooklyn singer-songwriter, Greenwich was impressed by Neil Diamond, who had transferred from Erasmus to Abraham Lincoln High School, where he had fallen under the spell of Neil Sedaka. "He had records out, and you could hear them on the radio," Diamond said. "Back then, you judged yourself against Sedaka." Greenwich played Diamond's songs for Barry, and together they persuaded Leiber and Stoller to give Diamond a short-term songwriting contract. When that expired and Diamond requested a raise, Leiber and Stoller balked. Barry, Greenwich, and Diamond formed Tallyrand Music to publish, produce, and exploit Diamond's songs and made a deal with Bert Berns. A songwriter and producer with a bad hairpiece and a worse heart that would give out when he was only thirty-eight, Berns was the "B" in Bang Records. (The "ang" in the Atlantic subsidiary were Ahmet and Nesuhi Ertegun and Gerald Wexler.) This new joint venture was like the house a couple buys or the baby it conceives to save a failing marriage, and in Barry and Greenwich's case, it was no more successful, although it launched Diamond's spectacular career.

Greenwich and Barry coauthored two singles in 1965 that they sang separately and released as solo records under their individual names. Morton joined them in writing "You Don't Know" and urged Greenwich to sing it. Dramatically juxtaposing intimate spoken passages with soaring vocal harmonies and heavy orchestration, "You Don't Know" sounded like a Shangri-Las record, while Greenwich's college-grad diction and noble refusal ever to betray her best friend even though she had a huge crush on her boyfriend evoked Lesley Gore and suburban rec rooms. (The Shangri-Las would never have stood on such sisterly, self-sacrificing ceremony.) The single was an intriguing hybrid and, according to Greenwich, prompted talk of promoting her as an American Dusty Springfield and perhaps even flying her to England. But the record never entered the charts.

Meanwhile, Barry recorded and released a dispirited and equally unsuccessful single, written with Greenwich, in which he urged:

> *I think that you*
> *Can learn to behave*
> *I know I can give*
> *More than I gave*
> *C'mon, let's try, c'mon, let's try*
> *Baby, don't say goodbye*
> *'Cause I think our love can still be saved.*

He didn't sound very convinced.

"We had too much happen to us too fast," Greenwich said. "The music did so well and we were so wrapped up in it that we never had time to get to know each other." The pressure of sustaining their extraordinary success was enormous. At a BMI banquet that presented them with several awards, Greenwich asked Barry, with tears in her eyes, what he felt about their future. He answered with "three words that ended our relationship, 'I don't know.'"

Greenwich was devastated. "It wasn't just a marriage," she said. "It was a partnership." For Barry that was part of the problem: "We had a creative partnership but not an overly romantic one. It was a good partnership but not a great marriage." And Barry regarded marriage as he did the recording studio: "He couldn't wait to get in and get out." As his relationship with Greenwich unraveled, Barry began to date Nancy Calcagno, who worked in a recording studio. Greenwich and Barry separated in October 1965, just before their third wedding anniversary, and obtained a Mexican divorce in December of that year.

Artie Resnick thought that Calcagno, whom Barry soon wed, was "a very sweet girl" but feared that Barry's attraction to the Calcagno family and his inconstancy reflected his unhappy childhood. "He had a bad life, and that's what a lot of this was about: always looking for something. Everything that Jeff would get, he would get sick of quickly. He would go through a lot of phases—bow and arrow, motorcycles, guns, a million things—and they would interest him one minute." Beverly Ross, on the other hand, ascribed Barry's short amorous attention span to his romanticism: "I think Jeff's a romantic, and if he feels a flicker of love, he'll marry that girl." The actress Jennifer O'Neill, who was briefly Barry's fourth wife, concurred, calling him "a romantic to the core."

Whatever the reasons for their divorce, Greenwich felt bereft. "I come from a very protected environment," she said. "I'm very ill-equipped to do this, and yet my husband and partner says, 'See ya!'" Gerry Goffin, whose marriage was also breaking up, spent an evening with Greenwich and realized, he said, "long before the night was over that this girl was too much for me. She wouldn't let me leave, and I was trying like hell to get out of her apartment." According to Greenwich, she was eager to get *him* out the door. "It must have been during his drug-taking days, and he wasn't exactly together. I was getting uncomfortable." She said she called Hank Medress and arranged for them to take a cab to visit him in Brooklyn, where she left Goffin and rushed home.

When word got out that they were parting, a mobster called Greenwich and asked if she wanted him to talk to Barry. He wouldn't kill him, he reassured her, but after he broke Barry's kneecaps, the tall, skinny guy would be shorter.

Thugs were showing up with increasing regularity at Red Bird's offices. "George had gotten himself deeply into debt with the bookies again," Ripp said, "and he compromised himself. The last thing that Leiber and Stoller wanted to do was deal with a group of wiseguys who said, 'George signed over his share of the company to us, and we're now your partners.' I think they were put in a position where the smart thing was just to get out of it, turn it over and don't be bothered with it. There was no upside."

Billboard announced on April 16, 1966, that Leiber and Stoller had sold Goldner their interest in Red Bird. According to them, the price was one dollar. "One day they said, 'Get your stock. We're going to sign it over,'" recalled Barry, joking that Leiber and Stoller still owed him a dime. "I said, 'Fine.' End of discussion." Greenwich remembered, "I was like Tinker Bell, floating around, writing my songs. And all of a sudden we no longer had a piece of the company."

Leiber and Stoller said good-bye not only to Red Bird but also, to a great extent, to the rock 'n' roll they felt they had outgrown. (Both men also shed their first marriages.) While they expanded their publishing company, becoming curators of their greatest hits and acquiring other catalogs, they concentrated most of their songwriting energies on trying to compose a Broadway show. They worked on something called *The International Wrestling Match* and made stabs at adapting Jean Giraudoux's play *The Madwoman of Chaillot* and Mordecai Richler's novel *The Apprenticeship of Duddy Kravitz*. "They came to me with ideas," Mitch Miller said, "and the music was never good enough."

Meanwhile, Goldner made short work of Red Bird, which quickly collapsed. By then the Shangri-Las, like the Dixie Cups and the Ad Libs before them, had left the label, in their case for Mercury Records. But they could not sustain their success and soon disbanded. The performers on Red Bird, like many on other labels, found fame fleeting at best and little if any fortune. They were as disposable as the Dixie Cups, who complained they received only one check, for less than $500, for "Chapel of Love."

"The performers were kids, and the adults were ripping everybody off," said Dick Fox, a manager (of Neil Sedaka at one point) and concert promoter who introduced his receptionist as one of the Shangri-Las. She looked young enough to be Mary Weiss's daughter. The group had never owned its name, which Fox registered and exploited. "And you know what's funny?" Fox continued, speaking of young artists generally during the 1950s and '60s. "You can talk to them today, and they didn't care! They say, 'We wanted to hear ourselves on the radio. We were driving in our car, we heard ourselves on the radio,' and that was it. Money? What was money? . . . They signed these contracts that said, 'You turn over all your royalties, you turn over your first-born, you turn over your house, you turn over your parents.' . . . They care now, but they didn't care then."

No performer ever blamed a writer for coming up with a hit song. "The one person who always comes off smelling like roses is the songwriter," Hank Medress said. "That's the purest part of it." At worst the writers were guilty of indifference toward the artists, a lack of concern or even of curiosity. "Literally, they were vehicles for the songs," Greenwich said, "so we knew them as far as rehearsing them, but *knowing* them? No." In another interview she commented: "The girls gave, and the girls took. They'd get fancy clothes, expensive dinners, all of that. Most of them didn't think in terms of a 'career.' It was just fun, and better than their alternatives, and they took what they could get. Most of them only wanted their couple of years, and then they wanted to get married and raise a family. They knew there were trade-offs, but it wasn't a one-sided exploitation, that's for sure."

Writers became more complicit in the impoverishment of performers when they assumed other roles, producing their records or owning the label that released them. The costs of production and promotion were deducted from artists' royalties, and these expenses and others were frequently inflated. "The record companies had a license to steal," Ripp explained.

> If I went out on a promotion trip and had five records in release, let's say I went into Philadelphia and spent $1,000. I now charge that $1,000 to each of the five records. I didn't charge a fifth and divide it because I may have worked on one record more. Who is to say I spent thirty minutes promoting this record and five minutes on this one? It's just simpler: Charge everyone $1,000. So if in fact you were paying for the promotion trips, you were paying for the advertising, you were paying for this, that, and the other thing, you were paying for the recording costs, traditionally the artists were getting fucked. . . . And the black artist and the young white kid artist, what would they know? They would just be happy making records.

In fact, many performers did feel frustrated. The Shirelles took Scepter Records and Florence Greenberg to court. The Chiffons sued Medress and the other Tokens to abrogate their contract with the Tokens' production company. After they won, in part because they were minors when they signed the contract, they discovered that no one else wanted to work with troublemakers. The group had little alternative but to return to their original producers and record company.

As a writer, producer, and label owner, Phil Spector controlled so many aspects of some performers' careers that he could exploit them to the brink of extortion, but by late 1965 he was running out of patsies and genius. Not only record buyers but Spector himself seemed to have lost interest in Philles's girl groups, and the Righteous Brothers had abandoned him. Deciding to follow up their blue-eyed soul with its brown-eyed inspiration, he leased Rhythm & Blues artists Ike and Tina Turner from their label, Warner Brothers, for $20,000, much as he had previously rented the Righteous Brothers from Moonglow. Not knowing or not caring that they were divorcing, he appealed to Greenwich and Barry, with whom he had not worked for nearly two years. Their collaborations had made Spector the "Tycoon of Teen," as Tom Wolfe dubbed him in a vivid article that was as impressionable as it was impressionistic. (An exemplar of the New Journalism, the piece was also inaccurate, claiming that Spector alone wrote the music and lyrics of his hit records.) When the success of the Dixie Cups' "Chapel of Love" cast a pall on their relationship, Spector dallied with Mann and Weil and Goffin and King, but now, when the chips were down, he wagered on the writers who had delivered most dependably for him in the past. Perhaps as a measure of his slipping stature, he accommodated Barry and Greenwich by traveling to New York instead of summoning them to Los Angeles at someone else's expense, as he had Mann and Weil.

Collaborating under strained circumstances was "a little weird," according to Greenwich, and "sad in a way, knowing that this was probably the last time we were going to work together. . . . But we were professional about it. I think if the music takes over, the circumstances don't matter at all." In less than a week she, Barry, and Spector managed to compose three songs. "It was like vomiting it out," Greenwich said.

The most important of these songs was "River Deep—Mountain High," a vehicle for the rumbustious Tina Turner. (Spector had no interest in Ike, Tina's dour, abusive husband, and kept the guitarist and bandleader at arm's length.) Since all three writers had grown apart, they came to the collaborative sessions with disparate bits. According to Greenwich, she provided the melody of the verse, Spector that of the chorus, and Barry most of the words. (Insisting that he never distinguished word-smithing from tune-smithing, Barry said he must have contributed to the melody as well.) "Lyrically, we just all jumbled, jumbled, jumbled on the chorus," Greenwich recalled. "When you think about 'River Deep–Mountain High,' that lyrically says a lot about where we were coming from at that time. It also was a big sound, almost a desperate sound—but exciting! It breaks out: freedom!"

It also broke down into frenetic incoherence. Spector started recording "River Deep–Mountain High" in Los Angeles's Gold Star Studio A in February 1966, just as the Righteous Brothers released Mann and Weil's No. 1–bound "(You're My) Soul and Inspiration." It took five marathon sessions and cost more than $22,000 to complete the song. On one date enlisting four guitarists, four basses, two drummers, and more than twenty background singers, Tina Turner felt so overwhelmed by the assembled multitude and so baffled by the song that she could not sing. A week later she returned and performed with no one in the studio but Spector and engineer Larry Levine. Spector pushed her so hard and so repeatedly that after midnight Turner stripped off her sweat-drenched blouse and sang in her bra in the pitch-dark studio.

Many listeners did not know what to make of the song, which sounded as if it had been produced under the influence of two clashing drugs, mixing steroidal ponderousness and amphetamine rush. When the single peaked at No. 88, the failure of what he was convinced was his masterpiece so demoralized Spector that he retreated to his twenty-one-room mansion in Beverly Hills and sulked, playing pool for days on end. Although he shared the rented estate with Veronica Bennett, he repeatedly called his ex-wife. Was he as big as Dylan? he would ask, pleading for reassurance. As the Beatles? The answer clearly was "no longer."

Spector could not bestir himself to produce another of the songs he had composed with Barry and Greenwich during their last writing session. "He was mad at the world because of 'River Deep,' " said Barry, who filled in at Spector's request and produced "I Can Hear Music," a gorgeous ballad, with the Ronettes. Fearing that a flagrant imitation of his Wall of Sound would anger Spector, Barry played down the echo and special effects. "I tried to make it sound like a Ronettes record without pissing him off," he recalled, "and ended up with a very mediocre record." Squeaking into the pop charts at No. 100, "I Can Hear Music" was the last single released by Philles Records in the United States, ending Spector's career as a tycoon with a whimper. Three years later, Brian Wilson, always a Spector fan, and the Beach Boys recorded a heartfelt version of "I Can Hear Music" that became a modest hit.

Greenwich and Barry's songwriting partnership went the way of their marriage, but they continued to collaborate in the recording studio and enjoyed phenomenal success in 1966 and 1967 as the producers of Neil Diamond's early hit singles. The pomposity of Diamond's later records makes it easy to forget how inventive and varied those initial singles were, running the gamut from folk to Latin to blues and nearly garage rock, plus a few pop ballads. The moody, minor-key "Solitary Man," which Diamond had written with Bobby Darin in mind, was graced with a fugue for trombones that Greenwich composed. Barry and Bert Berns convinced Diamond to change the title and lyrics of a song that rocked to a Latin riff from "Money, Money" to "Cherry, Cherry" because they thought love and sex appealed more to teenagers than lucre. The call-and-response of Barry and Greenwich's backing vocals enlivened "Cherry, Cherry" and other singles such as "I Got the Feelin' (Oh No, No)," "Thank the Lord for the Night Time," and "You Got to Me."

"Neil basically was not a Brill Building writer," Richard Gottehrer observed. "He had the ability to perform, and he wrote with a guitar. There's the change. . . . Prior to that it was piano-driven." Yet one musician who participated in those sessions, Artie Kaplan, gave much of the credit for Diamond's sound to Barry, a Brill Building veteran: "I believe the inflections, the mannerisms, the phrasing on all those records was really Jeff. If the name wasn't Neil Diamond, it might have been Jeff Barry."

After seven hit singles, ego and ambition led Diamond to part company with Bang Records, Barry, and Greenwich. Moving to California, he signed with Uni Records and began to produce his own records in Los Angeles. The litigation that ensued lasted for years. Although Diamond's defection did not confound Barry, now remarried to Nancy Calcagno and secure in his role as a producer, it left Greenwich at loose ends. Their interest in Diamond, monetary as well as musical, was her last tie to her ex-husband. After it was severed, she never found another partner in life or in music.

Chapter Eighteen

SWINGING LONDON

★

Mary Isobel Catherine Bernadette O'Brien was walking by the Colony record store at Broadway and Fifty-second Street in late 1962 when the blare of the Exciters' "Tell Him" stopped her in her tracks. The intensity of that hit single, produced by Leiber and Stoller, and of Dionne Warwick's "Don't Make Me Over" inspired the young English singer to part company with the folk-country trio for which she had assumed the stage name of Dusty Springfield and to embrace the urban rhythms emanating from the nearby Brill Building and 1650 Broadway. "I knew then what I wanted to do," she said. "Bacharach and David changed pop music, and 'Don't Make Me Over' changed my life."

In 1964, Dusty Springfield had a No. 3 single in England with "I Just Don't Know What to Do with Myself," the dramatic ballad that Bacharach and David had written and Leiber and Stoller had produced for Tommy Hunt. That same year she had a hit in the United States with Bacharach and David's "Wishin' and Hopin'," the neglected b-side of Dionne Warwick's second single, which Springfield released at Bacharach's urging. Her first British album included cover versions of Bacharach-David's "Anyone Who Had a Heart" and "Twenty-four Hours from Tulsa" as well as Goffin-King's "Will You Love Me Tomorrow." When Warwick and the Shirelles performed their original versions at Paris's Olympia Theatre, Springfield crossed the Channel to join the audience.

Other English singers recorded Bacharach and David in 1964—barefoot Sandie Shaw's rendition of "(There's) Always Something There to Remind Me" and Cilla Black's of "Anyone Who Had a Heart" both went to No. 1 in the British charts—but Springfield was not simply following the crowd. Although the arrangements and production of her recordings (especially of "I Just Don't Know What to Do with My-self") were cruder than the originals', her smoky vocals were urgent and heartfelt. The yearning she compressed into the staccato gerunds of "Wishin' and Hopin'" made Warwick's performance seem glib. War-wick was dispensing advice; Springfield was admonishing herself. A troubled woman whose mascara, wigs, and lacquered look concealed near-sightedness, lesbianism, and substance abuse, Springfield seemed able to bare herself only in song—or by shattering cheap crockery, as Mary Weiss watched her do methodically backstage at Brooklyn's Fox Theater.

Pomus and Shuman had noted when they sojourned in London years earlier that the British were more appreciative than Americans of songwriters. While Bacharach and David were still little known in the States, Springfield, England's most beloved female vocalist for most of the 1960s, helped make them household names on her home turf. "I think we broke through in England before we broke through in Amer-ica," David said. "The English popular music audience had a greater awareness of writers." In the fall of 1964, when most American song-writers felt shell-shocked by the British Invasion, Bacharach and David went on the counteroffensive. Bacharach rented an apartment in "swinging London," and David flew over as frequently as his family permitted. Although Bacharach allowed to the press that "beat is not exactly my kind of music" and said he preferred "more restful music" to "the rough sound" of many British bands, he was acclaimed as visit-ing royalty and influenced many English groups. The Zombies, for in-stance, who toured with Dionne Warwick, tried to emulate Bacharach's augmented chords in their hit single "Tell Her No."

Unlike most of their American peers, Bacharach and David also en-gaged actively in writing and producing music in London, most of it for movies that were less memorable than their songs. The ties to the film industry that David and Bacharach had formed at Famous Music were strengthened by Bacharach's romance with Angie Dickinson, whom he married on May 5, 1965, in Las Vegas's Silver Bell wedding chapel, attended by David Nelson (Ricky's older brother and costar in *The Adventures of Ozzie and Harriet*) and his wife. Charles K. Feldman, a flamboyant, free-spending producer who had represented Marlene Dietrich when he was an agent, met Bacharach and David in London

and engaged them in two projects involving the improbable international medley of Peter Sellers (for comedy), Peter O'Toole (for class),
Woody Allen (for neuroticism), and Ursula Andress (for eroticism).

The first film was *What's New, Pussycat?*, which was Allen's debut
as a screenwriter and actor, and Bacharach's first opportunity to score
an entire movie. The witless sex farce had been written for Warren
Beatty and took its title from the Lothario's habitual greeting. David
and Bacharach set it to song on an Easter Sunday morning in London.
Bacharach played the galumphing waltz for its designated singer, Tom
Jones, who had put Bacharach-David's "To Wait for Love," previously
recorded to little avail by Tony Orlando and Jay and the Americans, on
the b-side of his first hit single, "It's Not Unusual." The bawling Welsh
baritone thought Bacharach must be joking and asked him to play the
real song. Such silliness was unbecoming a sex symbol in leather pants.
Jones recorded "What's New, Pussycat?" at his manager's insistence.
Bacharach, though not the producer of record, took charge in the studio. "He had me singing better than I'd ever done before," said Jones.
His lusty exuberance and the song's comic ungainliness made "What's
New, Pussycat?" an even bigger hit than "It's Not Unusual."

Another Bacharach-David song in the film was less successful commercially yet intriguing because it marked one of the first and few occasions when the songwriters worked in the studio with an actual and
decidedly unrestful rock-and-roll band. "My Little Red Book (All I Do
Is Talk About You)" was, in the words of critic Geoffrey O'Brien,
"a fascinatingly stylized approximation of rock and roll, or perhaps a
veiled commentary on its limitations." Although Manfred Mann, the
leader of the group that bore his name, was a fairly sophisticated piano
player with a jazz background, he had difficulty pounding out the
song's unusual chords the way Bacharach wanted him to: without syn-
copating any of the beats. "Burt was terribly nice," Mann recalled, "and
slowly and tactfully edged me out, finally using the phrase: 'Manfred,
why don't I play it, and you can tell me if it's O.K.?'" A promotional
photo shows Bacharach and David in the recording studio with the
group, Bacharach front and center at a Steinway, looking collegiate and
casual in tennis shoes, a sweater draped over his shoulders. David,
wearing a sport coat, a tie, and a grin, could be an accountant on holiday. The only person who appears stiff and uncomfortable, while most
of his bandmates smile, is a bug-eyed Manfred Mann.

"My Little Red Book" was a flop for the high-flying group, which had soared with Barry-Greenwich's "Do Wah Diddy Diddy" and Goffin-King's "Oh No Not My Baby." A then little-known Los Angeles band, Love, released a version that became a modest hit, but to Bacharach's disgust they got the chords wrong. Bacharach came closer to approximating rock and roll several months after "My Little Red Book" when he deployed jangling guitars on the title songs of two other films, "Promise Her Anything" (sung once again by Tom Jones) and "Made in Paris" (sung by Trini Lopez).

The second movie that Bacharach scored for Charles Feldman and some of the same cast of characters was *Casino Royale*. Though Woody Allen correctly characterized the James Bond spoof (which he did not write) as "unfunny burlesque," it provided the template for Mike Myers's Austin Powers films. This time around the title song was a jaunty instrumental played by trumpeter Herb Alpert and the Tijuana Brass, while the showstopper was Dusty Springfield's performance of "The Look of Love." On the only occasion they ever actually worked in the recording studio together, Bacharach urged Springfield to sing more softly and in a higher register than usual, in the manner of Astrud Gilberto, and he added a breathy saxophone solo that invoked Stan Getz. "The Look of Love" was his homage to the bossa nova. Springfield's whispered vocal, which she didn't sing so much as exhale (taking literally David's lyric, "well, it takes my breath away"), and Bacharach's spare murmur of an arrangement were extraordinarily intimate pillow talk. Springfield's record company, fearing the number was too unadorned to win radio play, rerecorded it and added a string arrangement that swathed the song in satin sheets. Even then, no one expected "The Look of Love" to become a hit, and it was released as a b-side, which a disc jockey in Seattle discovered and started to play. "The Look of Love" made it to No. 22 in the United States in November 1967. Although Sergio Mendes and Brasil '66 had a much bigger hit (No. 4) with the song the following year, Springfield's version is the one everyone remembers.

"Alfie" was another Bacharach-David song that almost got away. Eddie Wolpin asked them to write a title song for Lewis Gilbert's film, a Paramount picture. The movie already had a swinging jazz score by the great tenor saxophonist Sonny Rollins, but Paramount, little suspecting that the sardonic British film would make Michael Caine a star,

felt it needed an additional boost. Although David had doubts about
the film's title ("It seemed like a joke, a music hall name"), they obliged
the man who had paired them a decade earlier. David read the script in
Long Island and Bacharach, then in Los Angeles, screened a cut of the
film and assured David that little had changed. Adapting a line from Jim
Naughton's screenplay, "What's it all about, anyway?" David wrote the
lyrics first and telephoned them to Bacharach. The ballad that Bacharach came up with "didn't fit my lyric exactly," David said. "In each
phrase he had added a line." David then added words to fill out the tune.

As critic Francis Davis has pointed out, *Alfie* opened the same year
Time magazine asked on its cover, "Is God Dead?" David's lyric vowed
that love was "something even non-believers can believe in" while
Bacharach's melody made octave leaps of faith. Cilla Black, who
recorded the song under the direction of Bacharach and her producer
(as well as the Beatles'), George Martin, had difficulty negotiating the
song's intervals and delivered a strident performance. It was replaced in
American prints of the film by Cher's attempt, produced by Sonny
Bono, but neither version received major radio play. Dee Dee Warwick
recorded the song, once again with little success. It wasn't until her sister, who could rise to any challenge a Bacharach-David song presented,
cut "Alfie" and performed it at the Oscar ceremonies that it became a
hit at last.

Dionne Warwick rejected another song that became one of David
and Bacharach's biggest singles. It took David a couple of years after his
initial inspiration for "What the World Needs Now" to complete the
song. When he finally came up with the line "Lord, we don't need another mountain," he said, "the lyric flowed with ease." Bacharach set
David's words to yet another waltz and played it for Warwick, who was
not impressed. Bacharach decided he didn't like it, either, and forgot
about "What the World Needs Now" until David and he were presenting material to Jackie DeShannon, whom they had contracted to produce. (After recording Goffin, King, and Weil's "Heaven Is Being with
You," DeShannon had scored hits with the songs "Needles and Pins"
and "When You Walk in the Room," which she had cowritten and written, respectively.) David reminded Bacharach of "What the World
Needs Now," urged him to play it for DeShannon, and she loved it.
"Jackie was the catalyst—she was really excited about doing that song,"

David said. They recorded the song in two takes in New York, and it became an international hit.

"What the World Needs Now" was the favorite protest song of people who did not like to protest too much as the United States unleashed Operation Rolling Thunder in the skies over North Vietnam and killed seven hundred Vietcong in the war's first major land battle in the south. For all the brilliance of Bacharach's production—the euphonium that introduces and concludes the song on little cat's feet, the hurtling return of the chorus after the song seems to be quieting to a close—the waltz time sounds schmaltzy and the lyrics sententious. You don't have to be a radical environmentalist to recognize that we *do* need more meadows, or a radical of any stripe to wonder whether the "love" DeShannon is singing about can conquer all the world's woes. (Compare this to the self-awareness, irony, and unsettling time signature of the Beatles' "All You Need Is Love.") DeShannon flew to London to record more songs with Bacharach and David, but none of them came anywhere near equaling the success of "What the World Needs Now."

By now Bacharach was a star in his own right in England. He had released a single on which Joel Grey sang "What's New, Pussycat?" and Tony Middleton sang "My Little Red Book." David and he composed "Trains and Boats and Planes," a song about intercontinental dislocation that reflected Bacharach's globe-trotting with Marlene Dietrich as well as his current cosmopolitanism, writing songs about London, Paris, and Rome. (Richard Chamberlain sang Bacharach-David's "Rome Will Never Leave You" on three successive episodes of *Dr. Kildare.*) Bacharach's simple yet sophisticated rendition of "Trains and Boats and Planes," featuring a reverberating electric piano and vocals by the British vocal trio the Breakaways, beat out Billy J. Kramer and the Dakotas' earnest, awkward single on the U.K. charts (though not in the United States, where Bacharach still enjoyed little name recognition). This led to an album, *Hit Maker!,* most of which Bacharach recorded in London. To promote it, Bacharach starred in a British television special, and his guests included none other than Dionne Warwick and Dusty Springfield. Soon he was a regular and good-looking presence on English TV.

"I now consider myself as having arrived properly," Bacharach told a British reporter after the success of "Trains and Boats and Planes." Finally, he said, he felt "in control of things." "England was always good to me," Bacharach said years later, noting that *Hit Maker!* "sold maybe 5,000 copies in the States, but it was Top Ten in England." After Bacharach and Angie Dickinson's first child was born three months prematurely and his wife as well as daughter nearly died, Bacharach composed and released a grateful instrumental single, "Nikki."

Bacharach's burgeoning stardom strained his relationship with David. By his own admission, Bacharach took his partner's contribution to their music for granted. He scarcely mentioned it in press interviews. "At the time that he was delivering what seemed brilliant lyrics," Bacharach later acknowledged, "I wasn't paying attention to them." Yet the duo remained steadfast in their dedication to Dionne Warwick, continuing to compose and produce remarkable songs for the singer who would always be their most nimble and sensitive interpreter. "Here I Am," featured and fragmented in *What's New, Pussycat?*, was an elegant come-hither as seductive as Springfield's "The Look of Love" in *Casino Royale*.

Warwick resolved to cut a Bacharach-David song, "Kentucky Bluebird (Send a Message to Martha)" that Marlene Dietrich, Jerry Butler, Lou Johnson, and Adam Faith had already recorded. Faith's version had even been a hit in his native England. Convinced they had written a man's song, David and Bacharach discouraged Warwick. Undeterred, she recorded her own vocal over a version by French singer Sasha Distel. "I thought it was a smash," said Steve Tyrell, who argued with Bacharach and David in the elevator and all the way to Times Square. The next day they relented and released it as a b-side. The record was quickly flipped over and "Message to Michael," as Warwick had adjusted the lyric, reached No. 8 in America. Years later David admitted, "Dionne's version was so brilliant that it was obvious we had subconsciously written the song for her even while we thought we were writing it for a man to sing."

Always the perfectionist, Bacharach also initially opposed releasing Warwick's original version of "I Say a Little Prayer." "I thought I blew it," he told an interviewer decades later. "The tempo seemed too fast." Calling for back-to-back swoops of more than an octave down and up the scale, darting from 4/4 to 2/4 and 3/4 time, the song does sound breathless, but how better to capture the racing heart of a young woman on the go and in love? The following year Jerry Wexler overheard Aretha Franklin and her backup singers, the Sweet Inspirations, "goofing" with the song during downtime in the studio, and "I Say a Little Prayer" became a hit all over again.

Warwick did not like "Do You Know the Way to San Jose?" which she thought was in Mexico, but she recorded it out of respect for David's judgment and won her first Grammy award. This fleet study in varied rhythmic effects—from the backup singers' ten introductory "whoa's" to Warwick's eight monosyllables on the same note to four beats on the bass drum—also contained one of David's most deftly compressed lyrics, a short story:

> *Weeks turn into years. How quick they pass,*
> *And all the stars that never were*
> *Are parking cars and pumping gas.*

★

The team of Bacharach, David, and Warwick, especially during its first five years, from 1963 to 1968, was one of the great collaborations in pop music, surpassing in originality and variety even Leiber and Stoller's run with the Coasters. "The great innovator of popular melody in our generation was Burt Bacharach," Jimmy Webb wrote. "His influence was a breath of fresh air to a public that had tired of schmaltz but could not completely surrender to three-chord rock 'n' roll. Bacharach punctuated his clean, classically influenced melodies with idiosyncratic accents and even introduced *polyrhythms* to the Top 40."

Bacharach and David withstood the shifts of taste and fashion, from the Beatles to Dylan and the rise of the singer-songwriter, more successfully than any of their songwriting peers. They did so by stubbornly going their own way. "Everyone was taking acid and everybody was flower children," Steve Tyrell observed, "and they were doing 'Do You Know the Way to San Jose?' They didn't join in."

But slowly, and with some dazzling exceptions, Bacharach and David's music grew precious and filigreed. Warwick's records became ships in bottles as artistry—Bacharach's, David's, and hers—for its own sake stifled the emotional expressiveness of early records like "Don't Make Me Over" and "Walk On By." It's not coincidental that this oc-

curred as Bacharach and David attenuated and severed their ties to the
rhythm and blues in which Leiber and Stoller had schooled them.
Marty Robbins, Perry Como, and Bobby Vinton had not brought out
the best in Bacharach and David. The songwriters had consistently
done their finest work for the Drifters, the Shirelles, Jerry Butler, Lou
Johnson, Warwick, and Gene Pitney (the white exception that proved
the rule). The performances of black artists grounded Bacharach and
David's compositions in deeply felt experience. David and Bacharach
did not lose their voice after they ventured to London and started writing primarily for white artists (apart from Warwick), but their voice
changed. As they tailored their songs to the mainstream media of
movies and television as much as, if not more than, to the more racially
integrated and youthful outlet of radio, and as Warwick herself evolved
ever further away from her gospel beginnings, their work became
pallid.

A case in point is "The Windows of the World," one of David's favorite songs. His lyric protested the war in Vietnam, where he feared
his older son might someday have to serve. "There are many message
songs being written," David observed in 1970. "More and more of them
are violent. I tend to take a gentler approach in my protest." But
Bacharach and David's approach, as well as Warwick's, is so dainty and
indirect, though undeniably lovely, that the song has the impact of a
thistledown. Many listeners missed its point altogether.

When it didn't seem precious, Bacharach and David's music began to
sound slack. Film, television, the success on record and in concert of instrumental redactions of their songs, and the constraints of Bacharach's
tentative baritone when he sang them himself impelled the songwriters
toward easy listening. So did easy living, as Bacharach began to spend
more time in California with his movie star wife, and age. Bacharach
was entering his forties, and David was pushing fifty.

Older than the other songwriters except Doc Pomus, Bacharach and
David were also anomalous because they enjoyed their biggest (not to
be confused with their greatest) hits later. Incredibly, Bacharach and
David did not have a No. 1 hit record until 1968, with Herb Alpert's
"This Guy's in Love with You," followed in 1969 by B. J. Thomas's
"Raindrops Keep Fallin' on My Head" and in 1970 by the Carpenters'
"(They Long to Be) Close to You." What unites these records and dis-
tinguishes them from No. 1 singles such as "Yakety Yak," "Save the

Last Dance for Me," "Will You Love Me Tomorrow," "Breaking Up Is Hard to Do," "Chapel of Love," and "You've Lost That Lovin' Feelin'"—as well as from the best of Bacharach and David's earlier work—is their vapidity. All those other records drew upon rhythm and blues and/or Latin music. "This Guy's in Love with You," "Raindrops Keep Fallin' on My Head," and "Close to You" expunged every trace of black or brown ethnicity—even the Brazilian rhythms in which Bacharach was adept—and, with that, any hope of excitement.

Bacharach and David succeeded, however, where Leiber and Stoller failed in writing a Broadway musical. *Promises, Promises,* with a book by Neil Simon based on Billy Wilder and I.A.L. Diamond's screenplay for *The Apartment,* opened on December 1, 1968, before an audience that a reporter described as "absolutely resplendent with eyebrow-raising short dresses and eye-blinding men's shirts, ruffled and starched and turtle-necked." (One wonders whether the composer's father, Bert Bacharach, honored in 1971 as Man of the Year by the Men's Apparel Club of New York City, fully approved.) The *New York Times* hailed "the Neil Simon and Burt Bacharach musical," deferring mention of David to the ninth paragraph even though he wrote the lyrics to most of the songs first, and Bacharach set them to music afterward. The show ran for more than three years and 1,281 performances, and spawned a hit single for Dionne Warwick, the sprightly "I'll Never Fall in Love Again." David and Bacharach dashed off the song while the show was trying out in Boston, where Bacharach had been hospitalized with pneumonia.

Bacharach enjoyed the triumph of *Promises, Promises* but was too much of a control freak ever to wish to repeat the experience. It infuriated him that when Richard Rodgers came to hear the show, eight substitute musicians, including the drummer, were in the pit. "The impermanence gets to you because everything shifts from night to night," he explained to one interviewer. "I mean, with a film, if you've got it right, it's embedded forever. . . . If you've got a great take on a record, it's there."

Returning to film, Bacharach and David signed on for a musical remake of Frank Capra's 1937 film adaptation of *Lost Horizon.* The movie was a disaster (casting Charles Boyer as the high lama should have been a tip-off) and led to the dissolution of Bacharach and David's partnership in 1973 and of their collaboration with Warwick as well.

The partings provoked a welter of suits and countersuits in which War-wick sought damages for David and Bacharach's failure to provide her with songs, and the songwriters squabbled over publishing.

Asked if he felt his music had become blander by the end of the 1960s, Bacharach replied, "I don't think that Leiber and Stoller could write a song like 'Yakety Yak' today any more than I could write an-other 'Don't Make Me Over.' It was a part of our lives."

It was the best part, and by the time Bacharach made the cover of *Newsweek* (without David) in 1970, he was no longer of great musical interest.

Chapter Nineteen

FROM THE MONKEES TO THOMAS MANN

★

Don Kirshner saw the future of rock and roll when he heard the Monkees, and he was on the money. He had nothing to do with conceiving the television show or casting the group. Bob Rafelson (who would go on to coauthor and direct the film *Five Easy Pieces*) and Bert Schneider (whose father just happened to be president of Columbia Pictures–Screen Gems) were responsible for that. Nor was Kirshner involved in developing the Monkees' sound. Two young songwriters, Tommy Boyce and Bobby Hart, created, performed, and produced the group's initial "folk & roll," which was a little bit Beatles and, since the project was developed in Los Angeles, a little bit Byrds.

Yet when Columbia Pictures–Screen Gems' television division sold the pilot for a musical situation comedy about a Beatlish but American rock band to NBC in 1966, the recently promoted president of Columbia Pictures–Screen Gems' music division grabbed the chance to mastermind the cross-promotional possibilities of TV and Top Forty radio, a commercial combo he had exploited at Aldon Music by peddling songs to Paul Petersen, Shelly Fabares, and other small-screen juvenile leads. Kirshner boasted that his group would outsell the Beatles and, briefly, it did. (It helped that as the Beatles became driven by their own perfectionism and riven by personal differences, their records were fewer and further between.) His victory was Pyrrhic, however, and led not only to his own undoing but also undermined some of the songwriters he had nurtured. In addition to Aldon alumni, Kirshner's downfall involved Jeff Barry and, on the periphery, Mike Stoller, Jerry Leiber, and even Doc Pomus. The rise and fall of the Monkees would qualify as pop trivia if it did not also mark the eclipse of a song-writing era.

Kirshner and his corporate colleagues made a deal with RCA to distribute the Monkees' records on a new label, Colgems. Distrusting Boyce and Hart as unproven tyros, Kirshner empowered Lester Sill as the group's West Coast music coordinator and persuaded a reluctant Snuff Garrett to produce them, offering him a new Pontiac as a bribe. One frustrating session with the foursome in the studio, at which he tried to add their vocals to a Goffin-King song, "Take a Giant Step," convinced Garrett that in addition to being incapable of playing their instruments, the Monkees could not sing. Garrett quit, warning Kirshner, "I think you got a bunch of fuckin' nitwits here."

Kirshner turned to British producer Mickie Most, whose efforts he evidently found wanting, and then to Carole King and Gerry Goffin. The Monkees were so unruly as well as untalented that the couple returned to New York after one session, King in tears.

Then Kirshner and Sill enlisted Jack Keller, who had not found as much film work as he had hoped after following Howie Greenfield to Los Angeles. Keller added his production expertise to Boyce and Hart's experience with the group, which had taught them, according to Hart, "never to bring more than one of the Monkees at a time into the studio." Kirshner said long-distance from New York, "Jack, I need you to be the heavy." Together the trio would wrestle records out of the obstreperous quartet.

"The Monkees were totally insecure," Keller recalled. "They were actors. They had already gotten into the personas of the people they were playing, which was all this wacky, goofy stuff on screen. They were doing it now in rehearsal. If they didn't goof off, then we'd get down to serious business, listening to how they sounded, who was going to sing what. You couldn't get them to do that. That's what everyone else was walking out on."

The situation was so tense and the stakes so high that Kirshner overcame his fear of flying and attended a Hollywood recording session at which one of the Monkees, Micky Dolenz, after recording the lead vocal for "Take a Giant Step," upended a Coke over Kirshner's head, splattering Keller as well. "Don sat there," Keller said, "and I could tell that he was thinking, 'I could kill him! Well, $400,000—everything's going to go up in smoke?'"

The vaguely psychedelic "Take a Giant Step" was the b-side of the first Monkees hit, Boyce and Hart's "Last Train to Clarksville," which was promoted on the television series and went all the way to No. 1 in November 1966. Even before that, Kirshner had decided to exert more control over the group's music. In an action that recalled Colonel Parker's hammerlock on Presley, he issued a peremptory memo, according to Monkee Mike Nesmith, forbidding anyone to submit a song to the Monkees that he had not cleared. And he decreed that except for a few songs Nesmith was contractually permitted to produce, instrumental tracks for the Monkees' records would be cut in New York, where he could supervise them more closely, and then sent to Los Angeles for the group to add its vocals. Not only would the Monkees not play on their records, but they would have next to no say in them.

Goffin and King set to work producing a couple of Monkees songs in Manhattan and were joined by Neil Sedaka, who produced and played piano on a cheerful ditty he had written with Carole Bayer. The Monkees would later record two songs by Mann and Weil as well. But none of Kirshner's protégés wrote or produced for the Monkees nearly as successfully as two newcomers to the fold: Neil Diamond and Jeff Barry.

When "Cherry, Cherry" caught his ear, Kirshner contacted Diamond and asked if he had any material suitable for the Monkees. Diamond played a song for him that he had written with country singer Eddie Arnold in mind, and Kirshner immediately heard a hit. He excitedly promised Diamond that if "I'm a Believer" reached No. 1, he could write the Monkees' follow-up, too. His excitement did not prevent Kirshner from insisting—indeed, it made him all the more adamant—that he control the publishing. Although Diamond eventually complied, Kirshner confessed he was "a nervous wreck for about a month because [Diamond] held out."

Kirshner hired Barry to produce "I'm a Believer." He cut the rollicking instrumental track, with its Crayola-bright organ lick, unassisted by Greenwich even while he continued to produce Diamond's own records with his ex-wife as partners with Diamond in Tallyrand Music. Barry flew to Los Angeles to play the Monkees the track, and Mike Nesmith sneered, "That ain't no hit." When the ebullient single, with Dolenz singing lead, became the Monkees' biggest record by far, it vindicated Kirshner's assertion of total control and established Barry as a major producer in his own right, unaccompanied by Greenwich. A month after "I'm a Believer" reached No. 1, Barry wed Nancy Calcagno.

Having previously produced records under Leiber and Stoller's supervision, Barry had a unique perspective on Kirshner, whom he compared to George Goldner.

> He was kind of Goldner-ish in that he loves hits. He can't sing, he can't dance. George had music in him. Don's body doesn't function, but he sure has ears. That's the only part of his body that works musically, and that's the only part you need.
>
> Leiber and Stoller can contribute musically. Don doesn't. He contributes to the situation in letting you do your thing. Coming in, he might have a comment: "I don't understand what they're saying there" or "You think that part's too long?" He might question something but not know the answer. Leiber and Stoller might say, "You know, that chord should be *dah-dart*!"—and show you what they think it should be.

When Kirshner made good on his promise and released Diamond's "A Little Bit Me, A Little Bit You" as the Monkees' next single, he designated a mediocre song that Barry had written, "She Hangs Out," as its flip side. At that point the Monkees revolted, demanding a bigger role in their records. When Kirshner presented each of them with a check for $250,000 at the Beverly Hills Hotel, an unmollified Mike Nesmith smashed his fist through the wall. "That could have been your face," he warned Herb Moelis, the Aldon attorney who had followed Kirshner to Columbia–Screen Gems and had become an executive vice president. "We're not recording for you anymore," Nesmith declared. "We want to do our own thing."

Bob Rafelson and Bert Schneider sided with the group they had created, and when Kirshner refused to accommodate them, Bert's father, Abe, fired him. Doc Pomus, who had just signed with Screen Gems and had yet to write a song for his new publisher, felt betrayed and abandoned by Kirshner: "He bullshitted me."

"I think they were getting sick of him for reasons of their own," Monkee Peter Tork suggested. An outraged Kirshner attributed his dis-

missal to corporate jealousy. He had a percentage of the Monkees' profits, and he claimed he was making three times as much money (five
times, in another interview) as Abe Schneider. Kirshner was also out-
performing other Columbia–Screen Gems executives on the corporate
bottom line. In the year running up to the Monkees' distribution deal
with RCA, he had picked and promoted sixty Top Ten records, ten of
them No. 1's, while Columbia's film division fared poorly. Kirshner
was showing up his boss as well as antagonizing his son. "That doesn't
make you friends," Moelis observed.

Moelis thought it absurd that four actors impersonating rock 'n'
rollers on television should demand to play on their records. "What
would happen if on the set of *Superman*, Christopher Reeves said, 'I
want to do the flying'?" Still, there might have been room for compromise, but "Donnie's ego wouldn't allow it." Al Nevins died in 1965,
and Kirshner no longer had an older mentor or partner to restrain him.
The kind of compromise that is a prerequisite in the corporate world
"is hard for an entrepreneur to understand," Moelis explained. "Even if
you're right, you can't fit in as a rebel in a corporation. You can be Martin Scorsese or Orson Welles, but you can't be Orson Welles, Executive
Vice President. Donnie lived like an entrepreneur, he spent like an entrepreneur, and he never changed."

Kirshner hired Edward Bennett Williams, one of Washington's top
attorneys, and sued for $68 million for breach of contract. The equally
high-powered Arthur Liman represented Columbia Pictures–Screen
Gems, and the suit was settled for an undisclosed amount. Kirshner's departure left the songwriters he never stopped thinking of as his kids in
the foster care of Screen Gems, and the Monkees to their own devices.

"The Monkees killed themselves," Keller said. "They killed the
goose that laid the golden eggs." "A Little Bit Me, A Little Bit You"
reached No. 2, but they had lost its producer, who went off to work on
his own projects and Kirshner's, and its author, who had become so big
a star that he no longer needed to write for anyone but himself. Working with various producers, the Monkees recorded more songs by Goffin and King, another by Sedaka and Carol Bayer, and a couple by
Mann and Weil. Only one of these was a hit, Goffin-King's "Pleasant
Valley Sunday," a mild-mannered put-down of suburbia, with "char-
coal burnin' everywhere," including the songwriters' West Orange
backyard, only a few blocks from Pleasant Valley Way. "The local rock

group down the street" could have been the Myddle Class, although the guitar riff on the No. 3 single sounded like the Beatles.

"I need a change of scenery," Micky Dolenz sang on "Pleasant Valley Sunday," and within a year Goffin and King were living apart in Los Angeles, though still collaborating on occasion. They wrote and Goffin produced "Porpoise Song," the theme song to the Monkees' feature film *Head.* It took six recording sessions and twenty musicians (including a twittering porpoise) to record this elephantine ballad that echoed "Lucy in the Sky with Diamonds." Concurrently, the Monkees produced a less laborious song by King and her new writing partner, Toni Stern.

Why could Goffin and King and Mann and Weil write hits for Paul Petersen and James Darren but not, just a few years later, for the equally factitious Monkees? Goffin dismissed the nearly dozen Goffin-King songs the Monkees recorded as "throwaways," but several were much better than that. Mann and Weil's attempts, an ornate ballad and a guitar-driven rocker in oddball 7/4 time, were quite ambitious.

One reason for their failure was what Bobby Hart described as "the evacuation of the record industry out of New York." "I don't know how or why it happened," Cynthia Weil recalled, "but suddenly you found that everybody you wanted to talk to was three hours earlier than you were." Ten years after Leiber and Stoller abandoned Los Angeles because the music business was concentrated in New York, power shifted to California as film, television, and music merged in the entertainment mega-business. Even though Kirshner foresaw and encouraged this merger, he resisted it by trying to retain authority and recording in New York. One by one or two by two, most of New York's pop songwriting teams eventually followed Keller and Greenfield to California. The same year Goffin and King moved separately to Los Angeles, Mann and Weil rented a house there for the summer. But when these writers arrived, they lost a home-court advantage and confidence. The music of the Brill Building and 1650 Broadway had an urban edge and anxiety that sprawling, laid-back Los Angeles dulled.

Second, although it may seem preposterous to describe songwriters on the near side of thirty as over the hill, the audience that Kirshner targeted with the Monkees consisted of teenyboppers. Like the contemporaneous Bee Gees, the Monkees appealed to a subgeneration too young to have gone berserk with Beatlemania and too inexperienced to keep pace with John, Paul, George, and Ringo as they recorded paeans to drugs and protests against war. Yet these youngsters were eager to re-capitulate, in however diluted and debased a form, the excitement that the Fab Four had inspired in their elder siblings. The Aldon songwrit-ers had been trained to go for the juvenile audience as if it were the jugular, but they were beginning to show their age.

Finally, the Monkees' insistence, however naïve, on performing, sometimes producing, and occasionally even writing their own songs challenged the very existence of songwriters like Goffin and King and Mann and Weil and impugned their art as inauthentic. Far from origi-nating this demoralizing trend, which began with the Beatles and Bob Dylan, the Monkees were on its tail end as songwriters became hard-pressed to justify their profession unless they could add to it the prefix "singer." It was time, as Cass Elliott of the Mamas and the Papas sang on one of the several modest hits that Mann and Weil composed for her, to "make your own kind of music, / Sing your own special song."

There was the occasional reprieve and epiphany. Gerry Goffin was walking out of an oyster bar in midtown Manhattan when he bumped into Jerry Wexler, who suggested a title, "Natural Woman," much as he had touted "Young Blood" to Pomus, Leiber, and Stoller a decade earlier. Goffin and King were "in a slump," Goffin recalled, and they "didn't know what to write about." Having found success writing about their teenage experiences, it wasn't easy to make the transition to adult-hood. "There was no audience for it."

"You can't write songs about writing songs," Goffin said, yet now he wrote one of his greatest lyrics about exactly that: "Looking out on the morning rain / I used to feel so uninspired." So began Aretha Franklin's regal "(You Make Me Feel Like) A Natural Woman." Franklin was everything the Monkees were not: mature, prodigiously talented, and black. King and Goffin rose to the occasion of writing for her as they had for the Shirelles and the Drifters, composing one of their most memorable songs. Wexler's production combined church and state, melding Franklin's spare, gospel piano with Arif Mardin's sumptuous orchestral arrangement.

Wexler and Franklin also gave Ellie Greenwich one last chance to strut her stuff. When Wexler played Franklin's torrid rendition of Don Covay's "Chain of Fools" for her, Greenwich, always the astute backup singer, suggested some ingenious fillips to the harmonies. At Wexler's urging, the woman who had wanted to be a Shirelle added her voice to those of the Sweet Inspirations. "Chain of Fools" followed "Natural Woman" and became an even bigger hit in early 1968. Greenwich was uncredited, unpaid, and proud.

Having rescued Franklin from oblivion at Columbia Records and enthroned her as the Queen of Soul, Wexler turned his attention to another female singer who had recently signed with Atlantic. He decided to record Dusty Springfield in Memphis (although the temperamental singer ended up adding her vocals to the instrumental tracks in New York) and chose four songs by Goffin-King, one by Mann-Weil, and one by Bacharach-David. "Jerry Wexler called me," Goffin remembered, "and said he went through our whole catalog. I said, 'You know, you picked the four best songs.'"

Dusty in Memphis might have been expected to be the zenith of these songwriters' careers. Their experience writing for black and British performers could have culminated in the ultimate blue-eyed soul album, and indeed today *Dusty in Memphis* is revered as a classic. But the only hit single it yielded when released was by two little-known Nashville writers. Springfield recorded John Hurley and Ronnie Wilkins's "Son of a Preacher Man" after Franklin, the daughter of a preacher man, turned it down. The album sold poorly in the United States and even worse in England. "We thought we were going to make a lot of money," Goffin said, "but we didn't."

Goffin and King's songs on *Dusty in Memphis* were not throwaways. "So Much Love," "I Can't Make It Alone," "Don't Forget About Me," and especially "No Easy Way Down," a haunting ballad that reflects on a failed marriage, a faltering career, a bad drug trip, or all of the above, are songs with heft. Yet they did not win a hearing even as revivals of "Will You Love Me Tomorrow" by the Four Seasons, "Up on the Roof" by the Cryan' Shames, and "Take Good Care of My Baby" and "Halfway to Paradise" by Bobby Vinton pimpled the charts. The popularity of their own "oldies" made it all the more difficult for the songwriters to mature gracefully.

The b-side of "Son of a Preacher Man" was Weil and Mann's frisky "Just a Little Lovin'," a waltz-time parody (in part) of "What the World Needs Now." Weil's lyric describing early-morning lovemaking, delivered in Springfield's sultriest bedroom voice, sounded a lot sexier than Hal David and Jackie DeShannon's sloganeering "love." Mann and

Weil's hits were trickling toward a halt, but their marriage helped them hang on. "We just always had this hunger to continue," Mann said. "I don't like losing. We always adjusted. And I'm not saying this to be egotistical, but I think I wrote the kind of melodies that are timeless. Some were out there in 1961 that you could have written in 1985."

"Or 1945," Weil added.

Mann and Weil remain unsurpassed as songwriters, Jeff Barry said, characterizing their music as "more serious" and "aimed at a little higher demographic" than his own. "I was always writing for the nine-year-old or the sixteen-year-old girl. Keeping it simple, happy, and repetitive." While Bacharach and David courted older audiences, and Goffin and King and Mann and Weil seemed betwixt and between, Barry pursued the youth market as low as it could go.

Barry continued to work with Kirshner, who, determined that his next hot property would not rebel against him, developed the Archies, a band that existed only in animated form. A Saturday morning cartoon show starring the comic book characters promoted songs that Barry cowrote and produced. The third single, "Sugar, Sugar," featured the voices of Ron Dante, one of the Detergents, who had lampooned "Leader of the Pack" as "Leader of the Laundromat," and Toni Wine, who had written "A Groovy Kind of Love" with Carol Bayer. Its title tipped its hat to Neil Diamond's "Cherry, Cherry" and evoked the sickly sweet cereals and treats advertised on children's television. The song was equally empty but addictive. Exemplary "bubblegum" rock, it became the biggest-selling record of 1969.

"I had three- and four-year-olds at the time," Barry said, explaining that the Archies "were aimed at preschoolers. So who else was I going to write for except little kids? To judge that material as simplistic kids' stuff is like some food reviewer reviewing a candy cane and saying the nutritional value is highly suspect."

But most of the other music that Barry cowrote and produced during the late 1960s was also cloying. Barry launched a record label, Steed, whose name recalled his childhood fondness for cowpokes and ponies. He housed it as well as a publishing company and a recording studio in a brownstone one block from 1650 Broadway, on Fifty-second Street. Andy Kim, a Canadian singer and songwriter with whom Barry wrote most of the Archies material, had a string of hit singles on Steed that included revivals of Greenwich and Barry's "Be My Baby" and "Baby,

I Love You" as well as several Barry-Kim compositions. Kim's thin, bland tenor was utterly anonymous, and Barry, formerly an adventurous producer, fell back on formulas.

"You don't need a protractor to draw a line from 'Da Doo Ron Ron' to 'Bang Shang-a-Lang,'" an admirer observed of the Archies' first single. The records Barry and Greenwich wrote were frequently and deliberately infantile, but there the comparison to Barry's subsequent collaborations with Kim and other writers ends. While Greenwich had no success without Barry—she never wrote or produced a song of consequence without him—Barry had no personality without Greenwich. The baby talk and nonsense syllables in the best Greenwich-Barry songs bubbled with individuality and spunk. "Do Wah Diddy Diddy" conjured up a walk, a talk, a whole world of sass. While Greenwich imbued songs with attitude, the songs Barry composed afterward were generic. They succeeded only in the short term as the shrinking market for singles was reduced to juveniles while older teenagers and young adults purchased albums. Andy Kim and Archies singles are seldom heard today, while the Greenwich-Barry songs recorded by the Ronettes, Tommy James and the Shondells, Manfred Mann, and others are continually replayed and revived.

★

Barry and Greenwich's former employers, Leiber and Stoller, were unlikely songwriters to become involved with the Monkees, but Lester Sill, the songwriters' original mentor and partner, remained at Columbia Pictures–Screen Gems after Kirshner's ouster. Leiber and Stoller had written and produced a song for the Coasters that combined the parodistic evangelism of LaVern Baker's "Saved" with the wino wit and wisdom of the Coasters' earlier "What Is the Secret of Your Success?" "D. W. Washburn" starred Billy Guy as a drunk who refused to be rescued from the gutter. The Coasters had left Atco and were now on a Columbia subsidiary that didn't know what to make of the record or how to market a group that had not had a hit in several years. Leiber and Stoller sent the unreleased recording to Sill. Although Carl Gardner was the sole survivor of the original group, the track brought back memories of the Robins when they cut "Riot in Cell Block #9" thirteen years earlier for Leiber, Stoller, and Sill's Spark label. Sill urged the Monkees to record the song, and though Micky Dolenz was no Billy

Guy and the group seemed to have little clue what they were singing about, "D. W. Washburn" was the last Monkees single to skulk into the Top Twenty.

By then Leiber and Stoller had lost interest altogether in teenyboppers and even, for the most part, in rock 'n' roll. While still struggling to compose a Broadway show, they entertained the British singer Georgia Brown, star of the musical *Oliver!,* and her music director, Peter Matz. (Small world: Matz had recommended Bacharach to Marlene Dietrich.) To Stoller's piano accompaniment, Leiber recited some snippets of prose. These weren't the talking blues. What Leiber and Stoller were doing sounded in no way black and did not draw on the African-American oral and musical traditions they had helped introduce into the pop musical mainstream. Leiber was adapting and sometimes quoting directly an 1896 short story by Thomas Mann. In fewer than five pages—no longer than a hit single—"Disillusionment" described a brief encounter in Venice with a man whose disappointed response to every event in his life, from a childhood fire to young romance, was "Is that all there is to it?" Even death, he was sure, would only prove to be "that last disappointment." So much for the apocalypticism of American teenage pop, from the urgency of Presley's "It's Now or Never" to the Shangri-Las' *"Liebestod."* When the narrator of Leiber and Stoller's song is abandoned by his or her lover, he/she "thought I'd die . . . / but I didn't . . . / and when I didn't I said to myself / 'Is that all there is to love?' "

It was a long way from alley music to the Piazza San Marco. Like Mort Shuman, Leiber and Stoller were forsaking American popular song for European art (or at least cabaret) song, but instead of Jacques Brel, they turned for inspiration to Kurt Weill, or the echoes of Weill in John Kander and Fred Ebb's musical *Cabaret.* Georgia Brown, who had performed in Brecht-Weill's *Threepenny Opera* in London and New York, applauded and encouraged Leiber and Stoller to come up with a chorus.

When they did, Leslie Uggams recorded it. The young black star of Mitch Miller's *Sing Along with Mitch* television series had graduated to supper clubs, Broadway, and her own TV specials. Leiber and Stoller produced an album hideously entitled *What's an Uggams?* that featured three of their own compositions in addition to four tracks by Bacharach-David (two of which Leiber and Stoller owned a piece of through U.S. Songs, the short-lived joint publishing venture the four of them had formed) and Greenwich-Barry-Spector's "River Deep–Mountain High" (which Leiber and Stoller also partly owned). Leiber and Stoller seemed as determined as Bacharach and David to woo an older audience, and they made even fewer commercial concessions. *What's an Uggams?* was sophisticated but staid. It didn't rock *or* swing. And Uggams lacked the experience, the irony, and the wiles to sing "Is That All There Is?" She could scarcely bring herself to sound the "z" in "booze," and it was too early in her career for her to feel, much less express, the song's disenchantment.

Age was no impediment to Peggy Lee, who understood "Is That All There Is?" perfectly. She had sung with Benny Goodman's band before Leiber and Stoller reached puberty, and she had scored a minor hit in 1963 with "I'm a Woman," their proto-feminist parody of Bo Diddley's "I'm a Man" that recycled the Chicago blues riff the songwriters had appropriated for "Riot in Cell Block #9." In 1969, Lee recorded "Is That All There Is?" with an arrangement by Randy Newman that was subtler and queasier than Pat Williams's banjo-heavy singalong chart for Uggams. She insisted that Capitol Records release it as a single despite the company's initial resistance, and she was rewarded with her last major hit, which also turned out to be Leiber and Stoller's last major hit with a new (or newish) song.

And that's all there was. By 1969 the songwriting community that Leiber and Stoller had helped foster a dozen years earlier had grown up, fallen apart, and dispersed. Partnerships and marriages dissolved. Power in the music industry migrated from New York to Los Angeles, and creativity to a variety of venues from Philadelphia to San Francisco to Miami. Black power and self-sufficiency superseded the racial integration that these songwriters had championed as African-American artists, producers, entrepreneurs, and audiences overcame their dependency and the need for white middlemen and -women. The influence of Afro-Cuban music waned and waxed repeatedly as Latinos became more independent and marketers sliced and diced the audience for popular music into narrower segments by ethnicity and age. Singer-songwriters and groups who composed their own material supplanted songwriters. Even though many of them could not sing or could not write, their music frequently made up in impact on listeners and profitability for the performers what it sometimes lost in artistry.

The Brill Building and 1650 Broadway inexorably turned from hives of musical activity into shells, just as Tin Pan Alley's earlier outpost on West Twenty-eighth Street had calcified. Today the elevators in the Brill Building are more likely to open on the offices of a film or video company than a music publisher. Those cubicles that remain contain computers, not pianos. But in 1650 you may still be able to find a receptionist who moonlights as a Shangri-La.

CODA

★

The end of the sixties sealed some songwriters' careers. Those who clung the most obstinately to New York fared the most poorly. Ellie Greenwich made a couple of unsuccessful stabs at a solo career, suffered a nervous breakdown, and turned to writing, producing, and performing advertising jingles. Doc Pomus all but stopped writing for nearly a decade, during which he supported himself in part by running poker games from his bedside. When he resumed composing, he returned to his beloved blues, writing songs with Mac Rebennack, "Dr. John," for the likes of B. B. King and crusading to win aging R&B performers the royalties, respect, and gigs they deserved. Shortly after becoming the first white person to receive the Rhythm and Blues Foundation's Pioneer Award, he died of cancer on March 14, 1991, at the age of sixty-five.

Leiber and Stoller became bicoastal and transatlantic. They produced a few albums, most notably Stealers Wheel's eponymous first album, which yielded the hit single "Stuck in the Middle with You," and the fractious Scots-English group's follow-up, *Ferguslie Park.* Although they became extremely successful publishers (naming one of their companies Alley Music), they never got anywhere with musicals. When they finally made it to Broadway in 1995, it was with *Smokey Joe's Café,* a wildly popular nostalgic revue of songs they had composed more than a quarter century earlier.

Hal David wrote only one big hit after breaking up with Burt Bacharach in 1973. With Albert Hammond he composed Julio Iglesias and Willie Nelson's mawkish 1984 duet "To All the Girls I Ever Loved Before." He made his greatest contribution to songwriting as president of ASCAP and chairman of the Songwriters Hall of Fame.

Jeff Barry also disappeared from the charts after collaborating with Peter Allen on the sentimental ballad "I Honestly Love You," a No. 1 hit for Olivia Newton-John in 1974. The producer of the Monkees and the Archies continued to prosper on television, cowriting the theme songs for *The Jeffersons, One Day at a Time,* and *Family Ties.*

Barry Mann and Cynthia Weil soldiered on, surviving even a marital separation in the 1980s and writing hits for artists as diverse as pop singer B. J. Thomas (the sublime "Rock and Roll Lullaby"), crossover country diva Dolly Parton (the spry "Here You Come Again"), R&B crooners James Ingram and Jeffrey Osborne, Brazilian bandleader Sergio Mendes, and teen rockers Hanson. Collaborating with Tom Snow, Weil updated the girl-group sound with the Pointer Sisters' delightful "He's So Shy." Together, Mann and Weil wrote the music for the animated film *An American Tail,* whose theme song, "Somewhere Out There," became a hit for Ingram and Linda Ronstadt in 1987. Although many of their later songs have been big, bland ballads, no pop music songwriting team has remained together, active, and successful as long as Weil and Mann.

Gerry Goffin might have seemed the least likely songwriter to survive, yet he managed to write two No. 1 songs with Michael Masser: Diana Ross's "Theme from Mahogany (Do You Know Where You're Going To)" in 1976 and Whitney Houston's "Saving All My Love for You" in 1985, as well as Top Ten hits for Gladys Knight and the Pips and the Partridge Family. He did not lose his ability to put words in women's mouths or his attraction to drugs. In the early 1990s, he wrote a few songs with Bacharach, who called it quits because he could not tolerate Goffin's cocaine habit. "Now I'm basically retired," Goffin said, noting that "after I split from Carole, most of the women I lived with didn't care for any of my music, and they always brought home the next Dylan album. . . . I've given up trying to be a great lyricist. I'm just trying to be an adequate one."

The writers who stepped into the spotlight and performed their own songs had better luck prolonging their careers or launching new ones. Carole King, with the encouragement of James Taylor, became one of the most popular singer-songwriters of the 1970s. Taylor's version of King's "You've Got a Friend" and her own rendition of "It's Too Late," written with Toni Stern, were No. 1 singles in 1971 (so was a remake by Donny Osmond of Goffin-King's "Go Away Little Girl"), and *Tapes-*

try was the biggest-selling album of the year and the decade. King wed Charles Larkey, from the Myddle Class, and when that marriage dissolved, she married another musician, Rick Evers, who died a year later of a heroin overdose. Throughout the ups and downs of her personal life she has continued to record and, less frequently, to perform, often on behalf of environmental causes and Democrats.

Neil Sedaka had never shied away from performing, but it took him longer to return to the limelight. Moving to England, he recorded there and won the friendship and backing of Elton John. In 1975, Sedaka had an astounding three No. 1 singles in the United States: his own "Bad Blood" and "Laughter in the Rain" plus "Love Will Keep Us Together," performed by the Captain and Tennille, who cheered as the song ended, "Sedaka's back." Two more of his records, as well as the Carpenters' "Solitaire," a gorgeous ballad, placed high in the charts.

One casualty of Sedaka's brief comeback was Howie Greenfield, whom Sedaka replaced as his principal lyricist with Phil Cody. "Love Will Keep Us Together" was the last Sedaka-Greenfield collaboration to become a hit, and Greenfield enjoyed little commercial success thereafter. He died of AIDS on March 4, 1986, and Tory Damon succumbed to the disease a few days later. Sedaka, who was performing in Bombay and unable to attend Greenfield's funeral, tours indefatigably to this day. In 2004 he gave a concert of Yiddish songs at Carnegie Hall, harking back to his performance of "*Mein Yiddische Mama*" on *The Ed Sullivan Show* forty-two years earlier.

The revival of fortunes that King and Sedaka enjoyed in the 1970s was remarkable but not as incredible as Mort Shuman's transformation. No longer satisfied with translating and performing Jacques Brel, Shuman decided to become him. He moved to France and became a major pop star there, singing in French and breaking only occasionally into English. He never disguised or denied his Jewish roots or Brooklyn origins. One of his hits even incorporated strains of "Hava Nagila" into a guided tour of his hometown: "*Si tu viens ici / C'est dans un taxi / Dis au driver,* 'Brighton Beach / Brooklyn by the Sea.'" Yet he reinvented himself once more, this time as "the new prince of French pop," he wrote, and "man of the year (*France-Soir* said it, so it must be true)." In the late 1980s, Shuman moved to London, where he died of complications following an operation for liver disease on January 2, 1991, three months before Doc Pomus. He was fifty-four years old.

Nineteen ninety-one was also the first year since 1955 that not a single song, old or new, by any of these songwriters appeared on the American pop charts. But as the century ended, the ever anomalous Burt Bacharach suddenly came back in vogue. After parting company with Hal David and then Angie Dickinson, he found a new lyricist and wife in Carole Bayer Sager, who had added Sager to her name and also married and divorced the songwriter and composer Marvin Hamlisch. Bacharach wrote three No. 1 songs with Sager: Christopher Cross's "Arthur's Theme" (for which Cross and Peter Allen shared credit) in 1981 and Dionne Warwick, Gladys Knight, Stevie Wonder, and Elton John's AIDS fund-raising anthem "That's What Friends Are For" and Patti LaBelle and Michael McDonald's duet "On My Own," both in 1986. Such celebrity schmaltz seemed to confirm that Bacharach had gone utterly Hollywood and was less committed to music than to his stable of thoroughbred horses.

Bacharach and Sager divorced, and the songwriter appeared headed out to pasture when the man whom the original *Rolling Stone Illustrated History of Rock & Roll* scarcely deigned to mention defied expectations by becoming an icon to a generation young enough to be his grandchildren. Just as the English had acclaimed Bacharach and David thirty years earlier, the buzz began once again in Great Britain. Elvis Costello had always appreciated Bacharach-David's songs and had performed "I Just Don't Know What to Do with Myself" early in his career. Now he was joined by young bands like Oasis that were seeking, however ineffectually, to restore melody to rock and to replicate the glamour and excitement of an era that had evaporated before they were born. Bacharach's cameo appearance in the first Austin Powers film not only evoked the nostalgia for swinging London that Mike Myers's movie exploited but also acknowledged its debt to *Casino Royale*. Meanwhile, in America a recidivist generation buoyed by the bubble of a high-tech economy and bored by feminism rediscovered the pleasures of cocktails and what it dubbed "lounge music." Suddenly Bacharach was swank.

He did not disappoint his admirers, who tended to forget—as Bacharach himself did—Hal David. Bacharach collaborated with Costello on a song and then an entire CD. Before Costello wed Diana Krall, the Canadian singer-pianist recorded "The Look of Love," the title track of a best-selling CD. Bacharach himself produced, arranged, and conducted live a 2003 CD on which Ronald Isley reinterpreted classic Bacharach-David material and made even "Close to You" sound soulful and sexy. And in 2004, Steve Tyrell, forty-five years after Leiber and Stoller's strings on "There Goes My Baby" inspired him "to get the fuck out of Texas and move to New York," released a popular CD of standards that included, alongside George and Ira Gershwin's "They Can't Take That Away from Me" and Cole Porter's "You'd Be So Nice to Come Home To," Bacharach and David's "I Just Don't Know What to Do with Myself" and "This Guy's in Love with You."

★

As this book entered its final editing stages, I was browsing for a card to condole with my brother on his fiftieth birthday when the store's sound system surprised me with a song that was forty-five years old: "Nobody but Me." Written by Pomus and Shuman, produced by Leiber and Stoller, it was to have been the a-side of a Drifters single until the flip side, "Save the Last Dance for Me," prevailed. The gospel call-and-response of the vocals, the rumba in the bass line, and the scintillation of the strings identified the song as a typical Brill Building smorgasbord of African-American, Afro-Cuban, and European flavorings even before I recalled its title.

One of the great appeals and legacies of the songs of the Brill Building era is their racial and ethnic integration—and how easy and irresistible they make such integration seem. Seldom in subsequent decades has music spoken to and spoken for so many different Americans. By the 1970s, when I taught in college, one of my freshman classes could not name a single pop song that everyone knew until we finally came up with "Let It Be"—which some black students, never having heard the Beatles' version, believed Aretha Franklin had originated. By 2001, when my daughter entered college, musical lines had been drawn not just between races but within them. A preregistration form asked what kinds of music she liked and did not like, for fear of assigning her an incompatible roommate.

But the songs of the Brill Building era blended more than black, brown, and white. They also struck a fine balance between words, melody, harmony, and rhythm that respected all four equally. You can dance to these songs, you can listen to their lyrics, you can savor their tunes and add your voice to their harmonies. This may not seem more difficult than patting your head and rubbing your stomach at the same time until you consider the diminished role that melody and harmony play in most contemporary popular songs. The stuttering beats and rapid-fire wordplay of hip-hop, by far the most innovative and influential genre of the past few decades, reduce melody to a drive-by hook or sample. Heavy metal and other abrasive forms of hard rock are often even less tuneful.

A great deal of music today is lopsided, emphasizing some elements of song over others, serving some purposes over others, targeting some audiences over others. Technology drives this differentiation and specialization relentlessly further. Sirius Satellite Radio offers forty-nine different pop, rock, country, hip-hop, R&B/urban, and dance/electronic channels. Computer downloading, file-sharing, and iPods take market segmentation to the ultimate extreme, narrowing the niche to an audience of one.

On the one hand, this is extremely liberating. No longer do we have to endure a deejay's dreary countdown or purchase an overpriced CD to hear the one song we desire. We can access or order on the Internet nearly everything that has ever been recorded. On the other hand, the conditions under which music is created and disseminated today can be alienating. The consolidation of the record industry into four multinational behemoths has constrained audiences and artists alike and threatens to turn infinite individual choice into an illusion: Bruce Springsteen's "fifty-seven channels and nothin' on."

Somewhere between the isolated individual consumer and mass-marketing conglomerates lies the ideal if not always the reality of community, at once intimate and inclusive. The songwriters in this book formed a family united by their youth, their Jewish roots, their upbringing in New York City's outer boroughs (for the most part), their employment in midtown Manhattan, their love of black and Latin music, the company they kept, and the publishing and record companies that kept them. Their music helped forge a far larger community that embraced much of America and extended overseas to England and beyond.

The songwriters of the Brill Building era created this community by making what Carole King called in one interview "an emotional connection" and by communicating their joy in this bond. "I think if there's not an emotional connection—if it's just business—fine; you can sell lots of records by making something that's commercial. If there's no emotional connection in it, I don't think it's art." King continued, "The primary purpose back then was to make money, but in the process, we had so much joy in it. We went into the areas of 'What do we want to say? Let's do this! Let's do that!' But it was out of the joy of making a great song."

The songwriters in the Brill Building and 1650 Broadway were not alone or unique. They were joined and in many ways emulated, as we have seen, by Motown and by the Beatles and their subalterns in the British Invasion. Music and community coalesced in the 1960s for a "magic moment, so different and so new," to borrow from another context a line from Pomus and Shuman. To celebrate the music of that decade is not necessarily to succumb to Wordsworthian nostalgia: "Bliss was it in that dawn to be alive, / But to be young was very heaven!" Because even if the music does not last, like Pomus and Shuman's bliss, "forever 'til the end of time," it still resounds a half century later.

ACKNOWLEDGMENTS

"It's a lot easier writing about dead people," my wife warned me. As usual, she was right. There are few reliable written accounts of the Brill Building era, and virtually none that corroborates one person's imperfect memory or vivid imagination with other people's recollections. Tracking down everyone I needed to speak to in order to write this book, wending my way through assistants and entourages, and wheedling interviews were extremely time-consuming, frequently frustrating, and occasionally humiliating. Far more often than not, however, persistence was ultimately rewarded with surprising courtesy and friendly cooperation.

Among the principals in this book, Barry Mann, Cynthia Weil, Jeff Barry, Ellie Greenwich, and Neil Sedaka were extraordinarily generous with their time and thoughts. So were the family and friends of "Doc" Pomus: Sharyn Felder, Will Bratton, Raoul Felder, Willi Epstein, and Shirlee Hauser. I would also like to thank Mike Stoller, Jerry Leiber, Burt Bacharach, Hal David, and especially Gerry Goffin for speaking to me, and Mort Shuman's widow and attorney, Maria Pia Shuman and Charles Negus-Fancey, for providing me with portions of Shuman's handwritten autobiographical sketch and permitting me to quote from them.

I am deeply indebted to scores of other people who talked with me at length, often invited me into their homes, responded to my e-mails and in many instances patiently answered pestering follow-up questions. First and foremost among these is the late Jack Keller, followed by Susan Aberbach, Stanley Applebaum, Al Aronowitz, Brooks Arthur, Dick Asher, Mark Barkan, Freddy Bienstock, Johnny Bienstock, Eric Blau, Maxine Brown, Artie Butler, Al Contrera, Ed Cramer, Jackie DeShannon, Paul Evans, Fabian Forte, Dick Fox, Snuff Garrett, Al Gorgoni, Richard Gottehrer, Bobby Hart, Hank Hunter, Larry Kolber, Judy Jeffreys Lotwin, Rod McBrien, Hank Medress, Mitch Miller, Herb Moelis, George "Shadow" Morton, Elaine Orlando, Tony Orlando, Jerry Ragovoy, Artie Resnick, Artie Ripp, Irwin Robinson, Beverly Ross, Jay Siegal, Mary Weiss Stokes, Meryl Stoller, Elly Stone, Charlie Thomas, Russ Titelman, Steve Tyrell, Kenny Vance, Stan Vincent, Ben Weisman, and Jerry Wexler.

Among secondary sources I am particularly grateful to Morgan Neville. No one contributed more to this book than the director of *Hitmakers: The Teens Who Stole Pop Music, Words and Music by Leiber & Stoller,* and *Burt Bacharach,* three superb documentaries that aired on the A&E cable television network's *Biography* series. Morgan kindly gave me transcripts of the interviews he conducted for these films, which frequently spared me the necessity and others the tedium of rehearsing yet again the same old questions and answers. He also provided many phone numbers, other contact information, and invaluable friendly advice.

I am also greatly beholden to Usha Popuri, librarian at Abraham Lincoln High School, and Jeffrey Litman at James Madison High School (both in Brooklyn), George Boziwick at the New York Public Library for the Performing Arts, and the rest of the staff at that library as well as those of New York City's Humanities and Social Sciences Library, Science, Industry and Business Library, and Mid-town Manhattan Library, and the New-York Historical Society Library, Montclair State University's Harry A. Sprague Library, and the Montclair (N.J.) Public Library.

I began to develop the ideas and conduct the research for this book at Princeton University as the Philip Anschutz Distinguished Visiting Fellow in American Studies. I am grateful to Mr. Anschutz and his daughters for this honor and opportunity, as well as to the friends I made at Princeton, especially Sean Wilentz, Dick Hartog, and Judith Ferszt.

For favors professional and personal, I would also like to thank Bill DeMain, Brian Gari, Gregg Geller, Jesse Goffin, Alex Halberstadt, Tony Heilbut, Floyd Mutrux, Bill Pepper, Randy Poe, Steve Scharf, Tony Scherman, Nizza Thobi, David G. Transom, and the intrepid investigative reporter Jennifer Weiss.

Sharyn Felder, Will Bratton, David Sanjek and BMI, Russ Titelman, Neil Sedaka, Brian Gari, and David G. Transom were extremely helpful with photographs, and I thank them one and all.

The enthusiasm, fine ear, and sharp eye of my editor, Rick Kot, and the conscientiousness of his assistant, Alessandra Lusardi, serendipitously a former student of mine, contributed greatly to this book, which is their creation nearly as much as it is mine.

Finally, as always, I would like to thank my agent, Gloria Loomis, my wife, Ellen, and my daughter, Maude, for their unfailing faith and support.

NOTES

INTRODUCTION

x   **"Get me another drink":** Nevil Shute, *On the Beach* (New York: Signet/New American Library, paper, 1958), 81–82.

xi   **"dreamed the usual Brooklyn dreams . . .":** Michael Chabon, *The Amazing Adventures of Kavalier & Clay* (New York: Picador, paper, 2000), 6.

xi   **"jumped into radio . . .":** Clark Whelton in the *New York Times,* quoted in Arnold Shaw, *Honkers and Shouters: The Golden Years of Rhythm and Blues* (New York: Macmillan, 1978), 512.

xii   **That's why Buddy Borsalino:** Richard Price, *The Wanderers* (Boston: Mariner, paper, 1999), 201–02.

xii   **The catch-all term:** Russell Sanjek, *American Popular Music and Its Business: The First Four Hundred Years,* Vol. 3, *From 1900 to 1984* (New York: Oxford University Press, 1988), 387; Timothy White, *Long Ago and Far Away: James Taylor, His Life and Music* (London, Omnibus, 2001), 161.

xiii   **"all but dead":** Charlie Gillett, *The Sound of the City: The Rise of Rock and Roll* (New York: Outerbridge & Dienstfrey, 1970), 77.

xiii   **"Rock and roll got very bad . . .":** Paul Simon, quoted in Patrick Humphries, *The Boy in the Bubble: A Biography of Paul Simon* (London: Sidgwick & Jackson, 1988), 15.

xiii   **"Things were pretty sleepy . . .":** Bob Dylan, *Chronicles: Volume One* (New York: Simon & Schuster, 2004), 5–6.

xiii   **"the dynamite . . .":** Gillett, *The Sound of the City,* 48.

xiii   **When Elvis Presley entered:** Sanjek, *American Popular Music,* 343.

xiii   **The market:** James Miller, *Flowers in the Dustbin: The Rise of Rock and Roll, 1947–1977* (New York: Simon & Schuster, 1999), 144; Marc Eliot, *Rockonomics: The Money Behind the Music* (New York: Franklin Watts, 1989), 27.

xiv   **"More than anyone else . . .":** Mark Ribowsky, *He's a Rebel: Phil Spector, Rock and Roll's Legendary Producer* (New York: Cooper Square Press, paper, 1989), 112.

xv   **"I always admire . . .":** Quoted in Bill DeMain, "Carole King: New Threads in the Tapestry," *Performing Songwriter* 79 (July/August 2004), 52.

CHAPTER ONE: THE ORIGINAL COOL CATS

1   **Presley sauntered:** Peter Guralnick, *Last Train to Memphis: The Rise of Elvis Presley* (Boston: Little, Brown, 1994), 273.

1   *Andrea Doria*: Mike Stoller's experience aboard the *Andrea Doria* and adrift is recounted in William Hoffer's *Saved! The Story of the* Andrea Doria—*the Greatest Sea Rescue in History* (New York: Summit, 1979) and Richard Goldstein's *Desperate Hours: The Epic Rescue of the* Andrea Doria (New York: John Wiley, 2001).

1   **a relieved and elated Leiber:** Mike Stoller, e-mail communication, 1 February 2005; Cleothus Hardcastle, "The Backpages Interview: Jerry Leiber and Mike Stoller, *Rock's Backpages,* 27 June 2001, http://www.rocksbackpages.com/news/3006_hardcastle_lands. html.

1   **reached No. 1:** Unless otherwise noted, all chart positions for single records are drawn from Joel Whitburn, *Joel Whitburn's Pop Annual 1955–1999* (Menomonee Falls, WI: Record Research Inc., paper, 2000).

2   **an exception:** Mike Stoller, e-mail communication, May 2002.

3   **"I identified . . .":** Quoted in Joe Smith, *Off the Record: An Oral History of Popular Music,* ed. Mitchell Fink (New York: Warner Books, 1990), 120.

3   **"Those radios . . .":** Quoted in Robert Palmer, *Baby, That Was Rock & Roll: The Legendary Leiber & Stoller* (New York: Harvest/Harcourt Brace Jovanovich, paper, 1978), 13.

3   **Mike Stoller was born:** Information regarding Stoller's childhood is drawn from Mike Stoller, interview, 14 May 2001; Ted Fox, *In the Groove: The People Behind the Music* (New York: St. Martin's, 1986), 158; Palmer, *Baby,* 16; and Harvey R. Kubernik, "A Yakety Yak with Leiber and Stoller," *Goldmine* 385, vol. 21, no. 9 (28 April 1995), 66.

3   **on the recommendation of a drummer:** Kubernik, 67–68.

3   **"It was like, 'Wow . . .' ":** Meryl Stoller, interview, 10 July 2002.

4   **"Assorted":** Freddy Bienstock, interview, 26 February 2002.

4   **"I was afraid . . .":** Kenny Vance, interview, 26 March 2002.

4   **"They were the original . . .":** Steve Tyrell, interview, 19 February 2002.

4   **Chet Baker:** Hardcastle, "The Backpages Interview: Jerry Leiber and Mike Stoller."

4   **b-side of a single:** "Alley Music" appeared in 1955 as the b-side of Spark 112, "My Four Women," by The Sly Fox. (Blues singer Eugene Fox was produced and accompanied by Ike Turner.)

4   **On the eve of World War I:** Richard Hadlock, *Jazz Masters of the Twenties* (New York: Collier, paper, 1974), 146–47, quoting an interview with Johnson by Tom Davin published in *The Jazz Review* in 1959.

4   **he listened surreptitiously:** Mike Stoller, interview, 14 May 2001; "Those Magic Moments: Doc Pomus Remembered by His Friends and Peers," *Goldmine* (19 April 1991), 9.

4   **"Alley, Alley, Alley":** Raoul Felder, interview, 2 March 2001.

5   **The city's black population:** Ralph Eastman, "Pitchin' Up a Boogie," in Jacqueline Cogdell DjeDje and Eddie S. Meadows, eds., *California Soul: Music of African Americans in the West* (Berkeley: University of California Press, paper, 1998), 95–96.

5   **"The big, first surge . . .":** Ralph Bass, quoted in Shaw, *Honkers and Shouters,* 245.

5   **"People talk . . .":** Steve Roeser, "Ain't Nobody's Business: The No Rollin' Blues

of Jimmy Witherspoon," *Goldmine* 413, vol. 22, no. 10 (24 May 1996), 88. Also see Charlie Gillett, *Making Tracks: Atlantic Records and the Growth of a Multi-Billion-Dollar Industry* (New York: E. P. Dutton, 1974), 11; and Barney Hoskyns, *Waiting for the Sun: Strange Days, Weird Scenes, and the Sound of Los Angeles* (New York: St. Martin's/Griffin, paper, 1999), 5–37.

5   **Witherspoon idolized:** Roeser, 86; Eastman, "Pitchin' Up a Boogie," in DjeDje and Meadows, 94.

5   **"He's a white guy . . .":** Shaw, *Honkers and Shouters,* 211–12.

5   **Witherspoon became the first . . .** Mike Stoller, e-mail communication, May 2002.

5   **"When Jerry and I . . .":** Smith, *Off the Record,* 122.

6   **"It was a *secret world* . . .":** Kubernik, 124.

6   **"a predilection . . .":** Walter Mosley, *Devil in a Blue Dress.* New York: Pocket Books, paper, 1997, 19.

6   **"*We did.*":** Hardcastle.

6   **"Jazz is orgasm . . .":** Norman Mailer, "The White Negro: Superficial Reflections on the Hipster," reprinted in Robert F. Lucid, ed., *The Long Patrol: Twenty-five Years of Writing from the Work of Norman Mailer* (New York: World Publishing, 1971), 212.

6   **"At lilac evening . . .":** Jack Kerouac, *On the Road* (New York: Penguin, paper, 1991), 179–80.

6   **"The way they are treating . . .":** Quoted in Gary Giddins, *Satchmo: The Genius of Louis Armstrong* (New York: Dolphin/Doubleday, 1988), 163.

6   **"old-fashioned spade kicks . . .":** Kerouac, *On the Road,* 251.

7   **"why white musicians . . .":** Milton "Mezz" Mezzrow and Bertram Wolfe, *Really the Blues* (New York: Random House, 1946), 82–83.

7   **"I felt black.":** David Fricke, "Leiber & Stoller," *Rolling Stone,* 19 April 1990 (unpaginated reprint).

7   **"Race, Negro.":** Mezzrow and Wolfe, 328, 301–6, 252–53, 5.

7   **"the first self-conscious *students* . . .":** Hadlock, 110.

7   **Under the gaze:** Palmer, 11; Dave "Daddy Cool" Booth, "Jerry Leiber & Mike Stoller: What Is the Secret of Your Success?," ed. Colin Escott, *Goldmine* 111, vol. 10, no. 20 (26 October 1984), 28.

8   **"We felt . . .":** Fricke.

8   **fifteen minutes to write:** Ibid.

8   **"novelty jump":** Palmer, 33; James M. Salem, *The Late Great Johnny Ace and the Transition from R&B to Rock 'n' Roll* (Urbana: University of Illinois Press, 1999), 79.

9   **"disappointed":** Hardcastle.

9   **"The idea was . . .":** Quoted by Randy Poe in his notes to *Leiber and Stoller Present the Spark Records Story* (Ace CDCHD 801).

10   **vaudeville and chitlin' circuit skits:** Steve Propes, "Johnny Otis," *Goldmine* 200, vol. 14, no. 7 (25 March 1988), 8.

10   **Leiber himself cited:** Kubernik, 67.

10   **the Robins had originally:** Propes, "Johnny Otis," 8.

10   **he heard Amos Wilburn:** Kubernik, 66.

10   **"a little company":** Booth, 28–30.

10   **"a collectively improvised . . .":** Mezzrow and Wolfe, 103.

11   **"Jerry Leiber would actually . . .":** Kenny Vance, interview, 26 March 2002.

11   **"Those voices just happened . . .":** Quoted in Fricke.

11   **"Never trust . . .":** D. H. Lawrence, *Studies in Classic American Literature* (New York: Viking, paper, 1964), 2.

11   **dallied with a left-wing commune:** Greil Marcus discusses this commune in *Dead Elvis: A Chronicle of a Cultural Obsession* (New York: Doubleday, paper, 1991), 100–101, 105. According to Jim Miller's *Flowers in the Dustbin* (p. 362), Marcus's account is based on an interview of Leiber and Stoller conducted by Michael Roloff. A close reading of this unpublished interview strongly suggests that only Leiber participated in this commune and not Stoller, contrary to Marcus's and Miller's accounts.

11   **Guy Endore:** See Carlos M. Larralde and Richard Griswold del Castillo, "Luisa Moreno and the Beginnings of the Mexican American Civil Rights Movement in San Diego," *Journal of San Diego History*, vol. 43, no. 3 (summer 1997), http://www.sandiegohistory.org/journal/97summer/moreno.htm.

11   **"like looks could kill . . .":** Hardcastle.

12   **You couldn't get three whiter people . . .":** The Bregman quote appears on www.thecheers.com, attributed to *Motion Picture Magazine* (January 1962).

12   **sold the song's foreign rights:** Shaw, *Honkers and Shouters*, 418.

13   **Leiber and Stoller worked extensively with the Cheers:** In addition to "Bazoom (I Need Your Lovin')," "Black Denim Trousers and Motorcycle Boots," and "Chicken," Leiber and Stoller wrote or cowrote "Bernie's Tune," "Can't We Be More Than Friends," "Blueberries," "Fancy Meeting You," and "Que Pasa, Muchacha" for the Cheers, who also recorded two Leiber and Stoller songs that the Robins recorded in 1955: "Whadaya Want?" and "I Must Be Dreamin'." This information is culled from Palmer, 120–31, and www.thecheers.com.

13   **"Every session . . .":** Meryl Stoller, interview, 10 July 2002.

14   **Nesuhi brought the record:** Ahmet Ertegun with Greil Marcus, Nat Hentoff, Lenny Kaye, Robert Gordon, Robert Christgau, Vince Aletti, Will Friedwald, David Fricke, and Barney Hoskyns: *"What'd I Say": The Atlantic Story: 50 Years of Music* (New York: Welcome Rain, 2001), 78, 100.

14   **Largely on Nesuhi's recommendation:** Jerry Wexler, interview, 25 July 2002.

14   **it stipulated that:** Fox, 167.

14   **If Leiber and Stoller were not the first:** Ertegun, 100; Mike Stoller, e-mail communication, May 2002.

14   **"Mr. Disorderly . . .":** Jerry Wexler and David Ritz, *Rhythm and the Blues: A Life in American Music* (New York: Knopf, 1993), 134.

15   **fifty-six takes:** Tony Allan with Faye Treadwell, *Save the Last Dance for Me: The Musical Legacy of the Drifters* (Ann Arbor, MI: Popular Culture, 1993), 64.

15   **Less than ten minutes:** Leiber and Stoller describe the recording of "Searchin'" in Randy Poe and Robert Palmer's notes to the Coasters' *50 Coastin' Classics* (Rhino Records R2 71090).

16   **"really funky . . .":** Ertegun, 110.

16   **"an expression of Jerry Leiber":** Jerry Wexler, quoted in Shaw, *Honkers and Shouters*, 412.

CHAPTER TWO: A BROADWAY DIVIDED

17   **"written for the most part by cretinous goons":** Quoted in Linda Martin and Kerry Segrave, *Anti-Rock: The Opposition to Rock 'n' Roll* (Hamden, CT: Archon, 1988), 46–47.

18   **"[I]f we do not get off our soft fannies . . .":** Kings County Criminal Court Judge Samuel S. Leibowitz, in *Juvenile Delinquency (The Effectiveness of the Juvenile Court System). Hearings before Subcommittee to Investigate Juvenile Delinquency of*

the Committee on the Judiciary, United States Senate, Feb. 12 and 19, 1959 (Washington, DC: U.S. Government Printing Office, 1959), 32.

18 New Yorkers founded: Joseph M. Hawes, *Children in Urban Society: Juvenile Delinquency in Nineteenth-Century America* (New York: Oxford University Press, 1971), 35–40.

18 juvenile arrests more than tripled: Robert M. MacIver, *The Prevention and Control of Delinquency* (New York: Atherton Press, 1966), 3–4.

18 "Never in our 180-year history . . .": Bill Davidson's article in the January 1957 *Collier's* is quoted in H. H. Remmers and D. H. Radler, *The American Teenager* (Indianapolis: Bobbs-Merrill, 1957), 251.

18 One poll indicated: *Juvenile Delinquency: Facts, Facets* 1 (Children's Bureau, Social Security Administration, U.S. Department of Health, Education and Welfare, 1960), iii.

19 His ABC television series flopped: Kitty Kelley, *His Way: The Unauthorized Biography of Frank Sinatra* (New York: Bantam, 1986), 251.

19 Named after its owners: For the Brill Building's architectural and historical details, see David W. Dunlap, *On Broadway: A Journey Uptown Over Time* (New York: Rizzoli, 1990), 184; "The History of a Sound Building," http://www.brillbuilding.com.

19 "the Parthenon": Dunlap, 175.

19 The Paradise: "Night Club to Seat 1000 Guests Is Planned for Brill Building," *New York Times*, 16 November 1932, 33; Dunlap, 186 (citing "Girls, Girls, Girls, Girls, Girls," *Fortune* [July 1939], 119).

19 A. J. Liebling: A. J. Liebling, *The Jollity Building* (New York: Ballantine, paper, n.d.), 30–38.

19 Wexler described: Wexler and Ritz, 57.

20 the first pop song: Ian Whitcomb, *After the Ball* (New York: Limelight Editions, paper, 1986), 4.

20 Racing season: Mike Stoller, interview, 14 May 2001.

20 A bookie would interrupt: Hal David recounts this in Al Kasha and Joel Hirschhorn, *Notes on Broadway: Conversations with the Great Songwriters* (Chicago: Contemporary Books, 1985), 91.

20 "If they had a song . . .": Ed Cramer, interview, 25 March 2002.

20 One major publisher nearly fired: Elaine Orlando, interview, 6 May 2002.

20 "The Turf was for people . . .": Artie Ripp, interview, 20 October 2001.

20 "There were about twenty phone booths": Kenny Vance, interview, 26 March 2002.

21 Jones wrote in his autobiography: Quincy Jones, *Q: The Autobiography of Quincy Jones* (New York: Doubleday, 2001), 99.

21 "I started knocking . . .": Paul Evans, interview, 16 November 2001.

21 "Some of them could not accept . . .": Ed Cramer, interview, 25 March 2002.

21 "The Brill Building was the real old-timers . . .": Larry Kolber, interview, 13 June 2003.

21 "They never let country songwriters in . . .": Mitch Miller, interview, 27 June 2002.

21 Gene Autry once complained: Sanjek, 429.

21 Sinatra's lawyer: Ibid.

22 "dropped in by helicopter": Jeff Barry, interview, 18 October 2001.

22 Hanson's Drug Store: For a description of Hanson's, see Al DiOrio, *Borrowed Time: The 37 Years of Bobby Darin* (Philadelphia: Running Press, paper, 1986), 57–59.

22 "vertical integration": Alan Betrock, *Girl Groups: The Story of a Sound* (New York: Delilah, 1982), 39.

22 A demo could cost: Arnold Shaw, *The Rockin' Fifties: The Decade That Transformed the Pop Music Scene* (New York: Hawthorn Books, 1974), 23; Jack Keller, interview, 3 June 2003.

22 **"Sixteen-fifty to me was the hip building":** Hank Medress, interview, 25 September 2001.

22 **"a little bit of a competitive thing":** Tony Orlando, interview, 24 April 2002.

22 **In his autobiography, Orlando wrote:** Tony Orlando with Patsi Bale Cox, *Halfway to Paradise* (New York: St. Martin's, 2002), 27.

23 **According to Jay Siegal:** Jay Siegal, interview, 11 September 2001.

23 **"You might aspire . . .":** Artie Ripp, interview, 20 October 2001.

23 **"Sixteen-fifty was more of a workman's place":** Ed Cramer, interview, 25 March 2002; Freddy Bienstock, interview, 26 February 2002.

23 **Jean Aberbach climbed the stairs:** Ben Weisman, interview, 17 October 2001.

23 **were now partners:** Mike Stoller, e-mail communication, May 2002.

23 **"Their philosophy . . .":** Elaine Orlando, interview, 6 May 2002.

23 **according to Jerry Wexler:** Quoted in Robert Stephen Spitz, *The Making of Superstars: Artists and Executives of the Rock Music Business* (Garden City, NY: Anchor/Doubleday, 1978), 255.

23 **On the first Monday of every month:** Wexler and Ritz, 129.

24 **"the best-looking Jewish gangster":** Jerry Leiber, telephone interview, 5 March 2001.

24 **Eddie Wolpin . . . had suggested:** Hal David, *What the World Needs Now and Other Love Lyrics* (New York: Trident, 1970), 42.

24 **"My whole history . . .":** Hal David, interview, 1 May 2003. Unless otherwise noted, all information and quotations concerning David's early life and career are drawn from this interview.

24 **"a form of Jewish culture":** Bruce Pollock, *In Their Own Words* (New York: Collier, paper, 1975), xx.

24 **"He was a role model . . .":** Ibid., xviii.

25 **Mack, one of the ASCAP writers:** Ed Cramer, interview, 25 March 2002.

25 **"authority on men's clothing":** Sam G. Riley, *Biographical Dictionary of American Newspaper Columnists* (Westport, CT: Greenwood Press, 1995), 16.

26 **It was . . . Irma Bacharach:** Burt Bacharach, interviewed by Morgan Neville for A&E's *Biography.*

26 **"I ate jars . . .":** Rex Reed, "Bacharach—No More 'Promises,' " *New York Times,* 15 December 1968, 3:2.

26 **he was too short:** Burt Bacharach, interviewed by Morgan Neville for A&E's *Biography.*

26 **"They always got to do . . .":** Reed, 3:2.

26 **A band member:** Burt Bacharach, interviewed by Morgan Neville for A&E's *Biography.*

26 **until he heard *Daphnis et Chloé*:** This account of Bacharach's adolescent musical tastes draws on Neville's interview; Kasha and Hirschhorn, *Notes on Broadway,* 2; Robert Hilburn, "What Burt Needs Now," *Los Angeles Times Calendar,* 12 April 1998, 79; Bill DeMain, "There's Always Something There to Remind Me: The Burt Bacharach Story," CD notes, *The Look of Love: The Burt Bacharach Collection* (Rhino R2 75339).

27 **"let the melody shine through":** DeMain, "There's Always Something There to Remind Me."

27 **"to be popular":** Reed, 3:2.

27 **"I have written practically nothing . . .":** Undated letters in the Henry Cowell Collection, Folder 11 (JPB 00–03), New York Public Library for the Performing Arts.

27 **shipped off to Germany:** Reed.

27   "I was probably . . .": Burt Bacharach, interview, 3 May 2002.
27   He also performed: Charles Moritz, ed., *Current Biography Yearbook 1970* (New York: H.W. Wilson, 1970), 71; Jack Kroll, "Burt Bacharach: The Music Man 1970," *Newsweek,* 22 June 1970, 53.
28   "My family knew . . .": Burt Bacharach, interview, 3 May 2002.
28   "a terrible song": Reed, 3:2.
28   "It may have been we guaranteed . . .": Burt Bacharach, interview, 3 May 2002.
28   While Bill Haley: "Frenzy 'n' Furor Featured at Paramount," *New York Times,* and " 'Don't Knock the Rock,' " *New York Herald Tribune,* 23 February 1957.
28   "I was lousy . . .": Alan Dale, *The Spider and the Marionettes* (New York: Lyle Stuart, 1965), 304.
29   "a 32-bar commercial": Mitch Miller, interview, 27 June 2002.
29   Robbins became: Eliot, 33–34.
29   "When we wrote . . .": Hal David, interview, 1 May 2003.
30   Richard Russo nailed: Richard Russo, *Empire Falls* (New York: Vintage, paper, 2002), 278–79.

CHAPTER THREE: LONELY AVENUE

31   He had made a demo: Doc Pomus was interviewed on videotape by Peter Guralnick in 1984. A copy of this interview was kindly provided to me by William Bratton and Sharyn Felder.
31   a ballad Pomus had written: The song was "My Happiness Forever." Doc Pomus, interviewed by Stuart Goldman, 3–4 April 1990. A videotape of this interview was kindly lent to me by William Bratton and Sharyn Felder.
31   Pomus excitedly telephoned: Joseph Sapia, "What's Up, Doc?: The Doc Pomus Interview," *Goldmine* 78 (November 1982), 7; Doc Pomus, interviewed by Dan Kochakian, liner notes, *Send for the Doctor: The Early Years, 1944–55* (Whiskey, Women, and . . . Record Company KM700); Doc Pomus, Goldman interview, 3–4 April 1990.
31   According to Leiber and Stoller: Kubernik, 62; Randy Poe and Robert Palmer, Notes for the Coasters, *50 Coastin' Classics* (Rhino Records R2 71090), 23.
31   Jerry Wexler insisted: Jerry Wexler, interview, 25 July 2002.
31   "a very average hack song": Doc Pomus, Goldman interview, 3–4 April 1990.
31   the only elevator building: Raoul Felder, interview, 2 March 2001.
32   When his parents raced: Willi Burke, interview, 4 June 2001; Shirlee Hauser, interview, 5 April 2002.
32   Felder family lore: Willi Burke, interview, 4 June 2001; Raoul Felder, interview, 21 August 2001.
32   "Master Jerome Felder": Mike Shadix, Roosevelt Institute, Warm Springs, GA, e-mail communication, 21 July 2001.
32   Pomus told of a surgeon: Shirlee Hauser, interview, 5 April 2002.
32   Jerry had to yell: Willi Burke, interview, 4 June 2001.
32   "the only decent piece . . . fall and fall": Raoul Felder, interviews, 2 March 2001 and 21 August 2001.
33   Felder protested that he was a singer: Doc Pomus, interviewed by Kochakian, liner notes, *Send for the Doctor.*
33   dubbed William Basie "Count": Count Basie, as told to Albert Murray, *Good Morning Blues: The Autobiography of Count Basie* (New York: Random House, 1985), 163.

33   **Felder reprised:** Doc Pomus, interviewed by Kochakian, liner notes, *Send for the Doctor.*

33   **"a poignant lament":** Gunther Schuller, *The Swing Era: The Development of Jazz, 1930–1945* (New York: Oxford University Press, 1989), 796.

33   **"I went home that night":** Quoted in *Hal Willner's Doc Pomus Project,* performed 7 November 2001 at St. Mark's Church, New York City.

34   **"I came from . . .":** Doc Pomus, interviewed by Kochakian, liner notes, *Send for the Doctor.*

34   **Cabs didn't cruise:** Raoul Felder, interview, 2 March 2001.

34   **hard and gritty:** Willi Burke, interview, 4 June 2001.

34   **"hip, midnight character":** Sharyn Felder, interview, 26 March 2001.

34   **"the indigo stuff":** Doc Pomus, "The World of Doc Pomus: Cookie's Caravan," *Whiskey, Women, and . . .*, no. 16 (spring 1987), 2.

34   **"Pomus . . . was a white Negro . . .":** Mort Shuman, unpublished autobiographical sketch (copyrighted 1991). Selections from this handwritten manuscript were kindly provided to me by Shuman's attorney, Charles Negus-Fancey, and widow, Maria-Pia Shuman, and are quoted with their generous permission.

35   **Newton had even played:** Mezzrow and Wolfe, 285–87.

35   **Dinah Washington paused:** Leonard Feather, *The Jazz Years: Earwitness to an Era* (New York: Da Capo, 1987), 26–31, 191.

35   **A 1940s *Journal of Pediatrics* article:** Edith Meyer, "Psychological Considerations in a Group of Children with Poliomyelitis," *Journal of Pediatrics* 31, no. 1 (July 1947), 46–47.

35   **"social taboo":** Edith Henrich, comp. and ed., *Experiments in Survival,* with commentary by Leonard Kriegel (New York: Association for the Aid of Crippled Children, 1963), postscript, 191–92.

35   **"I was never one . . .":** Quoted in *Hal Willner's Doc Pomus Project.*

35   **flicking unstubbed Chesterfields:** Raoul Felder, interview, 2 March 2001; Shirlee Hauser, interview, 5 April 2002.

35   **"To be doomed by illness . . .":** Leonard Kriegel, "In Kafka's House," *Falling Into Life: Essays by Leonard Kriegel* (San Francisco: North Point Press, 1991), 192.

35   **"a kind of discriminatory barrier":** Fred Davis, *Passage Through Crisis: Polio Victims and Their Families* (Indianapolis: Bobbs-Merrill, 1963), 41.

36   **"reached out and touched":** Raoul Felder, interview, 2 March 2001.

36   **"a huge army":** Doc Pomus, "The Journals of Doc Pomus (1978–91)," excerpted in *Antaeus: On Music* 71/72 (autumn 1993), 160, 178.

36   **"the only way":** Doc Pomus, interviewed by Kochakian, liner notes, *Send for the Doctor.*

36   **"The darkness . . .":** Shirlee Hauser, interview, 5 April 2002.

36   **Jerry rehearsed:** Raoul Felder, interview, 2 March 2001.

36   **"My legs were lifeless . . .":** Kriegel, *Falling Into Life,* 15.

36   **Pomus worked with an extraordinary number:** Doc Pomus, interviewed by Kochakian, liner notes, *Send for the Doctor.* See also Pomus's foreword to Fox, *In the Groove,* xiv.

37   **"Sometimes it was hilarious . . .":** Pomus, "The World of Doc Pomus: Cookie's Caravan," 2.

37   **"the kings of Bed-Stuy . . .":** Doc Pomus, "Otis Blackwell and Me," *Goldmine* 85 (June 1963), 19.

37   **"songwriting came very hard":** Sapia, 7.

37   **broke the fingers:** Raoul Felder, interview, 21 August 2001.

37 **Gatemouth Moore:** Doc Pomus, interviewed by Kochakian, liner notes, *Send for the Doctor.*

38 **forgot he was black:** Raoul Felder, interview, 21 August 2001.

38 **Pomus said he gave 15 percent:** Sapia, 7.

38 **Connie Kaye:** Michael Ruppli, compiler, *Atlantic Records: A Discography,* Vol. 1 (Westport, CT: Greenwood Press, 1979), 61.

38 **"the kids":** Shirlee Hauser, interview, 5 April 2002.

38 **the Pilgrim Travelers:** "Lonely Avenue" echoes the Pilgrim Travelers' "I've Got a New Home" and "How Jesus Died." See Tony Heilbut, *The Gospel Sound: Good News and Bad Times* (New York: Simon & Schuster, 1971), 116. I'm grateful to Tony Heilbut for sharing with me his knowledge of gospel music and the Pilgrim Travelers in a telephone interview on 24 October 2002.

39 **Pomus told an interviewer:** Pollock, *In Their Own Words,* 21.

39 **"There's a street . . .":** Pomus, "The Journals of Doc Pomus," 160.

39 **"You sing about the woman . . .":** Quoted in Michael Lydon, *Ray Charles: Man and Music* (New York: Riverhead, 1998), 275.

39 **"There's so much time . . .":** Jerry Wexler, interview, 25 July 2002.

40 **"I realized . . .":** Doc Pomus, Goldman interview, 3–4 April 1990.

40 **derelicts and hookers:** Sapia, 8.

40 **$540 a year:** Doc Pomus, Goldman interview, 3–4 April 1990.

40 **writing articles:** Doc Pomus, interviewed by Kochakian, liner notes, *Send for the Doctor.*

40 **new cases of the disease dropped:** Kathryn Black, *In the Shadow of Polio: A Personal and Social History* (Reading, MA: Addison-Wesley, 1996), 230.

40 **"[P]olio had ceased to be . . .":** Jane Smith, *Patenting the Sun: Polio and the Salk Vaccine* (New York: Morrow, 1990), 371.

40 **"I had no instinct . . .":** Doc Pomus, Goldman interview, 3–4 April 1990.

41 **Mortimer Shuman grew up:** Unless otherwise noted, all direct quotations of Mort Shuman and biographical details of his life are drawn from his unpublished autobiographical sketch.

41 **"dynamic and popular":** Neil Sedaka, interview, 30 April 2002.

41 **loitered in Andria's Pizzeria:** Ibid.

41 **"Everybody on my block . . .":** Norman Spizz, quoted in Myrna Katz Frommer and Harvey Frommer, *It Happened in Brooklyn* (New York: Harcourt Brace, 1993), 59.

41 **"the *fresser*":** Raoul Felder, interview, 2 March 2001.

41 **"I decided that . . .":** Doc Pomus, Goldman interview, 3–4 April 1990.

43 **Pomus married Wilma Burke:** Unless otherwise noted, all quotes from Willi Burke and details about her marriage to Doc Pomus are from a 4 June 2001 interview.

44 **"You'd come home . . .":** Doc Pomus, Goldman interview, 3–4 April 1990.

44 **R&B Records lacked:** Ibid.

44 **"we had no track . . .":** Ibid.

45 **pinched his cheeks:** Susan Aberbach, interview, 2 August 2002.

45 **"consummate music man":** Elaine Orlando, interview, 6 May 2002.

45 **"Paul always knew . . .":** Shirlee Hauser, interview, 5 April 2002.

45 **"The first time I heard Fabian . . .":** Doc Pomus, Goldman interview, 3–4 April 1990.

45 **"This little guy . . .":** Fabian Forte, interview, 15 July 2002.

46 **Pomus said as much:** Doc Pomus, Goldman interview, 3–4 April 1990; Jean-Marie Pouzenc, notes, Elvis Presley, *Elvis Chante Mort Shuman & Doc Pomus* (BMG France 74321 745962).

46 **the insistence of Fabian's manager:** Fabian Forte, interview, 15 July 2002.

46   **"I got hysterical . . .":** Paul Evans, interview, 16 November 2001.

46   **"Elvis had to be impressed . . .":** Fabian Forte, interview, 15 July 2002.

46   **"the meatballs":** Ibid.

46   **By 1959, Italian Americans:** Anthony J. Gribin and Matthew M. Schiff, *The Complete Book of Doo-Wop* (Iola, WI: Krause Publications, 2000), 55–56.

47   **Pomus resold:** Pomus, "The World of Doc Pomus," *Whiskey, Women, and . . .*, nos. 12/13 (December 1983), 6. Pomus told a different story about "Go, Jimmy, Go" on more than one occasion. According to that account, Atlantic had irritated him by delaying the release of the Drifters' recording of "Save the Last Dance for Me." In his frustration, Pomus rehearsed the song with Jimmy Clanton, who was about to record the song when Jerry Wexler called with news that the Drifters' original version was finally coming out. Thinking fast, Pomus dusted off "Go, Bobby, Go," retitled the song, and substituted it for "Save the Last Dance for Me." See Sapia, 10; Colin Escott, liner notes, The Drifters, *1959–1965: All-Time Greatest Hits and More* (Atlantic 81931-1). The story is too good be true: Clanton released "Go, Jimmy, Go" before the Drifters recorded "Save the Last Dance for Me."

47   **Pomus complained:** Pomus, "The World of Doc Pomus," 6.

47   **"We had no idea . . .":** Unless otherwise noted, the account that follows of Pomus and Shuman's dealings with the Mystics is taken from a 10 April 2002 interview with Al Contrera.

47   **"The new lyrics . . .":** Bob Shannon and John Javna, *Behind the Hits: Inside Stories of Classic Pop and Rock and Roll* (New York: Warner Books, paper, 1986), 52. Shannon and Javna write that Pomus and Shuman composed "Teenager in Love" expressly for Dion and the Belmonts, and the interview with Pomus that they quote seems to confirm this, but Al Contrera's detailed account of the song's origins is convincing and supported by "The Mystics: A Talk with the Mystics," *Goldmine* 90, vol. 9, no. 11 (November 1983), 61, as well as Norm N. Nite's *Rock On: The Illustrated Encyclopedia of Rock N' Roll, The Solid Gold Years* (New York: Popular Library, paper, 1977), 450.

48   **"like a dad":** "Those Magic Moments: Doc Pomus Remembered by His Friends and Peers," 8.

48   **"an amazingly talented guy":** Dion DiMucci with Davin Seay, *The Wanderer: Dion's Story* (New York: Beech Tree Books/Morrow, 1988), 84.

48   **Fordham Baldies:** Eric C. Schneider, *Vampires, Dragons, and Egyptian Kings: Youth Gangs in Postwar New York* (Princeton, NJ: Princeton University Press 1999), 120.

48   **first snort of heroin:** DiMucci, 51.

48   **"faggy":** Quoted by Mitchell Cohen in his liner notes to Dion and the Belmonts, *24 Original Classics* (Arista AL9-8206).

49   **"wary young man":** "The Sound," *The New Yorker* (22 April 1961), 36.

49   **Hank Williams:** DiMucci, 36–43.

49   **"[A]ll the time I thought . . .":** Sapia, 9.

49   **"As to a hierarchy . . .":** Pomus, "The Journals of Doc Pomus," 173.

50   **"If you're not writing . . .":** Doc Pomus, Goldman interview, 3–4 April 1990.

50   **"stepping away from the bawdy":** Scott Saul, *Freedom Is, Freedom Ain't: Jazz and the Making of the Sixties* (Cambridge, MA: Harvard University Press, 2003), 194.

50   **"I think he was trying . . .":** Shirlee Hauser, interview, 5 April 2002.

50   **Leiber and Stoller's twelve:** *Joel Whitburn's Pop Annual 1955–1999* indicates that Leiber and Stoller wrote eleven hits in 1959 (p. 62) but neglects to include "There Goes My Baby," which they coauthored.

50   **"The old-time Broadway . . .":** Doc Pomus, Goldman interview, 3–4 April 1990.

CHAPTER FOUR: "MY DAUGHTER BOUGHT IT. WHAT ARE YOU GOING TO DO ABOUT IT?"

51   *"Well, let's see . . .":* June Bundy, "NBC Spot Sales Blast at R&R Rouses Ire," *Bill-board* (14 July 1958), 3.

51   **"[W]e said that what we wrote . . .":** Quoted in Fox, 163.

51   **Lieber and Stoller followed:** Hardcastle; Mike Stoller, e-mail communication, May 2002.

51   **They opened their own office:** Mike Stoller, interview, 14 May 2001; e-mail communication, May 2002.

52   **after only six months:** Palmer, 23.

52   **"I couldn't even find . . .":** Booth, 22.

52   **"By the time you filled out . . .":** Quoted in Fox, 176.

52   **Leiber had the temerity:** Leiber's accounts of this episode, which differ slightly, appear in Fricke and in Guralnick, *Last Train to Memphis,* 448–49. The quotes from Nelson Algren's *A Walk on the Wild Side* appear in the paperback reissue (New York: Noonday Press/Farrar, Straus and Giroux, 1998), 288, 56.

53   **Colonel Parker pulled:** Guralnick, *Last Train to Memphis,* 453. See also Hardcastle.

53   **"It was demoralizing . . .":** Booth, 16.

53   **Leiber was boiling water:** Jerry Leiber and Mike Stoller, quoted in the notes to the Coasters' *50 Coastin' Classics;* Stoller, quoted in Fricke.

54   **"sixth voice":** Booth, 24.

54   **"bluegrass":** Mike Stoller, interview, 14 May 2001.

54   **"My daughter bought it . . .":** Committee on Interstate and Foreign Commerce, United States Senate, *Hearings on S.2834, a Bill to Provide That a License for a Radio or Television Broadcasting Station Shall Not Be Granted to, or Held by, Any Person or Corporation Engaged Directly or Indirectly in the Business of Publishing Music or of Manufacturing or Selling Musical Recordings* (Washington, DC: U.S. Government Printing Office, 1958), 1185–86.

55   **Leiber once partly attributed:** Kubernik, 67.

55   **George Barnes, a jazz guitarist:** Artie Butler, interview, 24 October 2001.

55   **He ran stone-faced:** Tom Dowd, interviewed by Morgan Neville for A&E's *Biography.*

56   **"I think the most fun . . .":** Quoted in Fox, 171, 166.

56   **"their shining hour":** Artie Butler, interview, 24 October 2001.

56   **Leiber's original lyrics sharpened:** Shannon and Javna, 121.

56   **Leiber once said:** Palmer, 26.

57   **"quite an honor":** Booth, 28.

57   **"LaVern Baker was *tough* . . .":** Booth, 28.

58   **replaced them with four of the five Crowns:** The best account of the transformation of the Crowns into the Drifters appears in *Marv Goldberg's R&B Notebooks,* "5 Crowns," http://home.att.net/~marvy42/5Crowns/5crowns.html.

58   **Treadwell, a former jazz trumpeter:** For Treadwell's background and relationship with Sarah Vaughan, see Leslie Gourse, *Sassy: The Life of Sarah Vaughan* (New York: Scribner's, 1993), 42–93.

58   **"The Drifters were not . . .":** Booth, 26.

59   **"I started playing . . .":** Mike Stoller, e-mail communication, May 2002; Ertegun, 110. The number of violins engaged for the "There Goes My Baby" session has wavered in Stoller's accounts between four and five.

59   Although the Orioles had used strings: Allan, 76.

59   Stoller was in distinguished company: "Music World: Series Is Saved," *New York Times*, 21 January 1962, II:11; "Music: Pollikiff's Series," *New York Times*, 25 January 1962, 24.

59   composers Morton Feldman and Earle Brown: Meryl Stoller, interview, 10 July 2002.

59   Applebaum "just came into our life . . .": Charlie Thomas, interview, 22 June 2002.

60   "an assignment that I did . . .": Stanley Applebaum, interview, 25 March 2002.

60   "striking realization . . .": Jimmy Webb, *Tunesmith: Inside the Art of Songwriting* (New York: Hyperion, 1998), 132.

60   "get the fuck out of Texas": Steve Tyrell, interview, 19 February 2002.

60   "a very simple, specific beat": Stanley Applebaum, interview, 25 March 2002.

60   *Anna*, a 1952 Italian tearjerker: Mira Liehm, *Film in Italy from 1942 to the Present* (Berkeley: University of California Press, 1984), 100; "Italian Import Makes Debut," *New York Times*, 2 February 1953, 20.

61   "They said I got shook up . . .": Charlie Thomas, interview, 22 June 2002.

61   "I was a baritone-bass . . .": Quoted in Smith, *Off the Record*, 124.

62   "I totally misprized . . .": Jerry Wexler, interview, 25 July 2002.

62   "It was not a favorite record . . .": Tom Dowd, interviewed by Morgan Neville for A&E's *Biography*.

62   Wexler said that in order to prevent: Jerry Wexler, interview, 25 July 2002.

62   "Wow! We hadn't even heard . . .": Charlie Thomas, interview, 22 June 2002.

63   "[I]t *is* a twelve-bar blues . . .": Stoller and Leiber quoted in Fox, 164.

64   "At least 60% of our stuff . . .": "Tin Pan Alley: Jailhouse Rock," *Time*, 20 April 1959, 48.

CHAPTER FIVE: PARTNERS IN CHUTZPAH

65   "Anyone who wrote . . .": Neil Sedaka, interviewed by Morgan Neville for A&E's *Biography*.

65   Sedaka and Greenfield descended: Both Sedaka and Kirshner have told this story slightly differently on different occasions. Sometimes, for instance, it is Kirshner who answered the door, and sometimes it is Al Nevins. See Neil Sedaka, *Laughter in the Rain: My Own Story* (New York: G. P. Putnam's, 1982), 64–65; Spitz, 31, 145.

65   suave Nevins: Artie Ripp, interview, 20 October 2001.

66   "I thought the whole world . . .": Neil Sedaka, interview, 30 April 2002.

66   she rode a roller coaster: *Neil Sedaka*, a documentary directed by Scott Lenz and shown on A&E's *Biography*, 12 November 2002.

66   "sissy": Robin Flans, "Neil Sedaka: He Never Really Left," *Goldmine* 100, vol. 10, no. 9 (25 May 1984), 21.

66   Listening to the radio: Sedaka, 26–27.

67   "I was thirteen . . .": Neil Sedaka, interview, 30 April 2002.

67   "bastardized bolero . . .": Sedaka, 41.

67   "Why are you writing songs with him?": Neil Sedaka, interview, 30 April 2002.

68   When Sedaka performed it: Ibid.; Sedaka, 45–46; *Landmark 1955* (Abraham Lincoln High School yearbook).

68   Ben Goldman: Frommer and Frommer, 196; Hank Medress, interview, 25 September 2001.

69   **he played hooky:** Neil Sedaka, interview, 30 April 2002.

69   **"permanent obligation":** *Landmark 1956* (Abraham Lincoln High School yearbook), 3.

69   **80 to 85 percent Jewish:** Abe Lass, quoted in Frommer and Frommer, 176.

69   **"a culture we knew nothing about":** Richard Gottehrer, interview, 13 November 2003.

69   **"We had to learn it":** Hank Medress, interview, 25 September 2001.

70   **"Howie was tone-deaf":** Neil Sedaka, interview, 30 April 2002.

70   **"Neil was always very cocky":** Jack Keller, interview, 3 June 2003.

71   **The Tokens performed:** Jay Siegal, interview, 11 September 2001.

71   **Sedaka was named:** "Top Music Students to Appear on WQXR," *New York Times,* 19 March 1956, 25.

71   **Rubinstein complimented him:** Sedaka, 61–62.

71   **"He would go on it over and over . . .":** Hank Medress, interview, 25 September 2001.

71   **He bought a copy:** Bruce Pollock, *When Rock Was Young: A Nostalgic Review of the Top 40 Era* (New York: Holt, Rinehart and Winston, 1981), 148.

72   **"I used to make demos . . .":** Flans, 21.

72   **Dick Clark:** Harry Finfer and Harold Lipsius owned Guyden, which released "Ring-a-Rockin' Music" and was the "sister" label of Jamie Records, in which Clark as well as Finfer and Lipsius owned an interest. See John A. Jackson, *American Bandstand: Dick Clark and the Making of a Rock 'n' Roll Empire* (New York: Oxford University Press, 1997), 117; *Jamie/Guyden History,* "The Early Days," http://www.jamguy.com/scripts/jamguycom.

72   **a messenger for National Cash Register:** Pollock, *When Rock Was Young,* 149.

72   **Don Kirshner had been more successful:** Unless otherwise noted, all information and quotations regarding Don Kirshner's childhood and early career are drawn from Spitz, 26–37, and an interview by Morgan Neville for A&E's *Biography.*

73   **Cassotto had not been expected to live:** DiOrio, 28–29, 85–86.

73   **"the brother I never had":** Quoted in Al Aronowitz, "The Dumb Sound," *Saturday Evening Post* (August 1963), available online in *The Blacklisted Journalist,* Column 84 (1 February 2003), http://www.bigmagic.com/pages/blackj/column84.html.

73   **"Bubblegum Pop":** Allan, 90.

73   **Kirshner was adrift:** Although Kirshner insisted Darin wanted him to be his manager but he "didn't want to carry his bags" (interviewed by Morgan Neville for A&E's *Biography*), a friend of Darin's cited in two biographies said that Kirshner burst into tears when Darin broke the bad news over dinner (DiOrio, p. 43; Dodd Darin and Maxine Paetro, *Dream Lovers: The Magnificent Shattered Lives of Bobby Darin and Sandra Dee by Their Son* [New York: Warner Books, 1994], 60–61).

73   **"idols were people like Walt Disney":** "So Far Away," *The New Yorker* (8 March 1993), 36.

74   **Pomus charitably suggested:** Doc Pomus, Goldman interview, 3–4 April 1990.

74   **To Leiber and Stoller's surprise:** Mike Stoller, interview, 14 May 2001.

74   **"he wasn't offering us enough money":** Doc Pomus, Goldman interview, April 3–4 1990.

74   **"Stampede":** William Bratton, interview, 26 June 2002.

74   **"reputation for palatable sounds":** Noel R. Kramer, liner notes, The Three Suns, *Soft and Sweet/Midnight for Two* (Collectables COL-CD-2742).

74   **"The guy who was the brains . . .":** Hank Medress, interview, 25 September 2001.

75   **"Al was a respected figure . . .":** Dick Asher, interview, 10 April 2002.

75   **"the complete opposite of Kirshner":** Larry Kolber, interview, 13 June 2003.

75   **If they could place one of the songs:** Betrock, 40; Pollock, *When Rock Was Young*, 149; Neil Sedaka, e-mail communication, 8 February 2005.

76   **A nervous Sedaka told Francis:** Neil Sedaka, interviewed by John Griffin for A&E's *Biography,* 9 June 1998. Sedaka wrote "Never Again," the song Dinah Washington recorded, with his sister's fiancé, Eddie Grossman. See Sedaka, 55–56, and Brian Gari's notes to Neil Sedaka, *The Brooklyn Demos (1958–1961)*, Original Cast Records OCR6060.

76   **"I knew there was no way ...":** Connie Francis, interviewed by Jerry Osborne in DISCoveries Magazine (September 1991).

77   **Kirshner gratefully acknowledged:** Don Kirshner, interviewed by John Griffin for A&E's *Biography*, 9 June 1998.

77   **"a very pushy little Jewish kid":** Flans, 13.

77   **Francis had suggested:** Neil Sedaka, interviewed by John Griffin for A&E's *Biography,* 9 June 1998; William Ruhlmann, "Connie Francis Sings Everybody's Favorites," *Goldmine* 334, vol. 19, no. 9 (14 May 1993), 19.

77   **Sedaka took Francis to Coney Island:** Neil Sedaka, interviewed by John Griffin for A&E's *Biography*, 9 June 1998.

77   **Richard Barrett substituted a song:** Dennis Garvey, "Little Anthony and the Imperials: Back in Harmony," *Goldmine* 358, vol. 20, no. 8 (15 April 1994), 52–54.

78   **the entire advance from RCA:** Sedaka, 74.

78   **"a pinnacle of musical taste":** Kramer, liner notes, The Three Suns, *Soft and Sweet/Midnight for Two.*

78   **"It just didn't sound like rock 'n' roll":** Sedaka, 74–75.

78   **"Those were terrible days ...":** Don Kirshner, interviewed by Morgan Neville for A&E's *Biography.*

78   **spent $100,000 promoting the record:** Neil Sedaka, interview, 30 April 2002

78   **"I'll tell you one thing ...":** Hank Hunter, interview, 10 November 2001.

79   **"I decided to write a song ...":** Sedaka, 84–85.

79   **"Neil and Howie would pick up ...":** Hank Medress, interview, 25 September 2001.

79   **Kirshner himself said he did:** Don Kirshner, interviewed by Morgan Neville for A&E's *Biography.*

79   **According to another Aldon songwriter:** Cynthia Weil, interview, 21 October 2001.

79   **the same man, Chuck Sagle:** Brian Gari, "Oh Carol," notes to Neil Sedaka , *Oh Carol: The Complete Recordings 1956–1966* (Bear Family Records BDC 16535 HK), 16.

80   **"an ode to my old high school girlfriend":** Sedaka, 85.

80   **Stephen Foster:** Spitz, 152. Sedaka and Greenfield eventually paid tribute to Foster with a song, "Stephen."

80   **with Frankie Avalon in mind:** Hank Hunter, interview, 10 November 2001.

80   **Keller had noted:** Jack Keller, interview, 3 June 2003.

80   **Greenfield was upset:** Hank Hunter, interview, 10 November 2001.

80   **Aldon attorney Dick Asher recalled:** Dick Asher, interview, 10 April 2002.

80   **Sedaka knew he was a star:** Sedaka, interviewed by Morgan Neville for A&E's *Biography.*

80   **buying a Thunderbird:** Sedaka, 87.

81   **The word itself dated back:** Jackson, 173.

81   **according to a Cleveland disc jockey:** Dick Clark and Richard Robinson, *Rock, Roll & Remember* (New York: Thomas Y. Crowell, 1976), 197.

81   **"legitimized payola":** Neil Sedaka, interview, 30 April 2002.

81   **It may indeed have been within the law:** Jackson, 185, 192.

81   "I personally don't see anything to hurt me . . .": *Responsibilities of Broadcasting Licensees and Station Personnel: Hearings Before a Subcommittee of the Committee on Interstate and Foreign Commerce, House of Representatives, Eighty-sixth Congress, Second Session, on Payola and Other Deceptive Practices in the Broadcasting Field,* Part 2 (Washington, DC: United States Government Printing Office, 1960), 1112.

81   while a deejay who testified: Kerry Segrave, *Payola in the Music Industry: A History, 1880–1991* (Jefferson, NC: McFarland & Co., 1994), 152.

81   "Promotion meant first of all . . .": Artie Ripp, interview, 20 October 2001.

82   According to his widow, Agnes Mammarella: Jackson, 167.

82   "the clean side": Linda Goldner, interviewed by Morgan Neville for A&E's *Biography.*

82   the Three Suns had fingered: Shaw, *The Rockin' Fifties,* 269.

82   "We couldn't control . . .": Don Kirshner, interviewed by Morgan Neville for A&E's *Biography.*

83   "It would amaze you . . .": Artie Ripp, interview, 20 October 2001.

83   The payola hearings briefly depressed: Eliot, 86–87; Ertegun, 63.

CHAPTER SIX: THE YOUNG LOVERS

84   Sedaka was impressed: Sedaka, 57–59.

84   "We used to do a half-tone . . .": Neil Sedaka, interview, 30 April 2002.

84   "She was a groupie . . .": Sedaka, 60.

85   "Her mother told me . . .": Pollock, *When Rock Was Young,* 146.

85   "Carol was enamored . . .": Hank Medress, interview, 25 September 2001.

85   Carole King denied indignantly: Quoted in David Kamp, "The Hit Factory," *Vanity Fair* (November 2001), 257.

85   Sedaka saw perform: Neil Sedaka, interview, 30 April 2002.

85   "from the mellow chords . . .": *Log,* James Madison High School 1958 yearbook.

86   "and marry[ing] some doctor": Quoted in Mike Patrick and Malcolm Baumgart, notes to *On Broadway: Hit Songs and Rarities from the Brill Building Era* (Westside WESD 216).

86   In addition to singing on these demos: Humphries, 7–11; James E. Perone, *Carole King: A Bio-Bibliography* (Westport, CT: Greenwood Press, 1999), 1.

86   "Just to Be with You": Nite, 473.

86   "tall, with a gangly air . . .": Julian Halevy, *The Young Lovers* (New York: Simon & Schuster, 1955), 8.

86   "I showed her the play . . .": Gerry Goffin, interview, 22 October 2001.

87   a Rodgers and Hammerstein musical: Ibid.

87   "like some kind of game": Interviewed in Pollock, *In Their Own Words,* 28.

87   "I never knew . . .": Gerry Goffin, interview, 22 October 2001.

87   Under her influence: Gerry Goffin, interviewed by Morgan Neville for A&E's *Biography.*

87   King became pregnant: Gerry Goffin, interview, 22 October 2001.

87   wed on August 30: Jesse Goffin, interviewed by Jennifer Weiss, 18 February 2005.

87   "We were having a ball": Gerry Goffin, interview, 22 October 2001.

88   "felt flattered": Neil Sedaka, interview, 30 April 2002.

88   "Donnie loved that side . . .": Gerry Goffin, interview, 22 October 2001.

88   "Gerry and I were in competition . . .": Quoted in Kamp, 257.

89   **"Gerry was a bit introverted . . .":** Don Kirshner, interviewed by Morgan Neville for A&E's *Biography.*

89   **Jo-Ann Campbell:** Richard J. Lorenzo, "Bobby Darin: Doing His Own Thing and Other Things," *Goldmine* 227, vol. 15, no. 7 (7 April 1989), 18; Pollock, *When Rock Was Young,* 94–96; DiOrio, 102.

89   **the piano they had purchased for $35:** Gerry Goffin, interview, 22 October 2001.

89   **"I don't know if Gerry . . .":** Orlando, 32.

89   **"I remember going into that house . . .":** Tony Orlando, interview, 24 April 2002.

89   **"They had a little four-track . . .":** Orlando, 33.

89   **One evening in the fall of 1960:** This account of the composition of "Will You Love Me Tomorrow" draws on the author's interview with Gerry Goffin, 22 October 2001, and Morgan Neville's interview with him for A&E's *Biography.*

90   **"a great song for Johnny Mathis":** Don Kirshner, interviewed by Morgan Neville for A&E's *Biography.*

90   **"a girl's lyric":** Tony Orlando, interview, 24 April 2002. Orlando has given confused and contradictory accounts over the years of how and when he came to record "Will You Love Me Tomorrow." Compare, for instance, Gillett, *Making Tracks,* 166, and Orlando, 40–41. I am hopeful my careful and lengthy questioning obtained an accurate account.

90   **Dixon had been urged:** Wayne Jancik, "Scepter-Wand Records," *Goldmine* 315, vol. 18, no. 17 (21 August 1992), 10.

90   **"I can't do this song . . .":** Shirley Reeves (formerly Shirley Owens), interviewed by Morgan Neville for A&E's *Biography.*

91   **"We had some pretty definite ideas . . .":** Gerry Goffin, interviewed by Morgan Neville for A&E's *Biography.*

91   **"our contradictory popular culture . . .":** Mailer, "The White Negro: Superficial Reflections on the Hipster," in *The Long Patrol,* 214.

91   **"the happy chore":** Gerry Goffin, interviewed by Morgan Neville for A&E's *Biography.*

91   **"We got a nice advance . . .":** Ibid. Memories differ over when Goffin quit his day job. According to Jack Keller (interview, 3 June 2003), Goffin left the chemical plant immediately after signing with Aldon.

CHAPTER SEVEN: PUTTING THE BOMP IN THE BOMP, BOMP, BOMP

92   **"I can read music":** Cynthia Weil described her first encounter with Carole King in an interview with Morgan Neville for A&E's *Biography* and in an October 21, 2001, interview with the author. Unless otherwise noted, all subsequent quotes of and information regarding Weil and Barry Mann are drawn from the latter interview.

92   **"a great rockabilly singer":** Dylan, 80–81.

93   **"I'm sure I screamed . . ."** Snuff Garrett, interview, 28 December 2003.

93   **"pimplefarms":** Susan Loesser, *A Most Remarkable Fella: Frank Loesser and the Guys and Dolls in His Life* (New York: Donald I. Fine, 1993), 238.

93   **"Three chords on the guitar":** Ibid., 239.

94   **Ross visited Weil:** Beverly Ross, interview, 4 June 2003.

94   **James Madison High School:** For historical information about James Madison High School as well as access to its yearbooks, I am indebted to the school's leadership teacher and Sing coordinator, Jeffrey Litman.

94   **"from a shtetl background":** Barry Mann, interview, 21 October 2001.

94 Barry's mother was "very influential": Artie Resnick, interview, 11 March 2002.

95 "I can barely read and write music": Jeff Tamarkin, "Barry Mann and Cynthia Weil . . . They Put the Bomp!" *Goldmine* 75 (August 1982), 13.

95 "He was very leery": Jack Keller, interview, 3 June 2003.

96 "I always wanted to be a songwriter . . .": Barry Mann, interview with Morgan Neville for A&E's *Biography*.

97 "It became almost like a factory . . .": Hank Hunter, interview, 10 November 2001.

97 "very reticent at the beginning": Larry Kolber, interview, 13 June 2003.

98 cut these at Kirshner's insistence: Ibid.

98 "Carole King sang harmonies . . .": Orlando, 40.

98 Suddenly a man: Larry Kolber, interview, 13 June 2003.

99 "little and squirrely": DiMucci, 81.

99 ""Every Breath I Take": For an account of the recording of "Every Breath I Take," see Ribowsky, 90.

99 "a funeral dirge": Larry Kolber, interview, 13 June 2003.

99 Spector told Kolber: Ibid.

100 recorded her first single for George Goldner's Gone Records: Brian Gari, "What the World Needs Now Is Jackie DeShannon," *Goldmine* 290, vol. 17, no. 18 (6 September 1991), 16.

100 John Gluck Jr.: Mark Barkan, interview, 4 October 2001.

100 never exchanged "more than five sentences": Larry Kolber, interview, 13 June 2003.

100 "two different countries": Jeff Tamarkin, "Barry Mann and Cynthia Weil," 14.

101 "I bring home this guy . . .": Cynthia Weil, interviewed by Morgan Neville for A&E's *Biography*.

101 "We used to kid . . .": Gerry Goffin, interview, 22 October 2001.

102 The Edsels: Gribin and Schiff, 404.

102 "Their relationship seemed to blossom . . .": Tony Orlando, interview, 24 April 2002.

102 "Jack Keller produced . . .": Ibid.

103 "It just wasn't working . . .": Ibid.

103 The first royalty check: Barry Mann and Cynthia Weil, interviewed by Terry Gross on *Fresh Air*, National Public Radio, 18 July 2000.

103 "You can still change your mind": Barry Mann and Cynthia Weil, interviewed by Morgan Neville for A&E's *Biography*.

CHAPTER EIGHT: IN THE GARDEN OF ALDON

104 "Maybe not better": Ruhlmann, 22.

104 submitted two different theme songs: Neil Sedaka, interview, 30 April 2002.

105 "Neil always thought . . .": Herb Moelis, interview, 10 April 2002.

105 he taught the Cookies: Sedaka, 108.

105 The Cookies were no longer the same: John Clemente, *Girl Groups: Fabulous Females That Rocked the World* (Iola, WI: Krause Publications, 2000), 64–67.

106 "You had only two hours . . .": Jack Keller, interview, 3 June 2003.

106 Nevins was "king": Tony Orlando, interview, April 24 2002.

106 "he had not a clue . . .": Jack Keller, interview, 3 June 2003.

106 "I wanted them to learn production . . .": Don Kirshner, interviewed by Morgan Neville for A&E's *Biography*.

106 Sedaka was "very professional": Stanley Applebaum, interview, 25 March 2002.

107 "There was a Neil Sedaka sound . . .": Neil Sedaka, interview, 30 April 2002.

107   "Rather than just writing songs . . .": Sedaka, 90, 107.

107   Strassberg had gotten a nose job, and Sedaka . . . losing his virginity: Ibid., 91–95, 111–15.

107   Tory Damon: Neil Sedaka, interview, 30 April 2002; Jack Keller, interview, 3 June 2003.

108   "Neil seemed to be a little 'up there' . . .": Larry Kolber, interview, 13 June 2003.

108   Greenfield "was warmer . . .": Hank Hunter, interview, 10 November 2001.

108   "We always fought . . .": Neil Sedaka, interview, 30 April 2002.

108   "a surgeon performing": Flans, 21.

108   Greenfield and Keller collaborated: Unless otherwise noted, all quotations of Jack Keller and other information describing his collaborations with Howard Greenfield are drawn from a June 3, 2003, interview with Keller.

108   "Everybody's Somebody's Fool": Connie Francis's recollection of the origins of "Everybody's Somebody's Fool" differs from Keller's in details but not in gist. See Connie Francis, *Who's Sorry Now?* (New York: St. Martin's, 1984), 229–30; Ruhlmann, 20.

109   Arnold Maxim pressed: Francis, 235–38.

109   flabbergasted by its "hokey" sound: Neil Sedaka, interviewed by John Griffin for A&E's *Biography.*

109   "There's Gold in Them Thar Hillbilly Tunes": Colin Escott, with George Merritt and William MacEwen, *Hank Williams: The Biography* (Boston: Little, Brown, 1994), 144, citing an article by Bill Davidson in *Collier's* (28 July 1951).

109   her father had convinced her: Ibid., 19.

109   Otis Blackwell . . . Tex Ritter: Tom Russell, "Otis Blackwell: Don't Be Cruel," *Goldmine* 183, vol. 13, no. 6 (31 July 1987), 16.

110   Dion . . . Hank Williams: DiMucci, 36–43.

110   "That's what was great . . .": Barry Mann, interviewed by Morgan Neville for A&E's *Biography.*

110   "It was not uncommon . . .": Dick Asher, interview, 10 April 2002.

110   "Jack could turn anything . . .": Larry Kolber, interview, 13 June 2003.

111   The Everly Brothers approached Aldon: Colin Escott, "The Everly Brothers: Brothers in Arms," *Goldmine* 337, vol. 19, no. 12 (25 June 1993), 28.

112   Don Everly hated: Ibid., 28.

112   "I smell fuckin' money": Snuff Garrett, interview, 28 December 2003.

113   "the triumph of suburban values . . .": Charlie Gillett, *The Sound of the City,* 124.

113   "It was almost like architecture . . .": Brooks Arthur, interview, 23 October 2001.

114   "do Broadway": Barry Mann, interview, 21 October 2001.

114   "We all wrote interchangeably . . .": Roy Carr and Andrew Tyler, "Leaders of the Pack," *New Musical Express* (3 November 1973), 30.

114   On the surface we got along . . .": Gerry Goffin, interviewed by Morgan Neville for A&E's *Biography.*

114   Paul Evans bumped into Mann: Paul Evans, interview, 16 November 2001.

114   "Our entire life . . .": Cynthia Weil, interview, 21 October 2001.

115   "It was really a hotbed . . .": Jeff Tamarkin, "Barry Mann and Cynthia Weil," 14.

115   "Nevins gave [Kirshner] a sense . . .": Ed Cramer, interview, 25 March 2002.

115   the company's "electricity": Artie Ripp, interview, 20 October 2001.

115   "We had this kind of sibling rivalry . . .": Cynthia Weil, interview, 21 October 2001.

115   He was like our surrogate father . . .": Neil Sedaka, interview, 30 April 2002.

115   "You became his follower . . .": Tony Orlando, interview, April 24 2002.

115   Kirshner was a "father figure": Don Kirshner, interviewed by Morgan Neville for A&E's *Biography.*

116   Nevins and Kirshner helped Goffin and King: Gerry Goffin, interview, 22 October 2001.

116   They lent another employee: Artie Ripp, interview, 20 October 2001.

116   Keller was floored: Jack Keller, interview, 3 June 2003.

116   "If he heard a song he liked . . .": Hank Hunter, interview, 10 November 2001.

116   "one of the best song pluggers": Jack Keller, interview, 3 June 2003.

116   "He always got us the records . . .": Gerry Goffin, interview, 22 October 2001.

116   "All the major labels . . .": Richard Gottehrer, interview, 13 November 2003.

117   "Donnie liked to use . . .": Jerry Wexler, interview, 25 July 2002.

117   "The family encompassed everything . . .": Jack Keller, interview, 3 June 2003.

117   eighteen writers on staff: Betrock, 42.

117   "the great thing about going in": Cynthia Weil, interviewed by Terry Gross on *Fresh Air,* 18 July 2000.

117   "It was like a bazaar . . .": Herb Moelis, interview, 10 April 2002.

118   "We wanted to go . . .": Ibid.

118   When Snuff Garrett hesitated: Bobby Vee, interviewed by Morgan Neville for A&E's *Biography;* Gerry Goffin, interviewed by Morgan Neville for A&E's *Biography.* Goffin's recollection differs from Vee's, incidentally. According to Goffin, rather than delaying the record's release, Snuff Garrett and Vee rejected the demo of "It Might As Well Rain Until September."

119   Eva Narcissus Boyd: Joe Haertel, "Little Eva: Doin' a Brand New Dance Now," *Goldmine* 248, vol. 16, no. 2 (26 January 1990), 20; Steve Propes, "Little Eva: From Babysitting to the Big Time," *Goldmine* 204, vol. 14, no. 11 (20 May 1990), 12; Clemente, 152.

119   "What's that?": Gerry Goffin, interview, 22 October 2001.

119   It's unclear whether: Haertel, 20.

119   By one account the label passed: Jackson, 235.

120   Nevins warned Goffin and King: Jack Keller, interview, 3 June 2003.

CHAPTER NINE: "IT WAS JUST JEWISH LATIN"

121   "All my writers idolized . . .": Don Kirshner, interviewed by Morgan Neville for A&E's *Biography.*

121   "Record Business 1-A": Artie Butler, interview, 24 October, 2001.

121   "Pomus loved the Drifters . . .": Willi Burke, interview, 4 June 2001.

122   "I always thought they were geniuses": Doc Pomus, Goldman interview, 3–4 April 1990.

122   the redemptive role that grace plays: See Daniel J. Wilson, "Covenants of Work and Grace: Themes of Recovery and Redemption in Polio Narratives," *Literature and Medicine* 13, no. 1 (Spring 1994), 22–41.

122   "I used to believe in magic . . .": Pomus, "The Journals of Doc Pomus," 157.

122   According to Burke: Willi Burke, interview, 4 June 2001.

122   Their daughter, Sharyn, found: Sharyn Felder, interview, 26 March 2001.

122   Pomus said it took only half an hour: Pollock, *In Their Own Words,* 23.

122   Leiber recounted: Ertegun, 127; Fox, 185.

122   "On their own those schmucks . . .": Sapia, 10.

123   **"Mortie was with us ..."**: Charlie Thomas, interview, 22 June 2002.

123   **within earshot of Puerto Ricans**: Raoul Felder, interview, 2 March 2001.

123   **"something like a translation"**: Mojo Nixon, "Elvis, Doc and Mojo Are Every-where," *Goldmine* 262, vol. 16, no. 16 (10 August 1990), 14.

123   **"mambonik"**: Shuman, unpublished autobiographical sketch.

123   **Anglo night**: "Latin-Music Patriarch Stays Hungry," *New York Times,* 30 April 2002, E:7.

123   **"Stars of stage ..."**: Shuman, unpublished autobiographical sketch.

123   **dated a Puerto Rican girl**: Mike Stoller, interview, 14 May 2001.

123   **"only Jewish pachuco"**: Bill Millar, *The Coasters* (London: Star Books, paper, 1974), 64; Mike Stoller, interviewed by Morgan Neville for A&E's *Biography.*

124   **"*Everybody* danced"**: José Torres, "The Palladium," *New York* (21–28 December 1987), 99.

124   **"The exciting stuff ..."**: Al Gorgoni, interview, 1 February 2002.

124   **"a little cha-cha song"**: Charlie Thomas, interview, 22 June 2002.

124   **According to Jerry Wexler**: Jerry Wexler, interview, 25 July 2002.

125   **Puerto Rican population more than doubled**: Joseph P. Fitzpatrick, *Puerto Rican Americans: The Meaning of Migration to the Mainland* (Englewood Cliffs, NJ: Prentice-Hall, 1987), 15.

125   **"to be vital, alive"**: Jack Kerouac, *The Subterraneans* (New York: Grove, paper, 1958), 70.

125   **"that crazy ... mambo"**: Kerouac, *On the Road,* 293.

125   **"neither black nor white"**: Jorge Duany, "Popular Music in Puerto Rico: Toward an Anthropology of *Salsa,*" in Vernon W. Boggs, lead author and ed., *Salsiology: Afro-Cuban Music and the Evolution of Salsa in New York City* (Westport, CT: Greenwood Press, 1992), 79.

125   **"The Palladium was the laboratory ..."**: Max Salazar, quoted in Steven Loza, *Tito Puente and the Making of Latin Music* (Urbana, IL: University of Illinois Press, paper, 1999), 68.

125   **"The Palladium opened the door ..."**: Quoted in Nina Siegal, "The New York Legacy of Tito Puente," *New York Times,* 6 June 2000, B:4.

125   **Ernie Ensley**: Quoted in Vernon W. Boggs, "Ernie Ensley, Palladium Mambero," in Boggs, 148.

125   **"Some of it was just one chord ..."**: Artie Butler, interview, 24 October 2001.

125   **"Cuban music is based on repetition"**: Brian Lynch, quoted in Ben Ratliff, "Latin-Music Patriarch Stays Hungry: Eddie Palmieri Dusts Off, and Polishes, His 1960's Sound," *New York Times,* 30 April 2002, E:7.

125   **"Mambo and Latin"**: Quoted in Pollock, *When Rock Was Young,* 146; *Landmark 1956,* p. 17; *Landmark 1955.*

126   **"The pulse of New York City ..."**: Cynthia Weill, interviewed by Morgan Neville for A&E's *Biography.*

126   **"If you were from Brooklyn ..."**: Tony Orlando, interview, 24 April 2002.

126   **A lifelong friend of Sedaka**: Frank Gershon, quoted in Frommer and Frommer, 126; Joyce Wadler, "Seymour Rexite, 91, Star of Yiddish Stage, Dies," *New York Times,* 16 October 2002, C:14.

126   **Bay Two**: Jay Siegal, interview, 11 September 2001; Hank Medress, interview, 25 September 2001.

126   **Machito entertained**: Vernon W. Boggs, "Salsa Music: The Latent Function of Slavery and Racism," in Boggs, 356.

126 **Hilton Ruiz:** Quoted in Loza, 118.

126 **Bandleaders Al "Alfredito" Levy:** John Storm Roberts, *The Latin Tinge: The Impact of Latin American Music on the United States* (New York: Oxford University Press, 2nd ed., paper, 1999), 130.

126 **Dick "Ricardo" Sugar:** Vernon Boggs, "Dick 'Ricardo' Sugar: Salsero *de* Salsero," in Boggs, 135–36.

126 **"it was just Jewish Latin":** Gerry Goffin, interviewed by Morgan Neville for A&E's *Biography.*

127 **Paul Case had introduced Spector:** Doc Pomus, Goldman interview, 3–4 April 1990.

127 **Spector had been pestering:** This account of the composition of "Spanish Harlem" draws on Ertegun, 129; Ribowsky, 72; Beverly Ross, interview, 4 June 2003; Artie Ripp, interview, 20 October 2001.

128 **"It's a great tune . . .":** Ben E. King, interviewed by Morgan Neville for A&E's *Biography.*

128 **Tindley . . . Franklin:** Heilbut, 60–61, 236; Allan, 87.

128 **"They were chance-takers":** Ben E. King, interviewed by Morgan Neville for A&E's *Biography.*

129 **"an insidious piece of work":** Fricke.

129 **"I never saw anybody so terrific . . .":** Burt Bacharach, interview, 3 May 2002.

129 **"I was opening her . . .":** Ibid.

129 **Peter Matz:** Marlene Dietrich, *Marlene,* trans. Salvator Attanasio (New York: Grove Press, 1989), 230–31.

129 **"Iz dot a cold?":** Reed, 3:2.

129 **"You'll be sorry":** Kroll, 53.

129 **"He was young . . .":** Dietrich, 229–55.

130 **"generalissimo":** Ibid., 255.

130 **"I never wrote a rock and roll song . . .":** Reed, 3:2.

130 **get a day job:** Ruhlmann, 26.

130 **"He couldn't really sing . . .":** Kenny Vance, interview, 26 March 2002. The Bacharach-David song "Little Betty Falling Star" later appeared on a Gene Pitney album.

130 **"loved rock 'n' roll . . .":** Pollock, *In Their Own Words,* xiii.

131 **"You guys know how to make hits . . .":** Leiber and Stoller, interviewed by Morgan Neville for A&E's *Biography.*

131 **"offbeat":** Mitch Miller, interview, 27 June 2002; Burt Bacharach, interview, 3 May 2002; Hal David, interview, 1 May 2003; Elaine Orlando, interview, 6 May 2002.

131 **Bacharach wrote with David:** Smith, *Off the Record,* 180.

131 **"Cowriting was like Russian roulette":** Hank Hunter, interview, 10 November 2001.

131 **Marlene Dietrich described:** Dietrich, 234.

132 **"Carole and Jerry idolized":** Tony Orlando, interview, 24 April 2002.

133 **"They were kind of like mythic figures . . .":** Gerry Goffin, interviewed by Morgan Neville for A&E's *Biography.*

133 **"When I was in college . . .":** Ibid.

133 **"Carole used to hang in there . . .":** Charlie Thomas, interview, 22 June 2002.

133 **According to Wexler:** Jerry Wexler, interview, 25 July 2002.

134 **"Carole came up with the melody . . .":** Gerry Goffin, interview, 22 October 2001.

134 **"blinking on the marquee":** Barry Mann, interview, 21 October 2001.

134 **"We were from the street":** Kenny Vance, interview, 26 March 2002.

134 **"Jerry Leiber hated it":** Cynthia Weil and Barry Mann, interview, 21 October 2001.

134   **Leiber denied this:** Jerry Leiber, e-mail communication, May 2002.

134   **Orlando observed:** Tony Orlando, interview, 24 April 2002.

135   **His "imagination caught fire":** Humphrey Burton, *Leonard Bernstein* (London: Faber and Faber, 1994), 249–50.

135   **All around me Puerto Rican kids . . .":** Meryle Secrest, *Leonard Bernstein: A Life* (New York: Alfred A. Knopf, 1994), 212. Brooks Atkinson's review is quoted in Secrest, 220.

135   **One day Weil saw:** Smith, *Off the Record,* 127.

135   **Using chords that Mann characterized:** Cynthia Weil and Barry Mann, interview, 21 October 2001.

135   **an estimated ten thousand mourners:** John Neville, *The Press, the Rosenbergs, and the Cold War* (Westport, CT: Praeger, 1995), 136.

135   **"I always felt that political noise . . .":** Barry Mann, interview, 21 October 2001.

136   **one of its veteran teachers was threatened:** Leonard Buder, " 'Refuse to Testify,' Einstein Advises Intellectuals Called In by Congress," *New York Times,* June 12, 1953, 1, reproduced in *Loyalty and Security in a Democratic State,* ed. Gene Brown, advisory ed. Richard H. Rovere, *The Great Contemporary Issues* series (New York: New York Times/Arno Press, 1977), 216.

136   **"clumsily, because I'm not a pianist":** Artie Ripp, interview, 20 October 2001.

136   **"He would make her do it . . .":** Cynthia Weil interview, 21 October 2001.

137   **"another of those songs I don't understand":** Cynthia Weil, interview, 21 October 2001.

137   **"two of the finest . . . in pop history":** Al Kasha and Joel Hirschhorn, "Anatomy of a Hit: Up on the Roof," *Songwriter* 5 (March 1980), 15.

137   **"They really loved it . . .":** This account of Mann and Weil's collaboration with Leiber and Stoller is drawn from Cynthia Weil and Barry Mann, interview, 21 October 2001; interview by Terry Gross on *Fresh Air,* 18 July 2000.

138   **Leiber and Stoller bumped into Spector:** Ertegun, 147.

139   **"In the wildest hipster . . .":** James Farrell, *The Spirit of the Sixties: Making Postwar Radicalism* (New York: Routledge, 1997), 66.

139   **"So we rewrote it . . .":** Barry Mann, interview, 21 October 2001.

139   **the song was "a sendup":** Fox, 180.

139   **According to Charlie Thomas:** Charlie Thomas, interview, 22 June 2002.

139   **"I killed the record":** Jerry Wexler, interview, 25 July 2002.

139   **Kenny Vance said:** Kenny Vance, interview, 26 March 2002.

140   **a spectacular afterlife:** This account of Jay and the Americans' recording of "Only in America" is based on Kenny Vance, interview, 26 March 2002, and Steve Kolanjian's notes to *Come a Little Bit Closer: The Best of Jay and the Americans* (EMI USA/United Artists CDP-7-934488-2).

CHAPTER TEN: BABY TALK

141   **Jerry Leiber heard a female voice:** This account of Leiber's first encounter with Greenwich is based on Ellie Greenwich, interview, 23 July 2001; Cub Koda, "Ellie Greenwich: America's Songwriting Sweetheart (and Then She Wrote)," *Goldmine* 361, vol. 20, no. 11 (27 May 1994), 38; Jerry Leiber, e-mail communication, May 2002.

141   **Ellie Greenwich was born:** Unless otherwise noted, all biographical information and quotations describing Ellie Greenwich's early life and career are drawn from three interviews conducted on 18 April and 23 July 2001 and 15 December 2004.

143   **"He was almost like an older brother . . .":** "Those Magic Moments: Doc Pomus Remembered by His Friends and Peers," *Goldmine,* 10.

143   **"She was bursting forth . . .":** Mark Barkan, interview, 4 October 2001.

145   **"you little prick":** Ibid.

145   **she slammed her Corvair:** Ellie Greenwich, interviewed by Morgan Neville for A&E's *Biography.*

145   **auguries of many songs to come:** The third Greenwich-Powers song that Spector produced, "My Heart Beat a Little Bit Faster," appeared on Bob B. Soxx and the Blue Jeans' 1963 album, *Zip-A-Dee-Doo-Dah.*

146   **"We went from having stuff . . .":** Jeff Barry, interview, 18 October 2001. Unless otherwise noted, all biographical information and quotations describing Barry's early life and career are drawn from this interview.

146   **Fellow student Al Contrera:** Al Contrera, interview, 10 April 2002.

147   **"I immediately had a great rapport . . .":** Beverly Ross, interview, 4 June 2003.

147   **Raleigh—a wizened older man:** Mark Barkan, *Almost Famous (or I Never Was Burt Bacharach),* unpublished autobiography, 17.

148   **"Jeff was crazy in love . . .":** Artie Resnick, interview, 11 March 2002.

149   **"like the Marlboro man":** Mike Stoller, e-mail communication, May 2002.

149   **"But she sort of smiled":** Gerry Goffin, interview, 22 October 2001. In an odd coincidence, a character in William Faulkner's *The Reivers,* published the same year that the Crystals recorded "He Hit Me," observed, "[W]hat better sign than a black eye or a cut mouf can a woman want from a man that he got her on his mind?" *The Reivers* (New York: Random House, 1962), 263.

150   *Rolling Stone* **magazine:** "The 500 Greatest Songs of All Time," *Rolling Stone* 963 (9 December 2004), 65–165.

150   **"the quintessential young record":** Doc Pomus, Goldman interview, 3–4 April 1990.

151   **Spector erased:** Ribowsky, 147–48.

151   **For the Ronettes:** Ronnie Spector with Vince Waldron, *Be My Baby* (New York: Harmony Books, 1990), 1, 3, 26–27, 47; Ellie Greenwich, interviewed by Morgan Neville for Peter Jones Productions.

152   **"thin out the palette":** Stanley Applebaum, interview, 25 March 2002.

152   **Phil was the first . . .":** Palmer, 28.

153   **"Those were the mono days":** Brooks Arthur, interview, 23 October 2001.

154   **"Everybody else was making out . . .":** Quoted in Patrick and Baumgart, notes to *On Broadway: Hit Songs and Rarities from the Brill Building Era.*

154   **two obscure girl groups:** Jay Siegal, interview, 11 September 2001; Hank Medress, interview, 25 September 2001; Clemente, 181.

154   **"I probably would have worked harder . . .":** Jeff Barry, interviewed by Morgan Neville for A&E's *Biography.*

CHAPTER ELEVEN: AT WORK IN THE ELVIS ATELIER

155   **"We never did a bit of work . . .":** Quoted in Ertegun, 127.

155   **"Those rooms . . .":** Beverly Ross, interview, 4 June 2003.

155   **"I used to dread . . .":** Elaine Orlando, interview, 6 May 2002.

156   **"At one time he had a contract . . .":** Freddy Bienstock, interview, 26 February 2002.

156   **"we were competing":** Ben Weisman, interview, 17 October 2001.

156   **"out of the swamps":** Doc Pomus, Goldman interview, 3–4 April 1990.

157   **"big for their britches":** Peter Guralnick, *Careless Love: The Unmaking of Elvis Presley* (Boston: Back Bay, paper, 2000), 162.

157   **Parker prevented Pomus:** Nixon, 13.

157 **"drifted by . . .":** Doc Pomus, Goldman interview, 3–4 April 1990.

158 **for the Flamingos:** Pouzenc, notes to *Elvis Chante Mort Shuman & Doc Pomus.*

158 **Garrett befriended Pomus:** Snuff Garrett, interview, 28 December 2003. According to Mort Shuman's unpublished autobiographical sketch, Hill and Range paid Pomus's airfare to Los Angeles and his, too.

159 **turned to their friend Bobby Darin:** Snuff Garrett, interview, 28 December 2003; Nixon, 13.

159 **"Latest Flame":** Pouzenc, notes to *Elvis Chante Mort Shuman & Doc Pomus*; Doc Pomus, Goldman interview, 3–4 April 1990; Sapia, 10; Nixon, 13.

159 **"I started fooling around . . .":** Pouzenc, notes to *Elvis Chante Mort Shuman & Doc Pomus.*

160 **Alan Jeffreys:** For information regarding Alan Jeffreys, I am indebted to Judy Jeffreys Lotwin, Jeffreys's widow and a singer under the name of Judy Scott, interviewed 6 November 2003.

162 **"no money, zilch":** Willi Burke, interview, 4 June 2001. Unless otherwise noted, all subsequent quotations and information regarding Pomus's marriage are drawn from this interview.

163 **"My experience has been":** Pollock, *In Their Own Words,* 16.

163 **"Doc felt he was someone . . .":** Shirlee Hauser, interview, 5 April 2002.

164 **"a dumpy little place":** Ertegun, 15.

164 **musical and show business clientele:** Shirlee Hauser, interview, 5 April 2002.

164 **Brooks Arthur remembered:** Brooks Arthur, interview, 23 October 2001.

164 **Spindletop Restaurant:** Phil Spector, "The Induction of Doc Pomus into the Rock and Roll Hall of Fame," *Antaeus: On Music,* no. 71/72 (autumn 1993), 153–54.

164 **"Sometimes Mortie wouldn't show up . . .":** Willi Burke, interview, 4 June 2001.

165 **dangling a joint over a secretary's desk:** Elaine Orlando, interview, 6 May 2002.

165 **"He was always stoned . . .":** Beverly Ross, interview, 4 June 2003.

165 **bedded a kibbutznik:** Mort Shuman, unpublished autobiographical sketch.

165 **Café Sahbra:** Ibid.; advertisement, *New York Post,* 15 April 1963, 20; Earl Wilson's column, *New York Post Sunday Magazine,* 5 May 1963, 3.

165 **a nightmare:** Mort Shuman, unpublished autobiographical sketch; Alfred Albelli, "Waiter Spills Piping Dish" and "Separation Won by Wife Despite Kiss 'n' Tell Pal," *Daily News,* 17 and 18 March 1964; Certificate of Disposition No. 0529, 1 June 2004, County Clerk, New York County.

165 **"Poor Mortie! . . .":** Paul Evans, interview, 16 November 2001; Brooks Arthur, interview, 23 October 2001; Mort Shuman, unpublished autobiographical sketch; Eric Blau, interview, 4 April 2002.

166 **"During the day M.S. was . . .":** Mort Shuman, unpublished autobiographical sketch.

166 **Shuman warned Barry Mann:** Barry Mann, interview, 21 October 2001.

166 **"Rock 'n' roll will never die":** Charlie Thomas, interview, 22 June 2002.

CHAPTER TWELVE: THE MAGICIAN AND THE MENSCH

167 **"regal elegance":** Clarence A. Moore, "Dionne Warwick: Forever Gold," *Goldmine* 248, vol. 16, no. 2 (26 January 1990), 8, citing an article that appeared in *Ebony* in the 1960s.

167 **Warrick's "piping voice":** Jerry Leiber, interviewed by Morgan Neville for A&E's *Biography.*

167 **"Burt and I were impressed . . .":** David, *What the World Needs Now and Other Love Lyrics,* 82.

168   "Tower of Strength": Joseph Laredo, notes to *A Hundred Pounds of Clay: The Best of Gene McDaniels* (Collectables COL-5646 S21-18546); Alec Cumming, with assistance from Paul Grein, "Let the Music Play: 75 Magic Moments," notes to *The Look of Love: The Burt Bacharach Collection,* 36; "Another Tear Falls," in the Collection of Lead Sheets of the Music Division of the New York Public Library for the Performing Arts at Lincoln Center, JPB 00–51, Box 1.

168   "mickey-mouse": Laredo, notes to *A Hundred Pounds of Clay: The Best of Gene McDaniels.*

168   Florence Greenberg: Ruth Brown with Andrew Yule, *Miss Rhythm* (New York: Donald I. Fine, 1996), 149; Freddy Bienstock, interview, 26 February 2002; Jancik, 10.

169   "She was a brave woman": Maxine Brown, interview, 29 April 2002.

169   "People would be afraid . . .": Steve Tyrell, interview, 19 February 2002.

169   Many people who worked with them confirmed: Gerry Goffin, interview, 22 October 2001; Freddy Bienstock, interview, 26 February 2002; Maxine Brown, interview, 29 April 2002.

170   "that dance he would do": Kenny Vance, interview, 26 March 2002.

170   Smokey Robinson: Bill Dahl, "Chuck Jackson: Suave, Debonair and Uptown," *Goldmine* 442, vol. 23, no. 14 (4 July 1997), 68.

170   "as if Burt was producing it": Cumming, "Let the Music Play: 75 Magic Moments," 35.

170   Vee Jay Records: The story of how "Make It Easy on Yourself" ended up at Vee Jay Records rather than Scepter is complicated by Ronald Isley's account, unconfirmed by Bacharach. According to Ronald Isley, the Isley Brothers, briefly signed to Scepter Records, set out to record "Make It Easy on Yourself" as the flip side of "Twist and Shout." When Luther Dixon changed some of Hal David's lyrics, an incensed Bacharach denied them permission, "took his music, and walked out of the studio"— or so Ronald Isley told "Boldface Names," *New York Times,* 20 November 2003, B:6.

170   Butler recalled: Jerry Butler with Earl Smith, *Only the Strong Survive: Memoirs of a Soul Survivor* (Bloomington: Indiana University Press, 2000), 116.

170   "I've always been grateful . . .": Burt Bacharach, interview, 3 May 2002.

170   Many of the flourishes . . .": Francis Davis, "The Man from Heaven," *Atlantic Monthly* (June 1997), 106.

171   when an A&R man told him: Hilburn, 6.

171   "That's how I started . . .": Burt Bacharach, interviewed by Morgan Neville for A&E's *Biography.*

171   "I was never so nervous . . .": Pollock, *When Rock Was Young,* 126.

172   Greenberg disliked Hunt: Jancik, 12.

172   "motion pictures surrounded us": Kasha and Hirschhorn, *Notes on Broadway,* 92.

173   it did not appear in the film: Wayne Jones, "Wayne Jones Talks with . . . Gene Pitney," *Goldmine* 80 (January 1983), 27.

173   "better than having a producer": Peter Doggett, "The Lost Hero of 60s Pop," *Record Collector* 267 (November 2001), 98.

174   fell out with Aaron Schroeder, whose aggressiveness: Cumming, "Let the Music Play," 54; Ben Weisman, interview, 17 October, 2001.

174   turned down "He's a Rebel": Pollock, *When Rock Was Young,* 118.

174   "To hell with the song . . .": Jancik, 12. By one account (Cumming, "Let the Music Play," 41), a demo of "It's Love That Really Counts" prompted Greenberg's negative response, but this is less convincing because Scepter Records' premier group, the Shirelles, proceeded to record it.

174   "Don't make me over, man!": Robin Platts, "Anyone Who Had a Heart: The Songs of Burt Bacharach and Hal David," *Discoveries* (December 1997), 49.

174   a misprint on the single's label: Smith, *Off the Record,* 181.
174   "She had to sing an octave . . .": Kroll, 52.
175   Weisman pleaded with Garrett: Ben Weisman, interview, 17 October 2001. Burt
      Bacharach said he could not recall this incident (interview, 3 May 2002), while Snuff
      Garrett disputed Weisman's account of the recording session and said that Liberty ini-
      tially promoted both sides of the single, intending to support whichever song won
      more airplay (interview, 28 December 2003).
175   *Rolling Stone Illustrated History of Rock & Roll:* Jim Miller, ed., *The Rolling Stone Il-
      lustrated History of Rock & Roll* (New York: Rolling Stone Press/Random House,
      1976).
175   "the delicacy and mystery": Quoted in Nat Hentoff's liner notes to *Dionne War-
      wick's Golden Hits—Part One* (Scepter SPS 565).
176   "Finish it!": David, *What the World Needs Now and Other Love Lyrics,* 4.
176   David always regretted: Ibid., 78–79.
176   "Hal is so intense": Burt Bacharach, interviewed by Morgan Neville for A&E's *Biog-
      raphy.*
176   When the house band at the Apollo: Webb, 301.
176   When Ben Weisman first heard: Ben Weisman, interview, 17 October 2001.
176   Greenberg preferred another song: Cumming, "Let the Music Play: 75 Magic Mo-
      ments," 49.
176   "the semi-bossa nova feel": Artie Butler, interview, 24 October 2001.
177   "There was nothing that Burt could write musically": Quoted in Sheryl Flatow,
      "What the World Needs Now," *Performing Arts* (April 1998), 16.
177   "The more that Hal and I wrote . . .": Burt Bacharach, interviewed by Morgan
      Neville for A&E's *Biography.*
177   "move beyond the boundaries": Hilburn, 79.
177   he wrote music in his head: Reed, 3:11.
177   "I wrote something on a fence": Elaine Orlando, interview, 6 May 2002.
178   Bacharach reflected: Quoted in Bill De Main, "Do You Know the Way to . . . Mon-
      terey? Santa Fe? Whitley Bay?" *Mojo* 28 (March 1996), 47.
178   "My nonsymmetrical phrasing . . .": Quoted in Webb, 301.
178   "I never felt his music was quirky": Hal David, interview, 1 May 2003.
178   "It just happened": Ibid.
178   "playboy of the Western world": Mark Barkan, interview, 4 October 2001.
178   "All my stuff was piled . . .": Hal David, interview, 1 May 2003.
179   bobbed and weaved and jerked: Al Gorgoni, interview, 1 February 2002.
179   retreated to the mens' room: Burt Bacharach, interviewed by Morgan Neville for
      A&E's *Biography.*
179   under the adoring eyes: Steve Tyrell, interview, 19 February 2002.
179   "I was coproducer": Hal David, interview, 1 May 2003.
179   "Hal sat in the studio . . .": Steve Tyrell, interview, 19 February 2002.
179   "The song was always the thing": Hal David, interview, 1 May 2003.
179   "a greater kick . . .": Quoted in Kroll, 51.
179   "Burt had a kind of genius quality . . .": Tony Orlando, interview, 24 April 2002.
180   "very tense and hyper . . .": Dionne Warwick in a 1982 interview with Mick Wright
      (http://www.merrymarketing.com/Dionne55.htm).
180   "we weren't so interested: Burt Bacharach, interview, 3 May 2002.
180   U. S. Songs: Ibid.; Hal David, interview, 1 May 2003; Leiber and Stoller, e-mail com-
      munication, May 2002.

180 **Richard Gottehrer explained:** Richard Gottehrer, interview, 13 November 2003.

181 **"competing with the last hit":** Burt Bacharach, interviewed by Morgan Neville for A&E's *Biography.*

181 **Brown approached Bacharach:** Maxine Brown, interview, 29 April 2002.

CHAPTER THIRTEEN: SELLING OUT

182 **intended for Bobby Rydell:** Tamarkin, "Barry Mann and Cynthia Weil," 15.

183 **"Some great work of American literature":** Gerry Goffin, interview, 22 October 2001.

183 **the writers read in the trade papers:** Bob Rolontz, "Nevins-Kirshner Sale to Disk Label Seems in Offing," *Billboard* (23 March 1963), 1; "Columbia Pix About to Sign Kirshner Deal," *Billboard* (30 March 1963), 1; Ren Grevatt, "Kirshner Named V.-P. As Deal Is Official," *Billboard* (27 April 1963), 1; Dick Asher, interviews, 4 April 2002 and 19 January 2004; Herb Moelis, interview, 10 April 2002.

183 **"twoscore writers":** "Columbia Pix About to Sign Kirshner Deal," *Billboard* (30 March 1963), 1.

183 **"Kirshner will concentrate . . .":** Grevatt, 1.

184 **"We were in the Garden of Eden":** Jack Keller, interview, 3 June 2003.

184 **A million dollars was not chump change:** Dick Asher interview, 10 April 2002; Richard Gottehrer, interview, 11 November 2003.

184 **"cardinal sin":** Don Kirshner, interviewed by Morgan Neville for A&E's *Biography.*

184 **"We thought it would be like calypso . . .":** Artie Butler, interview, 24 October 2001.

185 **sense of estrangement:** Cynthia Weil, interview, 21 October 2001; Herb Moelis, interview, 10 April 2002.

185 **"I have to know . . .":** Cynthia Weil and Barry Mann, interview, 21 October 2001.

185 **Goffin demanded a million-dollar guarantee:** Gerry Goffin, interview, 22 October 2001; Herb Moelis, interview, 10 April 2002.

185 **"we wanted to stay . . .":** Gerry Goffin, interview, 22 October 2001.

185 **Mann and Weil brought their German shepherd:** Cynthia Weil and Barry Mann, interview, 21 October 2001.

186 **Kirshner called Lester Sill:** Lester Sill, quoted in Smith, *Off the Record,* 187.

186 **The contracts:** Herb Moelis, interviews, 10 April 2002 and 19 January 2004.

186 **under the pseudonym:** Gari, notes for Neil Sedaka, *Oh Carol: The Complete Recordings 1956–1966,* 29–30.

187 **"It Hurts to Be in Love":** Tony Orlando, interview, 24 April 2002; Neil Sedaka, interview, 30 April 2002. Brian Gari gives a slightly different account of the origins and various versions of "It Hurts to Be in Love" in his notes for Neil Sedaka, *Oh Carol: The Complete Recordings 1956–1966* (p. 36).

187 **"very staid . . .":** Neil Sedaka, interview, 30 April 2002.

187 **"It doesn't?":** Neil Sedaka in Spitz, 147.

187 **Ben Sutter:** Sedaka, 104.

187 **"My father accepted it . . .":** Neil Sedaka, interview, 30 April 2002.

187 **Sedaka was less accepting:** Neil Sedaka, quoted in Pollock, *When Rock Was Young,* 153; Sedaka, 123–42; Gari, notes for Neil Sedaka, *Oh Carol: The Complete Recordings 1956–1966;* Neil Sedaka, interview, 30 April 2002.

188 **Australia:** Spitz, 148.

188 **eked out $30,000:** Flans, 22.

188 **"'Didn't you used to be . . .'":** Ibid., 13.

188   **"Howie and I wrote vanilla":** Jack Keller, interview, 3 June 2003.

189   **"Sinatra's next song":** Ibid.

189   **he bumped into Greenfield:** Artie Butler, interview, 24 October 2001.

189   **"We couldn't get it to work":** Gerry Goffin, interview, 22 October 2001.

190   **Enter the Tokens:** Clemente, 52; Hank Medress, interview, 25 September 2001; Jay Siegal, interview, 11 September 2001; Gerry Goffin, interview, 22 October 2001. Clemente and Michael Lydon (in *Boogie Lightning* [New York: Dial, 1974, 115–16]) wrote that the Tokens erased Little Eva's voice from the recording of "One Fine Day" that served as the basis for the Chiffons' record. Medress and Siegal said in separate interviews that they removed King's vocal, and no one could have been in a better position to know this than the record's producers.

190   **When Jackson rejected the song:** Dennis Garvey, "Freddie Scott: Soul Journeyman," *Goldmine* 329, vol. 19, no. 5 (5 March 1993), 54.

190   **living in a boxy house:** Gerry Goffin, interview, 22 October 2001; Jay Siegal, interview, 11 September 2001; Eugene Archer, "Bellhop Turned Millionaire, 30, Heads a Columbia Film Division," *New York Times,* 14 September 1964, 42; Gerry Goffin, interviewed by Morgan Neville for A&E's *Biography,* 28 September 2000.

191   **Russ Titelman:** Russ Titelman, interview, 11 October 2001; Ribowsky, 97–98.

191   **"Oh No Not My Baby":** Russ Titelman, interview, 11 October 2001; Maxine Brown, interview, 29 April 2002.

192   **"a separate subsidiary label":** "Columbia Pix About to Sign Kirshner Deal," 8.

192   **"Let's Turkey Trot":** Jack Keller, interview, 3 June 2003, and his notes to *Music for All Occasions,* a four-CD collection of his songs compiled for promotional use; Haertel, 24.

192   **"Gerry didn't want her . . .":** Herb Moelis, interview, 10 April 2002.

193   **Goffin "really had something . . .":** Barry Mann, interview, 21 October 2001.

193   **"I haven't really made a record . . .":** Russ Titelman, interview, 11 October 2001.

194   **"She was a great critic":** Ibid.

194   **Kirshner moved in high circles:** "Don Kirshner Has Been Named . . . ," *New York Post,* 2 September 1964, 87; "Place in History," *Billboard,* (9 November 1963), 1; Snuff Garrett, interview, 28 December 2003.

194   **The news reached:** Smith, *Off the Record,* 199; Elaine Orlando, interview, 6 May 2002.

CHAPTER FOURTEEN: SEESAW

195   **"She was afraid":** Gerry Goffin, interview, 22 October 2001.

195   **The Beatles' arrival:** Jay Siegal, interview, 11 September 2001; Perone, 3; Gerry Goffin, interview, 22 October 2001.

195   **When Snuff Garrett made his regular rounds:** Snuff Garrett, interview, 28 December 2003.

196   **after seeing A Hard Day's Night:** Gerry Goffin, interview, 22 October 2001; Russ Titelman, interview, 11 October 2001.

197   **The English onslaught:** Cynthia Weil, interview, 21 October 2001; Bob Dylan quoted in Howard Sounes, *Down the Highway: The Life of Bob Dylan* (New York: Grove Press, 2001), 117–18; Bob Dylan, notes to *Biograph* (Sony 65298); Dylan, *Chronicles,* 227.

197   **crossed paths at Carnegie Hall:** Gerry Goffin, interviews, 22 October 2001 and 21 January 2002; Gerry Goffin, interviewed with Carole King, Barry Mann, and Cynthia Weil by Morgan Neville for A&E's *Biography.*

197   **Going backstage:** Gerry Goffin, interview, 22 October 2001; Dylan, *Chronicles,* 48.

198   **Goffin's self-esteem:** Al Aronowitz, quoted in Sounes, 149; Goffin, interview, 22 October 2001; Goffin, interview, *Los Angeles Daily News,* September 1996 (accessible online at http://members.home.net/carolking/guideto.htm); Goffin, quoted in Pollock, *In Their Own Words,* 29.

198   **"After the Beatles . . .":** Goffin, quoted in Pollock, *In Their Own Words,* 29.

198   **World War III:** Jay Siegal, interview, 11 September 2001; Tony Orlando, interview, 24 April 2002.

198   **"a clear plan in mind":** Brooks Arthur, interview, 23 October 2001.

199   **"one among the millions":** DiMucci, 154; Barry Mann, interview, 21 October 2001.

199   **According to Goffin:** Goffin, interview, 22 October 2001; Al Aronowitz, interview, 5 November 2001.

199   **"trying to expand his mind . . .":** Steve Tyrell, interview, 19 February 2002.

200   **Crosby left the session in a huff:** Dave Zimmer, *Crosby, Stills & Nash: The Authorized Biography* (New York: Da Capo, paper, 2000), 54.

200   **Goffin also fought:** Barry Mann, interview, 21 October 2001; Jack Keller, interview, 3 June 2003.

200   **When the Tokens visited:** Hank Medress, interview, 25 September 2001; Jay Siegal, interview, 11 September 2001; Russ Titelman, interview, 11 October 2001.

200   **recommend a therapist:** This account of Goffin's breakdown is based on Barry Mann and Cynthia Weil, interview, 21 October 2001.

201   **the Myddle Class:** Al Aronowitz, "How I Nearly Made a Million Dollars in the Rock and Roll Business," *The Blacklisted Journalist* (15 January 2003), http://www.bigmagic.com/pages/blackj/column83.html; Al Aronowitz, interview, 5 November 2001.

201   **"part of the underbrush":** Barry Mann, interview, 21 October 2001.

202   **"trying to sound adolescent":** Tamarkin, "Barry Mann and Cynthia Weil," 14.

202   **in a single take:** Spector, *Be My Baby,* 101–2.

202   **"Listen to Phil Spector's records":** Jon Pareles, "Brian Wilson Speaks," in "Arts, Briefly," *New York Times,* 15 October 2004, E:6.

203   **"It's over":** Ribowsky, 217.

203   **Desperate to diversify:** Ibid., 184.

203   **At Kirshner's begrudged expense:** Barry Mann and Cynthia Weil, *They Wrote That?: The Songs of Barry Mann and Cynthia Weil,* a revue performed at the McGinn/Cazale Theatre, New York, 4 February 2004; Barry Mann, quoted in Smith, *Off the Record,* 127–28.

203   **Unusually:** Barry Mann and Cynthia Weil, interviewed by Terry Gross on *Fresh Air.*

203   **"[W]e are eavesdroppers":** Webb, 42, 121.

204   **It was Spector's idea:** Barry Mann and Cynthia Weil, interviewed by Terry Gross on *Fresh Air.*

204   **When Mann and Spector sang the song:** Bill Medley, quoted in Smith, *Off the Record,* 29; Cynthia Weil, interviewed by Morgan Neville for A&E's *Biography.*

204   **"working on a strategy . . .":** Ribowsky, 184–86.

204   **played at the wrong speed:** Barry Mann and Cynthia Weil, interviewed by Morgan Neville for A&E's *Biography.*

204   **Over the next four decades:** Ben Sisario, "Bobby Hatfield Dies at 63; Righteous Brothers Tenor," *New York Times,* 7 November 2003, C:10; Bill Medley, interviewed by Morgan Neville for A&E's *Biography.*

205   **Medley called Weil and Mann:** Jeff Tamarkin, "Righteous Brother and Sister: Bill Medley Meets Darlene Love—Again," *Goldmine* 355, vol. 20, no. 5 (4 March 1994), 64.

206   **ended their affair:** Darlene Love, with Rob Hoerburger, *My Name Is Love: The Darlene Love Story* (New York: William Morrow, 1998), 129.

206   **Demonstrating their mastery:** Hank Medress, interview, 25 September 2001; Cynthia Weil, interviewed by Terry Gross on *Fresh Air*; Al Gorgoni, interview, February 2002.

206   **composed with Gerry Goffin in mind:** Cynthia Weil, interview, 21 October 2001; Tamarkin, "Barry Mann and Cynthia Weil," 15.

206   **"We Gotta Get Out of This Place":** Barry Mann and Cynthia Weil, interviewed by Morgan Neville for A&E's *Biography*; Medley quoted in Len Scher, "The Righteous Brothers: Blue-Eyed Soul Brothers," *Goldmine* 99, vol. 10, no. 8 (11 May 1984), 52.

CHAPTER FIFTEEN: DOUBLE TROUBLE

208   **"All became clear . . .":** Mort Shuman, unpublished autobiographical sketch, 29.

208   **"found making transitions . . .":** Elaine Orlando, interview, 6 May 2002.

208   **Case urged Jerry Ragovoy:** "Those Magic Moments: Doc Pomus Remembered by His Friends and Peers," 10.

209   **Elaine Orlando's son:** Elaine Orlando, interview, 6 May 2002.

209   **Shuman's travels and dalliances:** Willi Burke, interview, 13 January 2004; Shirlee Hauser, interview, 5 April 2002.

209   **"Mortie was a free spirit":** Freddy Bienstock, interview, 26 February 2002.

209   **"I'm divorcing him, too":** Willi Burke, interview, 4 June 2001.

209   **Pomus took a bad spill:** Snuff Garrett, interview, 28 December 2003; Sapia, 9; Sharyn Felder, interview, 8 June 2001; Willi Burke, interview, 4 June 2001; Shirlee Hauser, interview, 5 April 2002; Raoul Felder, interview, 21 August 2001.

210   **While Pomus was recuperating:** Sapia, 9; Willi Burke, interview, 4 June 2001.

210   **Pomus was devastated:** Sapia, 9; Neil Sedaka, interview, 30 April 2002.

210   **"I'm not going to do this anymore":** Shirlee Hauser, interview, 5 April 2002.

211   **Jacques Brel distilled:** Barry Mann, interview, 21 October 2001; Eric Blau, interview, 4 April 2002; Mort Shuman, unpublished autobiographical sketch, 29–30.

211   **Shuman had such a flair:** Eric Blau, *Jacques Brel Is Alive and Well and Living in Paris* (New York: Dutton, paper, 1971), 13–15.

212   **Blau and Shumer soon set to work:** Ibid., 18.

212   **a rave review:** Clive Barnes's WQXR review and Mike Gross's 2 March 1968 *Billboard* review are reprinted in the notes to the CD reissue *Jacques Brel Is Alive and Well and Living in Paris* (Sony Classical/Columbia/Legacy SK89998).

212   **telephoned Brel in Paris:** Eric Blau, interview, 4 April 2002.

212   **Blau and Stone detected:** Eric Blau and Elly Stone, interviews, 4 April 2002.

CHAPTER SIXTEEN: GOLDEN GIRLS

214   **An audit they had requested:** Jerry Wexler, interview, 25 July 2002; Wexler and Ritz, 162; Jerry Leiber and Mike Stoller, interviewed by Morgan Neville for A&E's *Biography*.

215   **"Why are we making . . .":** Fox, 181.

215   **started Tiger Records:** Millar, 67.

215   **Billboard announced:** "Jerry Leiber, Mike Stoller Open Diskery," *Billboard* (2 November 1963), 6.

216   **the most positive result:** Millar, 158; Fox, 181; Dennis Garvey, "The Dixie Cups: Creole Bells," *Goldmine* 361, vol. 20, no. 11 (27 May 1994), 50.

217   **"We were about to go out of business":** Fox, 181.

217   **the fifty-dollar handshake:** Frederic Dannen, *Hit Men: Power Brokers and Fast Money Inside the Music Business* (New York: Crown, 1990), 52; Dorothy Wade and Justine Picardie, *Music Man: Ahmet Ertegun, Atlantic Records, and the Triumph of Rock 'n' Roll* (New York: W. W. Norton, 1993), 66.

217   **Goldner was dressed:** Jerry Leiber, interviewed in Richard Williams, "The Leiber-Stoller Story," *Melody Maker* (29 July 1972), 33; "Goldner Quits Roulette Again to Go on Own," *Billboard* (22 June 1963), 4; Fox, 182–83.

217   **Inspiration seized Lieber:** Kubernik, 124; Fox, 182–83. In a 23 March 2003 telephone interview, Hy Weiss denied Jerry Leiber's account of his encounter with Weiss and George Goldner at Al & Dick's, but poor health prevented him from supplying his own version of what transpired.

217   **When Leiber mentioned:** Fox, 183.

217   **"Chapel of Love":** Love, 91; Garvey, "The Dixie Cups," 50; Brooks Arthur, interview, 23 October 2001.

218   **created a rift:** Ribowsky, 172–73.

218   **"labor of love":** Ellie Greenwich, interview, 23 July 2001.

218   **"Iko Iko":** Ibid.; Garvey, "The Dixie Cups," 50; Brooks Arthur, interview, 23 October 2001; Jeff Barry, interview, 18 October 2001.

219   **"The most important thing . . .":** Artie Butler, interview, 24 October 2001.

219   **"He just loved sounds":** Brooks Arthur, interview, 23 October 2001; Jeff Barry, interview, 18 October 2001.

219   **"Jeff seemed to be more in charge . . .":** Jay Siegal, interview, 9 September 2001.

220   **Stoller insisted was a Long Island accent:** Mike Stoller, interview, 14 May 2001.

220   **"When a label starts . . .":** Ellie Greenwich, interview, 23 July 2001; Koda, 44.

220   **Most of the group disliked:** Greg Russo, *Mannerisms: The Five Phases of Manfred Mann* (Floral Park, NY: Crossfire Publications, paper, 1995), 22.

221   **"a camaraderie . . .":** Ellie Greenwich, interview, 23 July 2001.

221   **her "own little girls' group":** Ibid.

221   **Competition made conversation difficult:** Ellie Greenwich, interview, 18 April 2001.

222   **Leiber and Stoller rewarded:** Ellie Greenwich, quoted in Betrock, 98; Jeff Barry, interview, 18 October 2001; Leiber and Stoller, e-mail communication, May 2002; Artie Butler, interview, 23 January 2005.

222   **"The beauty of working for Leiber and Stoller . . .":** Ellie Greenwich, interview, 23 July 2001.

222   **"We only edited . . .":** Booth, 28.

222   **"They'd gotten too old . . .":** Meryl Stoller, interview, 10 July 2002.

222   **"I didn't dig it . . .":** Williams, 33.

223   **"an assembly line":** Jeff Barry, interview, 18 October 2001.

223   **Goldner brought more gusto:** Jerry Leiber, interviewed by Morgan Neville for A&E's *Biography*; Artie Butler, interview, 24 October 2001; Jeff Barry, interview, 18 October 2001.

CHAPTER SEVENTEEN: "SOMETHIN' DIED"

225   **The Shangri-Las were elusive:** Mary Weiss, interviewed by Morgan Neville for A&E's *Biography*; George "Shadow" Morton, interview, 30 May 2001; Artie Ripp, interview, 20 October 2001; Jeff Barry, interview, 18 October 2001; Mike Stoller, e-mail communication, May 2002.

225 **Relating the rise and fall:** Jerry Wexler, interview, 25 July 2002; Artie Ripp, interview, 20 October 2001.

225 **Mary Weiss and her older sister:** Kurt Loder, "Where Are They Now?: The Shangri-Las," *Rolling Stone* (12 September 1985), 50.

226 **organized crime:** Wade and Picardie, 117–19.

226 **Now Morton made a demo:** Rod McBrien, interview, 29 June 2001; George "Shadow" Morton, interview, 30 May 2001; Donna Gaines, "Girl Groups: A Ballad of Codependency," in ed. Barbara O'Dair, *Trouble Girls: The Rolling Stone Book of Women in Rock* (New York: Random House, 1997), 108.

226 **he presumed:** George "Shadow" Morton, interview, 30 May 2001; Ellie Greenwich, interview, 15 December 2004; Artie Ripp, interview, 20 October 2001; Brooks Arthur, interview, 23 October 2001.

226 **"Remember":** Jeff Barry, interview, 18 October 2001; Jeff Barry, quoted by Mike Patrick, notes for the Shangri-Las' *The Myrmidons of Melodrama* (RPM 136).

227 **Although Morton said:** Rod McBrien, interview, 29 June 2001; Jeff Barry, interview, 18 October, 2001.

227 **"shy person":** Mary Weiss, interviewed by Morgan Neville for A&E's *Biography*.

227 **A real motorcycle:** George "Shadow" Morton, interview, 30 May 2001; Brooks Arthur, interview, 23 October 2001.

228 **"The Shangi-Las were tough girls":** Quoted in Tommy West, notes, *I Can Hear Music: The Ellie Greenwich Collection* (Razor & Tie 7930182195-2).

228 **the Goodies:** George "Shadow" Morton, interviewed by Morgan Neville for A&E's *Biography*.

228 **a favorite of Mary Weiss:** Mary Weiss, e-mail communication, April 2002.

229 **At the height:** Wade and Picardie, 112–15; Leiber, quoted in Wexler and Ritz, 164.

229 **If Goldner was indulging:** Wade and Picardie, 111; Mike Stoller, e-mail communication, 1 February 2005; "Goldner Goes Independent with Goldisc," *Billboard* (13 July 1963), 3; "Jerry Leiber, Mike Stoller Open Diskery," 6; Kenny Vance, interview, 26 March 2002.

230 **Neil Diamond:** Neil Diamond, quoted in Smith, *Off the Record,* 187; Rich Wiseman, *Neil Diamond: Solitary Star* (New York: Dodd, Mead, 1987), 35–36.

231 **prompted talk of promoting:** Ellie Greenwich, interview, 23 July 2001; Betrock, 98.

231 **"We had too much happen . . .":** Ellie Greenwich, quoted in *Girl Groups: The Story of a Sound,* an MGM/UA home video presentation of a 1983 Delilah Films production.

231 **At a BMI banquet:** West, notes, *I Can Hear Music: The Ellie Greenwich Collection.*

231 **Greenwich was devastated:** Ellie Greenwich, interview, July 23, 2001; Jeff Barry, interview, 18 October 2001; Brooks Arthur, interview, 23 October 2001; Wiseman, 52.

231 **Artie Resnick thought:** Artie Resnick, interview, 11 March 2002.

232 **romanticism:** Beverly Ross, interview, 4 June 2003; Jennifer O'Neill, *Surviving Myself* (New York: William Morrow, 1999), 162.

232 **Whatever the reasons for their divorce:** Ellie Greenwich, interviews, 18 April 2001 and 15 December 2004; Gerry Goffin, interview, 22 October 2001.

232 **a mobster called:** Ellie Greenwich, interview, 23 July 2001.

232 **"into debt with the bookies . . .":** Artie Ripp, interview, 20 October 2001.

232 **Leiber and Stoller had sold:** Jerry Leiber, quoted in Fox, 184; Stoller, e-mail communication, 1 February 2005; Jeff Barry, interview, 18 October 2001; Ellie Greenwich, interview, 23 July 2001.

233 **trying to compose a Broadway show:** Williams, 33; Meryl Stoller, interview, 10 July 2002; Mitch Miller, interview, 27 June 2002.

233 **The Dixie Cups:** Jeff Tamarkin, "The Dixie Cups: Never Be Lonely Any-more," *Goldmine* 166, vol. 12, no. 25 (5 December 1986), 30; Jon Pareles, "A Happy Night for Old-Timers Still Singing the Blues," *New York Times,* 22 February 2003, B:17.

233 **"The performers were kids . . .":** Dick Fox, interview, 15 April 2002.

233 **No performer ever blamed:** Hank Medress, interview, 25 September 2001; Ellie Greenwich, interview, 23 July 2001; Ellie Greenwich, quoted in Betrock, 98.

234 **"a license to steal":** Artie Ripp, interview, 20 October 2001;

234 **The Chiffons sued:** Clemente, 54.

235 **Ike and Tina Turner:** Ribowsky, 219.

235 **Wolfe dubbed him:** Tom Wolfe, "The First Tycoon of Teen," in *The Kandy-Kolored Tangerine-Flake Streamline Baby* (New York: Noonday, 1965).

235 **"a little weird":** Ellie Greenwich, interview, 23 July 2001.

235 **disparate bits:** Ibid.; Jeff Barry, interview, 24 November 2004.

236 **Spector started recording:** Ribowsky, 220–22.

236 **so demoralized Spector:** Ibid., 198–99, 217–18; Spector, *Be My Baby,* 110.

236 **"He was mad at the world . . .":** Jeff Barry, interview, 18 October 2001.

237 **Diamond's early hit singles:** Wiseman, 37, 40; Jeff Barry, interview, 18 October 2001.

237 **"Neil basically was not . . .":** Richard Gottehrer, interview, 13 November 2003.

237 **"it might have been Jeff Barry":** Artie Kaplan, quoted in Wiseman, 46.

CHAPTER EIGHTEEN: SWINGING LONDON

238 **Mary Isobel:** Penny Valentine and Vicki Wickham, *Dancing with Demons: The Authorized Biography of Dusty Springfield* (New York: St. Martin's, 2000), 64, 72.

238 **at Bacharach's urging:** Burt Bacharach, interview, 3 May 2002.

238 **crossed the Channel:** Valentine and Wickham, 42.

239 **shattering cheap crockery:** Mary Weiss, interviewed by Morgan Neville for A&E's *Biography.*

239 **household names:** Hal David, interview, 1 May 2003; "Beat, Says Burt, Is Not My Kind of Music," *Melody Maker* (12 June 1965), 30; Claes Johansen, *The Zombies: Hung Up on a Dream* (London: SAF Publishing, 2001), 107–8.

239 **ties to the film industry:** "Earl Wilson on Broadway,"*New York Post,* 16 May 1965, 27; Eric Lax, *Woody Allen: A Biography* (New York: Knopf, 1991), 204; Cumming, "Let the Music Play: 75 Magic Moments."

240 *What's New Pussycat?:* Lax, 206; David, *What the World Needs Now and Other Love Lyrics,* 52; Lucy Ellis and Bryony Sutherland, *Tom Jones Close Up* (London: Omnibus, 2000), 67–68.

240 **"My Little Red Book . . .":** Geoffrey O'Brien, *Sonata for Jukebox: Pop Music, Memory, and the Imagined Life* (New York: Counterpoint, 2004), 19; Russo, *Mannerisms,* 29; Liz Jobey, ed., *The End of the Innocence: Photographs from the Decades That Define Pop* (Zurich: Scalo, 1997), 172.

241 *Casino Royale:* Lax, 222; Burt Bacharach, interview, 3 May 2002; David, *What the World Needs Now,* 67.

241 **"Alfie":** David, *What the World Needs Now,* 24; Hal David, interview, 1 May 2002.

242 *Alfie* **opened the same year:** Davis, "The Man from Heaven," 106; Cumming, "Let the Music Play: 75 Magic Moments"; Steve Tyrell, interview, 19 February 2002.

242 **"What the World Needs Now":** David, *What the World Needs Now,* 17; Smith, *Off the Record,* 181; Platts, 50; Jackie DeShannon, e-mail communication, 23 May 2001.

243 **By now Bacharach was a star:** Jim Pierson, notes, *Burt Bacharach Plays His Hits* (MCA MCAD-11681).

243 **"I now consider myself . . .":** "Beat, Says Burt," 30.

243 **"England was always good to me":** Hilburn, 79.

244 **wife as well as daughter nearly died:** Reed, 3:2.

244 **"At the time that he was delivering . . .":** Burt Bacharach, interviewed by Morgan Neville for A&E's *Biography.*

244 **"Kentucky Bluebird . . .":** Cumming, "Let the Music Play: 75 Magic Moments"; David, *What the World Needs Now,* 74.

244 **"I thought I blew it":** Hilburn, 79.

244 **Wexler overheard:** Wexler and Ritz, 214.

245 **Warwick did not like:** Moore, 12.

245 **"The great innovator . . .":** Webb, 169.

245 **"They didn't join in":** Steve Tyrell, interview, 19 February 2002.

246 **"The Windows of the World":** Bruce Pollock, *In Their Own Words,* xiv; Platts, 51; David, *What the World Needs Now,* 29.

247 *Promises, Promises:* Richard F. Shephard, "Anatomy of an Opening Night," *New York Times* (3 December 1968), 52; "Clothiers Honor Bacharach," *New York Times* (29 December 1970), 46; Clive Barnes, "Theater: Simon-Bacharach 'Promises, Promises,' Begins Run at the Shubert," *New York Times* (2 December 1968), 59; Kasha and Hirschhorn, 3–6; Louis Calta, "3 Broadway Musicals to Close This Weekend After Long Runs," *New York Times* (29 December 1971), 21.

247 **"The impermanence gets to you . . .":** Kasha and Hirschhorn, 9.

248 **"It was a part of our lives":** Burt Bacharach, interview, 3 May 2002.

CHAPTER NINETEEN: FROM THE MONKEES TO THOMAS MANN

249 **Two young songwriters:** Andrew Sandoval, "The True Story of the Monkees," notes to the Monkees, *Music Box* (Rhino R2 76706), 5; "Q&A with Bobby Hart," http://www.community.net/~tbaslier/hart.html.

250 **a reluctant Snuff Garrett:** Snuff Garrett, interview, 28 December 2003.

250 **Mickie Most:** Bobby Hart, interview, 8 June 2004.

250 **King in tears:** Jack Keller, interview, 3 June 2003.

250 **Kirshner and Sill enlisted:** Bobby Hart, interview, 8 June 2004; Jack Keller, interview, 3 June, 2003.

250 **"The Monkees were totally insecure":** Jack Keller, interview, 3 June 2003.

250 **upended a Coke:** Ibid.

251 **a peremptory memo:** Sandoval, "The True Story of the Monkees," notes to the Monkees' *Music Box,* 11.

251 **Kirshner contacted Diamond:** Wiseman, 50–51; "Interview: Don Kirshner," http://www.angelfire.com/sk/monkeerescue/kirs.

251 **"I'm a Believer":** Wiseman, 51; "Jeff Barry's Bubblegum Blues: Interview by Don Charles," in Kim Cooper and David Smay, eds., *Bubblegum Music Is the Naked Truth* (Los Angeles: Feral House, 2001), 128–29.

252 **"He was kind of Goldner-ish . . .":** Jeff Barry, interview, 18 October 2001.

252 **the Monkees revolted:** Don Kirshner and Mike Nesmith, interviewed in ed. Harold Bronson, *Hey, Hey, We're the Monkees* (Santa Monica, CA: General Publishing Group, 1996), and available online at http://www.geocities.com/monkeesincorp2/antikirshner.html.

252 **"He bullshitted me":** Sapia, 9.

252 "I think they were getting sick . . .": Peter Tork and Don Kirshner, interviewed in Bronson, ed.; "Interview: Don Kirshner;" Sanjek, 388–90; Herb Moelis, interview, 10 April 2002.

253 Moelis thought it absurd: Herb Moelis, interview, 10 April 2002.

253 Kirshner hired: "Interview: Don Kirshner"; Irwin Robinson, interview, 10 April 2002.

253 "The Monkees killed themselves . . .": Jack Keller, interview, 3 June 2003.

254 "throwaways": Gerry Goffin, interview, 22 October 2001.

254 "the evacuation of the record industry . . .": Bobby Hart, interview, 8 June 2004.

254 "I don't know how . . .": Cynthia Weil, interviewed by Morgan Neville for A&E's *Biography.*

255 "in a slump": Gerry Goffin, interviewed by Morgan Neville for A&E's *Biography.*

255 "You can't write songs . . .": Ibid.

255 "Chain of Fools": Ellie Greenwich, interviewed by Morgan Neville for A&E's *Biography;* Wexler and Ritz, 213–14.

256 "Wexler called me": Gerry Goffin, interview, 22 October 2001

256 *Dusty in Memphis:* Jim Feldman, notes, *Dusty in Memphis: Deluxe Edition* (Rhino R2 75580); Valentine and Wickham, 115; Gerry Goffin, interview, 22 October 2001.

257 "We just always had this hunger . . .": Barry Mann and Cynthia Weil, interview, 21 October 2001.

257 "I was always writing . . .": Jeff Barry, interview, 18 October 2001.

257 "I had three- and four-year-olds . . .": Ibid.

257 Barry launched a record label: "Jeff Barry's Bubblegum Blues: Interview by Don Charles," in Cooper and Smay, eds., 128.

258 "You don't need a protractor . . .": David Smay, "The Candy Ass Charisma of the Archies," in Cooper and Smay, eds., 43.

258 "D. W. Washburn": Leiber and Stoller, quoted in Randy Poe's notes for the Coasters' *50 Coastin' Classics;* Sandoval, "The True Story of the Monkees," notes to the Monkees' *Music Box,* 56–57.

260 "Is That All There Is?": Webb, 300; Thomas Mann, *Stories of Three Decades,* trans. H. T. Lowe-Porter (New York: The Modern Library, 1930), 23–27.

CODA

262 Ellie Greenwich: Koda, 46–47.

262 running poker games: Sharyn Felder, interview, 8 June 2001.

263 wrote a few songs with Bacharach: Gerry Goffin, interview, 22 October 2001; Burt Bacharach, interview, 3 May 2002.

264 Bombay . . . Carnegie Hall: Neil Sedaka, interview, 30 April 2002; Joseph Berger, "Vintage Pop Star with the Soul of a Bar Mitzvah Boy," *New York Times* (24 May 2004), E:1–4.

264 "the new prince of French pop": Mort Shuman, unpublished autobiographical sketch.

267 "an emotional connection": DeMain, "Carole King," 50–51.

BIBLIOGRAPHY

BOOKS

Algren, Nelson. *A Walk on the Wild Side.* Paper, New York: Noonday Press/Farrar, Straus and Giroux, 1998.

Allan, Tony, with Faye Treadwell. *Save the Last Dance for Me: The Musical Legacy of the Drifters.* Ann Arbor, MI: Popular Culture, 1993.

Basie, Count, as told to Albert Murray. *Good Morning Blues: The Autobiography of Count Basie.* New York: Random House, 1985.

Betrock, Alan. *Girl Groups: The Story of a Sound.* Paper, New York: Delilah, 1982.

Black, Kathryn. *In the Shadow of Polio: A Personal and Social History.* Reading, MA: Addison-Wesley, 1996.

Blau, Eric. *Jacques Brel Is Alive and Well and Living in Paris.* Paper, New York: Dutton, 1971.

Boggs, Vernon W., lead author and ed. *Salsiology: Afro-Cuban Music and the Evolution of Salsa in New York City.* Westport, CT: Greenwood Press, 1992.

Brown, Gene, ed., and Richard H. Rovere, advisory ed. *Loyalty and Security in a Democratic State.* In *The Great Contemporary Issues* series. New York: New York Times/Arno Press, 1977.

Brown, Ruth, with Andrew Yule. *Miss Rhythm.* New York: Donald I. Fine, 1996.

Burton, Humphrey. *Leonard Bernstein.* London: Faber and Faber, 1994.

Butler, Jerry, with Earl Smith. *Only the Strong Survive: Memoirs of a Soul Survivor.* Bloomington: Indiana University Press, 2000.

Chabon, Michael. *The Amazing Adventures of Kavalier & Clay.* Paper, New York: Picador, 2000.

Clark, Dick, and Richard Robinson. *Rock, Roll & Remember.* New York: Thomas Y. Crowell, 1976.

Clemente, John. *Girl Groups: Fabulous Females That Rocked the World.* Paper, Iola, WI: Krause Publications, 2000.

Committee on Interstate and Foreign Commerce, United States Senate. *Hearings on S.2834, a Bill to Provide That a License for a Radio or Television Broadcasting Station Shall Not Be Granted to, or Held by, Any Person or Corporation Engaged Directly or Indirectly in the Business of Publishing Music or of Manufacturing or Selling Musical Recordings.* Washington, D.C: U.S. Government Printing Office, 1958.

Cooper, Kim, and David Smay, eds. *Bubblegum Music Is the Naked Truth*. Los Angeles: Feral House, 2001.

Dale, Alan. *The Spider and the Marionettes*. New York: Lyle Stuart, 1965.

Dannen, Frederic. *Hit Men: Power Brokers and Fast Money Inside the Music Business*. New York: Crown, 1990.

Darin, Dodd, and Maxine Paetro. *Dream Lovers: The Magnificent Shattered Lives of Bobby Darin and Sandra Dee by Their Son*. New York: Warner Books, 1994.

David, Hal. *Hal David Songbook*. Paper, Milwaukee, WI: Hal Leonard Corporation, 1990.

———. *What the World Needs Now and Other Love Lyrics*. New enlarged edition, New York: Trident, 1970.

Davis, Fred. *Passage Through Crisis: Polio Victims and Their Families*. Indianapolis: Bobbs-Merrill, 1963.

Dietrich, Marlene. *Marlene*. Translated by Salvator Attanasio. New York: Grove Press, 1989.

DiMucci, Dion, with Davin Seay. *The Wanderer: Dion's Story*. New York: Beech Tree Books/Morrow, 1988.

DiOrio, Al. *Borrowed Time: The 37 Years of Bobby Darin*. Paper, Philadelphia: Running Press, 1986.

DjeDje, Jacqueline Cogdell, and Eddie S. Meadows, eds. *California Soul: Music of African Americans in the West*. Paper, Berkeley: University of California Press, 1998.

Dunlap, David W. *On Broadway: A Journey Uptown Over Time*. New York: Rizzoli, 1990.

Dylan, Bob. *Chronicles: Volume One*. New York: Simon & Schuster, 2004.

Eliot, Marc. *Rockonomics: The Money Behind the Music*. New York: Franklin Watts, 1989.

Ellis, Lucy, and Bryony Sutherland. *Tom Jones Close Up*. London: Omnibus, 2000.

Ertegun, Ahmet, with Greil Marcus, Nat Hentoff, Lenny Kaye, Robert Gordon, Robert Christgau, Vince Aletti, Will Friedwald, David Fricke, and Barney Hoskyns. *"What'd I Say": The Atlantic Story: 50 Years of Music*. New York: Welcome Rain, 2001.

Escott, Colin, with George Merritt and William MacEwen. *Hank Williams: The Biography*. Boston: Little, Brown, 1994.

Farrell, James. *The Spirit of the Sixties: Making Postwar Radicalism*. New York: Routledge, 1997.

Faulkner, William. *The Reivers*. New York: Random House, 1962.

Feather, Leonard. *The Jazz Years: Earwitness to an Era*. New York: Da Capo, 1987.

Fitzpatrick, Joseph P. *Puerto Rican Americans: The Meaning of Migration to the Mainland*. Englewood Cliffs, NJ: Prentice-Hall, 1987.

Fox, Ted. *In the Groove: The People Behind the Music*. New York: St. Martin's, 1986.

Francis, Connie. *Who's Sorry Now?* New York: St. Martin's, 1984.

Frommer, Myrna Katz, and Harvey Frommer. *It Happened in Brooklyn*. New York: Harcourt Brace, 1993.

Giddins, Gary. *Satchmo: The Genius of Louis Armstrong*. New York: Dolphin/Doubleday, 1988.

Gillett, Charlie. *Making Tracks: Atlantic Records and the Growth of a Multi-Billion-Dollar Industry*. New York: E. P. Dutton, 1974.

———. *The Sound of the City: The Rise of Rock and Roll*. New York: Outerbridge & Dienstfrey, 1970.

Goldstein, Richard. *Desperate Hours: The Epic Rescue of the Andrea Doria*. New York: John Wiley & Sons, 2001.

Gould, Tony. *A Summer Plague: Polio and Its Survivors*. New Haven, CT: Yale University Press, 1995.

Gourse, Leslie. *Sassy: The Life of Sarah Vaughan*. New York: Charles Scribner's, 1993.

Gribin, Anthony J., and Matthew M. Schiff. *The Complete Book of Doo-Wop.* Iola, WI: Krause Publications, 2000.

Groia, Philip. *They All Sang on the Corner: New York City's Rhythm and Blues Vocal Groups of the 1950s.* Branchport, NY: Edmonds Publishing Co., n.d.

Guralnick, Peter. *Careless Love: The Unmaking of Elvis Presley.* Paper, Boston: Back Bay, 2000.

———. *Last Train to Memphis: The Rise of Elvis Presley.* Boston: Little, Brown, 1994.

Hadlock, Richard. *Jazz Masters of the Twenties.* Paper, New York: Collier, 1974.

Halevy, Julian. *The Young Lovers.* New York: Simon & Schuster, 1955.

Hawes, Joseph M. *Children in Urban Society: Juvenile Delinquency in Nineteenth-Century America.* New York: Oxford University Press, 1971.

Heilbut, Tony. *The Gospel Sound: Good News and Bad Times.* New York: Simon & Schuster, 1971.

Henrich, Edith, ed. *Experiments in Survival.* With commentary by Leonard Kriegel. New York: Association for the Aid of Crippled Children, 1963.

Hoffer, William. *Saved! The Story of the* Andrea Doria—*the Greatest Sea Rescue in History.* New York: Summit, 1979.

Hoskyns, Barney. *Waiting for the Sun: Strange Days, Weird Scenes, and the Sound of Los Angeles.* Paper, New York: St. Martin's/Griffin, 1999.

Humphries, Patrick. *The Boy in the Bubble: A Biography of Paul Simon.* London: Sidgwick & Jackson, 1988.

Jackson, John A. *American Bandstand: Dick Clark and the Making of a Rock 'n' Roll Empire.* New York: Oxford University Press, 1997.

Jobey, Liz, ed. *The End of the Innocence: Photographs from the Decades That Define Pop.* Zurich: Scalo, 1997.

Johansen, Claes. *The Zombies: Hung Up on a Dream.* London: SAF Publishing, 2001.

Jones, Quincy. *Q: The Autobiography of Quincy Jones.* New York: Doubleday, 2001.

Juvenile Delinquency (The Effectiveness of the Juvenile Court System). Hearings before Subcommittee to Investigate Juvenile Delinquency of the Committee on the Judiciary, United States Senate, Feb. 12 and 19, 1959. Washington, D.C.: U.S. Government Printing Office, 1959.

Kasha, Al, and Joel Hirschhorn. *Notes on Broadway: Conversations with the Great Songwriters.* Chicago: Contemporary Books, 1985.

Kelley, Kitty. *His Way: The Unauthorized Biography of Frank Sinatra.* New York: Bantam, 1986.

Kerouac, Jack. *On the Road.* Paper, New York: Penguin, 1991.

———. *The Subterraneans.* Paper, New York: Grove Press, 1958.

Kriegel, Leonard. *Falling Into Life: Essays by Leonard Kriegel.* San Francisco: North Point Press, 1991.

Lawrence, D. H. *Studies in Classic American Literature.* Paper, New York: Viking, 1964.

Lax, Eric. *Woody Allen: A Biography.* New York: Knopf, 1991.

Leiber, Jerry, and Mike Stoller. *Leiber & Stoller Songbook.* Paper, Milwaukee: Hal Leonard Corp., n.d.

Liebling, A. J. *The Jollity Building.* Paper, New York: Ballantine, n.d.

Liehm, Mira. *Film in Italy from 1942 to the Present.* Berkeley: University of California Press, 1984.

Loesser, Susan. *A Most Remarkable Fella: Frank Loesser and the Guys and Dolls in His Life.* New York: Donald I. Fine, 1993.

Love, Darlene, with Rob Hoerburger. *My Name Is Love: The Darlene Love Story.* New York: William Morrow, 1998.

Loza, Steven. *Tito Puente and the Making of Latin Music.* Paper, Urbana: University of Illinois Press, 1999.

Lydon, Michael. *Boogie Lightning.* New York: Dial, 1974.

———. *Ray Charles: Man and Music.* New York: Riverhead, 1998.

MacIver, Robert M. *The Prevention and Control of Delinquency.* New York: Atherton Press, 1966.

Mailer, Norman. *The Long Patrol: Twenty-five Years of Writing from the Work of Norman Mailer.* Edited by Robert F. Lucid. New York: World Publishing, 1971.

Mann, Thomas. *Stories of Three Decades.* Translated by H. T. Lowe-Porter. New York: Modern Library, 1930.

Marcus, Greil. *Dead Elvis: A Chronicle of a Cultural Obsession.* Paper, New York: Doubleday, 1991.

Martin, Linda, and Kerry Segrave. *Anti-Rock: The Opposition to Rock 'n' Roll.* Hamden, CT: Archon, 1988.

Mezzrow, Milton "Mezz," and Bertram Wolfe. *Really the Blues.* New York: Random House, 1946.

Millar, Bill. *The Coasters.* Paper, London: Star Books, 1974.

Miller, James. *Flowers in the Dustbin: The Rise of Rock and Roll, 1947–1977.* New York: Simon & Schuster, 1999.

———, ed. *The Rolling Stone Illustrated History of Rock & Roll.* Paper, New York: Rolling Stone Press/Random House, 1976.

Moritz, Charles, ed. *Current Biography Yearbook 1970.* New York: H. W. Wilson, 1970.

Mosley, Walter. *Devil in a Blue Dress.* Paper, New York: Pocket Books, 1997.

Neville, John. *The Press, the Rosenbergs, and the Cold War.* Westport, CT: Praeger, 1995.

Nite, Norm N. *Rock On: The Illustrated Encyclopedia of Rock N' Roll, The Solid Gold Years.* Paper, New York: Popular Library, 1977.

O'Brien, Geoffrey. *Sonata for Jukebox: Pop Music, Memory, and the Imagined Life.* New York: Counterpoint, 2004.

O'Dair, Barbara, ed. *Trouble Girls: The Rolling Stone Book of Women in Rock.* New York: Random House, 1997.

O'Neill, Jennifer. *Surviving Myself.* New York: William Morrow, 1999.

Orlando, Tony, with Patsi Bale Cox. *Halfway to Paradise.* New York: St. Martin's Press, 2002.

Otis, Johnny. *Listen to the Lambs.* New York: W. W. Norton, 1968.

Palmer, Robert. *Baby, That Was Rock & Roll: The Legendary Leiber & Stoller.* Paper, New York: Harvest/Harcourt Brace Jovanovich, 1978.

Perone, James E. *Carole King: A Bio-Bibliography.* Westport, CT: Greenwood Press, 1999.

Pollock, Bruce. *In Their Own Words.* Paper, New York: Collier Books, 1975.

———. *When Rock Was Young: A Nostalgic Review of the Top 40 Era.* New York: Holt, Rinehart and Winston, 1981.

Price, Richard. *The Wanderers.* Paper, Boston: Mariner, 1999.

Remmers, H. H., and D. H. Radler. *The American Teenager.* Indianapolis: Bobbs-Merrill, 1957.

Responsibilities of Broadcasting Licensees and Station Personnel. Hearings Before a Subcommittee of the Committee on Interstate and Foreign Commerce, House of Representatives, Eighty-sixth Congress, Second Session, on Payola and Other Deceptive Practices in the Broadcasting Field. Part 2. Washington: U.S. Government Printing Office, 1960.

Ribowsky, Mark. *He's a Rebel: Phil Spector, Rock and Roll's Legendary Producer.* Paper, New York: Cooper Square Press, 1989.

Riley, Sam G. *Biographical Dictionary of American Newspaper Columnists.* Westport, CT: Greenwood Press, 1995.

Roberts, John Storm. *The Latin Tinge: The Impact of Latin American Music on the United States.* Second edition. Paper, New York: Oxford University Press, 1999.

Ruppli, Michael, compiler. *Atlantic Records: A Discography.* Vol. 1. Westport, CT: Greenwood Press, 1979.

Russo, Greg. *Mannerisms: The Five Phases of Manfred Mann.* Paper, Floral Park, NY: Crossfire Publications, 1995.

Russo, Richard. *Empire Falls.* Paper, New York: Vintage, 2002.

Salem, James M. *The Late Great Johnny Ace and the Transition from R&B to Rock 'n' Roll.* Urbana: University of Illinois Press, 1999.

Sanjek, Russell. *American Popular Music and Its Business: The First Four Hundred Years.* Vol. 3, *From 1900 to 1984.* New York: Oxford University Press, 1988.

Saul, Scott. *Freedom Is, Freedom Ain't: Jazz and the Making of the Sixties.* Cambridge, MA: Harvard University Press, 2003.

Schneider, Eric C. *Vampires, Dragons, and Egyptian Kings: Youth Gangs in Postwar New York.* Princeton, NJ: Princeton University Press, 1999.

Schuller, Gunther. *The Swing Era: The Development of Jazz, 1930–1945.* Paper, New York: Oxford University Press, 1989.

Secrest, Meryle. *Leonard Bernstein: A Life.* New York: Alfred A. Knopf, 1994.

Sedaka, Neil. *Laughter in the Rain: My Own Story.* New York: G. P. Putnam's, 1982.

Segrave, Kerry. *Payola in the Music Industry: A History, 1880–1991.* Jefferson, NC: McFarland & Co., 1994.

Shannon, Bob, and John Javna. *Behind the Hits: Inside Stories of Classic Pop and Rock and Roll.* Paper, New York: Warner Books, 1986.

Shaw, Arnold. *Honkers and Shouters: The Golden Years of Rhythm and Blues.* New York: Macmillan, 1978.

———. *The Rockin' Fifties: The Decade That Transformed the Pop Music Scene.* New York: Hawthorn, 1974.

Shute, Nevil. *On the Beach.* Paper, New York: Signet/New American Library, 1958.

Smith, Jane. *Patenting the Sun: Polio and the Salk Vaccine.* New York: Morrow, 1990.

Smith, Joe. *Off the Record: An Oral History of Popular Music.* Edited by Mitchell Fink. New York: Warner Books, 1990.

Sounes, Howard. *Down the Highway: The Life of Bob Dylan.* New York: Grove Press, 2001.

Spector, Ronnie, with Vince Waldron. *Be My Baby.* New York: Harmony Books, 1990.

Spitz, Robert Stephen. *The Making of Superstars: Artists and Executives of the Rock Music Business.* Garden City, NY: Anchor/Doubleday, 1978.

Turner, Tina, with Kurt Loder. *I, Tina.* New York: William Morrow, 1986.

Valentine, Penny, and Vicki Wickham. *Dancing with Demons: The Authorized Biography of Dusty Springfield.* New York: St. Martin's, 2000.

Wade, Dorothy, and Justine Picardie. *Music Man: Ahmet Ertegun, Atlantic Records, and the Triumph of Rock 'n' Roll.* New York: W. W. Norton, 1993.

Webb, Jimmy. *Tunesmith: Inside the Art of Songwriting.* New York: Hyperion, 1998.

Wexler, Jerry, and David Ritz. *Rhythm and the Blues: A Life in American Music.* New York, Knopf, 1993.

Whitburn, Joel. *Joel Whitburn's Pop Annual 1955–1999.* Paper, Menomonee Falls, WI: Record Research Inc., 2000.

Whitcomb, Ian. *After the Ball.* Paper, New York: Limelight, 1986.

White, Timothy. *Long Ago and Far Away: James Taylor, His Life and Music.* London: Omnibus, 2001.

Wiseman, Rich. *Neil Diamond: Solitary Star.* New York: Dodd, Mead, 1987.

Wolfe, Tom. *The Kandy-Kolored Tangerine-Flake Streamline Baby.* New York: Noonday, 1965.

Zimmer, Dave. *Crosby, Stills & Nash: The Authorized Biography.* Paper, New York: Da Capo, 2000.

ARTICLES

Albelli, Alfred. "Separation Won by Wife Despite Kiss 'n' Tell Pal." *Daily News,* 18 March 1964, 5.

———. "Waiter Spills Piping Dish." *Daily News,* 17 March 1964, 3.

Archer, Eugene. "Bellhop Turned Millionaire, 30, Heads a Columbia Film Division." *New York Times,* 14 September 1964, 42.

Barnes, Clive. "Theater: Simon-Bacharach 'Promises, Promises,' Begins Run at the Shubert." *New York Times,* 2 December 1968, 59.

"Beat, Says Burt, Is Not My Kind of Music." *Melody Maker,* 12 June 1965, 30.

Berger, Joseph. "Vintage Pop Star with the Soul of a Bar Mitzvah Boy." *New York Times* 24 May 2004, E:1.

Booth, Dave "Daddy Cool." "Jerry Leiber & Mike Stoller: What Is the Secret of Your Success?" Edited and introduced by Colin Escott. *Goldmine* 111, vol. 10, no. 20 (26 October 1984): 14.

Bundy, June. "NBC Spot Sales Blast at R&R Rouses Ire." *Billboard,* 14 July 1958, 3.

Calta, Louis. "3 Broadway Musicals to Close This Weekend After Long Runs." *New York Times,* 29 December 1971, 21.

Carr, Roy, and Andrew Tyler. "Leaders of the Pack." *New Musical Express,* 3 November 1973, 30.

"Clothiers Honor Bacharach." *New York Times,* 29 December 1970, 46.

"Columbia Pix About to Sign Kirshner Deal." *Billboard,* 30 March 1963, 1.

Dahl, Bill. "Chuck Jackson: Suave, Debonair and Uptown." *Goldmine* 442, vol. 23, no. 14 (4 July 1997): 62.

Davis, Francis. "The Man from Heaven." *Atlantic Monthly,* June 1997, 100–109.

DeMain, Bill. "Carole King: New Threads in the Tapestry." *Performing Songwriter* 79 (July/August 2004): 46–52.

———. "Do You Know the Way to . . . Monterey? Santa Fe? Whitley Bay?" *Mojo* 28 (March 1996): 42–50.

Doggett, Peter. "The Lost Hero of 60s Pop." *Record Collector* 267 (November 2001): 96–99.

"Don Kirshner Has Been Named . . ." *New York Post,* 2 September 1964, 87.

"Don't Knock the Rock." *New York Herald Tribune,* 23 February 1957.

"Earl Wilson on Broadway." *New York Post,* 16 May 1965, 27.

Escott, Colin. "The Everly Brothers: Brothers in Arms." *Goldmine* 337, vol. 19, no. 12 (25 June 1993): 14.

"The 500 Greatest Songs of All Time." *Rolling Stone* 963 (9 December 2004): 65–165.

Flans, Robin. "Neil Sedaka: He Never Really Left." *Goldmine* 100, vol. 10, no. 9 (25 May 1984): 12.

Flatow, Sheryl. "What the World Needs Now." *Performing Arts,* April 1998, 16.

"Frenzy 'n' Furor Featured at Paramount." *New York Times,* 23 February 1957.

Fricke, David. "Leiber & Stoller." Unpaginated reprint, *Rolling Stone,* 19 April 1990.

Gari, Brian. "What the World Needs Now Is Jackie DeShannon." *Goldmine* 290, vol. 17, no. 18 (6 September 1991): 16.

Garvey, Dennis. "The Dixie Cups: Creole Bells." *Goldmine* 361, vol. 20, no. 11 (27 May 1994): 50.

———. "Freddie Scott: Soul Journeyman." *Goldmine* 329, vol. 19, no. 5 (15 March 1993): 54.

———. "Little Anthony and the Imperials: Back in Harmony." *Goldmine* 358, vol. 20, no. 8 (15 April 1994): 52–54.

"Goldner Goes Independent with Goldisc." *Billboard,* 13 July 1963, 3.

"Goldner Quits Roulette Again to Go on Own." *Billboard,* 22 June 1963, 4.

Grevatt, Ren. "Kirshner Named V.-P. As Deal Is Official." *Billboard,* 27 April 1963, 1.

Haertel, Joe. "Little Eva: Doin' a Brand New Dance Now." *Goldmine* 248, vol. 16, no. 2 (26 January 1990): 20–27.

Hilburn, Robert. "What Burt Needs Now." *Los Angeles Times,* 12 April 1998, Calendar, 6.

"Italian Import Makes Debut." *New York Times,* 2 February 1953, 20.

Jancik, Wayne. "Scepter-Wand Records." *Goldmine* 315, vol. 18, no. 17 (21 August 1992): 10.

"Jerry Leiber, Mike Stoller Open Diskery." *Billboard,* 2 November 1963, 6.

Jones, Wayne. "Wayne Jones Talks with . . . Gene Pitney." *Goldmine* 80 (January 1983): 26.

Juvenile Delinquency: Facts, Facets. Children's Bureau, Social Security Administration, U.S. Department of Health, Education and Welfare. No. 1, 1960.

Kamp, David. "The Hit Factory." *Vanity Fair,* November 2001, 248–75.

Kasha, Al, and Joel Hirschhorn. "Anatomy of a Hit: Up on the Roof." *Songwriter* 5 (March 1980): 14–15.

Koda, Cub. "Ellie Greenwich: America's Songwriting Sweetheart (and Then She Wrote)." *Goldmine* 361, vol. 20, no. 11 (27 May 1994): 28.

Kroll, Jack. "Burt Bacharach: The Music Man 1970." *Newsweek,* 22 June 1970, 50–55.

Kubernik, Harvey R. "A Yakety Yak with Leiber and Stoller." *Goldmine* 385, vol. 21, no. 9 (28 April 1995): 60.

"Latin-Music Patriarch Stays Hungry." *New York Times,* 30 April 2002, E:7.

Lorenzo, Richard J. "Bobby Darin: Doing His Own Thing and Other Things." *Goldmine* 227, vol. 15, no. 7 (7 April 1989): 18.

Meyer, Edith. "Psychological Considerations in a Group of Children with Poliomyelitis." *Journal of Pediatrics* 31, no. 1 (July, 1947): 35–48.

Moore, Clarence A. "Dionne Warwick: Forever Gold." *Goldmine* 248, vol. 16, no. 2 (26 January 1990): 8.

"Music: Pollikiff's Series." *New York Times,* 25 January 1962, 24.

"Music World: Series Is Saved." *New York Times,* 21 January 1962, II:11.

"The Mystics: A Talk with the Mystics." *Goldmine* 90, vol. 9, no. 11 (November 1983): 61.

"Night Club to Seat 1,000 Guests Is Planned for Brill Building." *New York Times,* 16 November 1932, 33.

Nixon, Mojo. "Elvis, Doc and Mojo Are Everywhere." *Goldmine* 262, vol. 16, no. 16 (10 August 1990): 13.

Osborne, Jerry. Interview with Connie Francis. *DISCoveries Magazine,* September 1991.

Pareles, Jon. "Brian Wilson Speaks." In "Arts, Briefly," *New York Times,* 15 October 2004, E:6.

———. "A Happy Night for Old-Timers Still Singing the Blues." *New York Times,* 22 February 2003, B:17.

"Place in History." *Billboard,* 9 November 1963, 1.

Platts, Robin. "Anyone Who Had a Heart: The Songs of Burt Bacharach and Hall David." *Discoveries,* December 1997, 48–54.

Pomus, Doc. "The Journals of Doc Pomus (1978–91)." *Antaeus: On Music,* no. 71/72 (autumn 1993): 157–184.

———. "Otis Blackwell and Me." *Goldmine,* no. 85 (June 1963):19.

———. "The World of Doc Pomus." *Whiskey, Women, and . . .*, nos. 12/13 (December 1983): 6.

———. "The World of Doc Pomus: Cookie's Caravan." *Whiskey, Women, and . . .*, no. 16 (spring 1987): 1–3.

Propes, Steve. "Johnny Otis." *Goldmine* 200, vol. 14, no. 7 (25 March 1988): 8.

———. "Little Eva: From Babysitting to the Big Time." *Goldmine* 204, vol. 14, no. 11 (20 May 1990): 12.

Ratliff, Ben. "Latin-Music Patriarch Stays Hungry: Eddie Palmieri Dusts Off, and Polishes, His 1960's Sound." *New York Times,* 30 April 2002, E:1–7.

Reed, Rex. "Bacharach—No More 'Promises.' " *New York Times,* 15 December 1968, 3:2.

Roeser, Steve. "Ain't Nobody's Business: The No Rollin' Blues of Jimmy Witherspoon." *Goldmine* 413, vol. 22, no. 10 (24 May 1996): 84.

Rolontz, Bob. "Nevins-Kirshner Sale to Disk Label Seems in Offing." *Billboard,* 23 March 1963, 1.

Ruhlmann, William. "Connie Francis Sings Everybody's Favorites." *Goldmine* 334, vol. 19, no. 9 (14 May 1993): 15.

Russell, Tom. "Otis Blackwell: Don't Be Cruel." *Goldmine* 183, vol. 13, no. 6 (31 July 1987): 16.

Sapia, Joseph. "What's Up, Doc?: The Doc Pomus Interview." *Goldmine* 78 (November 1982): 7.

Scher, Len. "The Righteous Brothers: Blue-Eyed Soul Brothers." *Goldmine* 99, vol. 10, no. 8 (11 May 1984): 50.

Shephard, Richard F. "Anatomy of an Opening Night." *New York Times,* 3 December 1968, 52.

Siegal, Nina. "The New York Legacy of Tito Puente." *New York Times,* 6 June 2000, B:4.

Sisario, Ben. "Bobby Hatfield Dies at 63; Righteous Brothers Tenor." *New York Times,* 7 November 2003, C:10.

"So Far Away." *The New Yorker,* 8 March 1993, 36.

"The Sound." *The New Yorker,* 22 April 1961, 36–38.

Spector, Phil. "The Induction of Doc Pomus into the Rock and Roll Hall of Fame." *Antaeus: On Music,* no. 71/72 (autumn 1993): 153–54.

Tamarkin, Jeff. "Barry Mann and Cynthia Weil . . . They Put the Bomp!" *Goldmine* 75 (August 1982): 13–15.

———. "The Dixie Cups: Never Be Lonely Anymore." *Goldmine* 166, vol. 12, no. 25 (5 December 1986): 28.

———. "Righteous Brother and Sister: Bill Medley Meets Darlene Love—Again." *Goldmine* 355, vol. 20, no. 5 (4 March 1994): 52.

"Those Magic Moments: Doc Pomus Remembered by His Friends and Peers." *Goldmine* (19 April 1991): 8.

"Tin Pan Alley: Jailhouse Rock." *Time,* 20 April 1959, 48.

"Top Music Students to Appear on WQXR." *New York Times,* 19 March 1956, 25.

Torres, José. "The Palladium." *New York,* 21–28 December, 1987, 99.

Wadler, Joyce. "Seymour Rexite, 91, Star of Yiddish Stage, Dies." *New York Times,* 16 October 2002, C:14.

Williams, Richard. "The Leiber-Stoller Story." *Melody Maker,* 29 July 1972, 32–33.

Wilson, Daniel J. "Covenants of Work and Grace: Themes of Recovery and Redemption in Polio Narratives." *Literature and Medicine* 13, no. 1 (Spring 1994): 22–41.

ALBUM AND CD NOTES

Cohen, Mitchell. Notes for Dion and the Belmonts, *24 Original Classics.* Arista AL9-8206. Record album.

Dylan, Bob. Notes for Bob Dylan, *Biograph.* Sony 65298. Compact discs.

Escott, Colin. Notes for the Drifters, *1959–1965: All-Time Greatest Hits and More.* Atlantic 81931-1. Record album.

Feldman, Jim. Notes for Dusty Springfield, *Dusty in Memphis.* Deluxe Edition. Rhino R2 75580. Compact disc.

Fichera, Al, and Noel R. Kramer. Notes for the Three Suns, *Soft and Sweet/Midnight for Two.* Collectables COL-CD-2742. Compact disc.

Gari, Brian. Notes for Neil Sedaka, *The Brooklyn Demos (1958–1961).* Original Cast Records OCR6060. Compact disc.

———. Notes for Neil Sedaka, *Oh Carol: The Complete Recordings 1956–1966.* Bear Family Records BDC 16535 HK. Compact discs.

Hentoff, Nat. Notes for *Dionne Warwick's Golden Hits—Part One.* Scepter SPS 565. Record album.

Jay-Alexander, Richard. Notes for *Jacques Brel Is Alive and Well and Living in Paris.* Sony Classical/Columbia/Legacy SK 89998. Compact disc.

Keller, Jack. Notes for Jack Keller, *Music for All Occasions,* a collection of his songs compiled for promotional purposes. Compact discs.

Kochakian, Dan. Notes for Doc Pomus, *Send for the Doctor: The Early Years 1944–55.* Whiskey, Women, and . . . Record Company KM700. Record album.

Kolanjian, Steve. Notes for the Exciters, *Tell Him.* Collectables COL-5672, S21-18564. Compact disc.

———. Notes for *Come a Little Bit Closer: The Best of Jay and the Americans.* EMI USA/United Artists CDP-7-934488-2. Compact disc.

Laredo, Joseph. Notes for *A Hundred Pounds of Clay: The Best of Gene McDaniels.* Collectables COL-5646 S21-18546. Compact disc.

Milligan, Patrick, and Bill DeMain, Paul Grein, and Alec Cumming. Notes for *The Look of Love: The Burt Bacharach Collection.* Rhino R2 75339. Compact discs.

Patrick, Mike. Notes for the Shangri-Las, *The Myrmidons of Melodrama.* RPM 136. Compact disc.

———, and Malcolm Baumgart. Notes for *On Broadway: Hit Songs and Rarities from the Brill Building Era.* Westside WESD 216. Compact discs.

Pierson, Jim. Notes for *Burt Bacharach Plays His Hits.* MCA MCAD-11681. Compact disc.

Poe, Randy. Notes for *Leiber and Stoller Present the Spark Records Story.* Ace CDCHD 801. Compact disc.

———, and Robert Palmer. Notes for the Coasters, *50 Coastin' Classics.* Rhino Records R2 71090. Compact discs.

Pouzenc, Jean-Marie. Notes for Elvis Presley, *Elvis Chante Mort Shuman & Doc Pomus.* BMG France 74321 745962. Compact discs.

Sandoval, Andrew. Notes for the Monkees, *Music Box.* Rhino R2 76706. Compact discs.

West, Tommy. Notes for *I Can Hear Music: The Ellie Greenwich Collection.* Razor & Tie 7930182195-2. Compact disc.

ONLINE SOURCES

Aronowitz, Al. "The Dumb Sound." *Saturday Evening Post,* August 1963. Available online in *The Blacklisted Journalist,* Column 84 (1 February 2003). http://www.bigmagic.com/pages/blackj/column84.html.

———. "How I Nearly Made a Million Dollars in the Rock and Roll Business." *The Blacklisted Journalist,* Column 83 (15 January 2003). http://www.bigmagic.com/pages/blackj/column83.html. http://www.brillbuilding.com.

Bronson, Harold, ed. *Hey, Hey, We're the Monkees.* Santa Monica, CA: General Publishing Group, 1996. http://www.geocities.com/monkeesincorp2/antikirshner.html. http://www.thecheers.com.

Goffin, Gerry. Interview in *Los Angeles Daily News,* September 1996. http://members.home.net/caroleking/guideto.htm.

Goldberg, Marv. "5 Crowns." *Marv Goldberg's R&B Notebooks.* http://home.att.net/~marvy42/5Crowns/5crowns.html.

Hardcastle, Cleothus. "The Backpages Interview: Jerry Leiber and Mike Stoller." *Rock's Backpages,* 27 June 2001. http://www.rocksbackpages.com/news/3006_hardcastle_lands.html.

Hart, Bobby. "Q&A with Bobby Hart." http://www.community.net/~tbaslier/hart.html.

Jamie/Guyden History. "The Early Days." http://www.jamguy.com/scripts/jamguycom.

Kirshner, Don. "Interview: Don Kirshner." http://www.angelfire.com/sk/monkeerescue/kirs.

Larralde, Carlos M., and Richard Griswold del Castillo. "Luisa Moreno and the Beginnings of the Mexican American Civil Rights Movement in San Diego." *Journal of San Diego History,* vol. 43, no. 3 (summer 1997). http://www.sandiegohistory.org/journal/97summer/moreno.htm.

Wright, Mick. Interview with Dionne Warwick, 1982. http://www.merrymarketing.com/Dionne55.htm

UNPUBLISHED SOURCES

Bacharach, Burt. Undated letters to Henry Cowell in the Henry Cowell Collection, Folder 11 (JPB 00-03). Music Division, New York Public Library for the Performing Arts at Lincoln Center.

Barkan, Mark. *Almost Famous (or I Never Was Burt Bacharach).* Unpublished autobiography provided by the author.

Shuman, Mort. Unpublished autobiographical sketch, portions provided by Maria-Pia Shuman and Charles Negus-Fancey, copyright 1991 Mortimer Shuman Estate.

MISCELLANEOUS

"Another Tear Falls." Collection of Lead Sheets. JPB 00-51. Music Division, New York Public Library for the Performing Arts at Lincoln Center.

Burt Bacharach. Directed by Morgan Neville. A&E's *Biography.*

Girl Groups: The Story of a Sound. MGM/UA home video presentation of a 1983 Delilah Films production.

Hitmakers: The Teens Who Stole Pop Music. Directed by Morgan Neville. A&E's *Biography.*

Landmark 1955 and *1956.* Abraham Lincoln High School (Brooklyn, NY) yearbooks.

Log 1956 and *1958.* James Madison High School (Brooklyn, NY) yearbooks.

Mann, Barry, and Cynthia Weil. Interview by Terry Gross on *Fresh Air,* National Public Radio, 18 July 2000.

———. *They Wrote That?: The Songs of Barry Mann and Cynthia Weil.* Revue performed at the McGinn/Cazale Theatre, New York, 4 February 2004.

Neil Sedaka. Directed by Scott Lenz. A&E's *Biography.*

Willner, Hal. *Hal Willner's Doc Pomus Project.* Tribute performed at St. Mark's Church, New York, 7 November 2001.

Words and Music by Leiber & Stoller. Directed by Morgan Neville. A&E's *Biography.*

DISCOGRAPHY

The limited availability of old records, the swiftness with which CDs are repackaged and rush in and out of print, and the proliferation of opportunities to download music on the Internet reduce dramatically the usefulness of a discography. Still, the list that follows may at least head curious readers in the right directions.

Several record labels reissue music from the period, notably Collectables, Rhino, Sony/Columbia/Legacy, Varèse Sarabande, Taragon, and, overseas, Ace and Charly (U.K.), Bear Family (Germany), and Raven (Australia). I also discovered and purchased many recordings through Amazon, Roots & Rhythm (http://www.rootsandrhythm.com) and Collectors' Choice Music (http://www.ccmusic.com).

Unless noted otherwise, all recordings are CDs.

The Animals. *Animalization.* MGM E/SE-4384. LP.
———. *The Best of the Animals.* MGM E-4324. LP.
Bacharach, Burt. *Here I Am: Isley Meets Bacharach.* Dreamworks B0001005-02.
———. *The Look of Love: The Burt Bacharach Collection.* Rhino R2 75339.
———. *Plays His Hits.* MCA MCAD-11681.
———. *The Rare Bacharach 1: 53 Elusive Songs and Versions, 1956-1978.* Raven RVCD-150.
Baker, LaVern. *Soul on Fire: The Best of LaVern Baker.* Atlantic CD 82311.
———. *See See Rider/Blues Ballads.* Collectables COL-CD-6231.
Brel, Jacques. *Jacques Brel.* Polygram Distribution 816488-2.
Brown, Charles. *Driftin' Blues.* Collectables COL-5631 S21-18370.
Brown, Maxine. *Oh No Not My Baby: The Best of Maxine Brown.* Kent CDKEND 949.
Brown, Ruth. *Miss Rhythm: Greatest Hits and More.* Atlantic 7 82061-2.
Charles, Ray. *The Birth of Soul: The Complete Atlantic Rhythm & Blues Recordings, 1952-1959.* Atlantic 7 82310-2.
———. *Ultimate Hits Collection.* Rhino R2 75644.
The Chiffons. *Everything You Always Wanted to Hear by the Chiffons but Couldn't Get!* Laurie LES-4001. LP.
Clanton, Jimmy. *This Is Jimmy Clanton: 18 Original Classics from the '50s and '60s.* Music Club 50047.
The Clovers. *Their Greatest Recordings: The Early Years.* Atco SD 33-374. LP.

The Coasters. *50 Coastin' Classics.* Rhino R2 71090.

The Cookies. . . . *The Absolute Complete! (And Oh So Sweet!).* Chocolate Chip CCRD-4001.

Craddock, Billy Crash. *Boom Boom Baby.* Bear Family Records BCD 15610.

The Crystals. *The Best of the Crystals.* Phil Spector Records 72142.

The Cyrkle. *Red Rubber Ball (A Collection).* Columbia/Legacy CK 47717.

Darin, Bobby. *The Best of Bobby Darin, Vols. One (Splish Splash)* and *Two (Mack the Knife).* Atco 791794-2, 791795-2.

———. *The Bobby Darin Story.* Atco 33131-2.

———. *Twist with Bobby Darin.* Collector's Choice Music CCM-400-2.

Darren, James. *Teenage Tears: Original Colpix Recordings, 1959–1964.* Raven RVCD-42.

———, and Shelley Fabares and Paul Petersen. *Teenage Triangle.* Colpix CP 444. LP.

Davis, Skeeter. *The Pop Hits Collection.* Taragon Records TARCD-1102.

Diamond, Neil. *The Greatest Hits: 1966–1992.* Columbia C2K 52703/CK 52762.

The Diamonds. *The Best of the Diamonds: The Mercury Years.* Mercury 314-532 734-2.

Dion. *Bronx Blues: The Columbia Recordings (1962–1965).* Columbia/Legacy CGK 46972.

Dion and the Belmonts. *The Complete Dion & the Belmonts.* Collectors' Choice Music CCMO71-2/EMI Music Special Markets 72434-96374-2-9.

———. *24 Original Classics.* Arista AL9-8206. LP.

The Dixie Cups. *Chapel of Love.* Red Bird RB20-100. LP.

———. *The Complete Red Bird Recordings.* Varèse Sarabande 302 066 375 2.

The Drifters. *Let the Boogie-Woogie Roll: Greatest Hits 1953–1958.* Atlantic 7 81927-1. LP.

———. *1959–1965: All-Time Greatest Hits and More.* Atlantic 7 81931-1. LP.

———. *Rockin' & Driftin': The Drifters Box.* Rhino Records 72417.

———. *Save the Last Dance for Me/ The Good Life.* Collectables COL-CD-6417.

Evans, Paul. *I Was Part of the 50's.* S-Star Records SSR-1214.

The Everly Brothers. *24 Original Classics.* Arista AL9-8207. LP.

The Exciters. *Tell Him.* Collectables COL-5672 S21-18564.

Fabian. *Turn Me Loose!: The Very Best of Fabian.* Collectables COL-CD-6298.

Francis, Connie. *The Singles +.* BR Music BS 8141-2.

Franklin, Aretha. *Aretha Now.* Atlantic SD 8186. LP.

———. *Lady Soul.* Atlantic SD 8176. LP.

Gore, Leslie. *The Golden Hits of Leslie Gore.* Mercury SR 61024/MG 21024. LP.

———. *Start the Party Again.* Raven RVCD-31.

Greenwich, Ellie. *I Can Hear Music: The Ellie Greenwich Collection.* Razor & Tie 7930182195-2.

The Hollies. *Thirtieth Anniversary Collection: 1963-1993.* EMI Records USA 0777 7 99917 2 3.

Jackson, Chuck. *Golden Classics.* Collectables COL-CD-5115.

———. *The Very Best of Chuck Jackson, 1961–1967: Any Day Now.* Varèse Sarabande VSD-5777.

Jay and the Americans. *Come a Little Bit Closer: The Best of Jay and the Americans.* EMI/United Artists CDP-7-93448-2.

Keller, Jack. *Music for All Occasions.* A promotional compilation not for sale.

Kim, Andy. *Andy Kim's Greatest Hits.* Steed STS-37008. LP.

King, Ben E. *Spanish Harlem/Don't Play that Song.* Collectables COL-CD-6210.

King, Carole. *The Carnegie Hall Concert.* Ode/Epic/Legacy EK 64942.

———. *The Right Girl: Complete Recordings, 1958–1966.* Brill Tone Records CKW 222.

———. *Tapestry.* Ode EK 34946.

———. *Writer.* Epic/Ode EK 34944.

Kramer, Billy J. *Golden Legends.* Golden Legends Item GL 61502.

Lawrence, Steve. *The Best of Steve Lawrence.* Taragon Records TARCD-1002.

———, and Eydie Gorme. *The Greatest Hits, Volume 1.* GL Music GL 320.

Lee, Peggy. *Is That All There Is?* Capitol 386. LP.

Leiber, Jerry, and Mike Stoller. *Fine Gals, Fast Women and Wailin' Daddies: The First of Leiber and Stoller.* El Toro R&B 109.

———. *Leiber and Stoller Present the Daisy/Tiger Records Story: Everybody Come Clap Your Hands!!* Sundazed SC 11080.

———. *Leiber and Stoller Present the Spark Records Story.* Ace CDCHD 801.

———. *The Leiber and Stoller Story, Volume One: The Los Angeles Years, 1951–56.* Ace CDCHD 1010.

———. *There's a Riot Goin' On!: The Rock 'n' Roll Classics of Leiber & Stoller.* Rhino R2 70593.

Littlefield, Little Willie, and Friends. *Goin' Back to Kay Cee.* Ace CDCHD 503.

Love, Darlene. *The Best of Darlene Love.* Phil Spector Records 72132.

Lymon, Frankie, and the Teenagers. *The Very Best of Frankie Lymon & the Teenagers.* Rhino R2 75507.

Manfred Mann. *The Best of Manfred Mann: The Definitive Collection.* Ascot CDP-596096.

———. *Chapter Two: The Best of the Fontana Years.* Fontana 314 522 665-2.

Mann, Barry. *Barry Mann Songbook.* Universal UICY-4046.

———. *Soul & Inspiration.* Atlantic 83239-2.

———. *Who Put the Bomp (+4).* MCA MVCE-22057.

The McCoys. *Hang on Sloopy: The Best of the McCoys.* Legacy/Epic ZK 47074.

McDaniels, Gene. *The Best of Gene McDaniels: A Hundred Pounds of Clay.* Collectables COL-5646 S21-18546.

The Monkees. *Music Box.* Rhino R2 76706.

The Moody Blues. *Go Now.* London PS 428. LP.

Orlando, Tony. *Bless You and Seventeen Other Great Hits.* Collectables COL-5827/Sony #A 28263.

The Paris Sisters. *The Paris Sisters Sing their Greatest Hits & More.* Marginal Records MAR 087.

Pitney, Gene. *The Definitive Collection.* Charly CPCD 8196-2.

Pomus, Doc. *Send for the Doctor: The Early Years 1944-55.* Whiskey, Women, and . . . Record Company KM700. LP.

Pomus, Doc and Mort Shuman. *Turn Me Loose: The Songs of Doc Pomus and Mort Shuman.* A promotional compilation not for sale. Warner Chappell RA-002.

Presley, Elvis. *Elvis Chante Mort Shuman & Doc Pomus.* BMG France RCA 74321 745962.

———. *Elvis Presley Sings Leiber & Stoller.* RCA 3026-2-R.

The Raindrops. *The Raindrops.* Collectables COL-CD-6316.

Revere, Paul and the Raiders. *The Essential Ride: '63–'67.* Legacy/Columbia CK 48949.

The Righteous Brothers. *Anthology: 1962–1974.* Rhino R2 71488.

Robbins, Marty. *The Essential Marty Robbins: 1951–1982.* Columbia/Legacy C2K 48537.

Scott, Freddie. *Freddie Scott Sings and Sings and Sings.* Collectables COL-CD-5413.

Sedaka, Neil. *The Brooklyn Demos (1958–1961).* Original Cast OCR 6060.

———. *The Hungry Years.* Varèse Vintage VSD-5948.

———. *Legendary Neil Sedaka.* BMG Australia 74321913042.

———. *Oh Carol: The Complete Recordings, 1956-1966.* Bear Family Records BCD 16535 HK.

———. *Sings His Greatest Hits.* RCA 07863 53465-2.

The Shangri-Las. *I Can Never Go Home Anymore.* Red Bird RB20-104. LP.

———. *The Myrmidons of Melodrama.* RPM 136.

The Shirelles. *The Definitive Collection.* Charly CPCD 8190-2.

Shuman, Mort. *Ses Plus Belles Chansons.* Mercury France/Philips 536 039-2.

Shuman, Mort and Elly Stone, Shawn Elliott and Alice Whitfield. *Jacques Brel Is Alive and Well and Living in Paris.* Original cast recording. Sony Classical/Columbia/Legacy SK 89998.

Spector, Phil. *Back to Mono (1958–1969).* ABKCO 7118.

———. *Phil Spector's Greatest Hits.* Warner/Spector Records 0998. LP.

Springfield, Dusty. *Dusty in Memphis.* Deluxe Edition. Rhino R2 75580.

———. *The Very Best of Dusty Springfield.* Mercury 314 558 208-2.

The Three Suns. *Soft and Sweet/Midnight for Two.* Collectables COL-CD-2742.

The Tokens. *All Time Greatest Hits!!!* Taragon TARCD-1040.

Turner, Joe. *The Best of Joe Turner: The Best of Joe Turner.* Blues Forever CD 68015.

———. *Joe Turner/Rockin' the Blues.* Collectables COL-CD-64198.

———. *The Very Best of Big Joe Turner.* Rhino R2 72968.

Uggams, Leslie. *What's an Uggams?* Atlantic SD 8196. LP.

Van Dyke, Leroy. *Walk on By.* Mercury 314-526 541-2.

Various artists. *Best of Kansas City.* K-tel 3271-2.

———. *Beyond the Valley of the Dimension Dolls: Girls Will Be Girls, Volume 2.* West Side WESM 608.

———. *The Brill Building Sound: Singers and Songwriters Who Rocked the 60's.* 4 vols. ERA Records 3298-2.

———. *Let the Boogie Woogie Rock and Roll.* Ace CDCHD 718.

———. *On Broadway: Hit Songs and Rarities from the Brill Building Era.* Westside WESD 216.

———. *Spotlite on Melba Records, Volume 1.* Collectables COL-CD-5636.

———. *The Red Bird Story.* Charly 296-4.

———. *Till the Night is Gone: A Tribute to Doc Pomus.* Forward R2 71878.

Vaughan, Sarah. *Golden Hits.* Mercury 824 891-2.

Vee, Bobby. *A Bobby Vee Recording Session.* Liberty LRP-3232. LP.

———. *Bobby Vee's Golden Greats.* Liberty LRP-3245. LP.

———. *The Essential & Collectible Bobby Vee.* Liberty/ EMI 7243 4 97788 2 5.

———. *The Very Best of Bobby Vee.* United Artists UA-LA332-E. LP.

Vincent, Gene. *Gene Vincent: The Capitol Collector's Series.* Capitol CDP 7 94074 2.

The Walker Brothers. *The Collection.* Karussel 550 200-2.

Warwick, Dionne. *Dionne Warwick's Golden Hits—Part One.* Scepter SPS 565. LP.

———. *Dionne Warwick in Valley of the Dolls.* Scepter SPS 568. LP.

———. *Very Dionne.* Scepter SPS 587. LP.

Williams, Andy. *The Complete Columbia Chart Singles Collection.* Taragon TARCD-1093.

INDEX